Mary Jane Holmes

Edna Browning

The Leighton Homestead : A novel

Mary Jane Holmes

Edna Browning
The Leighton Homestead : A novel

ISBN/EAN: 9783743329591

Manufactured in Europe, USA, Canada, Australia, Japa

Cover: Foto ©ninafisch / pixelio.de

Manufactured and distributed by brebook publishing software (www.brebook.com)

Mary Jane Holmes

Edna Browning

POPULAR NOVELS.

By Mrs. Mary J. Holmes.

I.—TEMPEST AND SUNSHINE.
II.—ENGLISH ORPHANS.
III.—HOMESTEAD ON THE HILLSIDE.
IV.—LENA RIVERS.
V.—MEADOW BROOK.
VI.—DORA DEANE.
VII.—COUSIN MAUDE.
VIII.—MARIAN GRAY.
IX.—DARKNESS AND DAYLIGHT.
X.—HUGH WORTHINGTON.
XI.—CAMERON PRIDE.
XII.—ROSE MATHER.
XIII.—ETHELYN'S MISTAKE.
XIV.—MILLBANK.
XV.—EDNA BROWNING. (*New.*)

Mrs. Holmes is a peculiarly pleasant and fascinating writer. Her books are always entertaining, and she has the rare faculty of enlisting the sympathy and affections of her readers, and of holding their attention to her pages with deep and absorbing interest.

All published uniform with this volume. Price $1.50 each, and sent *free* by mail, on receipt of price by

G. W. CARLETON & CO.,
New York.

EDNA BROWNING;

OR,

THE LEIGHTON HOMESTEAD.

A Novel.

BY

MRS. MARY J. HOLMES,

AUTHOR OF

TEMPEST AND SUNSHINE. — 'LENA RIVERS. — MARIAN GREY. — MEADOW-BROOK. — ENGLISH ORPHANS. — COUSIN MAUDE. — HOMESTEAD. — DORA DEANE. — DARKNESS AND DAYLIGHT. — HUGH WORTHINGTON. — THE CAMERON PRIDE. — ROSE MATHER. — ETHELYN'S MISTAKE. — MILLBANK. — ETC. — ETC.

NEW YORK:
G. W. Carleton & Co., Publishers.
LONDON: S. LOW, SON & CO.
M.DCCC.LXXII.

Entered according to Act of Congress, in the year 1872, by
DANIEL HOLMES,
In the Office of the Librarian of Congress, at Washington.

Stereotyped at the
WOMEN'S PRINTING HOUSE,
Corner Avenue A and Eighth Street,
New York.

CONTENTS.

CHAPTER		PAGE
I.	Roy, Our Hero	7
II.	At Leighton Homestead	15
III.	Georgie's Telegram	25
IV.	Georgie	31
V.	Roy's Decision	40
VI.	News of Edna	44
VII.	Miss Pepper's Letter	50
VIII.	The Brave Little Woman	60
IX.	After the Accident	69
X.	Georgie and Jack	77
XI.	Edna's First Weeks at Mrs. Dana's	84
XII.	How Aunt Jerusha received the News	89
XIII.	Jack's Home	97
XIV.	Edna and Annie	101
XV.	Aunt Jerry	107
XVI.	Aunt Jerry and Edna	114
XVII.	Where Edna went	123
XVIII.	At Uncle Phil's	127
XIX.	Uncle Phil	135
XX.	Up in the North Room	150
XXI.	Miss Overton	158
XXII.	Maude's Visit	166
XXIII.	Paying Debts	181
XXIV.	Georgie and Jack	186
XXV.	In the Summer	199
XXVI.	After another Year	206

CONTENTS.

CHAPTER		PAGE
XXVII.	Edna Accepts	215
XXVIII.	Edna goes to Leighton	219
XXIX.	Georgie's Secret	232
XXX.	At Leighton	240
XXXI.	Over at Oakwood	246
XXXII.	The Croquet Party	252
XXXIII.	How the Engagement was received	270
XXXIV.	How they got on at Leighton	281
XXXV.	Letters	289
XXXVI.	Annie Heyford	299
XXXVII.	The Night of the Party	311
XXXVIII.	After Annie's Death	323
XXXIX.	Maude and Edna visit Uncle Phil	328
XL.	Getting ready for the Bridal	333
XLI.	The Burglar	343
XLII.	The Alarm	355
XLIII.	Roy	361
XLIV.	Last Days	371
XLV.	Death at Oakwood	378
XLVI.	Jack's Marriage and Jack's Story	381
XLVII.	Roy finds Edna	395
XLVIII.	Mrs. Churchill and Edna	407
XLIX.	The Wedding	411
L.	Conclusion	420

EDNA BROWNING;

OR,

THE LEIGHTON HOMESTEAD.

CHAPTER I.

ROY, OUR HERO.

"ROBERT, son of Arthur and Anna Leighton, born April 5th, 18——," was the record which the old family Bible bore of our hero's birth, parentage, and name, but by his mother and those who knew him best, he was always called *Roy*, and by that name we introduce him to our readers on a pleasant morning in May, when, wrapped in a heavy shawl, he sat in a corner of a car with a tired, worn look upon his face, and his teeth almost chattering with the cold.

A four-month's acquaintance with the chill fever, taken at the time the river rose so high, and he worked all day to save some of his tenants who lived along the meadows, had wasted him to a shadow, and he was on his way to the West, hoping that change of air and scene would accomplish what bottles and bottles of quinine, with all the usual remedies for fever and ague, had failed to do.

Beside him sat his mother, a fair-haired, proud-faced little lady of fifty, or more, who conducted herself with a dignity becoming the mistress of Leighton Homestead, her son's beautiful home on the Hudson.

Anna Leighton had been much younger than her husband, and at the time of her marriage there were rumors of another suitor in whose brown beard there were no threads of gray, and of whom Mr. Leighton had been fearfully jealous. If this were true, it accounted in part for his strange will, by which only a small portion of his large fortune was left to his wife, who was to forfeit even this in the event of a second marriage. In her case, love proved more potent than gold, and, two years after her husband's death, she married Charlie Churchill, who made up in family and blood what he lacked in lands and money. There was a trip to Europe, a *dolce far niente* dream of happiness for eighteen months amid the glories of the eastern hemisphere, and then, widowed a second time, Anna Churchill came one dreary autumn day to the Leighton Place, on the river side, where, six months after, she gave birth to a little boy, for whom Roy, then a mere lad, stood as one of the sponsors in the old ivy-grown church at the foot of the hill.

Since that time, Mrs. Churchill had lived at the Leighton Homestead, and been, with her younger son, altogether dependent upon her eldest born, who had made her, to all intents and purposes, the honored and welcome mistress of his house. Only one sore point was there between them, and that was handsome and winning, but unprincipled Charlie,—who, looking upon his brother's fortune as his own, would, if uncontrolled, have spent it with a recklessness which would soon have brought the Leighton Homestead under the auctioneer's hammer.

Charlie was a spoiled boy, the neighbors said; and when, at sixteen, he coolly appropriated his brother's gold watch, together with a hundred dollars in money, and went off to Canada, "to travel and see a little of the world," they shook their heads, and said Roy would be justified in never taking him again into favor.

But Roy did not think so, and when Charlie had fished all summer among the Thousand Islands, and spent his hundred dollars, and pawned his watch, and fallen sick in Montreal, Roy went for the young scamp, who cried like a child at sight of him, and called him "a brick," and a "dear old Roy," and promised he would never be bad again, and in proof thereof would, if Roy said so, join the church, or take a class in Sunday-school, or go through college, he did not care which. And so Roy took him to the Academy in Canandaigua, and said that to the teachers which resulted in Mr. Charlie's being kept rather closer than was altogether agreeable to him. After a time, however, the strict surveillance was relaxed, and by his winning ways, he grew to be very popular with both teachers and pupils, and many a slight misdemeanor was winked at and overlooked, so powerfully did his soft blue eyes and pleasant smile plead for him.

At the time our story opens he had been in Canandaigua nearly a year and a half, and Mrs. Churchill and Roy were intending to stop for a day at the hotel and visit him. There were but few passengers in the car occupied by Roy and his mother, and these were mostly of the quiet, undemonstrative kind, who nodded in their seats, or read the newspaper, and accepted matters, *air* included, as they found them; consequently, poor Roy, who, shaking with ague, had a morbid dread of open windows, had for hours luxuriated in an atmosphere which made a group of young girls exclaim with disgust, when at a station thirty miles or so from Canandaigua they came trooping in, their cheeks glowing with health and their eyes sparkling with excitement.

There were four of them, and appropriating the two seats directly opposite Roy, they turned one of them back, and to the great horror of the invalid opened both the windows, thereby letting in a gust of air which blew directly across Roy's face, while Mrs. Churchill received an ugly cinder in her eye, which nearly blinded her. In blissful ignorance of the discomfort they were causing, or of the very uncomplimentary things the sick man and his mother were thinking, the girls chattered on, and the cool wind blew the ribbons on their hats far out behind, and tossed their veils airily, and lifted the golden-brown curls of the one who seemed to be the life of the party, and who talked the most, and kept the others shrieking with laughter, while her bright eyes glanced rapidly around the car, noting everything and everybody, until at last they lighted upon the pair just across the aisle, Mrs. Churchill working away at the obstinate cinder, and Roy wrapping his shawl more closely about him, and wondering why girls would always persist in keeping the windows open when everybody else was freezing. Roy was not in a very amiable state of mind, and he showed it in his eyes, which flashed a savage glance at the girl with the curls of golden-brown, whom her companions addressed as Edna. She was the worst of them all, for she had opened both the windows, and then with the exclamation that she was "roasted alive," sat fanning herself briskly with the coquettish little hat she had taken from her head. As she met Roy's angry glance, the smile which a moment before had wreathed her lips, vanished suddenly, and she looked at him curiously, as if half expecting him to speak. But Roy was silent for a time; then, as the bright, restless eyes of the offender kept meeting his own inquiringly, he mustered courage to say:

"Young lady, you'll oblige me by shutting that window. Don't you see I am catching cold?" and a loud sneeze attested to the truth of what he said.

It was not like Roy Leighton thus to address any one, and he repented of his surliness in an instant, and wished he might do something to atone. But it was now too late. He had shown himself a savage, and must abide the result.

The window was shut with a bang, and the gay laughter and merry talk were hushed for a time, while the girl called Edna busied herself with writing or drawing something upon a bit of paper, which elicited peals of laughter from her companions to whom it was shown. Roy could not help fancying that it in some way related to himself, and his mother thought the same, and was mentally styling them "a set of ill-bred, impertinent chits," when the train stopped before the Canandaigua depot, where, as usual, a crowd of people was assembled. This was the destination of the girls, who, gathering up their satchels and parasols, hurried from the car in such haste that the bit of paper which had so much amused them was forgotten, and fluttered down at Mrs. Churchill's feet. Her first impulse, as she stooped to pick it up, was to restore it to its owner, but when she saw what it was, she uttered an angry exclamation, and thrust it into her son's hand, saying:

"Look, Roy, at the caricature the hussy has made of us."

No man likes to be ridiculed, and Roy Leighton was not an exception, and the hot blood tingled in his pale cheeks as he saw a very correct likeness of himself, wrapped in a bundle of shawls, with his eyes cast reproachfully toward a shadowy group of girls across the aisle, while from his mouth issued the words, "Shut that window, miss. Don't you see I am freezing?"

Beside him was his mother, her handkerchief to her eye, and the expression of her face exactly what it had been when she worked at the troublesome cinder. Instead of a hat, the mischievous Edna had perched a bonnet on Roy's head, and under this abominable picture had written, "Miss Betty and her mother, as they looked on their travelling excursion. Drawn by Edna Browning, Ont. Fem.- Sem.; May 10th."

It was only a caricature; but so admirably was it done, and so striking was his own likeness in spite of the bonnet, that Roy could not help acknowledging to himself that Edna Browning was a natural artist; and he involuntarily began to feel an interest in the young girl who, if she could execute this sketch in so short a time, must be capable of better things. Still, mingled with this interest was a feeling of indignation that he should have been so insulted by a mere school-girl, and when, as he alighted from the car, he caught the flutter of her blue ribbons, and heard her merry laugh as she made her way through the crowd to the long flight of stairs, and then with her companions walked rapidly toward Main street, he felt a desire to box her ears, as she deserved that they should be boxed.

Thrusting the picture into his pocket, he conducted his mother through the crowd, and then looked about in quest of his brother, who was to have been there to meet them; and who soon appeared, panting for breath and apologizing for his delay.

"Professor Hollister wouldn't let me out till the last minute, and then I stopped an instant to speak to some girls who came on this train. How are you, mother, and you, old Roy? I don't believe I should have known you. That ague has given you a hard one, and made you shaky on your legs, hasn't it? Here, lean on me, while we climb these infernally steep stairs. Mother, I'll carry that satchel. What ails your eye? looks as if you'd been fighting. Here, this way. Don't go into that musty parlor. Come on to No. —. I've got your rooms all engaged, the best in the hotel."

And thus talking, with his invalid brother leaning on his arm, Charlie Churchill led the way to the handsome rooms which overlooked the lake and the hills beyond. Roy was very tired, and he lay down at once, while his mother made some changes in her toilet, and from a travel-soiled, rather dowdy-looking woman in gray, was transformed into a fair, comely and stylish matron, whose rich black silk trailed far behind her, and whose frills of costly lace fell softly about her neck and plump white hands as she went in to dinner with Charlie, who was having a holiday, and who ordered claret and champagne, and offered it to those about him with as much freedom as if it was his money instead of his brother's which would pay for it all.

Roy's dinner was served in his room, and while waiting for it he studied Edna Browning's sketch, which had a strange fascination for him, despite the pangs of wounded vanity he felt when he saw what a guy she had made of him.

"I wonder if I do look like that," he said, and he went to the glass and examined himself carefully. "Yes, I do," he continued. "Put a poke bonnet on me and the likeness is perfect, hollows in my cheeks, fretful expression and all. I've been sick and coddled, and petted until I've grown a complete baby, and a perfect boor, but there's no reason why I need to look so confounded cross and ill-tempered, and I won't either. Edna Browning has done me some good at least. I wonder who the little wretch is. Perhaps Charlie knows; she seems to be here at school."

But Roy did not ask Charlie, for the asking would have involved an explanation, and he would a little rather not show his teasing brother the picture which he put away so carefully in his pocket-book. They drove that afternoon in the most stylish turn-out the town afforded, a handsome open barouche, and Roy declined the cushion his mother suggested for his back, and only suffered her to spread his shawl across his lap instead of wrapping it around him to his chin. His overcoat and scarf were all he should need, he said, and he tried to sit up straight, and not look sick, as Charlie, who managed the reins himself, drove them through the principal streets of the town, and then out into the country for a mile or two.

On their way back they passed the seminary just as a group of girls came out accompanied by a teacher, and equipped apparently for a walk. There were thirty or more of them, but Roy saw only one, and of her he caught a glimpse, as she tossed back her golden brown curls and bowed familiarly to Charlie, whose hat went up and whose horses sheered just enough to make his mother utter an exclamation of fear. She, too, had recognized the wicked Edna by her dress, had seen the bow to Charlie, with Charlie's acknowledgment of it, and when the gay horses were trotting soberly down the street, she asked,—

"Who was that girl you bowed to, Charlie? the bold-faced thing with curls, I mean."

Now if she had left off that last, the chances are that Charlie would have told her at once, for he knew just whom she meant. A dozen of the girls had bowed to him, but he had had but *one* in his mind when he lifted his hat so gracefully, and it hurt him to hear her called "a bold-faced thing." So he answered with the utmost nonchalance.

"I don't know which one you mean. I bowed to them all collectively, and to no one individually. They are girls from the seminary."

"Yes, I know; but I mean the one in blue with the long curls."

"Big is she?" and Charlie tried to think.

"No, very small."

"Dark face and turned-up nose?" was the next query.

"No, indeed; fair-faced, but as to her nose I did not notice. I think she was on the same car with us."

"Oh, I guess you must mean Edna Browning. She's

short, and has long curls," and Charlie just touched his spirited horses, causing them to bound so suddenly as to jerk his mother's head backward, making her teeth strike together with such force as to hurt her lip; but she asked no more questions with regard to Edna Browning, who had recognized in Charlie Churchill's companions her fellow-passengers in the car, and was wondering if that dumpy woman and that muff of a man could be the brother and mother whom Charlie had said he was expecting when she met him that morning in the street.

CHAPTER II.

AT LEIGHTON HOMESTEAD.

IT was a magnificent old place, and had borne the name of Leighton Homestead, or Leighton Place, ever since the quarrel between the two brothers, Arthur and Robert, as to which should have the property in New York, and which should have the old family house on the Hudson, thirty miles or so below Albany, and in plain sight of the Catskills. To Arthur, the elder, the place had come at last, while Robert took the buildings on Broadway, and made a fortune from them, and dying without family, left it all to his brother's son and namesake, who, after his father's death, was the richest boy for many miles around.

As Roy grew to manhood he caused the old place to be modernized and beautified, until at last there were few country seats on the river which could compete with it in the luxuriousness of its internal adorning, or the beauty of the grounds around it. Broad terraces were there, with mounds and beds of bright flowers showing among the soft green turf; gravel walks which wound in and out among clumps of evergreen and ran past cosey arbors and summer-houses, over some of which the graceful Wisteria was trailing, while others were gorgeous with the flowers of the wonderful Trumpet-creeper. Here and there the ripple of a fountain was heard, while the white marble of urns and statuary showed well amid the dense foliage of shrubbery and trees. That Roy had lived to be twenty-eight and never married, or shown a disposition to do so, was a marvel to all, and latterly some of the old dowagers of the neighborhood who had young ladies to dispose of had seriously taken the matter in hand, to see if something could not be done with the grave, impassive man. He was polite and agreeable to all the girls, and treated them with that thoughtful deference so pleasing to women, and so rarely found in any man who has not the kindest and the best of hearts. But he never passed a certain bound in his attentions, and the young ladies from New York who spent their summers in the vicinity of Leighton Place went back to town discouraged, and hopeless so far as Roy was concerned.

"It was really a shame, and he getting older every year," Mrs. Freeman Burton of Oakwood said, as on a bright October morning in the autumn succeeding the May day when we first met with Roy, she drove her ponies down the smooth road by the river and turned into the park at Leighton. "Yes; it really is a shame that there is not a young and handsome mistress to grace all this, and Georgie would be just the one if Roy could only see it," the lady continued to herself, as she drove to the side door which was ajar, though there was no sign of life around the house except the watch-dog Rover, who lay basking in the sunlight with a beautiful Maltese kitten sleeping on his paws.

Mrs. Freeman Burton, whose husband was a Wall-street *Bull*, lived on Madison Square in the winter, and in the summer queened it among the lesser lights in the neighborhood of Leighton Homestead. As thought Mrs. Freeman Burton of Oakwood, so thought Mrs. Anna Churchill of Leighton, and as Mrs. Burton knew that Mrs. Churchill was in all respects her equal, it came about naturally that the two ladies were on the most intimate terms,—so intimate indeed, that Mrs. Burton, seeing no one and hearing no one, passed into the house dragging her rich India shawl after her and knocking at the door of her friend's private sitting-room. But Mrs. Churchill was up in Roy's room in a state of great mental distress and agitation, which Roy was trying to soothe as well as his own condition would admit. He had been thrown from his horse only the day before and broken his leg, and he lay in a state of great helplessness and pain when, about half an hour before Mrs. Burton's call, the morning letters were brought in and he asked his mother to read them.

There were several on business, which were soon dispatched, and then Mrs. Churchill read one to herself from Maude Somerton, a relative of Mr. Freeman Burton, who had spent the last summer at Oakwood, and flirted desperately with Charlie Churchill all through his vacation. Roy liked Maude and hoped that in time she might become his sister. Once he said something to Charlie on the subject, hinting that if he chose to marry Maude Somerton, and tried to do well, money should not be wanting when it was needed to set him up in business. There had been an awkward silence on Charlie's part for a few moments, while he turned very red, and seemed far more embarrassed than the occasion would warrant. Then he had burst out with:

"Don't you mind about Maude Somerton. She will flirt with anybody who wears a coat; but, old Roy, maybe I shall want that money for somebody else; or at all events want you to stand by me, and if I do, you will; won't you, Roy?"

And Roy, without a suspicion of his brother's meaning, said he would, and the next day Charlie returned to Canandaigua, while Maude went back to her scholars about ten miles from Leighton; for she was poor, and earned her own livelihood. But for her poverty she made amends in the quality of her blood, which was the very best New England could produce; and as she was fair, and sweet, and pure as the white pond-lilies of her native State, Mrs. Freeman Burton gave her a home at Oakwood, and gave her Georgie's cast-off clothing, and would very much have liked to give her Charlie Churchill, after she heard that Roy intended to do something for his brother whenever he was married.

Maude's letter was a very warm, gushing epistle, full of kind remembrances of Roy, "the best man in the world," and inquiries after Charlie, "the nicest kind of a summer beau," and professions of friendship for Mrs. Churchill, "the dear sweet lady, whose kindnesses could never be forgotten."

"Maude writes a very good letter," Mrs. Churchill said, folding it up and laying it on the table, and as she did so, discovering another which had fallen from her lap to the floor.

It was from Charlie and directed to Roy, but Mrs. Churchill opened it, turning first scarlet and then pale, and then gasping for breath as she read the dreadful news. Charlie was going to be married; aye, was married that moment, for he had named the morning of the 7th of October as the time when Edna Browning would be his wife! At that name Mrs. Churchill gave a little shriek, and tossed the letter to Roy, who managed to control himself, while he read that Charlie was going to marry Edna Browning, "the nicest girl in the whole world and the prettiest, as Roy would think if he could see her." They had been engaged a long time; were engaged, in fact, when Roy and his mother were in Canandaigua, and he would have told them then, perhaps, if his mother.had not asked who " that brazen-faced thing " was, or something like it, when they passed the seminary girls in driving.

"Mother means well enough, I suppose," Charlie wrote, "but she is too confounded-proud, and if I had told her about Edna, she would have raised the greatest kind of a row, for Edna is poor as a church-mouse,—hasn't a penny in the world, and nobody but an old maid aunt who lives in Richmond, and treats her like a dog. Her father was an Episcopal clergyman and her mother was a music teacher, and that's all I know of her family, or care. I love her, and that's enough. I s'pose I may as well make a clean breast of it, and tell you I've had a fuss with one of the teachers; and I wouldn't wonder if they expelled me, and so I've concluded to take time by the forelock, and have quit on my own hook, and have persuaded Edna to cast in her lot with mine, a little sooner than she had agreed to do. They wrote to you about the fuss, but I paid the man who carries the letters to the office five dollars for the one directed to you, as I'd rather tell you myself, and it gives me time, too, for this other matter in hand. Fortune favors the brave. Edna went yesterday to Buffalo with her room-mate, who is sick, and wanted her to go home with her; and I am going up to-morrow, and Wednesday morning, the 7th, we shall be married, and take the early train for Chicago, where Edna has some connection living.

"And now, Roy, I want some money,—there's a good fellow. You remember you spoke of my marrying Maude Somerton, and said you'd give me money and stand by me, too. Do it now, Roy, and when mother goes into hysterics and calls Edna *that creature*, and talks as if she had persuaded me, whereas it was I who persuaded her, say a word for me, won't you? You will like Edna,—and, Roy, I want you to ask us to come home, for a spell, anyway. The fact is, I've romanced a little, and Edna thinks I am heir, or at least joint heir with you, of Leighton Homestead. She don't know I haven't a cent in the world but what comes from you, and I don't want her to. Set me up in business, Roy, and I'll work like a hero. I will, upon my word,—and please send me five hundred at once to the care of John Dana, Chicago. I shall be married and gone before this reaches you, so there's no use for mother to tear her eyes out. Tell her not to. I'm sorry to vex her, for she's been a good mother, and after Edna I love her and you best of all the world. Send the money, do. Yours truly,

"CHARLIE."

This was the letter which created so much consternation at Leighton Homestead, and made Mrs. Churchill faint with anger, while Roy's pale face flushed crimson and the great drops of sweat stood on his forehead. That Charlie should be disgraced in school was bad enough, but that to the disgrace he should add the rash, imprudent act of marrying, was far worse,—even if the girl he married had been in all respects his equal. Of that last, Roy did not think as much as his mother. He knew Charlie better than she did, and felt that almost any respectable girl was good enough for him; but it did strike him a little unpleasantly that the Edna Browning, whose caricature of himself was still preserved, should become his sister-in-law. He knew it was she,—the girl in the cars, and his mother knew it too. She had never forgotten the girl, nor could she shake off the impression that Charlie knew more of her than she would like to believe. For this reason she had favored his flirting with Maude Somerton, who, though poor, was highly connected, which was more than could be said for Edna.

During the summer, there had been at Oakwood a Miss Rolliston, a friend of Maude Somerton, and a recent graduate of Canandaigua Seminary. And without seeming to be particularly interested, Mrs. Churchill had learned something of Edna Browning, "whom she once met somewhere" she said. Did Miss Rolliston know her?"

"Oh, yes, a bright little thing, whom all the girls liked, though she was only a charity scholar, that is, she was to teach for a time in the Seminary to pay for her education."

"Indeed; has she no friends?" Mrs. Churchill asked, and Miss Rolliston replied: "None but an aunt, a Miss Jerusha Pepper, who, if rumor is correct, led her niece a sorry life."

It was about this time that Charlie commenced flirting so desperately with Maude Somerton, and so Mrs. Churchill for a time forgot Edna Browning, and what Miss Rolliston had said of her. But it came back to her now, and she repeated it to Roy, who did not seem as much impressed with Miss Pepper and the charity scholar part as his mother would like to have had him. Perhaps he was thinking of Charlie's words, "You'll stand by me, won't you, old Roy," and rightly guessing now that they had reference to Edna Browning. And perhaps, too, the shadow of the fearful tragedy so soon to follow was around him, pleading for his young brother whose face he would never see again.

"What shall we do? What can we do?" his mother asked, and he replied:

"We must make the best of it, and send him the money."

"But, Roy, the disgrace; think of it,—an elopement; a charity scholar, a niece of Miss Jerusha Pepper, whoever she may be. I'll never receive her, and I shall write and tell her so."

"No, mother, you'll do nothing of the kind," Roy said; "Charlie is still your boy, and Edna is his wife. She is not to blame for being poor or for having an aunt with that horrible name. Write and tell them to come home. The house is large enough. Maybe you will like this Edna Browning."

Before Mrs. Churchill could reply, Mrs. Burton's card was brought to her, and to that lady as her confidential friend did the aggrieved mother unbosom herself, telling all she knew of Edna, and asking what she should do. Mrs. Burton sat a moment thinking, as if the subject demanded the most profound and careful attention, and then said:

"I hardly know how to advise; different people feel so differently. If it were my son I should not invite him home, at present. Let him suffer awhile for his misdeed. He ought to be punished."

"Yes, and he will be punished, when he comes to his senses and sees what a *mésalliance* he has made, though of course she enticed him," Mrs. Churchill said, her mother's heart pleading for her boy; whereas Mrs. Burton, who had never been a mother, and who felt a little piqued that after knowing Maude Somerton, Charlie could have chosen so unwisely, was very severe in her condemnation of both parties, and spoke her mind freely.

"Probably this Browning girl did entice him, but he should not have yielded, and he must expect to pay the penalty. I, for one, cannot promise to receive her on terms of equality; and Georgie, I am sure, will not, she is so fastidious and particular. Maybe she will see them. Did I tell you she had gone West?—started yesterday morning on the early train? She expected to be in Buffalo last night, and take this morning's train for Chicago, where she is going to see a child, a relative of her step-mother, who died not long since. I am sorry she happens to be gone just now, when Roy is so helpless. She could read to him, and amuse him so much."

It was evident that Mrs. Burton was thinking far more of Georgie than of her friend's trouble; but the few words she had spoken on the subject had settled the matter and changed the whole current of Edna Browning's life, and when, at last, she took her leave, and went out to her carriage, Mrs. Churchill had resolved *to do her duty*, and set her son's sins before him in their proper light.

But she did not tell Roy so. She would rather he should not know all she had been saying to Mrs. Burton.

So to his suggestion that she should write to Charlie that day, she answered that she would, but added:

"I can't write a lie, and tell him he will be welcome here at once. I must wait awhile before doing that."

To this Roy did not object. A little discipline would do Charlie good, he believed; and so he signed a check for five hundred dollars, and then tried to sleep, while his mother wrote to Charlie. It was a severe letter, aimed more at Edna than her boy, and told of her astonishment and indignation that her son should have been led into so imprudent an act. Then she descanted upon runaway matches, and unequal matches; and said he must expect it would be a long time before she could forgive him, or receive "Miss Browning" as her daughter. Then she quoted Mrs. Burton, and Georgie, and Roy, whose feelings were *so outraged*, and advised Charlie to tell Miss Browning at once that every dollar he had came from his brother; "for," she added in conclusion,

"I cannot help feeling that if she had known this fact, your unfortunate entanglement would have been prevented.

"Your aggrieved and offended mother,
"ANNA CHURCHILL."

She did not show what she had written to Roy, but she inclosed the check, and directed the letter to "Charles Augustus Churchill. Care of John Dana, Chicago, Ill." With no apparent reason, Mrs. Churchill lingered long over that letter, studying the name "Charles Augustus," and repeating it softly to herself, as we repeat the names of the dead. And when, at last, she gave it to Russell to post, she did it unwillingly, half wishing, when it was gone past recall, that she had not written quite so harshly to her boy, whose face haunted her that day wherever she went, and whose voice she seemed to hear everywhere calling to her.

With the waning of the day, the brightness of the early morning disappeared, and the night closed in dark and dreary, with a driving rain and a howling wind, which swept past Mrs. Churchill's windows, and seemed screaming Charlie's name in her ears as she tried in vain to sleep. At last, rising from her bed and throwing on her dressing-gown, she walked to the window and looked out into the night, wondering at the strange feeling of fear as of some impending evil stealing over her. The rain was over, and the breaking clouds were scudding before the wind, which still blew in fitful gusts, while the moon showed itself occasionally through an angry sky, and cast a kind of weird light upon the grounds below, the flower-beds, and statuary, which reminded Mrs. Churchill of gravestones, and made her turn away at last with a shudder. Then her thoughts went again after Charlie, and something drew her to her knees as she prayed for him; but said no word for Edna, the young girl-wife, whose sun of happiness was setting in a night of sorrow, darker and more terrible than anything of which she had ever dreamed.

CHAPTER III.

GEORGIE'S TELEGRAM.

THERE was no trace of the storm next morning, except in the drops of rain which glittered on the shrubs and flowers, and the soaked condition of the walks and carriage-road. The sun came up bright and warm again, and by noon the hill-tops in the distance showed that purplish haze so common to the glorious October days. Everything about Leighton Homestead was quiet and peaceful, and in nothing was there a sign of the terrible calamity already passed, but as yet a *secret* to the mother, whose nameless terror of the previous night had faded with returning day. She was in Roy's room, where a cheerful fire was blazing to counteract any chill or damp which might creep in through the open window. They had had their early lunch, and Roy was settling himself to sleep when Russell appeared, bearing a telegram, a missive which seldom fails to set one's heart to throbbing with a dread of what it may have to tell. It was directed to Roy, but Mrs. Churchill opened it and read it, and then, with an agonizing shriek, fell forward upon Roy's pillow, moaning bitterly :

"Oh, Roy, my Charlie is dead,—my Charlie is dead!"

She claimed him for all her own then. It was *my* Charlie, her fatherless one, her youngest-born, her baby, who was dead; and the blow cut deep and cruelly, and made her writhe in agony as she kept up the faint, moaning sound,—"My Charlie, my boy."

She had dropped the telegram upon the floor, but Russell picked it up and handed it to Roy, who read :

"There has been a railroad accident, and Charlie is dead. His wife slightly injured. I await your orders.

"GEORGIE L. BURTON."

When Roy read his brother's letter the day before, there had been great drops of sweat upon his brow; but now his face was pale as death, and the tears poured over it like rain, as he held the paper in his hand and tried to realize the terrible sorrow which had fallen so suddenly upon him. The telegram was dated at Iona, a little town between Cleveland and Chicago, and nearer to the latter place. Georgie had said: "I await your orders," and that brought Roy from his own grief to the necessity of acting. Somebody must go and bring poor Charlie home; and as Roy was disabled, the task would devolve on Russell, the head servant at Leighton, who had been in the family for years. With a grave bow he received his orders, and the next train which left the Leighton depot carried him in it, while four or five hours later, Miss Burton, to whom Russell had telegraphed at once, read that "Russell would start immediately for Iona."

Stunned and utterly helpless, Mrs. Churchill could only moan and weep, as her maid led her to her room and made her lie down upon the bed. She was a good woman at heart, in spite of the foibles and errors which appeared on the surface, and far greater than her sorrow for her own loss was her anxiety for her boy's future. Was it well with him? Would she ever meet him again, should she be so fortunate as to gain heaven herself? She had taught him to pray, and back through the years which lay between that dreadful day and his childhood, her thoughts went swiftly, and she seemed to see again the fair head resting on her lap and hear the dear voice lisping the words "Our Father," or, "Jesus, gentle Shepherd, hear me," which last had been Charlie's favorite prayer. But he was a child then, a baby. He had grown to manhood since, and she could not tell if latterly he ever prayed; and if not, oh, where was he that autumn day, whose mellow beauty seemed to mock her woe, as, in the home to which he would never come alive, she made bitter mourning for him. Suddenly, amid her pain, she remembered the previous night when she had prayed so earnestly for her boy. Perhaps God had saved him for the sake of that prayer; His love and mercy were infinite, and she would trust it all to Him, hoping that as He saved the thief on the cross, so from Charlie's lips in the moment of peril there had gone up a prayer so sincere, and full of penitence and faith, that God had heard and answered, and had her boy safe with Him.

"If I only knew it was so," she moaned; but alas! she did *not* know, and her soul cried out for sight and knowledge, just as many a bleeding heart has cried out for some word or token to make belief a certainty. But to such cries there comes no answer back; the grave remains unopened; the mystery unexplained, and we, whose streaming eyes would fain pierce the darkness, and see if our loved ones are safe, must still trust it all to God, and walk yet a while by faith, as poor Mrs. Churchill tried to do, even when she had so little to build her faith upon.

They sent for Mrs. Burton, who came at once and did what she could to soothe and quiet her friend.

"It was such a comfort to know Georgie was there, and so providential too," she said, and then she asked if "that girl was hurt."

Mrs. Churchill knew she meant Edna, and answered faintly: "Slightly injured, the telegram said," and that was all that passed between her and her friend respecting *that girl*. Mrs. Churchill could only think of Edna as one who in some way was instrumental in Charlie's death. If she had not enticed him, he would not have done what he did, and consequently would not at that moment have been lying where he was, with all his boyish beauty marred and disfigured, until his mother would not have known him. It was the evening paper which had that last in it, and gave an account of the accident, which was caused by a broken rail.

The car in which Charlie and Edna were had been thrown down an embankment, and five of the passengers killed. Special mention was made of the young man who had been married in the morning, and though no name was given, Mrs. Churchill knew who it was, and wept piteously as she listened to Mrs. Burton reading the article to her.

Of Edna, however, she scarcely thought; Edna, the bride, who, the paper stated, seemed perfectly stunned with horror. No one thought of her until Maude Somerton came. She had heard of the accident, and as Saturday was always a holiday with her, she came on Friday night to Leighton, and brought with her a world of comfort, though Mrs. Churchill's tears flowed afresh at sight of the girl who, she had fancied, might one day be her daughter.

"Oh, Maude, my child," she said, as Maude bent over her. "He's gone, our Charlie. You were a good friend of his, and I once hoped you might—"

"Let me bathe your head. It is very hot, and aches, I know," Maude said, interrupting her, for she guessed what Mrs. Churchill was about to say, and did not care to hear it.

She had found it vastly pleasant to flirt with Charlie Churchill, but when the excitement was over, and she was back again in the school-room with her restless, active pupils, she scarcely thought of him until the news of his sudden death recalled him to her mind. That he was married did surprise her a little, and deep down in her heart there might have been a pang of mortified vanity that she had been so soon forgotten after all those walks upon the mountain side, and those moonlight sails upon the river; but she harbored no ill-will toward his wife, and almost her first inquiries after Mrs. Churchill had grown quiet were for her.

"Is she so badly hurt, that she will not be able to come home with the body?" she asked, and Mrs. Churchill started as if she had been stung.

"Come home! Come here! That girl! I'd never thought of that," she exclaimed; and then Maude knew just how "that girl" was regarded by her husband's mother.

She did not know how Roy felt; but she went to him next and asked if it was not expected that *Charlie's wife* would come to Leighton if she was able to travel, and Georgie's telegram "slightly injured" would indicate that she was. Although he knew it to be a fact, still Charlie's *wife* was rather mythical to Roy, and he had thought but little about her, certainly never that she was coming there, until Maude's question showed him the propriety of the thing.

"Of course she will come," he said. "I wonder if mother sent any message by Russell. Ask her, please."

Mrs. Churchill had sent no message. She did not think it necessary; the girl would do as she liked, of course.

"Then she will come; I should," Maude said; and next morning, as she combed and brushed Mrs. Churchill's hair, she casually asked:

"*Which* room is to be given to Charlie's wife?"

"I thought, perhaps, she would prefer the one he used to occupy in the north wing," she added, "and if you like I will see that it is in readiness for the poor girl. How I pity her, a widow in less than twenty-four hours. And such a pretty name too,—*Edna*. Don't you think it is pretty?"

"Oh, child, don't ask me. I want to do right, but I don't like to hear of her. It seems as if she was the means of Charlie's death," Mrs. Churchill sobbed, and Maude's soft hands moved caressingly over the grayish-brown hair as she spoke again for the poor girl lying stunned, and scared, and white, so many miles away.

"Charlie must have loved her very much," she said, "or he would never have braved your displeasure, and that of Roy. She may be a comfort to you, who have no other daughter. I begin to feel a great interest in her, and mean to be her friend."

Maude had espoused Edna's cause at once, and her heart was full of sympathy for the poor girl, for she foresaw just how lonely and dreary her life would be at Leighton, where every one's hand was against her.

"Mrs. Churchill will worry and badger her, and Roy without meaning to do it will freeze her with indifference, while Aunt Burton and Georgie will criticise and snub her awfully," she thought. "But I will do what I can for her, and make her room as attractive as possible."

So all of Saturday morning was spent by Maude in brushing up and righting Charlie's old room for the reception of the widowed Edna. There were many traces of the dead in there, and Maude's eyes were moist with tears as she put them away, and thought how Charlie would never want them again. It was a very pleasant room, and under Maude's skilful hands it looked still pleasanter and more inviting on the morning when the party was expected.

"I mean she shall come right in here with me at once," Maude said to herself, as she gave the fire a little poke, and then for the fourth time brushed the hearth and rug.

There was an easy chair before the fire, and vases of flowers on the mantel, and bracket, and stand, and a pot of ivy stood between the windows, the white muslin curtains of which were looped back with knots of crape, sole sign of mourning in the room. Maude had asked her employers for two days' vacation, and so she was virtually mistress of ceremonies, though Mrs. Burton bustled in and out, and gave the most contradictory orders, and made poor Mrs. Churchill's nerves quiver with pain as she discussed the proper place for Charlie to be laid, and the proper way for the funeral to be conducted.

And through it all Roy lay utterly helpless, knowing that

it was not for him to look upon his brother's face, or to join in the last tribute of affection paid to his memory. He knew that Maude confidently expected that Edna was coming to Leighton, and so he supposed she was, and he felt a good deal of curiosity with regard to the girl who had caricatured him in a poke bonnet, and stigmatized him as a Betty. Not a word concerning her had passed between himself and his mother since the receipt of the telegram. Indeed, he had scarcely seen his mother, for she had kept mostly in her room, and either Maude or Mrs. Burton had been the medium of communication between them. The latter had indulged in some very pious talk about resignation and all that, and then had descanted upon Georgie's great kindness and unselfishness in leaving her own business, and coming back to Leighton. She knew this from the second telegram received from Georgie, saying, "We shall reach Leighton sometime on Monday."

That Georgie was coming was of itself enough to take away half the pain, and in her blind fondness for her adopted daughter, Mrs. Burton wondered why Roy and his mother should look as white and grief-stricken as they did that October afternoon, when the carriage was waiting at the station for the living, and the hearse was waiting for the dead.

CHAPTER IV.

GEORGIE.

GEORGIE BURTON was a brilliant, fascinating woman, several years older than Maude Somerton, and wholly unlike her both in looks and disposition. She was not only very beautiful, but she had about her an air of culture and high breeding which would have atoned for the absence of all beauty.

Some said her chief attraction was in her great black eyes, which were so soft and gentle in their expression at times, and then again sparkled and shone with excitement; while it was whispered that they could on occasion blaze, and flash, and snap with anger and scorn.

Few, however, ever saw the flash and the blaze, and to most of the people in the neighborhood Georgie Burton was the kind, sympathetic, frank-hearted woman who, though a devotee of fashion, would always lend a listening ear to a tale of woe, or step aside from her own pleasure to minister to others.

She was very tall, and her blue-black hair fell in heavy masses of curls about her face and neck, giving her a more youthful appearance at first sight than a closer inspection would warrant. Her complexion, though dark, was clear, and smooth, and bright,—so bright in fact, that there had been whispers of artificial roses and enamel. But here rumor was wrong. Georgie's complexion was all her own, kept bright and fair by every possible precaution and care. Constant exercise in the open air, daily baths, and a total abstinence from stimulants of any kind, together with as regular habits as her kind of life would admit, were the only cosmetics she used, and the result proved the wisdom of her course.

She was not Mrs. Freeman Burton's daughter; she was her niece, and had been adopted five years before our story opens. But never was an own and only child loved and petted more than Mrs. Burton loved and petted the beautiful girl, who improved so fast under the advantages given her by her doting aunt.

For two years she had been kept in school, where she had bent every energy of mind and body to acquiring the knowledge necessary to fit her for the world which awaited her outside the school-room walls. And when at last she came out *finished*, and was presented to society as Mr. Freeman Burton's daughter and heir, she became a belle at once; and for three years had kept her ground without yielding an inch to any rival.

To Mr. Burton she was kind and affectionate, and he would have missed her very much from his household; while to Mrs. Burton she was the loving, gentle, obedient daughter, who knew no will save that of her mother.

"A perfect angel of sweetness," Mrs. Burton called her, and no person was tolerated who did not tacitly, at least, accord to Georgie all the virtues it was possible for one woman to possess. The relations between Maude and Georgie were kind and friendly, but not at all familiar or intimate. Georgie was too reserved and reticent with regard to herself and her affairs to admit of her being on very confidential terms with any one, and so Maude knew very little of her real character, and nothing whatever of her life before she came to live with her aunt, except what she learned from Mrs. Burton, who sometimes talked of her only sister, Georgie's mother, and of the life of comparative poverty from which she had rescued her niece. At these times Georgie would sit motionless as a statue, with her hands locked together, and a peculiar expression in her black eyes, which seemed to be looking far away at something seen only to herself. She was not at all communicative, and even her aunt did not know exactly what the business was which had called her so suddenly to Chicago; but she was aware that it concerned some child, and that she had left it undone and turned back with Charlie; and when at last she came and was ushered into Mrs. Churchill's room, where Mrs. Burton was, both ladies called her a self-denying angel, who always considered others before herself.

There was a flush on Georgie's cheeks, and then her eyes went through the window, and off across the river, with that far-away, abstracted look which Maude had noticed so often, and speculated upon, wondering of what Georgie was thinking, and if there was anything preying upon her mind.

Mrs. Churchill was very fond of Georgie, and she held her hand fast locked in her own, and listened with painful heart-throbs while she told what she knew of the terrible disaster which had resulted in Charlie's lying so cold and dead in the room below.

"I left Buffalo the same morning Charlie did," she said, "but did not know he was on the train until the accident."

"Were you alone?" Mrs. Churchill asked.

"No. You remember my half-brother Jack, who was at Oakwood two years ago; he met me in Buffalo, and after the accident remembered having seen some one in the front car who reminded him of Charlie, but it never occurred to him that it could be he until he found him dead."

Here Georgie paused, and wiped away Mrs. Churchill's tears and smoothed her hair, and then continued her story:

"It was a stormy night, a regular thunder-storm, and the rain was falling in torrents when the crash came, and I found myself upon my face with Jack under me, while all around was darkness and confusion, with horrible shrieks and cries of terror and distress. Our car was only thrown on one side, while the one Charlie was in was precipitated down the bank, and it was a miracle that any one escaped. Charlie was dead when Jack reached him; he must have died instantly, they said, and there is some comfort in that. They carried him into a house not far from the track, and I saw that his body had every possible care. I thought you would like it."

"I do, I do. You are an angel. Go on," Mrs. Churchill said, and Georgie continued:

"There's not much more to tell of Charlie. I had his body packed in ice till Russell came, and then we brought him home."

"But *Edna*, his wife, *Mrs. Charlie Churchill*, where is she? What of her? And why didn't she come with you?"

It was Maude who asked these questions; Maude, who, when the carriage came, had stood ready to meet the "girl-widow," as she mentally styled her, and lead her to her room. But there was no Edna there, and to the eager questionings Maude had put to Russell the moment she could claim his attention, that dignitary had answered gravely:

"You must ask Miss Burton. She managed that matter."

So Maude ran up the stairs to Mrs. Churchill's room, which she entered in time to hear the last of Georgie's story, and where she startled the inmates with her vehement inquiries for Edna. Mrs. Churchill had not yet mentioned her name, and it did not seem to her that she had any part or right in that lifeless form downstairs, or any claim upon her sympathy. Her presence, therefore, would have been felt as an intrusion, and though she had made up her mind to endure it, she breathed freer when she knew Edna had not come. The name, "Mrs. Charlie Churchill," shocked her a little, but she listened anxiously to what Georgie had to say of her.

"Hush, Maude, how impetuous you are; perhaps poor Mrs. Churchill cannot bear any more just now," Georgie said, and Mrs. Churchill replied:

"Yes, tell me all about the girl. I may as well hear it now as any time. O, my poor boy, that he should have thrown himself away like that."

Georgie had her cue now, and knew just how to proceed.

"The girl was by Charlie's side trying to extricate him, and that was how we found out who she was and that he was married that morning. She was slightly injured, a bruise on her head and shoulder, and arm, that was all, and she seemed very much composed and slept very soundly a good part of the day following. I should not think her one to be easily excited. I did what I could for her, and spoke of her coming home with me as a matter of course.

"She said, 'Did they send any word to me by that gentleman?' meaning Russell. I questioned Russell on the subject and could not learn that any message had been sent directly to her, and so she declined coming, and when I asked her if she did not feel able to travel so far, she burst out crying, and said: 'I could endure the journey well enough, though my head aches dreadfully, but they don't want me there, and I cannot go;' a decision she persisted in to the last. She seemed a mere child, not more than fifteen, though she said she was seventeen."

"And did you leave her there alone?" Maude asked, her cheeks burning with excitement, for she had detected the spirit of indifference breathing in every word Georgie had said of Edna, and resented it accordingly.

Edna had a champion in Maude, and Georgie knew it, and her eyes rested very calmly on the girl as she replied:

"I telegraphed to her aunt, a Miss Jerusha Pepper, who lives near Canandaigua, and also to her friends in Chicago, a Mr. and Mrs. John Dana, and before I left Mrs. Dana came, a very plain, but perfectly respectable appearing woman."

"Which means, I suppose, that you do not think she would steal, or pick a man's pocket, unless sorely pressed," Maude broke in vehemently. "For goodness' sake, Georgie, put off that lofty way of talking as if poor Edna was outside the pale of humanity, and her friends barely respectable. I am sorry for her, and I wish she was here, and I want to know if you left her with any one who will be kind to her, and say a comforting word."

"Maude, have you forgotten yourself, that you speak so to Georgie in Mrs. Churchill's and my presence?" Mrs. Burton said reprovingly, while Mrs. Churchill looked bewildered, as if she hardly knew what it was all about, or for whom Maude was doing battle.

In no wise disconcerted, Georgie continued in the same cool strain:

"This Mrs. Dana I told you of, seemed very kind to her, and I think the girl felt better with her than she would with us. She was going to Chicago with Mrs. Dana, and *Jack* was going with them. You remember Jack?"

Yes, Maude did remember Jack, the great, big-hearted fellow, who had been at Oakwood for a few weeks, two years before, and whom Georgie had kept in the background as much as possible, notwithstanding that she petted and caressed, and made much of him, and called him "Jackey" and "dear Jack," when none but the family were present to see him and know he was her half-brother.

"So good in Georgie, and shows such an admirable principle in her not to be ashamed of that great good-natured bear of a fellow," Mrs. Burton had said to Maude; and Maude, remembering the times when the "great, good-natured bear of a fellow" had been introduced to any of Georgie's fashionable friends who chanced to stumble upon him, simply as "Mr. Heyford," and not as "my brother," had her own opinion upon that subject as upon many others.

She had liked Jack Heyford very much, and felt that he was a man to be trusted in any emergency, and when she heard that Edna was with him, she said impulsively:

"I know she is safe if Mr. Heyford has her in charge. I would trust him sooner than any man I ever saw, and know I should not be deceived."

"You might do that, Maude, you might. Jack is the truest, noblest of men," Georgie said, and her voice trembled as she said it, while Maude actually thought a tear glittered in her black eyes, as she paid this unwonted tribute to her brother.

"That reminds me;" said Mrs. Burton, wiping her own eyes from sympathy with Georgie's emotion, "what about that little child, and what will your brother do, as you did not go on with him?"

The dewy look in Georgie's eye was gone in a moment, and in its place there came a strange gleam, half pain and half remorse, as she answered:

"I shall go to Chicago in a few days."

"Is that necessary?" Mrs. Burton asked, and Georgie replied:

"Yes, the child keeps asking for *me*, and I must go."

"What child?" Maude asked, with her usual impulsiveness.

There was a quivering of the muscles around Georgie's mouth, and a spasmodic fluttering of her white throat, as if the words she was going to utter were hard to say; then, with her face turned away from Maude's clear, honest blue eyes, she said very calmly:

"It is a little girl my step-mother adopted. Her name is Annie, and she always calls Jack brother, and me her sister Georgie. Perhaps mamma told you my step-mother had recently died."

"No, she didn't. I'd forgotten you had a step-mother living," Maude said, and Georgie continued:

"Yes, Jack's mother, you know. She died a month or so ago, and this child met with an accident,—hurt her back or hip, and it was to see her that I was going to Chicago."

Georgie finished her statement quietly, and then, turning to Mrs. Churchill, asked if she should not again wet the napkin and bathe her head and face. She was very calm and collected, and her white hands moved gently over Mrs.

Churchill's hot, flushed face, until she declared herself better, and bade Georgie go and rest herself. Georgie was not tired, and said she would just look in upon Roy, to whom she repeated, in substance, what she had told his mother of the dreadful accident. Roy had heard the most of the particulars from Russell, but they gained new force and interest when told by the beautiful Georgie, whose voice was so low, and tender, and sorrowful, and whose long lashes, half veiling the soft eyes, were moist with tears as she spoke of "dear Charlie and his poor young girl-wife." That was what she called her when with Roy, not "the girl," but "his poor young girl-wife." She had seen at once that with Roy she must adopt a different tone with regard to Edna, for Roy was eager in his inquiries and sorry that she had not come to Leighton, "her proper place," he said.

Georgie tried to be open and fair with Roy, who, she knew, hated a lie or anything approaching it, and so she incidentally mentioned the nature of her business to Chicago, and told of the recent death of her step-mother, of whom Mr. Leighton had, of course, heard. Roy could not remember, but supposed he had, and then Georgie told him of little Annie Heyford, her adopted sister, and said she must still go and see to her. And Roy thought how kind she was, and hoped the little Annie would not suffer for her absence, or her brother be greatly inconvenienced. Georgie reassured him on both points, and then, as he seemed to be very tired and his limb was beginning to pain him, she left him for a time, and returned to Mrs. Churchill.

CHAPTER V.

ROY'S DECISION.

DURING the time we have been introducing Georgie Burton, poor Charlie lay in the little reception-room below, with the terrible bruises on his face, and the night fell darkly around Leighton Place, and the stars came out and looked down into the open grave, where, early the next morning, they buried the young man who had been the darling of his mother, and a sad trial in so many ways to his only brother.

But Roy forgot all that now; and, as he lay helpless upon his bed and heard the roll of wheels which carried Charlie away, he wept like a child, and wished so much that no harsh word had ever been spoken by him to the boy whose face he would never see again.

And then his thoughts went after the young girl who had been Charlie's wife for only a few short hours. He could be kind to her, and he would, for Charlie's sake, and thus atone for any undue severity he might have shown his brother.

"As soon as I am able, I will go after her, and bring her home with me," he said to himself, and he tried to recall her face as he had seen it in the car, wondering if he should know her.

She had curls, he knew; for he remembered just how they were tossed about by the wind; and her eyes were large, and bright, and brown he thought, though he was not positive. At all events, they were handsome eyes, and he believed Edna was handsome, too; and perhaps he should like her very much. And then, as he heard a sweet, cooing voice in the hall, telling Mrs. Churchill's maid that her mistress wanted her, he found himself wondering how Georgie and

Edna would suit each other in case it came about that *both* should live at Leighton. He had heard so much said with regard to his making Miss Burton his wife, that he had come to think he might possibly do so some day, but there was no special cause for haste; at least, there had been none up to the present time. But if Edna came there to live, he felt that it might be well to have a younger mistress in the house,—one who would brighten up matters, and make life a little gayer than his mother, with her old-fashioned, quiet ways, was inclined to do.

Could Roy have had his choice he would rather not have had a change, for he greatly enjoyed his present mode of living, and his entire freedom to do as he pleased without consulting the wishes of any one. And yet he was not naturally selfish. He had only grown so from living so much alone with his mother and having all his tastes consulted and deferred to. A wife would have made a far different man of him, and have found him the kindest, most thoughtful of husbands. He had liked Georgie since she first came to Oakwood, and he thought her very kind and self-sacrificing to leave her own matters and come there to comfort his mother, who, as soon as the funeral was over, went to her bed, where she was cared for by Georgie with a daughter's tenderness.

When at last quiet had settled around the house, and the day was drawing to a close, Georgie left her patient for a little and went to see how it fared with Roy. His limb was paining him more than usual, for a storm was gathering, and the day had been long and trying, with no one to talk to but Russell and the doctor. Thus Georgie's visit was well timed, and she had never seemed so lovely to Roy, even when arrayed in full party splendor, as she did now in her plain dress of black alpaca, with a simple white linen band at her throat and linen cuffs at her wrist. She had dressed thus in honor of Charlie's funeral, and in her nun-like garb she seemed to belong to the house and be a part of the family. Her curls were put up under a net, but one or two of them had escaped from their confinement and almost touched Roy's face as she bent over him asking how he felt and what she could do for him.

She made his pillow more comfortable and pulled the covering smoothly around him, and pushed back a stray lock of hair which persisted in falling into his eyes, and made him feel so much better that by the time she had seated herself in the chair by his side he was nearer to speaking the words she had waited so long to hear than he had ever been before. But first he would talk with her a little about Edna, and see what she thought of his going after her or sending for her to come at once. Georgie, however, did not approve of Edna's coming. "Under some circumstances it would be very pleasant for you to have her here, and it would be so nice for Edna," she said in her softest, mellowest tones, "but just at present I do not believe it is best. Your mother is too much grieved and crushed to reason correctly on anything, and I fear the presence of Charlie's wife would make her very wretched. She cannot help it, I dare say, but she charges Charlie's death to Edna, and under these circumstances neither could at present be happy with the other. By and by it will be different of course, and then it may be well to consider the matter again. Pardon me, Mr. Leighton, if I have said too much, but your mother is so brokenhearted that I would not for the world have a drop added to her cup of sorrow. I am so sorry for Edna too. Poor girl! but she is young, you know, and can bear it better."

Georgie was very gentle, and her voice had trembled just as much when speaking of Edna as when talking of his mother, and Roy was wholly convinced, and thought it might be better not to send for Edna, but let his mother have time to overcome her aversion to the girl.

It was better also to give himself a little longer space of freedom as a bachelor; for if Edna did not come, there was no immediate necessity for him to take a wife to make the house inviting. He and his mother could still live on in their quiet way, which he enjoyed so much, and felt that he enjoyed all the more from the fact that he had come so near losing it; so he did not speak to Georgie then, but it was arranged that when she went to Chicago she should find Edna, and do for her whatever needed to be done, and ascertain if she cared to come to Leighton.

"I must trust it all to your management, for I am helpless myself," Roy said, offering his hand to Georgie, as she arose to leave the room. "Try and overcome mother's prejudice against Edna, won't you? Women have a way of doing these things which men know nothing about. Mother thinks the world of you; so do your best to bring her round, will you?"

Georgie's hand, though not very small, was soft, and white, and pretty, and Roy involuntarily pressed it a little, as he asked its owner to "try and bring his mother round."

And Georgie promised that she would, and then went away from Roy, who, in the gathering twilight, tried to imagine how the house would seem with that queenly woman there as its mistress, and while speculating upon it fell asleep, and dreamed that Edna Browning was freezing him to death with open windows, and tying a poke bonnet under his chin.

CHAPTER VI.

NEWS OF EDNA.

MRS. CHURCHILL had never been strong, and the suddenness of her son's death, together with the manner in which it occurred, shocked her nervous system to such an extent that for weeks she kept her room, seeing scarcely any one outside her own family except Mrs. Burton and Georgie.

As another proof of her utter unselfishness, Georgie had postponed her Chicago trip for an indefinite time, and devoted herself to Mrs. Churchill with all a daughter's love and care.

But alas for Edna! Her case was not in the best of hands; indeed, Roy could hardly have chosen one more unlikely to "bring his mother round" than Georgie Burton. That Edna would be in her way at Leighton, Georgie had decided from the moment she had looked upon the great, sad eyes brimming with tears, and the childish mouth, quivering in a way which made her big-hearted brother Jack long to kiss the grief away and fold the little creature in his arms as a mother would her child.

She seemed a mere child to both Jack and Georgie, the latter of whom in her surprise at hearing she was Charlie Churchill's wife had asked how old she was.

"Seventeen last May," was the reply, and Georgie thought with a sigh of the years which lay between herself and that sweet age of girlhood.

Roy liked young girls, she had heard him say so, and knew that he treated Maude Somerton, of nineteen, with far more familiarity than he did Georgie Burton, of,—she never told how many years. And Roy would like Edna, first as a sister and then, perhaps, as something nearer, for that the girl was artful and ambitious, she did not doubt, and to have her at Leighton was far too dangerous an experiment. In this conviction she was strengthened after her talk with Roy, and whenever Mrs. Churchill mentioned her, as she frequently did, wondering what she would do, Georgie always made some reply calculated to put down any feelings of pity or interest which might be springing up in the mother's heart. But she never said a word *against* Edna; everything was in her favor, and still she managed to harm her just the same, and to impress Mrs. Churchill with the idea that she could not have her there, and so the tide was setting in strongly against poor, widowed, friendless Edna.

It was two weeks now since the accident, and through Jack Heyford, Georgie had heard that she was in Chicago with Mrs. Dana, that she had been and still was sick, and Jack didn't know what she was going to do if the Leightons did not help her. Georgie did not read this letter either to Roy or his mother. She merely said that Jack had seen Edna, who was still with Mrs. Dana.

"Does he write what she intends doing?" Roy asked, and Georgie replied that he did not, and then Roy fell into a fit of musing, and was glad he had sent Charlie five hundred dollars, and he wished he had made the check larger, as he certainly would have done had he known what was to follow.

"Poor Charlie!" he sighed. "He made me a world of trouble, but I wish I had him back;" and then he remembered the unpaid bills sent to him from Canandaigua since his brother's death, and of which his mother must not know, as some of them were contracted for Edna.

There was a jeweller's bill for the wedding ring, and a set of coral, with gold watch and chain, the whole amounting to two hundred dollars. And Roy paid it, and felt glad that

Edna had the watch, and hoped it was pretty, and wished Charlie had chosen a more expensive one.

He was beginning to feel greatly interested in this unknown sister, and was thinking intently of her one morning, when Russell brought him his letters, one of which was from Edna herself. Hastily tearing it open he read:

"Mr. Robert Leighton: Dear Sir,—Please find inclosed $300 of the $500 you sent to Charlie.

"I should not have kept any of the money, only there were some expenses to pay, and I was sick and had not anything. As soon as I get well and can find something to do, I shall pay it all back with interest. Believe me, Mr. Leighton, I certainly will. Yours truly,

"EDNA BROWNING CHURCHILL.

"P.S.—You will find my note inclosed."

And there, sure enough, it was, Edna's note to Robert Leighton, Esq.:

"CHICAGO, October 18, 18—.

"For value received I promise to pay to Robert Leighton, or bearer, the sum of two hundred dollars, with interest at seven per cent per annum, from date.

"EDNA BROWNING CHURCHILL."

Roy read these lines more than once, and his eyes were moist with tears as he said aloud:

"Brave little woman. I like you now, if I never did before."

He did not want the money; he wished in his heart that Edna had it, and more too; and yet he was in some way glad she had sent it back and written him that letter, which gave him an insight into her character. She was not a mere saucy, frolicsome girl, given to making caricatures of men in poke bonnets; there was about her a courage and energy, and strict integrity, which he liked, and he felt some curiosity to know if she *would* pay the two hundred dollars as she had promised to do.

"I believe I'll let her alone for a while till I see what is in her," he said, "and, when I am satisfied, I'll go for her myself and bring her home. My broken leg will be well long before she can earn that money. Brave little woman!"

Roy sent this letter to his mother but withheld the one which came to him next day from Edna, full of intense mortification and earnest entreaties that he would not think her base enough to have accepted Charlie's presents if she had known they were not paid for. Somebody had written to her that the jeweller in Canandaigua had a bill against Charlie for a watch and chain, and coral set, which had been bought with promise of immediate payment.

"They say the bill will be sent to you," Edna wrote, "and then you will despise me more than you do now, perhaps. But, Mr. Leighton, I did *not* dream of such a thing. Charlie gave them to me the morning we were married, and I did not think it wrong to take them then. I never took anything before, except a little locket with Charlie's face in it. If you have not paid that bill, please don't. I can manage it somehow. I know Mr. Greenough, and he'll take the things back, perhaps. But if you have already paid it I shall pay you. Don't think I won't, for I certainly shall. I can work and earn money somehow. It may be a good while, but I shall do it in time, and I want you to trust me and believe that I never meant to be mean, or married Charlie because he had money, for I didn't."

Here something was scratched out, and after it Edna wrote:

"Perhaps you will get a wrong impression if I do not make some explanation. I did not care one bit for the money I supposed Charlie had, but maybe if I had known he had nothing but what you gave him, I should not have been married so soon. I should have told him to wait till we were older and had something of our own. I am so sorry, and I wish Mrs. Churchill had Charlie back and that I was Edna Browning. I don't want her to hate me, for she is Charlie's mother, and I did love him so much.

"Yours,   E. B. CHURCHILL."

This was Edna's second letter to Roy, who felt the great lumps rising in his throat as he read it, and who would like to have choked the person who could have been malicious enough to tell Edna about those bills.

"She did not mention the ring," he said. "I hope she knows nothing of that."

But Edna did know of it, and the bitterest pang of all was connected with that golden symbol which seemed to her now like a mockery. She could not, however, confess to Roy that her *wedding ring* was among the articles unpaid for, so she made no mention of it, and Roy hoped she knew nothing of it and never would.

"I'll write to her to-day," he said, "and tell her to keep that watch as a present from me, and I'll tell her too that by and by I am coming out to bring her home. She is made of the right kind of metal to suit me. Brave little woman."

This seemed to be the name by which Roy thought of Edna now, and he repeated it to himself as he went over her letter again, and pitied her so much, but he did not write to her that day as he intended doing. He was rather indolent in matters not of a strictly business nature. He hated letter-writing at any time, and especially now when exertion of any kind was painful to him; and so the days came and went until a week was gone, and still Edna's letter was unanswered, and "the brave little woman" was not quite so much in Roy's mind, for he had other and graver matters to occupy his attention and engross his thoughts. His mother was very sick, and Georgie staid with her all the time, and Maude Somerton came on Friday night and remained till Monday morning, and Roy himself hobbled to her room on crutches, and sat beside her for hours, while the fever burned itself out, and she talked deliriously of her lost boy and the girl who had led him to ruin.

"That girl will have two lives to answer for instead of one, I fear," Georgie said, with a sorrowful shake of the head, and an appealing look at Roy, who made no reply.

He did not charge Edna with his brother's death, and would feel no animosity toward her even if his mother died, but he could not then speak for her, and brave Georgie's look of indignation against "that girl." This, however, Maude Somerton did, and her blue eyes grew dark with passionate excitement as she turned fiercely upon Georgie and said:

"Better call her a murderess at once, and have her hung as a warning to all young girls with faces pretty enough to tempt a man to run away with them. You know, Georgie Burton, she wasn't a bit more to blame than Charlie himself, and it's a shame for one woman to speak so of another."

To this outburst Georgie made no reply, but Roy in his heart blessed the young girl for her defence of Edna, and made a mental memorandum of a Christmas present he meant to buy for Maude.

CHAPTER VII.

MISS PEPPER'S LETTER.

MRS. CHURCHILL was better, and Georgie was talking again of going to Chicago, and had promised to find Edna and render her any service in her power. Roy had written to Edna at last, but no answer had come to him, and he was beginning to wonder at her silence and to feel a little piqued, when one day early in December Russell brought him a letter mailed in Canandaigua and directed to his mother in a bold, angular handwriting, which stamped the writer as a person of striking originality and strongly marked character. In his mother's weak state it would not do to excite her, and so Roy opened the letter himself and glanced at the signature:

"Yours to command,
"JERUSHA AMANDA PEPPER."

And that worthy woman, who rejoiced in so euphonious a name, wrote from her own fireside in Richmond to Mrs. Churchill, as follows:

"RICHMOND, ALLEN'S HILL,
"ONTARIO CO., N.Y., *Dec. 4th,* 18—.

"MRS. CHURCHILL:

"*Dear Madam*—I've had it on my mind to write to you ever since that terrible disaster by which you were deprived of a son, who was taken to eternity without ever the chance for one last prayer or cry to be saved. Let us hope he had made his prayers beforehand and had no need for them. He had been baptized, I suppose, as I hear you are a church woman, but are you High or Low? Everything to my mind depends upon that. I hold the Low to be purely Evangelical, while the High,—well, I will not harrow up your feelings; what I want to say is, that I do not and never have for a single moment upheld my niece, or rather my great niece, Edna, in what she has done. I took her from charity when her father died, although he was *higher* than I in his views, and we used to hold many a controversial argument on apostolic succession, for he was a clergyman and my sister's son. His wife, who set up to be a lady and taught music in our select school, died when Edna was born, and I believe went to Heaven, though we never agreed as to the age when children should be confirmed, nor about that word regeneration in the baptismal service. I hold it's a stumbling block and ought to be struck out, while she said I did not understand its import, and confounded it with something else; but that's neither here nor there. Lucy was a good woman and made my nephew a good wife, though she would keep a girl, which I never did.

"When William died, twelve years ago, I took Edna and have been a mother to her ever since, and made her learn the catechism and creed, and thoroughly indoctrinated her with my views, and sent her to Sunday-school, and always gave her something from the Christmas-tree, and insisted upon her keeping all the fasts, and had her confirmed, and she turned out High Church after all, and ran away with your son. But I wash my hands of her now. Such a bill as I have got to pay the teachers in the seminary for her education! It was understood that after she graduated she was to stay there and teach to pay for her schooling, and what does she do but run away and leave me with a bill of four hundred dollars! Not that I can't pay it, for I can. I've four times four hundred laid up in Mr. Beals's bank, and like an honest woman, I took it out and paid the bill and have got the receipt in my prayer-book, and I showed it to her, for she's been here; yes, actually had the cheek to come right into my house on Thanksgiving-day, when I was at church; and a good sermon we had, too, if our new minister did bow in the creed, which rather surprised me, after telling him, as I did only the day before, that I looked upon that ceremony as a shred, at least, if not a rag of Popery. He lost a dollar by that bow, for I had twelve shillings of milk-money I calculated to give him, but when he bowed over so low right at me as if he would say, 'You see, Miss Pepper, I'm not to be led by the nose,' I just put on my fifty cents, and let it go at that.

"The stage came in while I was at church; but I never thought of Edna till I got home and smelled the turkey I had left in the oven more than I should have smelled it if somebody hadn't hurried up the fire; and there was the vegetables cooking, and the table set for two; and Edna, in her black dress, stood before the fire with her hands held tight together, and a look on her face as if she felt she'd no business there after all she had done.

"'Edna Browning,' I said, 'what are you doing here, and how dare you come after disgracing me so?'

"Then she said something about its being the only place she had to go to, and my being lonely eating dinner alone Thanksgiving-day, and began to be histericky, of course.

"If there's anything I pride myself on more than another, it's *firmness* and presence of mind, and I am happy to say I maintained them both, though I did come near giving way, when I saw how what I said affected her.

"I told her that to get into any family the way she did into yours was mean and disgraceful, and said she was to blame for the young man's death; and asked who was to remunerate me for that four hundred dollars I had to pay for her schooling; and who was to pay for all the trinkets at Greenough's in Canandaigua, and if she was not ashamed to wear a wedding-ring a stranger had to pay for.

"Up to this point, I must say Edna had not manifested much, if any feeling, and I really felt as if she was hardened and did not care; but when I spoke of the ring something about her made my flesh creep, and told me I had gone far enough.

"There came a kind of pale-gray look all over her face, and a steel-gray look in her eye, as she took off the ring and put it away in her purse, saying, in a queer, low voice:

"'You are right, Aunt Jerry. I am a murderess, and I ought not to wear this ring until I have paid for it myself, and I never will.'

"She did not eat a mouthful of dinner, but with that same look in her eyes sat staring out at a blighted rose-tree just opposite the window, and when I asked what she saw, she answered:

"'My future life.'

"And that was all she said till the dishes were washed and it began to get dark. I was going to light a candle, but she turned kind of fierce like toward me and said:

"'Don't, Aunt Jerry,—don't light that candle. I like the darkness. I want to talk to you, and I can do it better if I don't see your face.'

"'Twas a queer notion, but I humored her, and she told me about your son, and took all the blame to herself, and said she was sorry, and told me of the money Mr. Leighton sent, and how much she kept, and that she was going to pay it back.

"'And if I live I'll pay you that four hundred dollars too,' she said; and her voice was so strange that I felt shivery like, and wished the candle was lighted. 'I have sent Mr. Leighton my note for the first two hundred. I shall send him another to-morrow,' she went on, 'and give you one too.'

"And sure enough she did, and I have her 'promise to pay four hundred do s with interest from date,' so that makes a debt of $800 she's saddled herself with, and she only seventeen. And upon my word I believe she'll do it! She is a little bit of a girl, but there's a sight of grit and vim wrapped up in her, and she seemed to have grown into a woman all at once, so that, mad as I was, I liked her better than ever I did before.

"She staid all night, and told me that Mrs. Dana in Chicago died suddenly from paralysis, and the husband asked *her* to be Mrs. Dana 2d, and take care of his little children and a baby of six months, and his wife only dead two weeks. That started her from there, and where she is now I know no more than the dead. She left me next morning, bag and baggage, and when I asked where she was going, she said, '*to earn my living.*'

"Then I asked if she had friends, and she said, 'None but God,' and added after a minute, 'Yes, one more, but he can't help me.'

"Who she meant I don't know, nor where she's gone. I tried to make her stay, but she said, 'No, I am my own mistress now. Marriage has made me that, if not my age, and I am going away;' and she went in the stage, and after she was gone I sat down and cried, for I felt I was a little too hard on her, and I could not forget the look on her face as I came in from church, nor the look as I talked to her about the ring and killing her husband. I have no idea where she's gone, but feel sure she will keep out of harm. She's been well brought up, and though some of her notions do not suit me, she is thoroughly indoctrinated in the truth, and will come out all right; so my advice is to let her alone for a spell at any rate, and see what she'll do.

"My object in writing this to you is to give you some little insight into the character of the family you are connected with by marriage, and to let you know I don't take my niece's part, although it is natural that I should find more excuse for her than you, who probably think it a disgrace to be connected with the *Peppers*. But, if you choose to inquire hereabouts, you'll find that I am greatly respected and looked up to in the church, and if you ever come this way give me a call, and I will do the same by you. If you feel like it, write to me, if not, not.

"Wishing you all consolation in your son's death,
 "Yours to command,
  "JERUSHA AMANDA PEPPER."

Roy read this letter with mingled emotions of disgust and indignation, and finally of tolerance and even kindly feelings, toward the writer, who had commenced with being so hard upon her niece, but had softened as she progressed, and at last had spoken of her with a good deal of interest and even sympathy.

"Poor little thing," he called Edna now, and he longed to take her up in his arms as he would a child, and comfort her. From the tenor of the first part of Miss Pepper's letter, he could imagine, or thought he could, just how hard, and grim, and stern the woman was, and just how dreary and cheerless Edna's life had been with her.

"I don't wonder she married the first one that offered," he said, and then as he recalled the man Dana, who had asked Edna to be his wife, he felt a flush of resentment tinge his cheeks, and his fists clenched with a desire to knock the impudent Dana down. "And it is to such insults as these she is liable at any time; fighting her way alone in the cold, harsh world, though, by Jove! I don't blame her for leaving that Pepper-corn, goading and badgering her about the ring, and murdering Charlie. I wouldn't have spent so much as the night there after that; I'd have slept in the dog-kennel first."

Roy did not stop to consider that no such luxurious

appendage as a dog-kennel was to be found on Miss Pepper's premises. He only remembered her cruelty to Edna, and the "pale-gray look which came into her face," and the "steel-gray look in her eye," as she took off her wedding ring, and then sat looking out at the blighted rose-tree, seeing there her future life. Roy was not much given to poetry, or sentiment, or flowery speeches, but he saw the connection between Edna and the blighted tree, and knew why it should have had a greater fascination for her than her aunt's rasping tirade.

"She is a blighted rose herself," he said, "or rather a blighted bud, only seventeen, as much a girl as she ever was, a wife of a few hours, a widow turned out into the world to shirk for herself with an assumed debt of, let me see, that two hundred to me, four hundred more to that miserly old sanctimonious Pepper, prating about High Church and Low, and arrogating to herself all the piety of both parties, just because she stands up straight as a rail during the creed, and believes Lorenzo Dow as divinely appointed to preach as St. Peter himself; that makes six hundred, besides that bill in Canandaigua, which Pepper says she's resolved to pay. Eight hundred dollars. Before she gets all that paid there'll be a grayer look in her eyes and on her poor little face than there was when she looked at the blighted rose-tree. And here I have more money than I know what to do with. I'll go for her at once, go this very day," and forgetting his lame leg in his excitement, Roy sprang to his feet, but a sharp twinge of pain brought him to his senses, and to his chair again. "I can't go. Confound it. I'm a cripple," he said: then, as he remembered that he did not know where Edna was, he groaned aloud, and blamed himself severely for having indulged in his old habit of procrastination, and so deferred the writing of his letter to Edna until it was too late.

For of course she never got it. If she had, it might have changed her whole line of conduct. At least, she would have known that she had two friends, one Roy, and the other the one she had mentioned to her aunt as powerless to help her. Who was he? for she distinctly said *he.* "Not that ass of a Dana sure, else she had not fled from him and his offer," and with his sound leg Roy kicked a footstool as the combined representative of the audacious Dana and Miss Jerusha Pepper. He was glad that woman was no nearer relative to Edna than great aunt, and so was his mother, for after his ebullition of anger was over, he decided to take the letter to her, and tell her what Edna had written to himself.

As Georgie was not present, there was no counter influence at work, and Roy's voice and manner told plainly which way he leaned.

In this state of things, Mrs. Churchill went with the tide, and cried softly, and said there was more to Edna than she had supposed, and hoped Roy would never take a cent of pay, and suggested his sending a check for four hundred dollars to that abominable Pepper woman, who thought to make friends with them by taking sides against her niece!

"She's a perfect old shrew,—a Shylock, you may be assured, and will take every farthing of principal and interest. Write to her now, and have it done with."

"And suppose I do," said Roy; "what warrant have we that this woman will not exact it just the same of Edna, who has no means of knowing that we have paid it?"

"I know she will not do that," Mrs. Churchill replied. "Disgusting as her letter is, I think it shows her to be honest, at least. At all events, I should test her."

And so Roy wrote to Miss Pepper, inclosing his check for the four hundred dollars, and asking, in return, for her receipt, and Edna's note. His letter was not a very cordial one, and shrewd Miss Jerusha detected its spirit, and sent back the check forthwith, telling Roy that she could see through a millstone any time; that it was kind in him to offer to pay Edna's debts, but she did not see the necessity of insulting her with a suspicion of unfair dealing with her own flesh and blood. She guessed he didn't know her standing in the church, and had better inquire next time. As for Edna, he need not worry about her. She (Miss Pepper) did not intend to harm her. She only wanted to see how much grit there was in the girl; and he would find sometime, perhaps, that a Pepper could be as generous as a Leighton.

Roy could not complain of the last sentiment, for he had himself been conscious of a desire to let Edna alone for a time, and see what was in her. But he did not feel so now, and if he had known where she was, he would have gone for her at once and brought her home to Leighton. But he did not know. The last intelligence he had of her was received in a letter mailed at Albany, two days after the date of Miss Pepper's effusion. In this letter, Edna wrote that she had disposed of her watch and coral for one hundred and fifty dollars, one hundred of which she sent to Roy, together with a second note for the remaining hundred due for the jewelry.

"You will forgive me, Mr. Leighton, for not sending the whole. I would do so, but I must have something to begin my new life with. I don't exactly know what I shall do, but think I shall teach drawing. I have some talent for that, as well as music, and my voice is not a bad one, they said at Canandaigua. As fast as I earn anything, I shall send you a part of it. Mr. Leighton, I have another debt besides yours, and perhaps you won't mind if I try to pay that as soon as possible. It will only make your time a little longer, and I do so much want that other one off my mind."

"I don't wonder she does," Roy said, as he finished reading the letter to his mother, who with himself began to feel a deep interest in this "brave little woman," as Roy called her aloud.

"She writes a very fair hand and expresses herself well," Mrs. Churchill said, examining the letter, and wondering where Edna was. "We have done our duty at all events," she added, "and I do not think anybody could require more of us."

Roy did not tell all he thought. It would not have pleased his mother if he had, and so he kept silent, while she flattered herself that they had done every possible thing which could be expected of them. Roy had tried to pay Edna's debts, and that he had not done so was not his fault, while she harbored no unkindness now toward the poor girl, she said to Georgie Burton, who came over in the afternoon to say good-by, as she was going to Chicago at last. Roy would never have told Georgie of Edna's affairs, but his mother had no concealments from her, and repeated the whole story.

"Of course you have done your duty, and I would not give it any more thought, but try to get well and be yourself again," Georgie said, kissing her friend, tenderly, and telling her of her projected journey.

Mrs. Churchill was very sorry to have Georgie go away, and Roy was, after a fashion, sorry too, and he went down to the carriage with her, and put her in, and drew the Affghan across her lap, and told her how much he should miss her, and that she must make her absence as brief as possible.

"Remember me to your brother," he said, as he finally offered her his hand; then after a moment he added, "I did hope to have sent some message direct to our poor little girl. Maybe you can learn something of her present whereabouts. I am most anxious to know where she is."

He held Georgie's hand all the time he was saying this, and Georgie's eyes were very soft and pitiful in their expression as she bade him good-by, and promised " to find out all she could about the poor, dear child."

CHAPTER VIII.

THE BRAVE LITTLE WOMAN.

BACKWARD now we turn to Edna herself, who *was* a brave little woman, though she did not know herself of what she was capable, or how soon her capabilities were to be tested on that October morning when she entered the cars, at Buffalo, a happy bride,—save when something whispered to her that perhaps she had not done the wisest thing in marrying so *secretly*. What would her teachers say when they heard the use she had made of their permission for her to accompany her sick friend home? And what would Aunt Jerry say to the runaway match when she was so great a stickler for the proprieties of life?

"She'll charge it all to my High Church proclivities," Edna said to herself, trying to laugh as she recalled her aunt's peculiarities, and the probable effect the news would have on her. "I don't care! I'm glad to be free from her any way," she thought, as she remembered, with a shudder, all the dreariness and longing for something different which she had felt in that house by the graveyard where her childhood was passed.

It had never been hers to know the happiness which many children know. No mother had ever put her to bed, and tucked her up, with loving words and the good-night kiss.

No hand had smoothed her locks of golden brown, as she said her little prayer. No pleasant voice had waked her in the morning from her dreamless sleep, and found excuse when the slumber was so hard to break, the eyes so unwilling to unclose. No little extra pie or cake was ever baked for her on the broken bit of plate, or cracked saucer. No sled, with her name upon it, stood out by gate, or door-step; and no genuine doll-baby ever lay in any box, or basket, or drawer in that prim, silent house, for Aunt Jerry did not believe in such useless things. "She gave the child enough to eat of good, plain, wholesome food, and that was all any one could ask." She knew, too, that Edna said her prayers, and she saw that her Sunday-school lesson was always learned, and heard her say the Creed and Commandments every Sunday afternoon; but there were no gentle words and kind caresses, no tucking up on winter nights, no loving solicitude to see if the little hands and feet were warm. Edna knit or sewed till eight o'clock, and then, prompt with the first stroke, put by her work and took the tallow candle from the mantle-piece, and without a word stole up the steep back stairs to her little bed in the room which looked out upon the graveyard just across the lane, where the white headstones shining through the darkness seemed to her like so many risen ghosts. She was afraid of the graveyard; and many a night she crept trembling into bed, and hiding her face under the clothes, said her prayers, not from any sense of duty, but because of the question sure to be put to her next morning, " Did you say your prayers, Edna?"

At the time of her father's death Aunt Jerry had contended with his parishioners about his body, and, coming off victorious, had brought it home with her and buried it just by the fence under the shadow of her own cherry-tree, where regularly every Sunday in summer she took Edna and talked to her of her father, and told her how sorry he would be if he knew what a bad girl she was, and how he would rest better in his coffin if she would try to be good and learn the creed and catechism, so as to be confirmed the next time the Bishop came. And, more from fear than anything else, Edna learned the catechism and was confirmed, and hoped her father would be easy in his coffin, as Aunt Jerusha said he would.

As a child, Edna shunned her father's grave, and thought only with terror of him who slept there; but after a time there came a change, and she no longer stood in fear of that grassy mound, but tended it with the utmost care, and sometimes, when no one saw her, knelt or rather crouched beside it, and whispered softly:

"Dear father, I am trying to be good: but oh, it is so hard, and Aunt Jerry is so cross. I wish you had not died. Help me,—can't you, father?"

In this prayer there was no direct appeal to God; but He who knew all the trials and sorrow of the poor orphan girl, heard that cry for help, and the world was always brighter to Edna after a visit to that grave, and Aunt Jerusha's tongue had less power to sting.

Aunt Jerusha meant to do her duty, and thought she did it when she tried to repress her naturally gay, light-hearted niece, and make her into a sober, quiet woman, content to sew the blessed day through and knit the livelong evening.

But Edna was like a rubber ball,—she could be crushed, but she would not stay so, and the moment the oppressor's foot was removed she bounded back again as full of fun, and frolic, and life as ever! So when at the age of fifteen she became, in one sense, a charity scholar in Canandaigua Seminary, she recovered all her elasticity of spirits, and, freed from her aunt's scrutiny, seemed constantly bubbling over with happiness and joy.

She was very popular, and, in spite of her plain dress, became the goddess by whom every academy boy swore, dreaming of her by night, and devising ways and means of seeing her by day.

Charlie Churchill was in love with her at once,—desperately, irretrievably in love, and, though she snubbed him at first, and made laughable caricatures of him in his foppish clothes, with his eye-glass, which he carried for no reason except to be dandyish, she ended by returning his affection and pledging herself to him on the fly-leaf of her algebra, that being the only bit of paper available at the time.

Charlie had the reputation of being very rich,—heir, or joint-heir with his brother of Leighton Place, on the Hudson. And Edna fully believed him when he talked so largely of "my house, my horses, my hounds, my park." All *mine*, and nothing Roy's, "Old Roy," as he usually designated his brother, whom Edna thought of as a sober, middle-aged man, who was at Leighton rather on sufferance than as its rightful owner.

After her adventure in the cars, and she learned that the man she had caricatured was the veritable Roy, she thought him rather younger and better-looking than she had supposed, but still esteemed him a kind of supernumerary, who would be dreadfully in her way when she was mistress at Leighton, and of whom she would dispose as soon as possible.

She would do nothing unkind, she thought,—nothing for which any one could blame her; but it was so much better for young folks and old folks to live apart, that she would fit up some one of the numerous cottages which Charlie had told her were on his place.

There was one near the river, a Gothic cottage, he said, somewhat out of repair. This she would improve and beautify, and furnish tastefully, and move Roy and his mother thither, where they could not be disturbed by the gayeties at Leighton. For she meant to be very gay, and have the house full all the time, and had made out a list of those who were to be her guests.

Aunt Jerry was to come during *Lent*, and the carriage was to take her every day to morning service in the little church; while, every Friday, they would have omelets for breakfast, and baked salmon trout for dinner. Edna had the programme of her future life all marked out, even to the dresses she would wear on different occasions. And she knew just how beautiful her future home was; for Charlie had described it so minutely that she had made a little sketch of it, and, with Charlie to suggest, had corrected and improved and enlarged it, until it was a very accurate picture of the grounds and house at Leighton; with Edna herself on the steps, fastening a rose in Charlie's button-hole.

The likeness to Charlie was perfect, and Edna prized it most for this, and put it away in her portfolio of drawings; and went on dreaming her bright dreams of the glorious future opening so joyfully before her.

She was not mercenary, and would have loved and married Charlie all the same if he had not been rich, as she believed him to be. But she was very glad that he had money, for her tastes were naturally luxurious. She liked beautiful things about her; and then she could do so much good, and make so many happy, she said to Charlie, when he asked her once how she would feel to know he was poor as a church mouse.

Charlie had almost made up his mind to tell her the truth, for his conscience troubled him greatly; but when, among other things, she said: "I do not care for your money, Charlie; and should love you just the same if you had not a penny. The only thing that could change me toward you, would be losing confidence in you," he could not tell her that he was deceiving her; and so he let her dream on, and tried to remember if he ever had told her positively that he was the heir of Leighton, and concluded that he had not. She had taken it for granted, and he was not responsible for the mistake.

Then, he trusted much to Roy's generosity. Roy would let them live at Leighton, of course; and it would be Edna's home just the same as if he owned it, only he did not know about *moving* his mother and Roy into that cottage by the river.

But he would not worry; it would all be right; and, in any event, Edna would be *his*, and could not "go back on him," when she did find out; and he could easily persuade her it was all done from love and his fear of losing her.

So he silenced his conscience, and let her go on blindly toward her fate, and surprised her one day with a proposition to elope.

At first, Edna refused; but when the mail brought her a letter from Aunt Jerusha, she began to waver. She had asked her aunt for a dollar of pocket money, and her aunt had written a stinging reply, telling her she *had* a dollar when she left home three weeks ago, and asking what had become of that.

"I know," she wrote, "that if you follow my instructions, you have put five cents every Sunday on the plate; that makes fifteen cents; then, you may have wanted some bootlacings,—you always do,—and possibly some elastics, but that is *all* you have any business to want; and you ought to have on hand *fifty cents* at least, and still allow for some extravagance I can't think of. No; I shan't send you any dollar for three weeks to come; then, if the roads are not too muddy, I shall be in town with some butter, and eggs, and poultry, and, if I hear a good account of you, shall give you, maybe, seventy-five cents.

"P.S. I've been half sorry that I let you go back to school this winter, for I aint feeling very well, and I shouldn't wonder if I took you home with me for a spell. I've got stuff enough together to make a nice carpet, and you could cut and sew the rags."

Now Edna had not spent her dollar of pocket money in ways of which her aunt would at all approve. Fifteen cents had gone on the plate, and five cents more to Sunday-school. Fifteen more had gone for chocolates, and twenty-five more for the blue ribbon on her hair which Charlie liked so much; twenty-five more to a poor woman, carrying one child in her arms and leading another by the hand, while the remaining fifteen had been paid for a saucer of ice-cream which she shared with two of her companions; nothing for shoe-lacings, nothing for elastics, and only twenty cents for anything which would commend itself to her stern aunt, who would call the beggar woman an impostor, the blue ribbon trash and vanity, which Edna had promised to renounce, while the chocolates and cream would be classed under the head of *gormandizing*, if, indeed, the literal Miss Jerusha did not accuse her of "gluttony and stuffing."

All this Edna knew was in store for her whenever the state of the roads would admit of her aunt's journey to town with her butter, eggs, and poultry; but, aside from these, there was the dreadful possibility of being taken from school and compelled to pass the dreary winter in that lonely house by the graveyard, with no companions but the cat and her own gloomy thoughts, unless it were the balls of carpet-rags she hated so terribly. When Edna thought of all this, and then remembered that Charlie had said, "I shall see you again to-night, when I hope to find you have changed your mind and will go with me yet," she began to hesitate, and balance the two situations offered for her acceptance. One, the lonely house, the dreary winter, the rasping aunt, and the carpet-rags; the other, Leighton Place, with its freedom from all restraint, its life of perfect ease, and Charlie! Can we wonder that she chose the latter, and told Charlie yes instead of no, and planned the visit to Mrs. Dana, her mother's cousin, and looked upon the proposition to accompany her sick friend home as something providential. There was no looking back after that, and Edna hardly stopped to think what she was doing, or to consider the consequences, until she found herself a bride, and stepped with Charlie on board the train at Buffalo. She was very happy, and her happiness showed itself in the sparkle of her eye, and the bright flush on her cheeks, and the restlessness of her little head, which tossed and turned itself airily, and kept the golden brown curls in constant motion.

Charlie, too, was happy, or would have been, could he have felt quite sure that Roy would send some money, without which he would be reduced to most unpleasant straits, unless he pawned his watch. He could do that, and he decided that he would; but as it could not be done until he reached Chicago, and as his purse, after paying the clergyman, and paying for his tickets, and paying for the book which Edna wanted, was none the heaviest, he feigned not to be hungry when they stopped to dine, and so had only Edna's dinner to pay for, and contented himself with crackers and pop-corn for his supper; and when Edna proposed sharing them with him, he only made a faint remonstrance, and himself suggested that they should travel all night, instead of stopping at some *horrid hotel* where the fare was execrable.

And Edna consented to everything, and, as the evening advanced, and she began to grow weary, nestled her curly head down on Charlie's shoulder, and slept as soundly as if she had been at home in her own room looking out upon the graves behind the churchyard. Once, about midnight, as they stopped at some station, Charlie went out for a minute, and when he returned and took his seat beside her, he said, hurriedly, as if it were something for which he was not very glad:

"I have just recognized two old acquaintances in the rear car, Jack Heyford and Georgie Burton. I hope they won't see us. I like Jack well enough; but to have that Georgie's great big eyes spearing at you I could not bear."

"Who is Georgie Burton, and who is Jack Heyford?" Edna asked; and Charlie replied, "Georgie lives at Oakwood, near Leighton, and is the proudest, stuck-up thing, and has tried her best to catch old Roy. I think she'll do it, too, in time, and then, my ——, won't she snub you, because—"

He hesitated a moment, while Edna said:

"Because what? Tell me, please, why Georgie Burton will snub me."

"Well, because you are poor, and she is rich," Charlie jerked out; and Edna said, innocently:

"But I shall be rich, too, as rich as she, won't I, Charlie?"

Her clear, honest eyes were fixed upon his without a shadow of suspicion; and Charlie could not undeceive her, and tell her that ten dollars was all the money he had in the world; that to defray the expenses of that journey he had sold a diamond stud in Buffalo, and, if Roy did not come to the rescue, his watch must get them back to Leighton.

"Even if you were not rich you would be worth a hundred Georgie Burtons," he said, as he drew her closely to his side; and then he spoke of Jack Heyford, Georgie's half-brother, and the best fellow in the world, and Edna listened awhile, until things began to get a little mixed in her brain, and her head lay again on Charlie's shoulder, and her eyes were closed in sleep.

The day had been very warm and sultry, and although somewhat out of season, a heavy thunder-storm had come up, and the darkness without grew darker as the rain beat against the windows, and flashes of lightning showed occasionally against the inky sky. Faster and faster the train sped on ; and Charlie's head drooped till his locks mingled with Edna's curls of golden brown, and in his sleep his arm tightened around her waist, and he was dreaming perhaps of Roy and his mother, and what they would say to his wife, when suddenly, without a moment's warning, came the fearful crash, and the next flash of lightning which lit up the gloom showed a dreadful sight of broken beams, and shattered boards, and shivered glass, and a boyish form wedged tightly in, its white face upturned to the pitiless sky, while beside it crouched the girlish bride, trying in vain to extricate her lover, as her quivering lips kept whispering, "Charlie, oh, Charlie!"

CHAPTER IX.

AFTER THE ACCIDENT.

IT was Jack Heyford who found our heroine; big-hearted Jack, who, after shaking himself loose from Georgie's nervous, terrified grasp, and ascertaining that neither she nor himself was injured, went at once to the rescue of the poor wretches shrieking and dying beneath the wreck. A man from a house near by came out with a lantern, and Jack stood beside him when its rays first fell upon Edna, kneeling by her husband and trying to get him free. Something in the exceeding beauty of her face, together with its horrified expression, struck deep at Jack's heart, and bending over her, he said softly as a mother would address her child:

"Poor little one, are you hurt? and is that your brother lying there?"

Edna recognized the genuine kindness and sympathy in the voice, and answered:

"Oh, Charlie, Charlie, get him out. He is my husband. We were married this morning."

A look of surprise and incredulity flitted over Jack's face; she seemed so young, so like a child, this girl who was married that morning, and whose husband lay dead before him. But he asked her no more questions then, and set himself at once to release the body from the heavy timbers which held it fast. There was a terrible gash across the temple, and the blood was pouring from it so that recognition was impossible until the body was taken to a house near by, and the white, marred face made clean. Then, with a start, Jack exclaimed:

"Oh, Georgie, come quick! It's Charlie Churchill. Don't you remember my telling you that I saw some one in the front car who resembled him?"

In an instant Georgie was at his side and bending over the lifeless form of the young man.

"Yes, 'tis Charlie," she said, "and who is this girl clinging to him and kissing him so?"

Her voice showed plainly that she thought *this girl* had no right to be "clinging to him and kissing him so," and her black eyes had in them a look of virtuous indignation as they scrutinized poor Edna, who shrank back a little when Georgie, wholly disbelieving Jack's answer that she was Charlie's wife, married the previous day, laid her hand firmly on the girl's shoulder and demanded sternly:

"Who are you, and what do you know of Mr. Churchill? He is a friend of mine."

In a kind of frightened, helpless way, Edna lifted up her tearful eyes, and with lips quivering with pain, replied:

"Charlie was my husband. I am Edna Browning. We ran away and were married in Buffalo, and now he is killed."

She had told her story, and her eyes fell beneath the cold gaze bent upon her, while as one woman reads another, so Edna, though ignorant of the world and of such people as Georgie Burton, read doubt and distrust in the proud face above her; and with a moan like some hunted animal brought to bay, she turned appealingly to *Jack*, as if knowing instinctively that in him she had a friend. And Jack bent down beside her, and laid his great warm hand upon her head, and smoothed her tangled hair, and wiped from one of the curls a drop of blood which had come from Charlie's wound. Edna answered all Jack's questions unhesitatingly, and when he asked if she was not hurt, she told of the blow on her head and shoulder, and offered no remonstrance when he proposed that she should lie down upon the lounge the woman of the house prepared for her. She was not seriously hurt, but the pain in her head increased, and she found it impossible to sit up when once she had lain down upon the pillow, which Jack himself arranged for her.

Georgie was busy with Charlie for a time, and then when it was certain that he was past recall, she went to Edna and asked what she could do for her.

Edna knew that she was Georgie Burton, the proud woman whom Charlie disliked, and she shrank from her advances and answered rather curtly:

"Nothing, thank you. No one can do anything for me."

Towards Jack, however, she felt differently. Charlie had spoken well of him, and even if he had not, Edna would have trusted that honest face and kindly voice anywhere, and when he said to her, "We have telegraphed to your husband's family, and if you will give me the address of your

Chicago friends I will also send a dispatch to them," she told him of Mrs. Joseph Dana, and of her aunt in Richmond, to whom she wished both letter and telegram to be forwarded.

When Edna knew the dispatch had gone to Charlie's brother, she turned her face to the wall and wept bitterly as she thought how different her going to Leighton would be from what she had anticipated, for that she should go there she never for a moment doubted. It was Charlie's home, and she was his wife, and when she remembered Aunt Jerusha and the house by the graveyard, she was glad she had a refuge from the storm sure to burst upon her head.

Edna was very young, and sleep comes easily to such, and she fell asleep at last and slept heavily for two or three hours, while around the work of caring for the dead and ministering to the living went on.

Georgie was very busy, and with her own hands wiped the blood from some flesh wound, and then bandaged up the hand or arm with a skill unsurpassed by the surgeons in attendance. She could do this to strangers who thought her a perfect saint, and remembered her always as the beautiful woman who was so kind, and whose voice was so soft and pitiful as she administered to their wants. But when she passed the room where Edna lay, there came a look upon her face which showed she had but little sympathy with that poor girl. Edna had concealed nothing in her story, and Georgie, judging from a worldly point of view, knew that Charlie Churchill had made a terrible *mésalliance*, and said so to Jack, when for a few moments he stood by her near the door of Edna's room.

"A poor girl with no family connections, what will poor Mrs. Churchill say, and she so proud. I think it a dreadful thing. Of course, they never can receive her at Leighton."

"Why not?" Jack asked, a little sharply, and Georgie replied:

"There can be nothing in common between this girl and people like the Leightons. Besides that, she really has no claim on them, for you know that Charlie had not a cent in the world of his own."

"No, I did not; Charlie's talk would lead one to a different conclusion," Jack said, and Georgie continued:

"Yes, I know Charlie used to talk to strangers as if it was all his, when the facts are that the property came through the Leighton line, and neither Charlie nor his mother have anything except what Roy gives them. This girl thought otherwise, I dare say, and married for money more than anything else."

"Heaven help her then, poor little thing," Jack said, as he moved away, and his ejaculation was echoed in the faint cry which the "poor little thing" tried to smother as she, too, whispered gaspingly, "yes, Heaven help me, if all that woman has said is true."

Edna was awake, and had been an unwilling listener to a conversation which made her at first grow angry and resentful, and then quiver and shake with a nameless terror of something coming upon her worse even than Charlie's terrible death. To lose confidence in him whom she had trusted so implicitly; to know he had deceived her; aye, had died with a lie in his heart, if not on his lips, was terrible, and Edna felt for a moment as if she were going mad. From the lounge where she lay she could see a corner of the sheet which covered her dead, and with a shudder she turned herself away from that shrouded form, moaning bitterly:

"Oh, Charlie, is it true, and was it a lie you told me all the time. I didn't care for your money. It isn't that which hurts me so. It's losing faith in you. Oh, Charlie, my lost, lost Charlie."

One of the women of the house heard her, and catching the last words went in to comfort her. Her story was generally known by this time, and great was the sympathy expressed for her and the curiosity to see her, and there was a world of pity for her in the heart of the woman, who, feeling that she must say something, began in that hackneyed kind of way some people have of talking to one in sorrow:

"Don't give way so, poor little dear. Your husband is *not* lost; he has only gone a little while before. You will meet him again some time. He is not lost forever."

Edna fairly writhed in anguish, and could have screamed outright in her agony.

"Don't, don't," she cried, lifting up both her hands. "Please go away. Don't talk. I can't bear it. Oh I wish I had never been born."

"She was getting out of her head," the woman thought, and she went after Jack Heyford, who seemed to be more to her than any one else.

But Edna was not crazy, and when Jack came to her, there were no tears in her eyes, no traces of violent emotion on her face,—nothing but a rigid, stony expression on the one, and a hopeless, despairing look in the other.

She did not tell him what she had heard, for if it were true she did not wish him to know how she had been deceived. Of her own future she did not think or care. Charlie had not been true and honest with her. Charlie had died with his falsehoods unforgiven; that was the burden of her grief, and if prayers of the living can avail to save the dead, then surely there was hope for Charlie in the ceaseless, agonized prayers which went up from Edna's breaking heart all that long, terrible day, when Georgie thought her asleep, so perfectly still she lay with her hands folded upon her breast and her eyelids closed tightly over her eyes. She knew they had telegraphed to Charlie's friends, and she heard Miss Burton telling some one that an answer had been received, and *Russell* was then on his way to Iona. Who Russell was she did not know; and at first she felt relieved that it was not Roy coming there to look at her as coldly and curiously as Miss Burton did. Then her feelings underwent a change, and she found herself longing to see some one who had been near and dear to Charlie, and she wondered if a message would not be sent to her by Russell,—something which would look as if she was expected to go back to Leighton, at least, for the funeral. She wanted to see Charlie's old home; to hear his mother's voice; to crouch at her feet and ask forgiveness for having been instrumental in Charlie's death; to get the kind look or word from Roy, and that would satisfy her. She would then be content to go away forever from the beautiful place, of which she had expected to be mistress.

But Russell brought no message, and when she heard that, Edna said, "I cannot go," and turned her face again to the wall, and shut her lids tightly over the hot, aching eyes which tears would have relieved. When Mrs. Dana came from Chicago and took the young creature in her motherly arms, and said so kindly, "Don't talk about it now," her tears flowed at once, and she was better for it, and clung to her cousin as a child clings to its mother in some threatened peril. Russell was very kind to her too, for her extreme youth and exceeding great beauty affected even him, and he spoke to her very gently, and urged her to accompany him back to Leighton. And perhaps she might have yielded but for Georgie, who said to Russell:

"You know your mistress as well as I, and that just now this girl's presence would only augment her grief." This remark was overheard by Mrs. Dana, who reported it to her cousin, and that settled the matter; Edna would not go, and lay with her hands clasped over her eyes when they took Charlie away. Jack Heyford had come to her side, and asked if she wished to see her husband again, and with a bitter cry she answered him:

"No, I could not bear it now. I'd rather remember him as he was."

And so they carried him out, and Edna heard them as they went through the yard to the wagon which was to take the coffin to the station, and the house seemed so lonely now that all were gone, and she missed Jack Heyford so much, and wondered if she should ever see him again to thank him for all his kindness to her. He was a clerk in one of the large dry-goods stores in Chicago, and Mrs. Dana said she had occasionally seen him there, and they were talking of him and wondering how his sister chanced to be so unlike him, when a rapid step came up the walk, and Jack's voice was heard in the adjoining room. He had never intended going to Leighton, he said, in reply to Edna's remark, "I supposed you had gone with your sister."

He seemed very sad indeed as he sat a few moments by the fire kindled in Edna's room, and as she lay watching him, she fancied that she saw him brush a tear away, and that his lips moved as if talking to some one. And he was talking to a poor little crippled girl, waiting so anxiously in Chicago for his coming, and whose disappointed voice he could hear asking, "Where is sister?"

"Poor Annie! Sister is not here. There! there! Don't cry. She is coming by and by."

That was what Jack Heyford was saying to himself, as he sat before the fire, with that tired, sad look upon his face, and his heart was very sore toward the woman who had shown herself so selfish.

CHAPTER X.

GEORGIE AND JACK.

CHICAGO, Sept. —, 18—.

DEAR Sister:—I write in great haste to tell you of little Annie's accident, and that you must come out and see her, if only for a few days. It happened the week after mother died. Her foot must have slipped, or hit on something, and she fell from the top of the stairs to tbe bottom, and hurt her back or hip; I hardly think the doctor knew which, or in fact what to do for her. She cannot walk a step, and lies all day in bed, or sits in her chair, with no other company than old Aunt Luna, who is faithful and kind. But Annie wants you and talks of you all the time, and last night, when I got home from the store, she told me she had written to you, and gave me this bit of paper, which I inclose.

"And now, Georgie, do come if possible, and come at once. There are so many things I want to consult you about now that mother is gone. I can ill afford to lose the time; but if you will start the —th day of October, I will meet you in Buffalo, so that you will not have far to travel alone. I shall expect your answer, saying yes.

"Your brother, JACK."

This letter, or rather the slip of paper it contained, had taken Georgie Burton to Buffalo, and on to Iona, where the accident occurred. She might have resisted Jack's appeal, and thought it one of his scares, and that Annie was not much hurt, and would do well enough with the old negress, Luna; but Annie's letter was a different thing from Jack's, and Georgie wept passionately when she read it. It was a little child's letter, and some of the words were printed, for

Annie was just beginning to learn to write of Jack, who was her teacher in all things.

"Dear sister Gorgy," the note began, "mother is dead and I've hurted my back and have to ly all day stil, and it do ake so hard, and I'me so streemly lonesome, and want to see my sweet, pretty sister so much. I ask Jack if you will come and he don't b'leeve you will, and then I 'members my mother say, ask Jesus if you want anything, and I does ask him and tell him my back akes, and mother's gone to live with him. And I want to see you, and won't he send you to me for Christ's sake, amen. And I know he will. Come, Gorgy, pleas, and bring me some choklets.
"Annie Heyford."

Georgie could not withstand that appeal, and when Mrs. Burton tried to dissuade her from going, she paid no heed whatever. Indeed, she scarcely heard what her mother was saying, for her thoughts were far away with a little golden-haired child, for whom she stowed away in her trunk the chocolates asked for, and the waxen doll and the picture book and pretty puzzle found that day at the shop in the little town near Oakwood.

Jack met her in Buffalo as he had said he would, and took her to the hotel for the night, and, in the privacy of her room she said things she never would have said had there been other ears to listen than those of Jack,—faithful, trusty Jack, who knew that of *her* which no other living creature knew. Alone with him she needed no disguise, and her voice was not as soft and sweet and bird-like as it always was at Oakwood; but it sounded much like any ordinary voice, as she asked after Annie, and if it really was necessary to send for her and compel her to take that long, tiresome journey.

"Perhaps it was not necessary; Aunt Luna and I could take care of her, of course; but, Georgie, she wanted you so badly, and I thought maybe"—here Jack's chin quivered a little, and he walked to the window, and stood with his back to Georgie—"I thought you might want to see her. It's two years almost since you did see her. And mother's being dead, and all, we feel so lonely and broken up, and don't know what to do. A man's nothing with a little child like Annie. I say, Georgie,"—and Jack suddenly faced about—"I thought maybe you'd stay with us a spell. We want a head; somebody to take the lead. Won't you, Georgie? It is not like Oakwood, I know; and you'll feel the change; but it is a great deal better than it used to be when you were there; for Annie's sake, maybe, you'll do it, and I'll work like a horse for you both. I'm getting good wages now,—better than ever before. I can give you some luxuries, and all the comforts, I guess. Mother thought you would. She told me to tell you it was your duty——"

Jack stopped suddenly, arrested by something in the expression of his sister's face, which he did not like. She had listened in silence, and with a good deal of softness in her eyes, until he spoke of her staying with him. Then there was a sudden lifting of her eyebrows, and she shot at him a look of surprise that he should presume to propose such a thing. When he reached his mother's message touching her duty, her face flushed with resentment, and she broke out impulsively:

"Don't go any further, Jack. You can work upon my feelings when you talk of Annie's wanting me, but when you try to preach *duty* to me, you fail of your object at once. I parted company with duty and principle, and everything of that sort, years ago; and *you*, who know me so well, ought to know better than to try and reach me through any such channel. I am going to see Annie, to do what I can for her, and then return to Oakwood. The kind of life I have led there, since leaving you, has unfitted me for—for—"

"For our four rooms on the second floor of a tenement house," Jack said, a little bitterly, and then there was silence between them; and Georgie sat, thinking of Oakwood, with all its luxurious elegance, and Jack's presumption in supposing she would voluntarily give it up for those four rooms on the second floor, with their plain furniture and still plainer surroundings.

And while she was thus employed, Jack, who had come back from the window, was leaning upon the mantel and intently looking at the beautiful woman with marks of culture and high breeding in every turn of her graceful head, and motion of her body,—the woman whose charms were enhanced by all the appliances of wealth, and who looked a very queen born to adorn some home as elegant and beautiful as herself. She *would* be out of place in the four rooms which constituted his home, he thought; and yet her natural place was there, and in his heart he felt for a moment as if he despised her for her selfishness and lack of all that was womanly and right. But she was his sister. They had called the same man father; they had been children together, and though he was the younger of the two, he had always assumed a kind of protecting air toward the little girl whose beauty he admired so much, and whom he once thought so sweet and lovely.

As she grew toward womanhood, and her marvellous beauty expanded day by day until it became the remark of even passers-by, who saw her at the window, he worshipped her as a being infinitely superior to himself, and when a great and crushing sorrow came upon her early in life, he stood bravely by her, shielding her as far as possible from disgrace, and took her to his own fireside, and, boy though he was in years, told her she was welcome then and forever, and overtasked his strength and gave up his hopes of an education, that she might be warmed and fed and clothed, even in dainty apparel which suited her brilliant beauty so well. Latterly their lives had lain apart from each other, hers at Oakwood, where, the petted idol of her indulgent aunt, she had no wish ungratified; and his in the noisy city of the West, where, at the head of a family, he toiled for his mother and the little Annie who was like a sister to him, and whom he loved with a deeper love than he had given to Georgie, inasmuch as she was more worthy of his love. His mother was now dead; Annie was a cripple; and in his loneliness and perplexity his heart went after Georgie as the proper one to help him. She had acceded to his wishes in part, but refused him where he had the greatest need, and his heart was very sore as he stood looking at her and thinking of all that was past in her life, and of the possible future.

She suspected his thoughts, and with her old, witching smile and manner, arose and stood by him, and parting his hair with her white hand, said coaxingly:

"Don't be angry with me, Jack. I cannot bear that, for you are the best, the truest friend I have in the world, and I love you so much, and will do anything for you but that; I cannot stay with you. I should neither be happy myself nor make you so; and then my remaining in Chicago would seriously interfere with my plans, which may result in bringing us all together beneath one roof. Trust me, please, and believe I am acting for the best."

She was thinking of Roy Leighton, and how her staying in Chicago might prevent what she so ardently desired. The living together beneath one roof was a thought of the instant, and nothing she had ever considered for a moment, or ever would. But it answered her purpose just as well; and she smoothed Jack's hair so lovingly, and looked at him with so soft, beseeching eyes, in which there was a semblance of tears, that Jack began to forgive her, and feel that she was right after all, and it was not of any use to make her unhappy by insisting upon her staying where she did not wish to stay.

This was in Buffalo, where he met her. Then followed the catastrophe, and Jack uttered no word of remonstrance against staying till Russell came, although he knew just how the little girl at home was longing for them. He wrote her a note, telling her to be patient, as sister Georgie was coming, and then gave himself to the suffering ones around him, with Georgie as a most valuable aid. He had no thought of her turning back to Leighton, and the fact that she was intending to do so, came like a thunderbolt. He could see no reason for it, and when she pleaded Mrs. Churchill's grief, which she could quiet better than any one else, he was guilty of swearing a little about the whole Leighton tribe, Roy not excepted; and he made Georgie cry, and didn't care either, and would not ask her *when* she was coming, but received the chocolates, and the doll, and the puzzle in silence, and put them away in his travelling bag, with a half-muttered oath as he thought of Georgie's selfishness, and a choking lump in his throat as he remembered the little one at home, and her disappointment. Georgie was all sweetness to the last, and her face wore an injured, but still a forgiving, angelic look, as she bade Jack good-by and said to him:

"I shall be with you almost before you know it. Tell Annie not to cry, but be a good girl till sister comes."

Jack did not reply, and his face was very sad when he went back to Edna, and asked what he could do for her. He had done for her already something she would never know, but which, nevertheless, was just as great a kindness. After hearing from Georgie of Charlie's entire dependence upon

Roy, it had occurred to him to take charge of the dead youth's pocket-book, and see how much it contained. Ten dollars,—that was all,—and Jack's heart gave a great throb of pity, as he counted out the little roll, and thought how much Edna would need.

"Oh, I do so wish I was rich," he said; and then he drew out his own purse and counted its contents,—twenty-five dollars, and twenty of that he had mentally appropriated for the purchase of a coat, to be worn in the store, as the one he was wearing now was getting shabby and old. "Maybe Aunt Luna can fix it up," he said to himself. "It is not threadbare; it's only shiny-like in spots. I'll wear it another quarter, and here goes for that poor, little frightened thing."

He put fifteen dollars in Charlie's purse, and ten back into his own; then he looked at Charlie's watch, but when he saw upon it, "Presented by his mother, Christmas, 18—," he said this must go back to Leighton, and the watch was reverently laid aside to be given into Russell's care, but the purse he kept for Edna, telling Georgie that he had it, and when she asked how much was in it, answered, "twenty-five dollars," but said nothing of his coat and generous self-denial. He was used to such things; he would hardly have known himself with no one to care for, and when Georgie was gone with Charlie's body, he turned to Charlie's wife, and began to plan for her comfort. It never occurred to him that much as he desired to be at home, he could leave her alone with only a woman to look after her. If it had, he might have gone that night, but he chose to wait till the next day, when he hoped Edna would be able to bear the journey.

She was very weak and feverish when the morrow came, and Jack lifted her in his arms as if she had been Annie, and carried her into the car, where by turning two seats together he improvised a very comfortable bed, with his own and Mrs,

Dana's travelling shawl. Nor did he say good-by until he had carried her into Mrs. Dana's house, and deposited her upon a lounge around which four little children gathered wonderingly.

"I shall run in and see how you are to-night or to-morrow. Now I must go to Annie," he said; and Edna felt drearier, more desolate than ever, as the door closed upon him, and she heard his footsteps going from her, and leaving her there in that strange place alone, with the children huddling around her, and the baby screaming loudly at the sight of its mother.

CHAPTER XI.

EDNA'S FIRST WEEKS AT MRS. DANA'S.

MRS. DANA did not live in a block, but in a little wooden house standing by itself in the suburbs of the city. John Dana, who was a carpenter by trade, though he now kept a small grocery, had built the house himself at odd hours of leisure, fashioning it after no particular style, but rather according to his means, which were somewhat limited. It was neither pretty nor commodious, but very comfortable, and nicely kept by his thrifty wife, who tried to make Edna feel that she was not in the way, notwithstanding the smallness of the quarters and the hosts of children which seemed to fill every nook and corner of the kitchen, and followed even into the spare room, where, though dignified with the name of parlor, there was a bed on which poor Edna laid her aching head, feeling more desolate and homesick than she had ever felt in her life before, and in her desolation even longing for the old familiar chamber at Aunt Jerusha's which looked out upon the graveyard. She was not accustomed to city ways of living, and the house seemed so small and the noise in the street so great that she felt it was impossible for her to stay there. But what should she do and where should she go? To return to Aunt Jerusha was not to be thought of, and so she did not consider that for a moment; but her thoughts did keep straying away toward Leighton, Charlie's home. Perhaps Georgie had been mistaken and Charlie had a right there after all, or if he had not, possibly his mother and brother would take some interest in her for Charlie's sake, and ask her to come to them or try to help her in some way.

"And if they do, I'll accept their overtures," she thought to herself, as she held her throbbing head with both hands, and tried to keep back the scalding tears.

The children had been quieted down by this time. The baby was asleep in its cradle; Rachel, the girl who in Mrs. Dana's absence had cared for the family, had gone home, and Mrs. Dana, having laid aside her travelling suit, was busy putting things to rights and preparing supper for her husband, the master of the house, whom Edna had not yet seen, and whose approach was hailed by the children with a perfect storm of joy.

"Papa's comin'. I seen him, I did."

"I mean to tell him first ma's here."

"You shut, 'cause I'm goin' to. You're always doin' everything and me nothin'."

These and similar outcries fell on Edna's ears, and she began to feel a little curiosity about this man, who, finding her there in the capacity of a poor, sick relation, might consider her in the light of an intruder. But she did not know John Dana. Everybody was welcome so long as he had a crust, and as soon as he had been made a little more presentable by a fresh collar and neck-tie, and had washed his hands to get off what his wife called "a mackerel smell," he went to Edna's room and spoke very kindly to her, and said he hoped Susan had made her comfortable, and that the youngsters would not drive her crazy.

He had one in his arms then, and two more were holding to his coat skirts and climbing up his knees, and Edna felt at once just how kind and generous and unselfish he was, and the terrible pain lessened a little, and the home-sickness was not so great as before. He had a letter for her, he said, or rather one directed to Mr. Churchill, and placing in her hands the letter written by Mrs. Churchill to her son, he called his troop of children to come out while "Cousin Edna read her letter."

His wife had brought in a lamp, and sitting up in bed Edna held the letter a moment while her hand grew icy cold and her heart beat almost audibly. For a single moment she thought, "I will not open it. I will send it back unread;" then there came over her an intense desire to know what Mrs. Churchill or Roy thought about the marriage. Charlie had said to her on the morning of the bridal, "I have written to Roy and told him we were coming home after a little;" and this, of course, was the reply.

"Maybe I shall know if what Miss Burton said was true or false, if I read this," Edna thought, and with a hope for the best she opened the envelope and read the letter through, knowing when she had finished it how contemptuously Charlie's mother looked upon the girl who had entangled her son into a *mésalliance*, and how mercenary her motives were regarded.

"I cannot help feeling that if she had known all, your unfortunate entanglement would have been prevented," Mrs. Churchill had written, and Edna commented sadly upon it:

"Yes, if I had known all, it would have been prevented; but it is not the money,—no, not the money; oh, Charlie, it is losing faith in you which hurts me the worst," she moaned; then, resentment toward Mrs. Churchill got the better of her grief, and she said, "I'll write to that woman, and tell her how mistaken she is."

But only for an instant did she harbor such a thought. She would not wound Mrs. Churchill more deeply than she was already wounded. She would not write her at all, but to Roy, the heir,—Roy, the master of Leighton. The money came from him, and to him it should be returned, but not all at once. Fortunately for her Roy had sent a check payable to the bearer, and so she had no trouble in getting it cashed, and she decided that she must keep a part and pay it afterward. She had seen enough of the arrangements of the house to know that while there was not poverty, there was not a great plenty, and the owners could ill afford any additional expense.

"I may be sick for weeks," she thought, "and I shall need money, and that twenty-five dollars in poor Charlie's purse will not go very far. Oh, if only Aunt Jerusha was kind and forgiving; she has means; she could help me, if she would."

At this point Mrs. Dana came in, bringing Edna's supper, which she had tried to make as inviting as possible. But Edna could not eat; and, as the evening advanced, she grew so hot and feverish, and said such queer things, that Mrs. Dana sent for a physician, who managed by dint of bleeding, and blistering, and pills, to reduce his patient to a desirable state of weakness and keep her an invalid for two weeks or more; during which time Jack Heyford came many times to inquire after her, and bring her some little present which he thought might please her. Now it was an orange, or a bunch of grapes, and again a bouquet of flowers, which he left; and Edna liked these the best, and always cried over them, and thought of the little patch of flowers which, after a vast amount of pleading, she had been permitted to have for her own in Aunt Jerusha's garden.

From Aunt Jerusha there had as yet come no reply to the message sent from Iona, and Edna began to feel that she was alone in the world; with herself to care for, unaided by any one. And with returning strength she felt equal to it. The blow which had taken Charlie from her and opened her eyes to Charlie's defects, and showed her the estimation in which Charlie's mother held her, seemed to have cut her loose from all that was giddy, and weak, and foolish in the Edna Browning of old. All the lightness and thoughtlessness of her young girlhood fled away and left her at seventeen a woman, self-reliant, and determined to fight her own way in the world independent of friend or foe.

And so her first act when able to do anything was to send the three hundred dollars back to Roy, with her note for the balance. How proud and strong she felt as she wrote that note, and then read it aloud to see how it sounded, and how she anticipated the time when she could pay it even to the utmost farthing. Once she thought to sell her watch and corals, the pretty gifts which Charlie had brought her just before she went with him to the house of the clergyman. He had come into the room after she was dressed, and stealing up behind her, had laid the chain across her neck, and with his arms around her had held the watch before her eyes and said:

"Look here, my darling! see what I have brought you."

With boyish delight, he fastened it in her belt, and put the delicate pink jewels in her ears, and then bade her look at herself in the mirror to see the effect. That scene was as vividly in her mind as if it had occurred but yesterday; the happy, blushing face which the mirror reflected, and behind the young girl the tall young man whose lips touched her glowing cheeks as they whispered, "My beauty, my wife!"

She could not part with the bridal gift, so she kept a part of Roy's money, and put the coral away as unsuited to her black dress, but she wore the watch, and its muffled ticking beneath her belt seemed like some friendly human heart throbbing against her own. This was before she received Aunt Jerusha's effusion, which came to her the same day on which she sent her first letter to Roy, and which deserves a place in another chapter.

CHAPTER XII.

HOW AUNT JERUSHA RECEIVED THE NEWS.

AUNT JERUSHA had never heard of Charlie Churchill, or dreamed of her niece's love affair, and she sat milking Blossom, her pet cow, with her skirts tucked up around her, and an old sun-bonnet perched on her head, when the boy from Livonia station came furiously round the corner of the church, and reined up his panting, hard-driven horse so suddenly, that Blossom, frightened out of her usually grave, quiet mood, started aside, and in so doing upset the pail, and came near upsetting the highly scandalized woman, who, turning fiercely to the boy, demanded what he wanted, and what he meant by tipping over all that milk, which was as good as a quarter right out of her pocket.

The boy, who knew the contents of the telegram, made no reply with regard to the milk, except a prolonged whistle as he saw the white liquid streaming along upon the ground, and then glanced curiously at the tall, grim woman confronting him so angrily.

"Here's a telegraph," he said, "and there's two dollars to

pay on it, 'cause I had to fetch it so far; and your nephew, or niece, Edna, I forgot which, is dead, killed by the cars."

At the mention of the price she must pay for that bit of paper, Miss Pepper bristled at once, and began to revolve the propriety of not taking it from the boy, who could not compel her to pay for what she never received; but when, boy-like, he blurted out the contents, making a great blunder, and telling her Edna was dead, she grew whiter than the milk which Tabby, her cat, was lapping at her feet, and forgetting the two dollars leaned up against the fence, and taking the telegram in her hands, began to question the boy as to the *when* and *how* of the terrible catastrophe.

"Edna killed!" she gasped, and to do her justice, she never thought of the piles of carpet-rags the girl was to have cut that winter; for she had made up her mind to bring her home when she went with her poultry to Canandaigua; but she *did* think of the dreary look she had so often seen in the young girl's face; of the tears, which Edna had shed so plentifully when under discipline; and there arose in her heart a wish that she had been less strict and exacting with the girl who was said to be dead. "How came she near the cars to get killed?" she asked, and the boy replied:

"Read for yourself, and you'll know all I do."

It was growing dark, and Miss Pepper led the way into the house, and bade the boy sit down while she hunted up a tallow-candle and lighted it from a coal taken from the hearth. There was certainly a tear on her hard face as she blew the coal to a blaze, and the pain in her heart kept growing until with the aid of the candle she read:

"IONA, *October 8th,* 18—.

"TO MISS JERUSHA PEPPER:
"ALLEN'S HILL, ONTARIO Co., N.Y.
(*via* LIVONIA STATION.)

"There has been a railroad accident, and your niece

Edna's husband was killed. They were married yesterday morning in Buffalo. MISS GEORGIE BURTON."

"Edna's husband! Married yesterday morning in Buffalo! What does it mean?" she exclaimed, forgetting the dreary look, and the tears, and the harsh discipline, and in her amazement seizing the boy by the collar, as if he had been the offending Edna, and asking him again "what it meant, and where he got that precious piece of news, and who Edna's husband was, and how he knew it was true, and if it was not, how he dared come there with such ridiculous stuff and tip her milk over and charge her two dollars to boot?"

She had come to herself by this time, and the milk and the money were of more importance to her than the story, which she believed was false; and she continued to shake the boy until he twisted himself loose from her grasp and retreated toward the door.

"Goll darn ye," he said, "a pretty actin' woman you be, with some of yer relations dead. What do I know about it? Nothin', only it was telegraphed to the office this afternoon, and they posted me off to once to tell you 'bout it. I'll take the two dollars, or if you won't they'll send you a writ to-morry;" and the boy, grown bold from the fact that he was standing on the door-step and out of the vixen's reach, began to whistle "Shoo Fly" with a great deal of energy.

People like Miss Pepper usually have a great terror of a *writ*, and without stopping to consider the probabilities of the case, the good woman reluctantly counted out two dollars, and handing them to the boy, bade him be off and never darken her door again. Once alone, Miss Pepper read and *re-read* the telegram, which gave her no further intelligence than that first imparted to her. There had been a railroad accident out west and Edna's husband was killed. What could it mean, and who was Edna's husband? Then as she thought of Canandaigua and reflected that somebody there knew something about it, she resolved upon going to town on the morrow and ascertaining for herself what it all was about. But the next morning was ushered in with a driving rain, which came in under Miss Jerusha's front door, and drove into the cellar and through that patch of old shingles on the roof, and kept the old dame hurrying hither and thither with mop, and broom, and pail, and drove Canandaigua from her mind as utterly impracticable.

The next day, however, was tolerably clear; and having borrowed a neighbor's horse, and arrayed herself in an old water-proof cloak, with the hood over her head, she started for town, where the news had preceded her, and produced a state of wild excitement among the seminary girls, who pounced upon Miss Pepper at once, each telling what she knew, and sometimes far more than she knew. First, they had heard that Charlie Churchill had run away from the academy, then of the marriage in Buffalo, and then the last evening's papers had brought the news of the fearful tragedy, which changed the public feeling of blame into pity for poor Edna. But Aunt Jerusha knew no pity. That four hundred dollars which she must now pay for Edna's education precluded the possibility of pity in a nature like hers, and she felt only anger and resentment towards her luckless niece who had thrown such a bill of expense upon her. Not that the principal spoke of the bill so soon; he had no fears of its being unpaid, and would have waited till a more fitting time, before touching upon so delicate a point. It was Miss Pepper herself who dragged in the subject and insisted upon knowing *about* how much it was, even if she could not know exactly, and showed so much bitterness that Mr. Stone threw off fifty dollars and made it an even four hundred, and told her not to trouble herself, and a good deal more meant to conciliate her.

But he might as well have talked to the wind, for any effect his words had upon the excited woman. Everything which it was possible to learn with regard to Charlie Churchill she learned, and in her secret heart felt that if it had turned out well, she should be a little proud of the Leighton family; but it had not turned out well, and she expressed herself so freely, that a few of the girls who had always been envious of Edna, and Charlie's attentions to her, dropped a hint of a rumor they had heard about some bill at Greenough's, and forthwith the incensed Jerusha drove to the jeweller's, and by dint of questioning and cross-questioning, learned about the watch, and the coral, and the ring; then hurrying back to the Seminary, she picked up the clothes Edna had left, and cramming them into a little square hair-trunk which had held Henry Browning's wardrobe when he first went to college, carried it to the buggy by the gate, and putting her feet upon it, drove back to the Hill in a state of greater mental excitement than she had ever been in before.

Two days after Jack's letter came, telling her the particulars, and saying " Mrs. Churchill sends her love and will write herself when she is able. She is very sorry to make you feel as badly as she knows you must, and hopes you will forgive her."

This letter, instead of conciliating Miss Pepper, threw her into a greater rage than ever. This might have been owing in part to the fact that she was suffering from an attack of neuralgia, induced by a cold taken the day she went to Canandaigua in Edna's behalf. Neuralgia is not pleasant to bear at any time, and Miss Pepper did not bear it pleasantly, and looked more like a scarecrow than a human being as she crouched before the fire, with her false teeth out, a hasty pudding poultice on her face, a mustard paste on the back of her neck, and an old woollen shawl pinned over her head to keep it warm.

"Mrs. Churchill! Mrs. Fiddlesticks! That chit of a child," she said, when she finished reading Jack Heyford's letter, "sends her love, and is sorry, and hopes I'll forgive her! Stuff! I hope I won't! Brought up religiously as she was, confirmed and all that, and then ran away with a beggar who breaks his neck. No, I shan't forgive her; leastwise not for a spell. She ought to suffer awhile, and she needn't think to wheedle me into asking her home right away. By and by, when she is punished enough, I may take her back, but not now. She has made her bed and must lie in it."

This was Miss Pepper's decision, and taking advantage of a few minutes when her face was easier, she commenced a letter to Edna, berating her soundly for what she had done, telling her she could not expect her friends to stand by her when she disgraced herself by "marrying a man or boy who did not own so much as the shirt on his back, and who was mean enough to buy a lot of jewelry and never pay for it. Greenough told me about the watch, and coral, and ring, and he's going to send the bill to Mr. Leighton. I should think you'd feel smart wearing the jimcraks. Yes, I should."

Edna was better when the letter came to her, and the world did not look one half so dreary as it had done when viewed from her sick bed in that little front room of Mrs. Dana's. For the first time since the accident, she had given some thought to her toilet, and had brushed and arranged her beautiful hair, and thought of Charlie with a keen throb of pain as she wound round her fingers the long curls he used so to admire. Edna was proud of her hair, which so many people called beautiful, but which Aunt Jerusha had set herself so strongly against. Twice had that maiden's scissors been in dangerous proximity to the mass of golden brown, but something in the girl's piteous expression had reminded her of the dead man under the shadow of the cherry-trees, and the curls had not been harmed. Edna thought of Aunt Jerusha now, as she shook back the shining ringlets, which rippled all round her neck and shoulders, and with the thought came a desire to know what that worthy woman would say, and a wonder as to why she did not write. She was beginning to long for some expression with regard to her conduct, even though it should be anything but commendatory. She knew she would be blamed; she deserved it, she thought, but she was not quite prepared for the harsh tone of Aunt Jerusha's letter, and she felt for a moment as if her heart would burst with a sense of the injustice done to her.

One piece of information which the letter contained hurt her cruelly, and that was the news concerning the jewelry, which Roy Leighton must pay for, even to her wedding ring which she clutched at first with an impulse to tear it from her finger and thrust it from her forever. But the solemn words—" With this ring I thee wed "—sounded again in her ears, and brought back that hour when she stood at Charlie's side, loving him, believing in him, trusting him implicitly. She did not ask herself how much of that faith, and trust, and love was gone; she dared not do that, for fear of what the answer might be. Charlie was dead, and that was enough; and she wrung her hands helplessly and looked at the ring, the seal of her marriage, but could not take it off then, even though Roy Leighton must pay for it. She wrote to him again that very day, with what sore heart and utter humiliation we have seen in her letter to him, but with a firm determination to do what she promised him she would do, namely: liquidate her indebtedness to him and arrange if possible with the jeweller.

"I must go to work now," she said to herself. "I can be idle no longer."

But what to do, and where to seek employment in that city, where she was an utter stranger, was the point which puzzled her greatly; and when Jack Heyford came next to see her, she told him of her plans and asked him for advice. Had he been rich, Jack would have offered to pay her debts and make her free from want, for never was there a more generous, unselfish heart than that which beat under his old worn coat. But Jack was not rich, and his salary, though comparatively liberal, could not at present warrant any additional expense to those he already had to meet; and when she asked him if he knew of any scholars either in music or drawing, which she would be likely to get, he replied that he *did* know of *one*, and it would be just the thing for her, too, and help to relieve the tedium of sitting all day long in her chair, or reclining on the couch. Annie should take lessons of Mrs. Churchill, and commence to-morrow, if that would suit, and meantime he would inquire among his friends, and tell them Edna's story.

And so it was arranged that Edna should go to little Annie Heyford the next day, at two o'clock, and give her first lesson in drawing.

"You will have no difficulty in finding your way," Jack said. "I would come for you myself, but might not be able to leave the store at the hour." Then, just before leaving, he added: "Suppose you make it one, instead of two, and lunch with Annie. That will please her vastly, she complains of eating alone so often."

As there was no special reason why Edna should decline this invitation, she accepted it readily; and that night, just as she was falling away to sleep, and dreaming that she had more scholars than she could well manage, and that her debt to Roy was nearly paid, Jack was conferring with old Luna concerning the lunch of the next day.

"Get up a tip-top one, auntie," he said, handing her a bill. "She was half-starved in the seminary, I'll warrant, and I don't believe those Danas know much about good cooking; anyway they *fry* their beefsteak, for I've smelled it, and that I call heathenish. So scare up something nice, irrespective of the expense."

CHAPTER XIII.

JACK'S HOME.

JACK'S four rooms on the second floor, No. 30 —— street, though plain and poor, compared with the splendors of Oakwood, were very pleasant rooms at all times; and on the morning of the day when Edna was expected, they were swept and dusted, and put in order much earlier than was usual for Aunt Luna, who was not gifted with remarkably swift powers of locomotion.

The front room answered the double purpose of parlor by day and sleeping room by night, the bed disappearing in the shape of a broad, luxurious-looking sofa, or lounge, whose neat covering of green and white chintz, with the soft, motherly cushions, gave no hint of the bedding stowed carefully away beneath. The carpet also was green, of a light, cheerful pattern, while the easy chairs were covered with the same material. Plain muslin curtains were draped gracefully back from the windows, in one of which a bird-cage was hanging, and in the other a wire basket of moss, from which the German ivy hung in festoons, and then was trained back to the wall, making for both the windows a beautiful cornice, and reaching still further on to a pretty chromo which it surrounded with a network of leaves. Over the mantel was another and a larger-sized chromo, and on the wall opposite two or three first-class engravings. These, with a few brackets and vases, a book-case of well-chosen books, and a head of Schiller and Dante, completed the furniture of the room, if we except the bright fire blazing in the grate and the pretty lion's-head rug lying before the fender.

To the left of the front windows was a door opening into the hall bedroom, Jack's room, with its single bed, its strip of carpeting, its one chair, its little square stand, and on the wall a porcelaintype of Georgie, whose black eyes, though soft and beautiful, seemed to have in them a look of contempt, as if they scorned their humble surroundings.

A narrow passage, with closets and shelves on either side, divided the parlor from the room in the rear, which also did double service as dining-room and kitchen, where Luna baked, and washed, and ironed, and served her master's meals with as much care and attention as if he had been the richest man in the city, and dined each day from solid plate.

Old Luna's sleeping apartment was the little room or closet off from the kitchen, which she kept so neat and tidy that few would have shrunk from resting there in her easy chair, or even from sleeping, if need be, in her clean, wholesome-looking bed.

And here Jack lived content and happy till his mother died. With her death a great light had gone from his dwelling, for the mother and son were tenderly attached; but whatever Jack suffered, he suffered alone, in the privacy of his own room, or out in the dark streets, which he often traversed at night after his work was done. There was seldom a trace of sadness in his genial, good-natured face when he went back to Annie, who, since her accident and his mother's death, had at times been given to fits of weeping and depression.

"I want somethin', and I don't know," was what she had said at first when questioned as to the cause of her grief.

Gradually the want had resolved itself into an intense longing for "sister Georgie," whom the child regarded as little less than an angel, almost worshipping the beautiful picture which she sometimes had brought to her bed, where she could see it and talk to it when Jack was away and Luna busy in the kitchen.

With all the eagerness of a child, she had waited for Georgie's coming; and when Jack's telegram from Iona had told her there must necessarily be a delay, she cried herself into a headache, and finally went to sleep with her white cheek pressed against the portrait of Georgie, who was not worthy of this child's pure love, and whose heart was as cold and hard as the block of porcelain which shadowed forth her marvellous beauty.

It was a very sad heart which Jack Heyford carried up the stairs to his home on that day of his return, for he knew how bitter was the disappointment in store for the expectant little one, who had been dressed and waiting so long, and whose blue eyes shone like stars when the familiar step was heard upon the stairs. One look of welcome they gave to Jack, and then darted past him out into the passage,—out into vacancy; Georgie was not there.

"Oh, Jack," and the eyes were like Georgie Burton's, when looking afar off. "Where is sister? Didn't she come with you?"

Jack told her where Georgie was as gently as possible, and without a word or tone which sounded like blame, and Annie listened to him; and when he said, "she bade me tell you not to cry, but be a good girl, and she will soon come to you," the pretty lip quivered in a grieved kind of way, and the breath came in quick gasps as the child tried to do her sister's bidding.

"Is it naughty to cry? then I won't. I will try and be a good girl, but oh, I am sorrier than Georgie can guess,"

Annie said at last, and Jack felt something rising to his lips like a curse upon the heartless woman this little child loved so much.

He gave her the chocolates, and the doll, and the puzzle, and the book, and sighed to see how quietly she put them away without so much as tasting her favorite candies. And then he told her about the terrible accident, and of Edna, who, he said was so young, and pretty, and who was suffering such terrible sorrow. Annie was interested, and the tears she had repressed to please Georgie, flowed in torrents now, as she said:

"I am so sorry for the lady, and I want to see her so much, and I mean to pray for her that Heaven will make it better for her sometime;" and that night, while Edna in her lonely bed at Mrs. Dana's was weeping over her desolation and feeling so friendless and alone, a little crippled child lay on its back, and with hands clasped reverently, prayed for the poor lady whose husband was killed; prayed that "Heaven would bring it right some day, and make it better, and make her well, and make her happy, and make her another husband for Christ's sake." "I reckon that will do," Annie whispered softly. "Mother said, 'ask for Christ's sake, and believe you'll have it, and you will,' but then"—and here a dark doubt of unbelief began to creep in—"if that is so, why didn't sister come? I asked God to send her, and I believed He would just as hard, and He didn't. Maybe it's that lie I told the other day;" and again the waxen hands were folded, while the little trusting child asked, as she had done many times, to be forgiven for the falsehood told to Jack two weeks before.

She had confessed it to Jack, and he had forgiven her, and promised not to tell Georgie when she came. She had also confessed it to God many times, and asked Him not to let her do such naughty things; and now when she told Him about it again, she felt as if that one sin was forgiven, but away down in her heart was a shadow of unbelief, the first she had ever known. She had trusted Heaven, and her faith was firm as a rock that Georgie would come. But the contrary had been the case; Georgie had not come; Heaven had not heard and answered her, and she could not account for it. Poor child, she is not the first or the only one who has found it hard to understand just what Christ meant when He said, "What things soever ye desire when ye pray, believe that ye shall receive them, and ye shall have them."

CHAPTER XIV.

EDNA AND ANNIE.

BRIGHT and cheery as was the parlor at No. 30 on that autumnal morning when Edna was expected, the brightest, prettiest thing by far in it was the little girl whom Aunt Luna had dressed with so much care, and who sat propped with cushions and pillows in her easy chair, with her hair falling in soft curls about her face, and her eyes shining with eager expectancy. She was a little vain, and as she settled herself among her cushions and saw Aunt Luna's evident admiration, she asked:

"Do I look nice, Aunt Luna? Do I make a pretty picture? I hope so, for Mrs. Churchill is an *arterist*, you know, and 'preciates such things."

Aunt Luna's reply was satisfactory, and after making some change in the adjustment of the shawl on the arm of her chair, and lifting her dress so as to show her high-heeled slipper with its scarlet rosette, Annie was ready for her visitor. Nor had she long to wait ere a step was heard on the stairs, and Aunt Luna opened the door to Edna. Jack had said she was young and small, but neither Aunt Luna nor Annie was prepared for any one so very young looking and so small as the little lady who asked if Mr. Heyford lived there, and announced herself as Mrs. Churchill.

"Yes, he do live here," a blithe voice replied, and Edna walked straight up to the chair whence the voice came, and bending over the little girl kissed her tenderly, saying:

"And you are Annie, I know."

"And you are Mrs. Churchill," Annie said, winding her arms around Edna's neck. "Jack said I'se sure to love you, and I know it, without his saying so."

That was their introduction to each other, and they grew familiar very fast, so that before lunch was ready, Annie had told Edna how funny it seemed to think her a big married woman, and how glad she was she had come, and how sure she was to love her.

"I think I begin to know what Aunt Luna meant by God's making it up to me," she said, after a moment's silence, during which she had been holding and caressing Edna's hand.

Edna looked inquiringly at her, and she continued:

"I was so sorry about Georgie,—that's sister, you know. You seen her, Jack said."

"Yes."

And Edna gave a little shiver as she recalled the face which had looked so coldly and proudly upon her.

It had evidently never looked thus to this little child, who went on:

"I cried so hard when she didn't come, and was kind of mad at Heaven, I guess, and Aunt Luna talked and said how He'd make it up some way, if I was good, and so He sent me you, though it's funny you didn't go back with that poor man. He was your beau, wasn't he?"

"Yes, my husband," Edna faltered, adding: "I was sick, hurt, you know."

She could not explain why she had not gone with her husband's body, as it seemed natural that she should have done. Neither did Annie wait for any explanation, but went on talking in her old-fashioned way, which greatly surprised Edna, who was not much accustomed to children. Annie was an odd mixture of childish simplicity and womanly maturity. From having lived all her life with no other companions than grown-up people, she was in some respects much older than her years, and astonished Edna with her shrewd remarks and her mature ways of thinking. Georgie was the theme of which she never tired, and Edna found herself feeling more lenient toward the haughty woman whom she had instinctively disliked. There must be something good in her, or this little child would not love her so devotedly.

"The bestest sister and the beautifulest," Annie said, and when Edna, who had gathered from Jack that it was nearly two years since Georgie had been in Chicago, remarked that she should hardly suppose Annie could remember how she looked, Annie replied: "Oh yes, I 'members 'stinctly, or thinks I do. Any way, I has her picture and her letters; they are so nice. I want to show you one."

She touched a little bell on the table beside her, and summoning Luna from the kitchen, bade her bring the portfolio which held sister's letters.

"There they are; read any of them," she said.

And more to please the child than from curiosity, Edna did read one of the notes, bearing date six or seven months before, and as she read she felt a growing interest and even liking for Georgie Burton, who, however cold and proud she might be to strangers, showed a deep interest in Annie's well-being.

One thing struck Edna forcibly, and that was the hope Georgie expressed that her dear little sister would grow up truthful, and break herself of the habit she had of sometimes equivocating. At Annie's request Edna read the letter aloud, and when she had finished it she saw that Annie's face was crimson with a look of sorrow and shame.

"I didn't know as 'twas that one," she said, "and I don't want you to hate me. I did use to tell lies, oh, so many"—and the voice sank to a whisper—"and mother spanked me once and wrote it to Georgie, and told me how wicked it was, and I do try not to now, so much, though Jack says I will *romance* a little, that's what he calls it, meaning, you know, that I made up *some*. It's my blood; I heard Jack tell mother so. Bad blood, he said, though that time I cut my finger so and bleeded so much, it looked like Jack's did when he had the nose-bleed."

She had taken the matter literally, and Edna could not repress a smile at her interpretation of *bad blood*, while she began to wonder how much of this same blood, if any, was in Jack Heyford's veins. Georgie was only his half-sister she knew, while Annie was still further removed, although she called him brother. Any questions, however, which she might have put to Annie with regard to the relationship, were prevented by the appearance of Luna with the lunch.

It was a very tempting lunch, and Edna felt her lost appetite returning when she saw the oysters fried to just the brown she liked, the slices of rich baked ham, the delicate rolls, home-made and fresh from the oven, the creamy butter, the pot of raspberry jam, and the steaming chocolate which Annie liked so much and was occasionally allowed to drink. A dish of apples and oranges with clusters of rich purple grapes completed the bill of fare, and Annie proved herself a very competent little hostess, as she did the honors of the table and urged the good things upon Edna, who enjoyed it nearly as much as Annie herself, and forgot in part the dark shadow which had fallen upon her life. As if they had been princes lunching in some palatial mansion, old Luna waited upon them, showing a skill and readiness which rather surprised Edna until she heard from the negress herself that she had been a house servant in her late mistress's family in St. Augustine, Florida, that her duties had been wholly confined to the dining-room and its appointments until three years since, when she came to Mrs. Heyford.

Since then, to use her own words, "she has done little of everything, tend here, tend there, bake, and wash, and iron, and do what only low-lived trash does at home."

She seemed a very capable, intelligent woman, and evidently regarded "Master Jack and Miss Annie" with feelings amounting almost to adoration. Of Georgie she said but little, and that little showed conclusively her opinion of a young lady "who would turn her back on her own flesh and blood, and never come a nigh even when they sickened and died, just because they was poor and couldn't give her all the jimcracks she wanted."

"She was here oncet, two years or so ago," she said to Edna, who, after lunch, went with her to the kitchen for a moment. "She staid about three weeks, and seemed to think it was such a piece of condescension on her part to do even that. And we waited on her as if she'd been a queen, and Master Jack's bill for the ices, and creams, and fruit, and carriages, which he got for her was awful, and pinched us for three months or more. I must say though that she took wonderfully to Miss Annie. Never seen anything like it. Don't understand it, no how, and 'taint none of my business if I did."

Here Aunt Luna broke off abruptly, and Edna went back to Annie, to whom she gave the first lesson in drawing. Annie bade fair to prove an apt pupil, and Edna felt all her old ambition and love for the work coming back as she directed the child's hand, and then with a few rapid curves and lines made a little sketch of her pupil's face. The likeness was perfect, and Annie screamed with delight as she took it in her hand and inspected it more closely.

"It looks some like Jack," she said, "but none like Georgie. I wish I was like her, but Jack says I'm most like my father."

"How long has he been dead?" Edna asked, and Annie replied:

"Oh, ever so many years; before I was born, I guess. I never 'member him."

Edna laughed heartily at this characteristic reply, and as the afternoon was drawing to a close, she bade her pupil good-by, promising to come again the next day if Annie felt equal to another lesson so soon.

Regularly each day after this Edna went to Annie Heyford, who improved rapidly and evinced almost as much talent for drawing as Edna herself. Jack, who sometimes came in while Edna was there, became greatly interested and tried to secure other pupils for Edna. But his immediate friends were mostly too poor to incur any additional expense, while the ladies whom he only knew as he served them behind the counter did not care to patronize a total stranger who had no recommendation save that given her by her enthusiastic admirer, Jack. And so poor Edna was not making money very fast, and Jack was contemplating taking lessons himself by way of adding a little to her store, when an event occurred which changed the whole tenor of Edna's life and drove her to seek a home elsewhere than in Chicago. Without a shadow of warning, Mrs. Dana was suddenly smitten with paralysis, and after three days of silent suffering, died, leaving her five children to such care as the motherless poor can find. For a week or two Edna devoted herself to them entirely, and then the father startled her with an offer of marriage, saying, by way of excuse for his haste, that he must have a housekeeper, that he preferred her to any one he knew, and that in order to save talk they might as well be married then if she was willing.

Edna did not leave his house at once as some would have done, for she knew he meant well, though he had erred greatly in his judgment of her. Firmly, but kindly, she declined his offer, and then again stunned and bewildered, sat down to think what she should do next, and as she thought, her heart began to go out longingly for that old house by the graveyard. It was her home, the only one she had ever known, and Aunt Jerusha, with all her peculiarities, had many excellent traits of character, and would perhaps be glad to see her by this time.

Since that first letter, no communication whatever had passed between them, and Edna did not know how much Aunt Jerry might have softened toward her. As she could no longer remain with Mr. Dana, and as she could not afford to board elsewhere, and would not accept of the home which Jack Heyford offered her temporarily, it seemed that the only thing left for her was to go back to Aunt Jerry until some better situation presented itself to her. Jack himself advised it, after he found she would not stay with him, and so Edna bade adieu to Chicago, and with a sad heart turned her face toward Aunt Jerry, feeling many misgivings with regard to her reception the nearer she came to home.

CHAPTER XV.

AUNT JERRY.

EDNA had planned it so as to reach home on Thanksgiving day, thinking within herself:

"Her heart will be softer on that day, sure, and she will not be so hard on me."

Fortunately for her she saw no one in Canandaigua whom she knew, for the morning train, which was a little behind time, arrived just before the departure of the stage which would take her to the Hill. She was the only passenger, and as she rode along over the rough, uneven road, she had ample time for reviewing the past, and living over in fancy all she had experienced since last she traversed that route, drawn by Deacon Williams's old white horse, with Aunt Jerry beside her, prim and straight, and grimly silent, save when she gave her niece some wholesome advice, or reproved her for what she had not done quite as much as for what she had. Then she was Edna Browning, the happy school-girl, who knew no care sharper than Aunt Jerry's tongue, and from that she was escaping for a time, for she was going back to school, to all the fun and frolic which she always managed to extract from her surroundings; and Charlie was there to meet her,—aye, did meet her right by the gate, as the old white horse drew up, and would have helped her out, but for the signal she gave that he must not notice her. Aunt Jerry was death on academy boys, and her face assumed a still more vinegary expression as she asked:

"What young squirt was that who looked as if he was going to speak?"

Edna had not replied, as she was busily occupied in climbing over the wheel, and so Aunt Jerry had never heard of Charlie Churchill until the telegram was brought to her announcing his death. That scene was very fresh in Edna's mind, and her tears flowed like rain as she thought of herself as she was then, and as she was now, scarcely three months later. A wife, a widow, friendless and alone, going back to Aunt Jerry as the only person in the world on whom she had a claim.

"She won't turn me off," she said to herself. "She can't,

when I've nowhere to go; and I mean to be so humble, and tell her the whole story, and I'll try to please her harder than I ever did before.

Thus Edna reasoned with herself, until from the summit of a hill she caught sight of the tall poplars, and saw in the distance the spire of St. Paul's. Behind it was Aunt Jerry's house; she was almost there, and her heart beat painfully as she tried to think what to say, how to word her greeting so as not to displease. It did not occur to her that probably Aunt Jerry was at church, until the stage left her at the gate, and she tried the door, which was locked. Fortunately, she knew just where to look for the key, and as she stooped to get it, Tabby, who had been sitting demurely on the window-sill, with one eye on the warm room from which she was shut out, and one on the church whence she expected her mistress to come, jumped down, and with a *meow* of welcome came purring and rubbing against Edna's dress, and showing,—as much as a dumb creature can show,—her joy at seeing her young playmate again. Edna took the animal in her arms, and hugging it to her bosom, let fall a shower of kisses and tears upon the long, soft fur, saying aloud:

"You, at least, are glad, old Tabby, and I'll take your welcome as a good omen of another."

She let herself into the house, and with Tabby still nestled in her arms, stood looking around the familiar room. It seemed to her years since she was there, and she found herself wondering to find it so unchanged. The same rag carpet which she had helped to make, with what weariness and tears she could not recall without a shudder. The same calico-covered lounge, with Aunt Jerry's work-basket and foot-stove tucked away under it, the same fall leaf table with its plaid spread of red and green, Aunt Jerry's straight-back chair by the oven door, the clock upon the mantel, and could she believe her senses, a picture of herself upon the wall above the fire-place; a photograph taken three years before by a travelling artist, whose movable car had ornamented the common in front of the church, a terror to all the horses, and a thing of wonder and fascination to all the school boys and girls, most of whom first and last saw the inside of the mysterious box, and came out reproduced. Edna had picked blackberries to pay for her picture, and sat unknown to Aunt Jerusha, whose comment on the likeness was, "Better have saved the money for something else. You ain't so handsome that you need want to be repeated. It looks enough sight better than you do."

Edna knew that the picture did not look half as well as she did. The mouth was awry, the chin elevated, the hands immense, and the whole body indicative of awkwardness, and lack of taste on the artist's part. But it was herself, and Edna prized it and kept it hidden away from Aunt Jerry, who threatened to burn it when she found her niece looking at it instead of knitting on her stocking. Latterly, Edna had ceased to care for it, and did not know where it was, but Aunt Jerry had found it and put it in a little frame made of hemlock twigs, and hung it over the mantel; and Edna took heart from that, for it showed that Aunt Jerry had a warm place for her memory at least, or she would not preserve that horrid caricature of her.

"She is not so hard after all," Edna said, as she laid aside her wraps, and then, as she remembered something she had read about there being a parlor and a kitchen in every person's heart, and the treatment one received depending very much upon which room they get into, she thought, "I guess I've always been in the kitchen, but hereafter I'll stay in the parlor."

The stove, which Aunt Jerry used in winter, was closed tightly, but Edna caught the odor of something cooking in the oven, and opening the door, saw the nicely dressed turkey simmering slowly in preparation for Miss Pepper's dinner, and then the impulse seized her to hasten the fire, and have the dinner ready by the time her aunt came in from church. The vegetables were prepared and standing in pans of water, and Edna put them on the stove, and basted the turkey, and set the table with the best cloth and dishes, just as she used to do on Thanksgiving day, and felt her old identity coming back as she moved about among the familiar things, and wondered what Aunt Jerry would say, and how long before she would come.

Church was out at last, she knew by the pealing of the organ, and by seeing Mr. Swift go behind the church and unhitch his gray horses. There was a brisk step outside the gate ; Aunt Jerry was coming, and with her hands clasped together, and her head slightly bent forward in the attitude of intense expectancy, Edna stood waiting for her.

There was a heightened color on her cheek, and her eyes shone with such brilliancy as to make them seem almost black, while her long curls fell forward and partly covered her face like some bright satin veil.

To say that Miss Pepper was surprised, would but faintly express the perfect amazement with which she regarded the apparition which met her view as she hastily opened the door, her movements accelerated by the mysterious smells of savory cooking which had greeted her olfactories when outside the gate. And yet Edna had really been much in the spinster's mind that Thanksgiving morning, when she bustled about here and there and made her preparations for her solitary dinner,—solitary unless Miss Martha Ann Barnes, the only intimate friend Miss Pepper had, could be induced to spend the remainder of the day with her.

"It will seem more Christian-like and pleasant to have somebody sit opposite you at table on such a day as this, won't it, Tabby?" Miss Pepper said to her cat, to whom she was sometimes given to talking, and who showed her appreciation of the remark by a friendly mew and by rubbing against her mistress' dress.

And then Miss Pepper's thoughts went straying back into the past, forty years ago, and she saw a group of noisy, happy children, of which she had been the merriest, the ringleader, they had called her at first, and afterward the flirt, who cared but little how many hearts she broke when, at the gay Thanksgiving time, she joined them at her grandfather's house among the Vermont hills, and with her glowing beauty, set off by some bright bit of ribbon or string of beads, made sad havoc with the affections of her young male relatives. There was a slight jerking of her shoulders, and a bridling of her head, as Miss Pepper remembered those far-off days, and then her thoughts came a little nearer to the present time, to thirty-five years ago that Thanksgiving day, and the dress of white brocade, with its bertha of dainty lace, and the orange flowers sent by a city cousin who "could not be present on the happy occasion." The flowers were never worn, neither was the lace, nor the brocade; and yellow and soiled with time, they lay together, far down in the old red chest, where the linen sheets and the sprigs of lavender were, and where no one had ever seen them but Miss Pepper herself.

As regularly as Thanksgiving day came round, she opened the red chest, and undoing the precious parcel, shook out the heavy folds of the brocade, and held the orange flowers a moment in her hands, and wondered where *he* was to-day, and if he thought of thirty-five years ago, and what had almost been.

As she had always done so, Miss Pepper did now on the day of which we write; and did it, too, earlier than had been her wont. Usually her visit to the chest was reserved for the afternoon, but this morning there was a strange yearning at her heart, a longing for something her life had missed, and before her breakfast dishes were washed she had made her yearly visit to the chest, and sitting down beside it, as by an open grave, with the faded brocade across her lap, and the orange flowers in her hand, said softly to herself, " If this had come to pass I mightn't have been alone to-day." And then, as she remembered the girl of thirty-five years ago, and thought of herself as she was now, she arose, and going to the glass, inspected, with a grim kind of resignation, the face which met her view; the thin, sharp features, the straight nose, with its slightly glaring nostrils, the firmly compressed lips, the broad, low forehead, and the round black eyes which age had not dimmed one whit, though it had given them a sharper, harder expression than in their youth they had worn.

"And they called me handsome," she said, as she stood contemplating herself. "I was Jerry then, pretty Jerry Pepper, but now I'm nobody but Aunt Jerush, or worse yet, old Mother Pepper, as the school-boys call me."

And with a sigh, the lonely woman locked up her treasures till another year, and went back to her household cares and her lonely life. But there was a softer look upon her face, and when, as she was dusting, she came to Edna's picture, which from some unaccountable impulse she had only a few days before framed and hung upon the wall, she held her feather duster suspended a moment, and looked earnestly at the face of the young girl who for twelve years had been with her on Thanksgiving day. And as she looked there arose a half wish that Edna was there now, disgraced though she thought her to be by her unlucky marriage.

"She bothered me a sight, but then it's kind of lonesome without her. I wonder what she's doing to-day," she said, as she resumed her dusting and thought again of Martha

Ann Barnes, who might be induced to occupy Edna's old seat at the table.

But Martha Ann was not at church. Miss Pepper must eat her dinner alone; and with the thought that "it did not pay to buy that head of celery and make a parade just for herself," she turned to the Prayer Book and minister, and felt her ire rise so high at his bowing so low in the creed, that, as she wrote to Mrs. Churchill, she withheld a dollar and gave as her offering only fifty cents; taking care as she came out of church to tell what she had done to one who she knew would communicate it to her pastor. Excellent Miss Pepper! the Thanksgiving sermon must have done her a world of good, and she went home prepared to enjoy as best she could her solitary dinner, but not prepared to find her niece waiting there for her.

CHAPTER XVI.

AUNT JERRY AND EDNA.

IF Miss Pepper had owned the truth, she was not sorry to see Edna, and the feeling of loneliness which all the morning had been tugging at her heart, began to give way at once; but she was one of those people who feel bound to "stick to their principles," whether right or wrong, and as one of her principles was that her niece had behaved very shabbily and deserved punishing, she steeled her heart against her, and putting on her severest look and manner, said to her:

"Edna Browning, how dare you come here after disgracing me so?"

This was the speech with which Miss Pepper had intended to greet her niece if she ever came back unannounced, and she had repeated it many times to herself, and to Tabby, and to the teakettle boiling on the stove, and the clock ticking upon the mantel, and from having said it so often, she had come to repeat it without any great amount of genuine indignation; but this Edna did not know, and the eager, expectant look on her face died out in a moment as she heard the words of greeting.

"Oh, aunty," she cried, and her little hands clasped each other more tightly as she took a step forward, "don't speak so to me. I am so desolate, and I had not anywhere else to go. I thought you would be lonely eating dinner alone, and might be glad to see me."

"Glad to see you after all you've done! You must think me a saint, which I don't pretend to be," was the harsh reply, as Aunt Jerusha hurried past Edna, without noticing the hand involuntarily stretched out toward her.

Going into her bed-room to lay her bonnet and cloak aside, Miss Pepper's lip quivered a little as she said to herself,—

"The child has suffered, and no mistake, but I'm not going to be talked over at once. She deserves a good lesson. If she was a youngster, I'd spank her smartly and be done with it, but as I can't do that I shall carry a stiff upper lip a spell, till she's fairly cowed."

With this intention Miss Pepper returned to the attack, and once having opened her volley of abuse,—reproof she called it,—she did not know where to stop, and said far more than she really felt or had at first any intention of saying. The runaway match with a mere boy; the meanness, aye the dishonesty of breaking the contract with the principal of the seminary, and leaving that four hundred dollars for some one else to pay; the littleness of wearing jewelry which a stranger must pay for, and the wickedness of decoying a young man into marriage, and thereby causing him to lose his life, and making her a murderess, were each in turn brought up and eloquently handled; while Edna stood with bowed head and heard it quietly, until her aunt reached the *ring*, and asked if she was not ashamed to wear it. Then it was that the "pale-gray look came over her face and the steel-gray look in her eye," as she took the golden band from her finger, and laid it away in her purse, saying in a voice Miss Pepper would never have recognized as Edna's,—

"You are right, aunty. I am a murderess, and I ought not to wear this ring until I have paid for it myself, and I never will."

Something in her tone and manner stopped Miss Pepper, and for a moment she gazed curiously at this young girl who seemed to expand into a dignified, self-assured woman as she drew off her wedding ring, and, putting it away from her sight, walked quietly to the window, where she stood looking out upon the dull November sky from which a few snow-flakes were beginning to fall. Miss Pepper was puzzled, and for an instant seriously contemplated taking back a part, at least, of what she had said, but that would not have been in accordance with her theory of managing young people, and so she contented herself with doing instead of saying. She made the kind of gravy for the turkey which she remembered Edna liked, and put an extra lump of butter in the squash, and brought from the cellar a tumbler of cranberry jelly and a pot of peach preserves, and opened a bottle of pickled cauliflower, and warmed one of her best mince-pies, and made black tea instead of green, because Edna never drank the latter, and then, when all was ready, said, in a half-conciliatory tone, "Come now, the victuals is ready."

Then Edna came away from the window and took her seat at the table, and took the heaped-up plate offered to her, and made some casual remarks about the *price of butter*, and asked if Blossom gave as much milk as ever, but she did not eat. She had been very hungry, but the hunger was gone now, and so she sipped her tea and toyed with her fork, and occasionally put it to her lips, but never with anything on it which Aunt Jerusha could see. In short, the dinner was a failure; and when it was over Aunt Jerry removed her turkey nearly as whole as when it went upon the table, and carried back her cranberries and peaches untouched, and felt as if she had been badly used that her dinner was thus slighted. Edna did not offer to help her as she cleared the dinner away, but sat with folded hands looking out to where a brown, blighted rose-bush was gently swayed by the wind.

Once when Aunt Jerry could endure the silence no longer, she said:

"What under the sun do you see out there? What are you looking at?"

"My future life," Edna replied, without so much as turning her head, and Aunt Jerry gave an extra whisk to her dish towel as she went on washing her dishes.

As it began to grow dark, Miss Pepper brought out her candle, and was about to light it, when Edna started suddenly, and turning her white, stony face toward her aunt, said:

"Don't light the candle now. I like the dark the best. I want to talk with you, and can do it better if I do not see your face."

There was a ring in the voice which puzzled Aunt Jerry a little, but she humored her niece, and felt glad that at last Edna was going to talk. But she was not quite prepared for what followed when her niece, who had suddenly outgrown all fear of her aunt, spoke of some things in the past, which, had they been different, might have borne a different result and have kept her from doing what she had done.

"I believe you meant well, Aunt Jerry," she said, "and perhaps some would say you did well. You gave me a home when I had none; gave me food and clothes, and taught me many things; but for the one great thing which children need the most and miss the most, I did hunger so terribly. I wanted some love, auntie; some petting, some kind, caressing act which should tell me I was more to you than the poor orphan whom you took from charity. But you never gave it, never laid your hand upon me fondly, never called me a pet name, never kissed me in your life, and we living together these dozen years. You chide me for turning so readily to a stranger whom I had only known for a few months, and preferring him to my own flesh and blood. Auntie, in the few months I knew Charlie Churchill, he gave me more love, more kindness than I had ever known from you in the twelve years we lived together, and when he asked me to go with him, as I did, I hesitated, for I knew it was wrong; but when your letter came threatening to bring me home, the thought of the long, dreary winter during which scarcely a kind, pleasant word would be spoken to me, was more than I could bear, and so I went with Charlie."

Edna paused a moment with the hope that what she had said might bring some expression of regret from the woman sitting so straight, and prim, and silent in the chair near by. But it did not, and as Edna could not see her face she never dreamed of the effect her words had produced, and how the great lumps were swelling in her aunt's throat, as that peculiar woman forced down the impulse of her better nature which did prompt her to say she had been to blame. To confess herself in error was a hard thing for Miss Pepper to do, and glad that the darkness prevented her niece from seeing the tear which actually rolled down her cheek, she maintained a perfect silence while Edna told her more of Charlie, and of her life in Chicago, and her indebtedness to Roy, and her resolve to cancel it as well as to pay for her education if her aunt would wait patiently till she could earn it.

"I am very tired," she said, when she had finished her story. "I rode all night, you know, and if you don't mind being left alone so early, I think I'll go to bed. I shall find my room the same as ever, I suppose."

Then Aunt Jerry arose and struck a light, and without looking at her niece, said to her : "Hadn't you better go up to the front chamber? It's a nicer bed, you know ; nicer every way. I guess you better try it."

This was a great concession on Aunt Jerry's part, and Edna was touched by it, but she preferred her old room, she said ; she should not feel at home elsewhere, and taking the candle from Aunt Jerry's hand she said good-night, and went up the steep, narrow stairs she had so often climbed in childhood. As she reached the landing, Aunt Jerry called after her :

"You'll find a blanket in the chest if there ain't clothes enough. You better take it, any way, for it is cold to-night."

This was another olive branch, and Edna accepted it as such, and took the blanket more to please her aunt than because she needed it. Her room was the same as ever, with the exception of a few rolls of carpet-rags which were lying in one corner, and at which Edna looked with a kind of nervous dread, as if they had been cut and sewed by her own unwilling hands. It was too dark outside to distinguish more than the faint outline of the tombstones in the graveyard, but Edna singled out her father's, and putting out her candle knelt down by the low window and gazed long and earnestly at the spot where her father slept. She was bidding his grave farewell, it might be forever, for her resolution was taken to go away from there, and find a place among entire strangers.

"It is better so," she said, as she leaned her hot forehead

against the cool window-pane. "'Tis better so, and father would bid me go, if he could speak. Oh, father, if you had not died, all this might have been spared to me."

Then, as she remembered her other Father, her Heavenly one, and His promise to the orphan, she clasped her hands over her face and prayed earnestly for His protection and blessing upon her wherever she might go. And then she thought of Aunt Jerry, and asked that God would bless her, too, and if in what she had said that night there was anything harsh and wrong, He would forgive her for it, and help her to make amends. Her prayers ended, she crept into her bed, which seemed, with its softness and warmth, to embrace and hold her as a mother might have done, and so embraced and held, she soon fell away to sleep, and forgot all that was past, and ceased to dread what might be in store for her.

Meantime Aunt Jerry sat in the room below, with her feet on the stove hearth, her hands locked together around her knees, and her head bent forward until her forehead almost touched her dress. Perhaps she maintained this attitude to accommodate Tabby, who had mounted upon her back and nestled across her neck, and perhaps she did it the better to think intently, for she was thinking of all Edna had said to her with reference to her childhood, and wondering if, after all, her theory was wrong, and children were like chickens, which needed brooding from the mother hen.

"But sakes alive, how was I to know that,—I, a dried-up old maid, who never had a baby of my own, and never held one either, except that young one of Mrs. Atwood's that I stood sponsor for, and almost dropped when I presented it? If things had turned out different, why, I should have been different."

And with a little sigh as she thought of the yellow brocade in the chest upstairs, Miss Pepper put Tabby from her neck, and bringing out her prayer-book read the Gospel and Epistle and Collect for the day, and then kneeling by her chair said the Creed and the Lord's Prayer, and a few words of her own improvising, to the effect that if she was too hard the Lord would thaw her out and make her softer, and help her somehow to make it up to Edna, and then she went to bed.

Edna was hungry the next morning, and did full justice to the cold roast turkey and nicely browned potato, and when her aunt asked if she would like some cranberry jelly, she said she would, for she felt that her aunt wanted her to have it, and did not begrudge the journey to the cellar in quest of it. There was but little talk on either side, until Edna asked if the stage went out the same hour as usual, and announced her intention of going away. Then Aunt Jerry spoke her mind again, and said Edna "was a fool to go sky-larkin' off alone, when she was welcome there, and could get plenty of scholars too, if that was what she wanted;" and she even went so far as to say "they might as well let bygones be bygones, and begin anew, and see if they couldn't pull together a little better."

But Edna was not to be persuaded from her purpose. She did not know exactly where she was going, she said, but would let her aunt know when she was located, and if she did not succeed she might perhaps come back.

"That is, if you will let me. This is all the home I have at present, you know," she added, looking wistfully up in her aunt's face, as if for some token that she was cared for by that undemonstrative woman, who scolded the driver for bringing in so much snow and mud when he came for Edna's trunk, and scolded the boy who came to help him for leaving the door open, and did it all to hide what she really felt at parting with her niece.

"Of course I'll let you. I'd be a heathen to turn out my

own flesh and blood," she said, in reply to Edna's remark, and then as the driver's shrill "all ready" was heard, she gave her hand to Edna, who would have kissed her but for the forbidding look upon her face, and the pin between her teeth.

Aunt Jerry went with her to the stage, and stood looking on until she was comfortably seated, and then, as the driver mounted to his box and gathered up his reins, she said, "Wall, good-by again," with a tone in her voice which made Edna throw back her veil to look at her more closely. But the horses, obedient to the lash, had started forward, and Aunt Jerry was left, feeling more alone than she had ever before felt in her life.

"I wonder if she would have staid if I'd been more outspoken, and told her how much I really wanted her?" Aunt Jerry said, as she returned to the house and began to put it to rights. "But that's the way with me. I can't say what I feel. I guess I'm ugly, if I do belong to the Church. I let him go when a word would have kept him, only I was too proud to speak it; and now I've lost her, just as I was beginning to know that I did like her some. I wish she knew how near crying I was when she said so queer-like, 'You never kissed me, auntie, in my life, and we living together these dozen years.' Don't she know I ain't the kissing sort? Still, I might have kissed her when a little child, and not hurt myself."

She was dusting the clock and the mantel, and when she came to the little picture in the rustic frame, she stopped, and continued her soliloquy:

"I wonder if she noticed that. If she did, she must know I think something of her, if I never did kiss her, and make a fuss. The likeness ain't much like her, any way, but still it's her picture, and I've half a mind,—yes, I b'lieve I will;" and reaching up her hand, the strange woman, who in twelve years had never shown her orphan niece a single mark of genuine affection, took down that photograph and kissed it.

That was a great deal for her to do, and being done, she began to feel as if she had made atonement for all that had been wrong in herself heretofore, and that Edna really ought now to come back. But Edna had gone, and as the days went by and brought no news of her, Aunt Jerry began to grow indignant, and finally relieved herself by writing to Mrs. Churchill the letter we have seen. Roy's reply and the check threw her into a violent rage, and after letting him know her mind, she washed her hands, as she said, of the whole of them, and settled back into her lonely life, sharper, harsher than before, and more disposed to find fault with her clergyman and battle with his decided tendency to High Church and Ritualism.

CHAPTER XVII.

WHERE EDNA WENT.

TO Canandaigua first, but not to the seminary, nor yet the jeweller's, as she had once thought of doing. She had heard from her aunt that Mr. Greenough was paid, and she shrank from meeting him face to face, or from seeing any of her old friends. So she sat quietly in the ladies' room, waiting for the first train going east, and thinking it would never come. She had bought her ticket for Albany, but, with her thick black veil drawn closely over her face, the ticket agent never suspected that she was the gay, light-hearted girl he used sometimes to see at the station, and who recently had become so noted for the tragic ending of her marriage.

No one recognized her, for it was not the hour when the seminary girls were ever at the depot, and when, at last, the train came and took her away with it, nobody was the wiser for her having been there.

And *where* was she going? Have you, my reader, ever crossed the mountain range between Pittsfield and Albany? And if you have, do you remember how many little villages you saw, some to the right, some to the left, and all nestled among and sheltered by those tall mountains and rocky hills, with here and there a stream of water, as clear and bright as crystal, rippling along under the shadow of the willow and the birch, or dancing headlong down some declivity?

Edna was bound for one of these towns, where Uncle Phil Overton had lived for many years. He was her great uncle on her mother's side, though she had never heard of him until she met her cousin, Mrs. Dana, in Chicago. Mrs. Dana had known Mr. Overton well, and had lived with him for a few months while she taught in the little academy which stood upon the common. He was an eccentric old man, who for years had lived among the mountains, in the same yellow farm-house, a mile, or more, from the village, which represented to him the world, and which we call Rocky Point.

Edna could not tell why her thoughts kept turning to Uncle Phil as they did. In her utter despair, while listening to Aunt Jerry's abusive greeting, her heart had cried out:

"Oh, what shall I do?"

"Go to Uncle Phil," was the answer which came to her cry, and she had clung to that as a drowning man to a straw.

Mrs. Dana had said he was kind and generous, if you touched the right chord. He had no wife, or children, but lived alone with a colored woman, who had been in the family for years. He was getting to be old,—sixty, if not more,—

and, perhaps, he would be glad of some young creature in the house, or, at all events, would let her stay till she could look about and find something to do. Maybe she could teach in the academy. Mrs. Dana had done so, and Edna felt that her acquirements were certainly equal to those of her cousin. And so she was going to Rocky Point, and Albany lay in her way, and she stopped there until Monday, and took her watch and coral to a jeweller's, and asked what they were worth.

It was a beautiful little watch, and the chain was of exquisitely wrought gold; and, as the jeweller chanced to be an honest man, he told her frankly what it was worth, but said, as it was second-hand, he could not dispose of it so readily, and consequently could not afford to give her quite so much as if it were new. Edna accepted his offer, and, with a bitter pang, left the watch and coral lying in the glass case, and, going back to the hotel, wrote a letter to Roy, and sent him one hundred dollars.

How near Roy seemed to her there in Albany, which was not so very far from Leighton Place, and how she was tempted to take the New York train, and go to Charlie's home; not into it, but to the town, where she could see it and visit Charlie's grave. But a few moments' reflection showed her the inexpediency of such an act. She had no money to waste in useless trips. She should need it all, and more, unless Uncle Phil opened his door to her; and so she put the scheme aside, and took, instead, the Boston train, which long before noon left her upon the platform at Rocky Point. Everybody knew Uncle Phil Overton, and half a dozen or more answered her questions at once, and wondered who she was, and what the queer old chap would do with such a dainty bit of femininity as she seemed to be. One man, a farmer, whose road homeward lay past the Overton place, offered to take her there, and she was soon riding along through scenery so wild and romantic, even in early December, as to elicit from her many an exclamation of surprise and delight, while her fingers fairly ached to grasp her pencil and paper and sketch some of the beautiful views with which the neighborhood abounded. The man was very respectful, but rather inquisitive; and as his curiosity was in no wise abated by the sight of her glowing face when, at the top of a hill, she threw back her veil, and asked him to stop a moment while she gazed at the scenery around her, he began to question her, and found that she was Phil Overton's grand-niece, an orphan without friends, and that she had come to Rocky Point, hoping to find something to do. Did he know whether they were in want of a teacher in the academy, and did any of the scholars take lessons in drawing or music? She could teach both, though drawing was her preference.

Mr. Belknap was very sorry to tell her that the old academy was closed,—"played out," he said; and the "Deestrict" School had been commenced for a week, or more. "But then," he added, as he saw the look of disappointment on Edna's face, "maybe we could scare up a s'leck school. We had one last winter, kep' by a man in a room of the academy; but he was a poor stick, and the boys raised the very old Harry with him. They wouldn't with you, a slip of a girl. Ain't you pretty young to teach?"

"Yes, perhaps so; but I must do something," Edna replied.

She did not tell him she was a widow; and, seeing her clothed in so deep mourning, the man naturally concluded it was for her parents, and he began to feel a deep interest in her, telling her she might count on his children if she opened a school; that he would also help her to get scholars, if needful, and then he asked if she had any idea of the kind of man Uncle Phil Overton was. Something in Mr. Belknap's question set Edna's heart to beating rapidly, but before she could reply, they turned the corner in the road and came close to the house.

"I wish you success with Uncle Phil," Mr. Belknap said, as he handed Edna from the wagon and deposited her trunk upon the stoop. "Maybe I and the girls will drop in to-night and see how you get on," he added, as he climbed over the wheel, and chirruping to his horse, drove off, leaving Edna standing by the door, whose huge brass knocker sent back a dull, heavy echo, but did not for some little time bring any answering response.

CHAPTER XVIII.

AT UNCLE PHIL'S.

IT was one of those old-fashioned farm-houses rarely found outside of New England, and even there growing more and more rare, as young generations arise with cravings for something new, and a feeling of having outgrown the old homestead with its "front entry" and crooked stairway leading to another "entry" above; its two "square rooms" in front and its huge kitchen and smaller sleeping apartment in the rear. Those who do not emigrate to some more genial atmosphere, where their progressive faculties have free scope to grow, have come to feel a contempt for the old brown houses which once dotted the New England hills so thickly; and so these veterans of a past century have gradually given way to dwellings of a more modern style, with wide halls and long balconies and bay-windows, and latterly the much-admired French roofs.

But Uncle Phil Overton was neither young nor a radical, nor was there anything progressive in his taste. As his house had been forty years ago, when by his father's death and will it came to him, so it was that day when Edna stood knocking at the door. It had been yellow then and it was yellow now; it had been void of shade-trees then and it was so now, if we except the horse-chestnut which grew near the gate, and which could throw no shadow, however small, upon the house or in the great, glaring rooms inside.

Uncle Phil did not like trees, and he did like light, and held it a sin to shut out Heaven's sunshine; so there never was a blind upon his house; and the green-paper shades and curtains of Holland linen, which somehow had been smuggled in and hung at a few of the windows, were rolled up both day and night. Uncle Phil had no secrets to shut out, he said, and folks were welcome to look in upon him at any time; so he sat before the window, and washed before it, and shaved before it, and ate before it, and dressed before it; and when his housekeeper, old Aunt Becky, remonstrated with him, as she sometimes did, and told him "folks would see him," he answered her, "Let 'em peek, if they want to;" and so the curtains remained as they were, and the old man had his way.

Many years ago, it was said that he had thought to bring a wife to the farm-house, which he had brightened up a little, putting a red and green carpet on the floor of the north room, painting the wood-work a light blue, and covering the walls with a yellowish paper of most wonderful design. Six chairs, and a looking-glass, and bureau, and table, had completed the furnishing of that room, to which no bride ever came; and, as Uncle Phil had been wholly reticent with regard to her, the story came gradually to be regarded as a mere fabrication of somebody's busy brain; and Uncle Phil was set down as one whose heart had never been reached

by anything fairer than old black Becky, who had lived with
him for years, and grown to be so much like him that one
had only to get the serving-woman's opinion to know what
the master's was. Just as that stiff, cold north room had
looked years ago, when made ready for the mythical bride,
so it looked now, and so, too, or nearly so, looked the south
room, with its Franklin fireplace, its painted floor, and the
two strips of rag carpet before the fire, its tall mantel-piece,
with two cupboards over it, holding a most promiscuous
medley of articles, from a paper of sage down to the almanacs for the last twenty years. Uncle Phil didn't believe in
destroying books, and kept his almanacs as religiously as he
did his weekly paper, of which there were barrels full, stowed
away in the garret. Besides being the common sitting-room,
the south room was also Uncle Phil's sleeping apartment,
and in one corner was his turned-up bed, with its curtain
of copperplate, and beyond it the clock-shelf and the clock,
and a tall writing-desk, where Uncle Phil's valuables were
kept. Two or three chairs, one on rockers, and one an old-
fashioned wooden chair with arms and a cushion in it, completed the furniture, if we except the table, on which lay
Walker's Dictionary, and the big Bible, and a book of sermons by some Unitarian divine, and Uncle Phil's glasses.
The pleasantest room in the whole house was the kitchen,
where Aunt Becky reigned supreme, even Uncle Phil yielding to her here, and never saying a word when she made
and put down a respectable rag carpet at the end of the
long room in which she kept her Boston rocker for company, and her little stuffed sewing-chair for herself, and her
square stand covered with a towel, and on it a pretty cushion of blue, which matched the string of robins' eggs ornamenting the little glass hanging beside the window, with its
box for brush and combs made of pasteboard and cones.
This was Aunt Becky's parlor, and her kitchen was just as

neat and inviting, with its nicely painted floor, and unpainted wood-work, scoured every week, and kept free from dust and dirt by daily wipes and dustings, and a continued warfare against the luckless flies and insects, to whom Becky was a sworn foe. Out in the back room there was a stove which Becky sometimes used, but she would not have it in her kitchen; she liked the fireplace best, she said, and so in winter nights you could see from afar the cheerful blaze of the logs Becky piled upon the fire, giving the "forestick" now and then a thrust by way of quickening the merry flames, which lit up her old black face as she stooped upon the hearth to cook the evening meal.

And this was the house where Edna stood knocking for admission, and wondering why her knock remained so long unanswered. Old Becky was at the barn hunting for eggs with which to make her master's favorite custard pie, and never dreamed that she had a guest, until, with her woollen dress pinned up around her waist, and a wisp of hay ornamenting her hair, she returned to the house, and entering the kitchen by the rear door, heard the knock, which by this time was loud and imperious. No one but strangers ever came to the front door in winter, consequently Aunt Becky, who had a good deal to do that morning, bristled at once, and wondered "who was making that *to do*, and why they didn't come to the kitchen door, and not make her all that extra trouble."

"Whale away," she said, as Edna again applied herself vigorously to the knocker. "I shan't come till I've put up my *aigs* and let my petticoats down."

This done, she started for the door, and, catching sight through the window of Edna's trunk, exclaimed:

"For Heaven's sake, if thar ain't a chist of clothes, a visitor; Miss Maude, perhaps, and I nothin' for dinner but a veal stew, or,—yes, I can open a bottle of tomarterses, and roast some of them fall pippins."

And with this consoling reflection, old Becky undid the iron bolt and opened the door; but started back when, instead of the possible Miss Maude, she saw a young girl dressed in black, "with just the sweetest, sorriest, anxiousest face you even seen, and which made my bowels yearn to oncet," she said to Miss Maude, to whom she afterward related the particulars of her first introduction to Edna.

"Does Mr. Philip Overton live here?" Edna asked, so timidly that Becky, who was slightly deaf, could only guess at what she said from catching the name Overton.

"Yes, miss, he does; walk in, please," and she involuntarily courtesied politely to the young lady, who, save that she was shorter and smaller every way, reminded her of her favorite Miss Maude. "You'll have to come right into my kitchen, I reckon; for when master's out all day we never has a fire in the south room till night," she continued, as she led the way through the "south room" into her pleasant quarters, which, in spite of the preparations going on for dinner, looked home-like and inviting, especially the bright fire which blazed upon the hearth.

Edna went up to this at once and held her cold hands near the blaze, and Becky, who was a close observer, noticed first the cut of her dress, and then decided that "it had as long a tail as Miss Maude's" (the reader will bear in mind that this was before the days of short dresses), "but was not quite as citified." She noticed, too, the little plump, white hands which Edna held up to the fire, and said within herself,—

"Them hands has never done no work; I wonder who she can be?"

Edna told her after a moment that she had come from

Chicago, from Mrs. Dana's, whom Becky might perhaps remember, as she was once an inmate for a time of the farmhouse. Becky did remember Miss Susan, and after expressing her surprise and regret at her sudden death, she continued:

"You've come to visit yer uncle,—have you ever seen him?"

Edna had never seen him, and she had not exactly come visiting either. In fact she hardly knew why she had come, and now that she was here, and had a faint inkling of matters, she began to wish she had staid away, and to wonder herself why she was there. To her uncle she intended to tell everything, but not to Becky, though she instinctively felt that the latter was a person of a great deal of consequence in her uncle's family, and must have some explanation, even though it was a very lame one. So she said:

"I lived with Mrs. Dana when she died. I have lost all my friends. I have no home, and so I came to Uncle Overton, hoping he would let me stay till I find something to do. Mrs. Dana said he was kind and good."

"Yes, but mighty curis in his ways," was Becky's rejoinder, as she wondered how her master would receive this stranger, who had no home nor friends unless he gave her both. "It's jest as the fit catches him," she thought, as she asked Edna to lay aside her wrappings, and then told her to make herself at home till the "marster came." "He's gone over to Millville, six or eight miles or so, and rode old Bobtail, who never trots faster than an ant can walk, so he won't be home till three o'clock, and I'm goin' to have dinner and supper all to oncet, but if you're hungry, and I know you be, I'll jest clap on a cold bite and steep a drawin' of tea," she said.

But Edna was not hungry; she had breakfasted at the station not many miles from Albany, and could wait until her uncle came.

"I'll fetch yer things in, only I dunno whar marster'll have 'em put. Any ways, I'm safet in the back bed-room," Becky continued, and with Edna's help, the trunk was brought into the house and carried up the back stairs to a little room directly over the kitchen, where the bare floor and the meagre furniture struck cold and chill to Edna's heart, it was so different from anything she had ever known.

That room at Aunt Jerry's, looking out upon the graveyard, was a palace compared to this cheerless apartment; and sitting down upon her trunk after Becky left her, she cried from sheer homesickness, and half resolved to take the next train back to—she did not know where. There was no place for her anywhere, and in utter loneliness and despair she continued to cry until Becky came up with a pitcher of warm water and some towels across her arm. She saw that Edna was crying, and half guessing the cause, said very kindly:

"I reckon you're some homesick, and 'tain't to be wondered at; this room ain't the chirkest in the house, and 'tain't no ways likely you'll stay here, but I dassen't put you in no other without marster's orders; he's curis, and if he takes to you as he's sure to do, you're all right and in clover right away. He sarves 'em all dis way, Miss Maude an' all, but now nothin's too good for her."

Edna did not ask who Miss Maude was, but she thanked Becky for her kindness, and after bathing her face and eyes, and brushing her hair, went down to the kitchen to wait with fear and trembling for the coming of the " marster who was so curis in his ways."

Becky did not talk much that morning. She had "too many irons in the fire," she said, and so she brought Edna a book which Miss Maude had left there more than a year ago, and which might help to pass the time. It was "Monte-Cristo," which Edna had never read, and she received it thankfully, and glancing at the fly-leaf saw written there, "Maude Somerton, New York, May 10th, 18——."

Becky's Miss Maude, then, was Maude Somerton, who lived in New York, and whom some wind of fortune had blown to Rocky Point, where she seemed to be an immense favorite; so much Edna inferred, and then she sat herself down to the book, and in following the golden fortunes of the hero she forgot the lapse of time until the clock struck two, and Becky, taking a blazing firebrand from the hearth, carried it into the south room, with the evident intention of kindling a fire.

"Marster always has one thar nights," she said, "and when we has company we sets the table thar. His bed ain't no 'count, turned up with the curtain afore it."

And so in honor of Edna the table was laid in the south room, and Aunt Becky, who had quietly been studying the young girl, and making up her mind with regard to her, ventured upon the extravagance of one of her finest cloths, and the best white dishes instead of the blue set, and put on napkins and the silver-plated forks and butter-knife, and thought how nicely her table looked, and wished aloud that "Marster Philip" would come before her supper had all got cold.

As if in answer to her wish there was the sound of some one at the gate, and looking from the window Aunt Becky joyfully announced that "marster had come."

CHAPTER XIX.

UNCLE PHIL.

FEELING intuitively that it would be better for Aunt Becky to announce her presence, Edna made some excuse for stealing upstairs, where from the window she had her first view of Uncle Phil, as he rode into the yard and round to the barn on Bobtail's back. He was a short, fat man, arrayed in a home-made suit of gray, with his trouser legs tucked in his boots, and his round, rosy face protected by lappets of sheepskin attached to his cap and tied under his chin. Taken as a whole, there was nothing very prepossessing in his appearance, and nothing especially repellent either, but Edna felt herself shaking from head to foot as she watched him dismounting from Bobtail, the old fat sorrel horse, who rubbed his nose against his master's arm as if there was perfect sympathy between them. Edna saw this action, and saw Uncle Phil, as he gently stroked his brute friend, to whom he seemed to be talking as he led him into the barn.

"He is kind to his horse, anyway. Maybe he will be kind to me," Edna thought, and then she waited breathlessly until she heard the heavy boots, first in the back room, then in the kitchen, and then in the south room, where Becky was giving a few last touches to the table.

The chamber door was slightly ajar, and as Uncle Phil's voice was loud, Edna heard him distinctly, as he said:

"Hallo, Beck, what's all this highfalutin for. What's up? Who's come,—Maude?"

Becky's reply was inaudible, but Uncle Phil's rejoinder was distinct and clear:

"Umph! A poor relation, hey? Where is she? Where have you put her?"

Becky was now in the kitchen, and Edna heard her say

"In the back chamber, in course, till I know yer mind."

"All right. Now hurry up your victuals and trot h[er] out. I'm hungry as a bear."

After overhearing this scrap of conversation, it is n[o] strange if Edna shrank from being "trotted out," bu[t] obedient to Aunt Becky's call, she went downstairs and in[to] the south room, where with his back to the fire, and h[is] short gray coat-skirts pulled up over his hands, stood Unc[le] Phil. He did not look altogether delighted, and his litt[le] round twinkling eyes were turned upon Edna with a curio[us] rather than a pleased-expression as she came slowly i[n]. But when she stood before him and he saw her face di[s]tinctly, Edna could not help feeling that a sudden chang[e] passed over him: his eyes put on a softer look, and h[is] whole face seemed suddenly to light up as he took h[er] offered hand.

"Becky tells me you are my kin, grand-niece, or gran[d] aunt, or grandmother. I'll be hanged if she made it o[ut] very clear. Maybe you can explain what you are to me?"

He held her hand tightly in his own, and kept looking [at] her with an earnest, searching gaze, before which Edn[a] dropped her eyes, as she replied:

"I can claim no nearer relationship than your gran[d] niece. My mother was Lucy Fuller."

"Who married the parson and died from starvation?" Uncle Phil rejoined.

And with a heightened color, Edna answered quickly:

"She married my father, sir, an Episcopal clergyma[n] and died when I was a few days old."

"Yes, yes, all the same," Uncle Phil answered, goo[d] humoredly. "I dare say she was half-starved most of th[e] time; ministers' wives mostly are, Episcopal ones esp[e]cially. I take it you are of the Episcopal persuasion, too?"

"I am."

And Edna spoke up as promptly as if it were her mother she was acknowledging.

"Yes, yes," Uncle Phil said again; and here releasing Edna's hand, which he had been holding all the time, he took a huge pinch of snuff, and then passed the box to Edna, who declined at once. "What, don't snuff? You miss a great deal of comfort. It's good for digestion and nervousness, snuff is. I've used it this thirty years; and you are an Episcopalian, and proud of it, I see: jest so. I've no great reason to like that sect, seeing about the only one I ever knew intimately turned out a regular hornet, a lucifer match, the very old Harry himself; didn't adorn the profession; was death on Unitarians, and sent the whole caboodle of us to perdition. She'll be surprised to find me settin' on the banks of the river Jordan when she comes across, paddlin' her own canoe, for she *will* paddle it, I warrant you. Nobody can help her. Yes, yes. Such is life, take it as you find it. Maude is an Episcopal, red-hot. I like her; maybe I'll like you; can't tell. Yes, yes; sit by now, and have some victuals."

During this conversation, Becky, who had put the dinner upon the table, was standing in respectful silence, waiting until her master was ready, and trembling for the fall of her light snowy crusts which she had made for her pot-pie. But her fears were groundless; the dinner was a great success, and Uncle Phil helped Edna bountifully, and insisted upon her taking more gravy, and ordered Becky to bring a bottle of cider from the cellar.

"Cider was 'most as good as snuff for digestion," he said, as he poured Edna a glass of the beverage, which sparkled and beaded like champagne.

On old Becky's face there was a look of great satisfaction as she saw her master's attentions to the young lady, and as soon as her duties were over at the table, she stole up the back stairs to the little forlorn room where Edna's trunk was standing,

"I know I kin ventur so much," she said to herself as she lifted the trunk and carried it into the next chamber, which had a pleasanter lookout, and was more pretentious every way, than its small dark neighbor.

This done Becky retired to the kitchen until dinner was over, and her master, who was something of a gormandizer, was so gorged that three or four pinches of snuff were requisite to aid his digestion; and then like a stuffed anaconda he coiled himself up in his huge arm-chair and slept soundly, while Becky cleared the table and put the room to rights.

The short wintry afternoon was drawing to a close by the time Uncle Phil's nap was over. He had slept heavily and snored loudly, and the last snore awoke him. Starting up, he exclaimed:

"What's that? Yes, yes; snored, did I? Shouldn't wonder if I got into a doze. Ho, you, Beck!"

His call was obeyed at once by the colored woman, who came and stood deferentially before him.

"I say, Beck, I'm 'bout used up, what with eatin' such an all-fired dinner on top of jouncing along on Bobtail,—might as well ride a Virginia fence and done with it. Can't you do the chores? Bobtail is fed, and the cows too."

Becky signified her readiness to do anything her master liked, and after bringing a tall tallow candle and adding a stick to the fire, she departed, leaving Edna alone with Uncle Phil, who was wide-awake now, and evidently disposed to talk.

"Now tell me all about it," he said, suddenly facing toward Edna. "Tell me who you are in black for, and what sent you here, and what you want, and how you happened to know of me, when I never heard of you; but first, what is your name? I'll be hanged if I've thought to inquire."

"Edna Louise Browning was my name until I was married."

"Married! Thunder!" and springing from his chair, Uncle Phil took the candle, and bringing it close to Edna's face, scrutinized it closely. "You married? Why, you're nothing but a child. Married? Where was your folks, to let you do such a silly thing? and where is he?"

"My husband is dead, was killed the very day we were married,—killed in the cars,—and I have no folks, no home, no friends, unless you will be one to me," Edna replied, in a choking voice which finally broke down in a storm of tears and sobs.

Uncle Phil did not like to see a woman cry, especially a young, pretty woman like the one before him, but he did not know at all what to say: so he took three pinches of snuff, one after the other, sneezing as many times, blew his nose vigorously, and then going to the door which led into the kitchen, called out:

"Ho, Beck! come here,—I want you."

But Beck was watering old Bobtail, and did not hear him, so he returned to his seat by the fire; and as Edna's tears were dried by that time, he asked her to go on and tell him her story. Edna had determined to keep nothing back, and she commenced with the house by the graveyard, and the aunt, who perhaps meant to be kind, but who did not understand children, and made her life less happy than it might otherwise have been; then she passed on to Canandaigua and Charlie Churchill; and while telling of him and his friends, and where they lived, she thought once Uncle Phil was asleep, he sat so still, with his eyes shut, and one fat leg crossed over the other, and a pinch of snuff held tightly between his thumb and finger. But he was not asleep, and when she mentioned Leighton Place, he started up again and went out to Becky, who by this time was moving in the kitchen.

"I say, Beck," he whispered in her ear, as he gave his snuff-box a tap with his finger, "move that gal's band-box into the northwest chamber, d'ye hear?"

Becky did not tell him that she had already done that, but simply answered, "Yes, sar," while he returned to Edna, who, wholly unconscious of her promotion or the cause of it, continued her story, which, when she came to the marriage and the accident, was interrupted again with her tears, which fell in showers as she went over with the dreadful scene, the gloomy night, the terrible storm, the capsized car, and Charlie dead under the ruins. Uncle Phil too was excited, and walked the room hurriedly, and took no end of snuff, and blew his nose like a trumpet, but made no comment until she mentioned Mrs. Dana, when he stopped walking, and said:

"Poor Sue, if she'd had a different name, I believe I'd kept her for my own, though she wan't over clever. Dead, you say, and left five young ones, of course; the poorer they be the more they have. Poor little brats. I'll remember that. And John wanted to marry you? You did better to come here; but where was that aunt, what d'ye call her? I don't remember as you told me her name."

"Aunt Jerusha Pepper," Edna said; whereupon something dropped from Uncle Phil's lip which sounded very much like "the devil!"

"What, sir?" Edna asked; and he replied:

"I was swearin' a little. Such a name as that! Jerusha Pepper! No wonder she was hard on you. Did you go back to her at all? and what did she say?"

He took four pinches of snuff in rapid succession, and scattered it about so profusely, that Edna received some in her face and moved a little further from him, as she told him the particulars of her going back to Aunt Jerusha, and what the result had been. She intended to speak just as kindly and cautiously of Aunt Jerry as was possible; but it seemed as if some influence she could not resist was urging her on, and Uncle Phil was so much interested and drew her out so adroitly, that, though she softened everything and omitted many things, the old man got a pretty general impression of Aunt Jerusha Pepper, and guessed just how desolate must be the life of any one who tried to live with her.

"Yes, yes, I see," he said, as Edna, frightened to think how much she had told, tried to apologize for Aunt Jerry, and take back some things she had said. "Yes, yes, never mind taking back. I can guess what kind of a firebrand she is. Knew a woman once, as near like her as two peas; might have been twins; pious, ain't this peppercorn?"

Edna did not quite like Uncle Phil's manner of speaking of her aunt, and she began to defend her, saying she was in the main a very good woman, who possessed many excellent qualities.

"Don't doubt it in the least. Dare say she's a saint; great on the creed and the catechism. And she is your aunt? Ho, Beck, come here; or stop, I'll speak to you in the kitchen," he said, as Becky came to the door.

The woman retreated to the kitchen fireplace, where Uncle Phil joined her, speaking again in a whisper, and saying,—

"Look here, Beck. Take that girl's work-bag, or whatever she brought her things in, and carry it into the north chamber."

"Maude's room, sar!" Becky asked, with glistening eyes.

"Yes, Maude's room," Uncle Phil replied, and then went back to Edna, who had but little more to tell, except of her resolve to come to him as the only person in the world who was likely to take her in, or on whom she had any claim of relationship.

"I don't wish to be an incumbrance," she said. "I want to earn my own living, and at the same time be getting something with which to pay my debts. Mr. Belknap, who brought me from the depot, thought I might get up a select school, and if I do, maybe you will let me board here. I should feel more at home with you than with strangers. Would you let me stay if I could get a school?"

There certainly was something the matter with Uncle Phil's eyes just then.

"The pesky wind made them water," he said, as he wiped them on his coat-sleeves and then looked down at the girl, who had taken a stool at his feet, and was looking anxiously into his face, as she asked if she might stay.

"Let me be, can't you. I've got a bad cold. I've got to go out," he said; and rising precipitately he rushed into the kitchen, and again summoning old Becky, began with, "I say, Beck, make a fire in the north chamber, a good rousing one too. It's cold as fury; and fetch down a rose blanket from the garret, and warm the bed with the warming-pan; the sheets must be damp; and make some cream-toast in the morning; all cream,—girls mostly take to that, and stew some *crambries* to-morrow, and kill a hen."

Having completed his list of orders Uncle Phil returned to Edna, while Becky, who, in anticipation of some such *dénouement* had already made a fire in the north and best chamber in the house, went up and added fresh fuel to the flames, which roared, and crackled, and diffused a genial warmth through the room. Meanwhile Uncle Phil, without directly answering Edna's question as to whether she could stay there, said to her:

"And it's seven hundred dollars you owe, with interest: three to Mr. Leighton, and four to that Peppery woman, and you expect by teaching to earn enough to pay it, child; you never can do that, never. Schoolma'ams don't get great wages round here."

"Then I'll hire out as a servant, or go to work in the factory. I'm not ashamed to do anything honorable, so that it gives me money with which to pay the debt," Edna said, and her brown eyes were almost black with excitement, as she walked hastily across the floor to the window, where she stood for a moment, struggling to keep back the hot tears, and thinking she had made a great mistake in coming to a man like Uncle Phil, who, having regaled himself with two pinches of snuff, said:

"Look here, girl. Come back to the fire and let's have it out."

Something in his voice gave Edna hope that after all he was not going to desert her, and she came back, and stood with her hand on the iron fireplace, and her eyes fixed on him, as he said:

"You spoke of Mr. Belknap. Did he inquire your name?"

"No, sir," was the reply.

"Did anybody inquire your name down to the depot?"

"No, sir."

"Has Beck asked it?"

"No, sir, but I think I told her."

"Thunder you did. Why will women tell all they know, and more too; ten chances though she didn't understand, she's so blunderin'. I'll go and see."

And again Uncle Phil went into the kitchen, and while pretending to drink from the gourd, casually said to the servant:

"Ho, Beck, what's this girl's name in 'tother room; hanged if I want to ask her."

Becky thought a moment and then replied: "don't jestly

remember, though I b'lieve she told me; but I was so flustified when she came. Specks, though, it's Overton, seein' she's yer kin."

"Yes, yes, certainly;" and Uncle Phil went back to the south room with a very satisfied look upon his face. "See here, miss," he began. "Your name is *Overton*,—LOUISE OVERTON. Do you understand?"

Edna looked at him too much surprised to speak, and he continued:

"You are my niece, *Miss Overton, Louise Overton*, not Browning, nor Churchill, nor Pepper-pod, nor Edna, but Louise Overton. And so I shall introduce you to the folks in Rocky Point."

Edna saw that he meant her to take another name than her own, and she rebelled against it at once.

"My name is not Overton," she said, but he interrupted her with—

"It's *Louise* though, according to your own statement, Edna Louise."

"I admit that, but it is not Overton, and it would be wrong for me to take that name, and lose my identity."

"The very thing I want you to do," said Uncle Phil, "and here are my reasons, or a part of them. I like you, for various things. One, you seem to have some vim, grit, spunk, and want to pay your debts; then, I like you because you have had such a hard time with that Pepper woman. I don't blame you for running away; upon my soul I don't. Some marry to get rid of a body, and some don't marry and so get rid of 'em that way. You did the first, and got your husband's neck broke, and got into debt yourself, and seas of trouble. And you are my great-niece. And Lucy Fuller was your mother, and Louise Overton was your grandmother, and my twin sister. Do you hear that, my twin sister, that I loved as I did my life, and you must have been named for her, and there's a look like her in your face, all the time, and that hair which you've got up under a net, but which I know by the kinks is curly as a nigger's, is hers all over again, color and all, and just now when you walked to the window in a kind of huff, I could have sworn it was my sister come back again from the grave where we buried her more than thirty years ago. Yes, you are a second Louise. I'm an old man of sixty, and never was married, and never shall be, and when Susan was here years ago, 1 thought of adopting her, but I'll be hanged if there was snap enough to her, and then she took the first chap that offered, and married Dana, and that ended her. There wasn't a great many of us, and for what I know you are all the kin I have, and I fancy you more than any young girl I've seen, unless its Maude, and she's no kin, which makes a difference. I've a mind to adopt you, to give you my name, Overton, and if you do well I'll remember you in my will. Mind, I don't propose to pay your debts. I want to see you scratch round and do it yourself, but I'll give you a home and help you get scholars, or if you can't do anything at that, help you get a place in the factory at Millville, or in somebody's kitchen as you mentioned."

Uncle Phil's eyes twinkled a little as he said this last, and looked to see what effect it had on Edna. But she never winced or showed the slightest emotion, and he continued:

"Nobody knows that you are a Browning, or a Churchill, or a widow, and it's better they shouldn't. I saw the account of that smash-up in the newspaper, but never guessed the girl was Louise's grandchild. Folks round here read it too; the papers were full of it. Charlie Churchill hunted up in my woods one season; he's pretty well known hereabouts."

"Charlie, my Charlie, my husband; was he ever here, and did you know him?" Edna asked, vehemently, and Uncle Phil replied:

"Yes, I knew him when he was a boy, though he couldn't be much more than that when you run off with him. His brother owns the hotel in town. We are on different roads, but ain't neither of us such a very great ways from Albany, you know."

Instantly Edna's countenance fell.

"Roy Leighton own the hotel! then he will be coming here, and I don't want to see him till he is paid," she said, in some dismay, and Uncle Phil replied:

"He don't often bother himself to come to Rocky Point. Never was here more than two or three times. His agent does the business for him, and that agent is *me*. He was here once, and I believe his mother was up the mountain at a kind of hotel where city folks sometimes stay and make b'lieve they like it. But this Charlie stayed in town at the tavern, and folks——"

Here Uncle Phil stopped abruptly, and Edna, after waiting a moment for him to proceed, said:

"Folks did not fancy Charlie. He was not popular. Is that what you want to say? If it is, don't be afraid to say it. I have borne much harder things than that," and there came a sad, sorry look upon her face. She was thinking of her lost faith in Charlie's integrity, and Uncle Phil of the scandalous stories there had been about the fast young man of eighteen who had made love to the girls indiscriminately, from little Marcia Belknap, the farmer's daughter, to Miss Ruth Gardner, whose father was the great man of Rocky Point, and whose influence would do more to help or harm Edna than that of any other person in town. But Uncle Phil could not tell Edna all this, so he merely replied, after a little:

"No, he wan't very popular, that's a fact. Young men from the cities are different, you know, and Charles was sowing his wild oats about those days. He passed for rich, you see; called it *my hotel*, my tenants, and all that, when it was his brother's."

A sound from Edna like a sob made Uncle Phil pause abruptly and mentally curse himself for having said so much. The truth was he had never quite forgiven Charlie for inveigling him into loaning fifty dollars with promises of payment as soon as he could get a draft from home. The draft never came, but Roy did, and settled his brother's bills and took him away while Uncle Phil was absent, and as Charlie made no mention of his indebtedness in that direction, the debt remained uncancelled. Several times Uncle Phil had been on the point of writing to Roy about it, but had neglected to do so, thinking to wait until he came to Rocky Point again, when he would speak to him about it. But after the news of Charlie's tragical death was received, he abandoned the idea altogether:

"Fifty dollars would not break him," he thought, and it was not worth while to trouble Roy Leighton any more by letting him know just what a scamp his brother was. So he tore up Charlie's note and threw it into the fire, and took a great deal of snuff that day, and stayed till it was pitch dark at the hotel where they were discussing the accident, and commenting upon poor Charlie, whose virtues now were named before his faults. Mention was made of him in the minister's sermon the next Sunday, and it was observed that Miss Ruth Gardner cried softly under her veil, and that pretty Marcia Belknap looked a little pale, and after that the excitement gradually died away, and people ceased to talk of Charlie Churchill and his unfortunate end. But they would do so again, and the whole town would be alive with wonder if it once were known that the young girl in black at Uncle Phil Overton's was Charlie Churchill's widow. Ruth Gardner's pale-gray eyes would scan her coldly and harshly, while even Marcia Belknap would, perhaps, draw back from one who all unknowingly had been her rival. This Uncle Phil foresaw, and hence his proposition that Edna should bear his name and drop that of Churchill, which was pretty sure to betray her. And after a time he persuaded her to do it."

"You are already Louise," he said, as Edna questioned the right in the matter. "And inasmuch as I adopt you for my daughter, it is right and proper that you take my name, is it not?"

"Perhaps so," Edna replied faintly; "but I shall have to tell Aunt Jerry, and Mr. Heyford too. I promised him I would write as soon as I was located in business."

To this, Uncle Phil did not object, provided Jack Heyford kept his own counsel, as Edna was sure he would. With regard to Miss Pepper, he made no remonstrance. He did not seem to fear *her*, but surprised Edna with the question,

"What sort of a looking craft is this Pepper woman?"

Edna, who felt that she might have told too much that was prejudicial to her aunt, gladly seized the opportunity to make amends by praising her personal appearance.

"Aunt Jerry dresses so queerly that one can hardly tell how she does look," she said, "but if she only wore clothes like other people, I think she'd be real handsome for her age. She was pretty once, I'm sure, for she has a nice, fair complexion now, and her neck and arms are plumper and whiter than a Mrs. Fosbook's, whom I saw barenecked and short-sleeved at a sociable in Canandaigua. Her hair is soft and wavy, and she has so much of it, too, but will twist it into such a hard knot always, when she might make such a lovely waterfall."

"Do you mean those things that hang down your back like a work-bag?" Uncle Phil asked, laughing louder and longer than Edna thought the occasion warranted, especially as he did not know Miss Pepper, and how out of place a waterfall would be upon her.

"What of her eyes?" he asked, and Edna replied—"bright and black as jet beads."

"And snap like a snap-dragon, I'll bet," Uncle Phil rejoined, adding, after a moment, "I'd really like to see this kinswoman of yours. Tell her so when you write, and say she's welcome to bed and board whenever she chooses to come, and there's an Episcopal meeting-house over to Millville, and she can have old Bobtail every saint's day in the calendar."

There was a perfect shower of snuff after this, and then Uncle Phil questioned Edna as to what she thought she could teach, and how much she expected to get for each scholar; then he summoned Becky and ordered cider, and apples, and fried cakes, and butternuts, and made Edna try them all, and told her about her grandmother Louise when she was a girl, and then, precisely as the clock pointed to nine, called Becky again, and bade her show *Miss Overton* to her room.

"I breakfast sharp at half-past seven," he said to Edna; "but if you feel inclined, lie as long as you please, though I can't say but I'd like to see a fresh young face across the table. Maude generally was up."

"I shall be up too," Edna said, as she stood a moment in the door looking at her uncle; then, as she remembered all the kindness he had shown to her, there came over her with a rush the hunger she had always felt for something missed in childhood, and without stopping to think, she walked boldly up to the little man, and said, "Uncle Phil, nobody ever kissed me good-night since I can remember; none of my relatives I mean; will you do so?"

Uncle Phil was confounded. It was more than thirty years since he had kissed anybody, and he began to gather up his short coat skirts and hop,—first on one foot, then on the other, and look behind him toward the door in a kind of helpless way, as if meditating flight. But Edna stood her ground, and put up her full, red lips so temptingly, that with a hurried "bless me, girl, bless me, I don't know 'bout this. Yes, yes, I feel very queer and curis," Uncle Phil submitted, and suffered Edna's kiss, and as her lips touched his, he clasped both arms about her neck, and kissed her back heartily, while with a trembling voice, he said, "Heaven bless you, my child, my daughter, Louise Overton. I'm a rough old fellow, but I'll do my duty to you."

There was a tear on Edna's cheek; left there by Uncle Phil, and Edna accepted it as the baptism for her new name, and felt more resigned to "Louise Overton," as she followed Becky upstairs to the north room, where the bright fire was making shadows on the wall, and diffusing a delightful feeling of warmth throughout the apartment.

CHAPTER XX.

UP IN THE NORTH ROOM.

"OH, how pleasant and nice. Am I to sleep here?" Edna asked, as she skipped across the floor, and knelt upon the hearth-rug in front of the fire. "What's become of that little room? I thought——"

She did not say what she thought, for Becky interrupted her with:

"Oh, dat's no 'count room; jes' put folks in thar when they fust comes, then moves 'em up higher, like they does in Scripter. Marster's mighty quare."

"How long have you lived with him?" Edna asked, and Becky replied:

"Oh, many years. I was a slave on the block, in Car'lina, and Marster Phil comed in and seen me, and pitied me like, and bid me off, and kep' me from gwine South with a trader, an' brought me home and sot me free, and I've lived with him ever since, an', please Heaven, I will sarve him till I die, for all he's done for me. Is you gwine to stay, Miss Overton?"

Edna told her that she was, and that she was sure she should like it very much if she could get something to do.

"You likes to work then, and so did Miss Maude, though she 'pears more of a lady than 'nough I've seen what wouldn't lift thar finger to fotch a thing," Becky said, and Edna asked:

"Who is Maude? Uncle Phil has spoken of her once or twice."

"Why she's Maude Somerton, from New York," Becky replied; "and she came fust to Prospect Cottage, as they call a house way up on the hills whar the city gentry sometimes stay summers for a spell, and whar Miss Maude's Aunt Burton was onct with her daughter called Georgie, though she was a girl."

Edna was interested now, and moved a little nearer to Becky, who continued:

"I know precious little 'bout them Burtons, only they was mighty big feelin', and Miss Maude was a kind of poor relation, I s'pects; leastwise she wanted to teach school, and Uncle Phil was committee-man and let her have it, and she was to board round, and didn't like it, and went at Marster Phil till he took her in, though he hated to like pison, and it was allus a mystery to me how she did it, for he don't hanker after wimmen much, and never could bar to have 'em 'round."

Here Aunt Becky paused a moment, and taking advantage of the pause, we will present our readers with a picture which Aunt Becky did not see, else she would have known just how Maude Somerton persuaded Uncle Philip to let her have a home beneath his roof. The time, five o'clock or thereabouts, on a warm summer afternoon: the place, a strip of meadow land on Uncle Phil's premises: the *Dramatis Personæ*, Uncle Phil and Maude Somerton: She, with the duties of the day over, wending her way slowly toward the small and rather uncomfortable gable-roofed house up the mountain road, where it was her fate to board for that week, aye, for two or three weeks, judging by the number of children, who seldom left her alone for a moment, and who each night contended for the honor of sleeping with the "school-marm." He, industriously raking up into mounds the fragrant hay, and casting now and then a wistful glance at a bank of clouds which threatened rain; when suddenly, across the field, and bearing swiftly down upon him, came an airy form, her blue linen dress held just high enough to clear the grass, and at the same time show her pretty boots, with the Broadway stamp upon them, and her dainty white petticoat, whose tucks and ruffles were the envy of all the girls in Rocky Point, and the bane of the wash-woman's life. Uncle Phil saw the apparition, and saw the tucks and ruffles, and thought what pretty feet Miss Somerton had, and what tall boots she wore, and wondered why she was coming toward him in such hot haste.

"Most likely some of those Beals' boys have been raisin' Cain, and so she comes to me as committee-man. I'll be blamed if I don't throw up the office, for I can't have wimmen taggin' after me this way," he thought, and pretending not to see the young girl, now so near to him, he kept on with his raking, until right before his very face came the vision of blue and white, and a little, fat, dimpled hand was laid upon his rake, and a pair of soft, blue eyes looked up into his with something like tears in them, while a pleading voice told him how terrible it was to board round, to eat the best cake every day, to be company all the time, and never feel at home; besides, having from one to three children fighting to sleep with you every night, when you wanted so much to be alone. And then, still grasping the rake, Maude asked if she might stay altogether at his house, where everything was so nice, and cool, and quiet, and she could have a room to herself, undisturbed by children.

"You will, I know you will, Mr. Overton," and she stopped for his reply.

Uncle Phil was more astounded than when asked by Edna to kiss her. Of his own accord, he would quite as soon have taken a young alligator into his family as a *girl*, a *woman;* but there was something about this one standing there before him, and now actually grasping his hand instead of the rake, which completely unmanned him. Those eyes, and the touch of the white fingers clinging so closely to his own, could not be resisted, and with a quick, nervous motion, he began to step backwards, and sideways, and then forwards, ejaculating meanwhile, "Lord bless me,—yes, yes! I feel very queer; yes I do. Let go my rake. This is sudden. Yes, yes. You don't like sleepin' with all the young ones in the deestrict. Don't blame you. I'd as soon sleep with a nest of woodchucks. Yes, yes. This is curis. I must have some snuff."

He got his hand free from Maude, took two or three good pinches of his favorite Macaboy, offered her some, and then, giving a hitch to his suspender, replied to her question, repeated, "May I stay with you, Mr. Overton?"

"Yes, yes; I s'pose you'll have to, if Beck is willin'. I'll see her to-night, and let you know."

He said this last by way of giving himself a chance to

draw back, for already he began to repent, and feel how terrible it would be to have a young woman in his house all the time,—to-day, to-morrow, and next day. It was a great deal worse than sleeping with every child in town, and he brought up Beck as the pack-horse who was to carry the burden of his refusal on the morrow. But Maude outwitted him there.

"Oh, thank you, thank you!" she cried. "You are the dearest man in the world. Becky is all right. I saw her first, and she said if you were willing, she was. I shall move this very day, for I cannot stay with Mrs. Higgins another hour. Thank you again, ever so much, you dear, darling man."

She was tripping off across the fields, leaving the enemy totally routed and vanquished, and sick at his stomach, and dizzy-headed, as he tried to think how many more weeks there were before vacation.

"Nine, *ten*, TWELVE!" he fairly groaned. "I can't stand it. I won't stand it. I'll put a stop to it,—see if I don't. Yes, yes; to have them boots trottin' up and down the stairs, and them petticoats whiskin' through the doors, and makin' me feel so curis. I'll go crazy,—I feel like it now."

He tried snuff,—six pinches; but that didn't answer. Then he tried raking hay so fast, that to use his own words, "he sweat like a butcher;" then he tried cooling his feet in the brook near by, and wiping them on his bandanna; but nothing was of avail to drive away "that curis feelin' at the pit of his stomach," and long before sunset he left his work, and wended his way homeward.

The enemy was there before him, or, at least, a part of her equipments, for two of the Higgins' boys had brought over Maude's satchel, and sun-umbrella, and water-proof, and two or three books, and a pair of overshoes; all of which were on the kitchen-table, while the boys were swinging on the gate in the front yard.

Uncle Phil ordered the boys home, and "the traps" up in the little "back chamber."

"That'll start her. She'll find that worse than sleepin' with the Higginses," he thought, as he gave the order, and then went and took a dose of something he called "jallup."

"He had an awful headache," he said to Aunt Becky, when she inquired what was the matter; and his headache increased, and sent him to bed before Maude arrived, flushed, delighted, and full of spirits that her boarding 'round was over.

He heard her go up to her little hot back room, and wondered how she liked it, and how long she'd stay in it, and half wished he had nailed the window down so she could not open it.

She was up bright and early the next morning, and drove the cows to their pasture, a distance of half a mile, and brought back a bunch of flowers, which she arranged upon the table; and she looked so fresh and pretty in her blue gown, which just matched her eyes, and ate cold beans so heartily, that Uncle Phil began to relent, and that night she slept in the *north-west* room instead of the little back one. There she stayed a week; and then, after having helped Uncle Phil rake up his hay one day when a shower was coming up, she was promoted to the *north*, and best chamber, and some nice striped matting was bought for the floor, and a pretty chestnut set took the place of the high-post bedstead and old-fashioned bureau; and some curtains were hung at the windows, for Uncle Phil said "he didn't want the whole town to see the *girl* undress, if they did him."

And here for weeks Maude reigned, a very queen, and cheered and brightened up the old farm-house until, when in the fall she left and went back to Oakwood, Aunt Becky cried for sheer loneliness, and Uncle Phil took a larger dose of "jallup" to help the feeling at his stomach, than when she first came to him.

And this was how Maude Somerton chanced to be an inmate of Uncle Phil's family, and enshrined in his heart, as well as in old Becky's, as a kind of divinity, whom it was not so very wrong to worship.

"'Pears like we never could get over hankerin after her," Becky said to Edna, "she was so chirk and pert-like, and made the house so different."

Edna was longing to ask another question, but did not quite know how to get at it. At last she said:

"Does Miss Somerton live in New York all the time? Has her Aunt Burton no country residence?"

"Yes, bless you, a house as big as four of this, down to Oakwood, whar thar's looking-glasses as long as you be, Miss Maude said, and furniture all covered with satin."

Edna was no nearer her point than before, and so she tried again.

"Have they any neighbors at Oakwood, any families they are intimate with?"

"Yes, thar's the Leighton's, to my way of thinkin' quite as sot up as the Burtons, and thar place, Miss Maude say, is handsomer and bigger than the one to Oakwood."

"Oh, indeed, Mrs. Leighton must be a happy woman. Did you ever see her?" Edna asked, and Becky replied,

"Thar ain't no Miss Leighton; she's Miss Churchill, married twicet; her oldest boy, Mr. Roy, owns the property, and is the nicest man I reckon you ever seen. He stayed to the hotel oncet a few weeks, and I done his washin', 'case he couldn't find nobody handy, and Marster Phil let me do it and keep the pay. He wore a clean shirt a day, and cuffs and collars, and white vests, and pocket handkerchiefs, and socks without end; and gave me seventy-five cents a dozen just as they run, which made me a nice handful of money."

"Yes," Edna said, musingly; "I suppose he must be very rich? Is he the only child?"

"Ne-oo," and Aunt Becky spoke a little scornfully, while Edna moved so as to hide her burning face.

She had reached the point at last, and her heart beat almost audibly as Aunt Becky continued:

"Or he wasn't the only child when they was here. Thar was a younger one, a Charles Churchill, who got killed on the railroad a spell ago. You should speak well of the dead, and I mean to; but I reckon he wasn't of so much 'count in these yer parts as Master Roy."

"Did he do anything bad," Edna asked, and her voice was very low and sad.

"No, not bad, only wan't of much 'count. He druv fast horses, and smoked all the time, and bragged about his money when he hadn't a cent, and flirted with the girls awfully. Thar's Miss Ruth Gardner, all of three years older than him, thought she should catch him sure, and little Marcia Belknap was fairly bewitched; and both on 'em cried when they heard he was dead, though he left a wife, the papers said, married that very day."

"Oh, dreadful," and Edna groaned aloud, for she saw again that awful scene, and the white, still face upturned to the angry sky, and it seemed wrong to sit there and make no sign while Becky went on.

"I hain't seen Miss Maude since, so I don't know nothin' about his wife, who she was, nor whar she is. Down to the Leighton Place, maybe, though it's been surmised that she warn't much,—kind of poor white folksy, I reckon; and if that's so, Miss Churchill ain't a-goin' to own her, 'case she's mighty big feelin', and turned up her nose at Miss Ruth, and took her boy home to git shet of her. But Miss Ruth is enough for her, and I've hearn she talked awful about that wife of Charlie's, and said she jest wished she could see her long enough to tell her she had the best and fustest right to her husband. Oh, she's a clipper, Miss Ruth is."

Edna's hands were locked firmly together, and the nails were making red marks upon her flesh, while she longed for Aunt Becky to leave her. She had heard enough, and she looked so white and tired, that Becky noticed it at last, and asked if she was sick.

"No, only tired," she said; and then Becky said good-night, and left her alone with her sad thoughts, which, however, were not all sad and bitter.

She had lost her first love in more ways than one, and as, with her head bent down, she sat thinking of him and all she had heard, she felt a fresh pang of remorse cut through her heart at her own callousness in feeling that perhaps for herself it was better that Charlie died. But only for herself. When she thought of *him*, and what he might have been, had space for repentance been granted him, her tears flowed like rain, and, prone upon her face, she prayed that if the prayers of the living for the dead could avail, hers might be heard and answered for her lost, wayward Charlie.

CHAPTER XXI.

MISS OVERTON.

TO the young and healthy sleep comes easily, and notwithstanding her excitement, Edna slept soundly in her new home; and when the first signs of daylight began to be visible in her room, and she heard sounds of life below, she arose with a feeling nearer akin to happiness than she had known since Charlie died. Aunt Becky soon appeared, chiding her for getting up before her fire was made, and finally coaxing her back to bed, while she kindled a blazing fire upon the hearth, and then brought a pitcher of hot water for her young lady's ablutions. Breakfast would be ready in half an hour, she said, as she left the room; and then Edna rose again, and remembering what Uncle Phil had said about her grandmother's hair, and inferring therefrom that he liked curls, she brushed and arranged her own thick tresses in masses of wavy curls, and then went down to Uncle Phil, who, after bidding her good-morning, said, softly, as he held his hand on her flowing hair:

"Wear it so always; it makes me think of my sister."

"I am going to town," he said, when breakfast was over, "to see what I can do towards scarin' up a school, though I haint a great deal of confidence; but if I fail, there's still the factory to Millville, and the hired-girl business, you know."

He gave Edna a knowing wink, offered her a pinch of snuff, told her "to keep a stiff upper lip," and then rode off on old Bobtail to Rocky Point.

Long before noon everybody in town knew that the young lady in black was Miss Louise Overton, Uncle Phil's niece, who wanted a school, and could teach music and drawing and everything, and Miss Ruth Gardner's name was actually down as a pupil in drawing, while Squire Gardner headed the list with his two youngest children. It was a stroke of policy on Uncle Phil's part to get the Gardners interested, especially Miss Ruth, whose name as a pupil in drawing was the direct means of gaining several more, so that when at noon Uncle Phil went home to dinner, it was settled that a select school should be opened at once in one of the rooms of the old Academy, Uncle Phil pledging himself to see that it was thoroughly cleaned and put in order, besides supplying the necessary fuel. Twenty scholars were promised sure, and Uncle Phil rode home in great spirits, and gave Bobtail an extra amount of hay, and then went in to Edna, to whom he said:

"I dunno 'bout the school, but there's a place you can have at Squire Gardner's as second girl, to wait on the door and table, and pass things on a little silver platter; wages, two dollars a week and found. Will you take it?"

"Certainly, if nothing better offers. I told you I would do anything to earn money," Edna replied, whereupon Uncle Phil called her a "brick," and said:

"He'd like to see her waiting on Ruth Gardner, yes he would," and took a pinch of snuff, and told her the exact truth, and that Miss Ruth was to call on her that afternoon and see some of her drawings, and talk it over with her.

Miss Ruth, who was very proud and exclusive, was at first disposed to patronize "Miss Overton," whose personal appearance she mentally criticised, deciding that she was very young and rather pretty, or would be if she had a little more style. Style was a kind of mania with Ruth, who, being rather plain, said frankly, that "as she could not be handsome, she *would* be stylish, which was next best to beauty;" and so she studied fashion and went to the extreme of everything, and astonished the Rocky Pointers with something new every month, and carried matters with a high hand, and queened it over all the young people, whom she alternately noticed and snubbed, and did more to help Edna by being a pupil herself than any six other young ladies could have done. She liked Edna from the first, and being of a romantic turn of mind, she liked her the more because she fancied her to be suffering from some other cause than the mere loss of friends. "A love affair, most likely," she thought; and as one who knew how to sympathize in such matters, she took a great interest in her young teacher, and, after a time, grew confidential, and in speaking of marriage, said with a sigh and a downcast look in her gray eyes, that "her first and only love was dead, that the details of his death were too dreadful to narrate, and had made so strong an impression upon her that it was not at all probable she should ever marry now."

And Edna listened with burning cheeks, and bent her head lower over the drawing she was making from memory of a bit of landscape seen from Aunt Jerry's upper windows. Edna stood somewhat in awe of Miss Ruth with her dash and style, and flights of fancy, but from the moment little Marcia Belknap called and looked at her with her great, dreamy eyes, and spoke with her sweet low voice, she was the young girl's sworn friend, and when the two grew so intimate that Marcia, who was also given to sentiment and fancies, and had a *penchant* for blighted hopes and broken hearts, told her teacher one night, just as Ruth had done, of *her* dead love, Edna caressed her bowed head and longed to tell her how foolish she was, and how the lost fruit, if gathered, would have proved but an apple of Sodom.

"Charlie was not worthy of so much love," was the sad refrain ever repeating itself in her heart, until at last the old soreness began to give way, and she felt that the blow which had severed his life from hers had also set her free from a load she would have found hard to bear as the years went on, and she saw more and more the terrible mistake she had made.

The school was a great success, thanks to Uncle Phil, who worked like a hero to get her scholars, and who carried her each day to and from the old academy, while Becky vied with him in caring for and petting her young mistress. And Edna was very happy. Her school, including her pupils in drawing, was bringing her in over one hundred and fifty dollars a quarter, and as she had no outgoing expenses she was confidently expecting to lessen her debt to Roy in the spring, besides sending Aunt Jerry a draft which should surprise her.

As soon as her prospects were certain she wrote her aunt a long letter, full of Rocky Point and Uncle Phil, whose invitation for Aunt Jerry to visit him she gave word for word.

"I have no idea she'll come," Edna said to herself as she folded up the letter, "but maybe she will feel better for the invitation."

And Aunt Jerry did, though the expression of her face was a study for an instant as, by her lone evening fire, with only Tabby for company, she read her niece's letter. She did not exactly swear as Uncle Phil had done, when he first heard *her* name and knew that Edna was her niece, but she involuntarily apostrophized the same personage, addressing him by another name.

"The very old Harry!" she exclaimed, and a perceptible pallor crept into her face, as, snuffing her tallow dip, she commenced again to see if she had read aright.

Yes, there it was in black and white. Philip Overton was Edna's great uncle, to whom in her distress she had gone, and he had taken her as his daughter, and given her his name, and sent a friendly message to her, Jerusha Pepper, asking her to visit him, and couching his invitation in language so characteristic of the man that it made the spinster bristle a little with resentment. She sent more than a quart of milk that night to the minister's wife, whose girl, as usual, came for it, and wondered with her mistress to find her pail so full; and next day at the sewing society she gave five yards of cotton cloth to be made into little garments for the poor children of the parish, and that night she wrote to Edna, telling her, "she was glad to know she was so well provided for, and hoped she would behave herself, and keep the right side of her uncle, and not go to the Unitarian meeting if she had any regard for what her sponsors in baptism promised for her, let alone what she took on herself the time she renewed the promise. The Orthodox persuasion was a little better, though that was far enough from right; and if she couldn't be carried over to Millville, and it wasn't likely Mr. Overton was one to cart folks to church, she'd better stay at home and read her prayer-book by herself and one of Ryle's sermons. She would send the book as a Christmas gift." The letter closed with, "'Thank your uncle for inviting me to his house, but tell him I prefer my own bed and board to anybody's else. I've toughed it out these thirty years, and guess I can stand it a spell longer."

Uncle Phil brought the letter to Edna, and when she had finished reading it, asked:

"What does the Pepper-corn say? or maybe you wouldn't mind letting me see for myself. I own to a good deal of curiosity about this woman."

Edna hesitated a moment, and then reflecting that the letter was quite a soft, friendly epistle for Aunt Jerry to write, gave it to Uncle Phil, who, putting on his glasses, read it through carefully till he came to the part concerning the proper way for Edna to spend her Sundays. Then he laughed aloud and said, more to himself than Edna, as it would seem:

"Yes, yes, plucky as ever. Death on the Unitarian church to the end of her spine; Orthodox most as bad; Ryle and the prayer-book; good for her."

Then, when he reached the reply to his invitation to visit him, he laughed so long and loud, and took such quantities of snuff, that Edna looked at him with a half fear lest he had suddenly gone mad. But he had not, and he handed the letter back, saying as he did so:

"Tough old knot, isn't she?"

Edna made no reply, for something in his manner made her sorry that she had shown him Aunt Jerry's letter, and she resolved never to do so again. She had written to Jack Heyford, telling him of her new name and prospects, and her proximity to Charlie's friends, and Jack had replied in a long, kind, brotherly letter, in which he told her that Georgie was at present with him, but he did not know how long she would stay.

"Annie is better," he wrote, "but we fear will never be able to walk again without the aid of crutches. She talks of you a great deal, and wonders where you are. I have not told her, for I thought it better not to do so while Georgie is here, as I fancy your uncle has some reason for not wishing the Leightons to know where you are at present. I am thinking of changing my quarters from Chicago to Jersey City, where I have a chance in an Insurance Company, but nothing is decided yet. Will let you know as soon as it is, and perhaps run up for a few days to Rocky Point, as there is something I wish to say to you, which I would rather not put on paper. I was there once with Roy Leighton some years ago; his mother was at the Mountain House, and Georgie was there too. Strange how matters get mixed up, is it not?"

Jack signed himself "yours truly," but something in the tone of his letter made Edna's heart beat unpleasantly, as she guessed what it was Jack Heyford had to say to her, which he would rather not commit to paper, and thought of the disappointment in store for him.

There was no Christmas tree at Rocky Point that winter. The Unitarians thought of having one, but gave it up on account of the vast amount of labor which must necessarily fall upon a few, and contented themselves with a ball, while the Orthodox portion of the community, who did not believe in dancing, got up a sleigh-ride to Millville, with a hot supper at the hotel, followed by a game of blind man's buff, in which Marcia Belknap bruised her nose until it bled, and had the back breadth of her dress torn entirely from the waist, in her frantic endeavors to escape from Uncle Phil

For Uncle Phil, though a Unitarian to his very marrow, cast in his lot for once with the other side, and hired a fancy team, and went to the sleigh-ride, and took Edna with him, and astonished the young people with his fun and wonderful feats of agility.

But, if there was no Christmas *tree* at Rocky Point, Santa Claus came to the old farm-house, and deposited various packages for "Miss Overton." There was a pretty little muff, and the box which contained it had "Chicago" marked upon it; and Edna felt a keen pang of regret as she thought how much self-denial this present must have cost the generous Jack, and how poorly she could repay it. Another package from Aunt Jerry, contained the promised book of sermons, and a pair of lamb's-wool stockings—"knit every stitch by myself and shaped to my own legs," Aunt Jerry wrote; adding, in reference to a small square box which the package also contained: "The jimcracks in the box, which to my mind are more fitting for a South Sea Islander than a widow, who has been confirmed, was sent to me by Roy Leighton, who deigned to say they was for his sister, Mrs. Charles Churchill,—a Christmas gift from himself; and he wanted me to give them to you, if I knew where you was, as he supposed of course I did by this time; and asked me to give him your address. Maybe you'll think I did wrong, but I just wrote to him that I'd got the toggery, and would see that you had it,—that you was taking care of yourself, and earning money to pay your debts, and inasmuch as you did not write to him, it was fair to suppose that you wanted to stay *incog.*, and I should let you. You can write to him yourself, if you wish to."

The box when opened was found to contain a full set of beautiful jets,—bracelets, ear-rings, pin, chain, and all,—with a note from Roy, who called Edna "My dear little sister," and asked her to accept the ornaments as a Christmas gift from her "brother Roy." There was a warm, happy spot in Edna's heart for the remainder of that day, and more than once she found herself repeating the words, "my dear little sister." They were constantly in her mind, both at home and on the way to Millville, when the sleigh-bells seemed to chant them, and the soft wind, which told of rain not far away, whispered them in her ears, as it brushed her hair in passing. But as her heart grew warmer with the memory of those words written by Roy Leighton, so the little hands clasped together inside Jack Heyford's muff, grew colder and colder, as she wished he had not sent it, and thought of the *something* he was to say when he came to Rocky Point.

CHAPTER XXII.

MAUDE'S VISIT.

TWO weeks after the ride to Millville, Uncle Phil received a letter from Maude, who said that as it was vacation with her now, she was coming for a few days to the farm-house. "So, dear Mr. Overton," she wrote, "give Bobtail an extra supply of oats, for if it chances to be sleighing, I mean to make you into a gay cavalier, a second Sir Launcelot, of whom all the Guineveres and Elaines of Astolat shall be jealous, as we go driving through the country. Tell dear Aunt Becky to get out her warming pan, and hold her fattest chicken in readiness. She knows my taste. Aunt Burton has sent for me to the parlor, so, dear, darling Mr. Overton, *au revoir* till next Thursday night. I can scarcely wait for thinking of that *north* room with the wood fire on the hearth, and Becky waiting upon me as if I were a queen instead of a poor Yankee schoolmistress. Yours, forever, Maude."

Uncle Phil read this letter three times to himself, and then three times to Becky, who was almost as much excited as her master. Edna, on the contrary, thought of Maude's visit with dread. She had no wish at present to be recognized by any friend of the Leightons. The Miss Overton *rôle* suited her now that she had become accustomed to it, and began to see that it was for the best. Sometime she meant to see Roy Leighton and his mother, and if she could do so without their knowing who she was, it would add greatly to the interest and excitement of the meeting; but if Maude should discover her secret, her pretty project would be spoiled. Still, the more she reflected upon it, the more she saw how improbable it was that Maude should suspect her of being other than Miss Overton, and her unwillingness to meet Miss Somerton gradually gave way until, at last, she was almost as anxious as Becky herself for the arrival of their guest, who came a train earlier than she was expected, and took them by surprise.

Edna walked home from school that day, and seeing no one as she entered the house, went directly to her chamber, where Maude was sitting in her blue flannel dressing-gown, with her bright, beautiful hair rippling over her shoulders, and the brush lying forgotten on the floor, as she sat gazing into the fire upon the hearth. As Edna entered unannounced, she started to her feet, and shedding back her luxuriant tresses, exclaimed with a merry laugh:

"Oh, you must be Miss Overton, I know; my rival in Becky's heart, and Mr. Overton's too; but you see I am not to be vanquished, and have come right back into my old quarters, trusting to your generosity to divide with me the towels and the hooks for my dresses. Let me help you, please. You look tired."

And she walked up to Edna, who was vainly trying to undo her waterproof. At sight of Maude, who had known Charlie so well, there had swept over Edna a faint, dizzy feeling, which made her for a moment very pale and weak; then the hot blood came surging back to her cheeks, which were bright as carnations by the time the troublesome knot had been untied by Maude Somerton's skilful fingers.

"What a little dot of a girl you are," Maude said, when at last Edna was disrobed and stood before the fire.

"And you are so much taller than I had supposed," Edna replied, looking up into the sunny blue eyes, which were regarding her so intently.

"Yes; I must seem a perfect amazon to one as *petite* as yourself. I used to want to stop growing, and once actually thought of tying a stone to my head, as Charlie Churchill teasingly suggested."

Edna felt a great heart throb at the mention of that name, but made no reply, and Maude continued:

"I suppose it is time now to dress for dinner. Becky tells me that on 'Miss Louise's' account, they dine after your school hours, by which I see that your position with Uncle Phil is in all respects '*comme il fait*,' but you must have commenced on the lower round. Did you try the little back chamber?" and Maude's eyes brimmed with mischief as she asked the question.

"Yes, and nearly froze for half an hour or so. Were you put in there, too?"

"Yes, and nearly melted. Of course you were promoted to the north-west room next."

Edna, who knew nothing of the gradation by which she had reached her present comfortable apartment, pleaded *not guilty* to the north-west room, whereat Maude professed to feeling terribly aggrieved at the partiality shown.

"It must be because you are a *little dot*," she said;

"and because—," she hesitated a moment, and then added, softly, "because of your deep mourning and trouble. That always opens one's heart. Mr. Overton told me all about you."

Maude's face was turned away from Edna, and so she did not see the violent start, as Edna asked:

"What did he tell you about me?"

"Oh, nothing improper," and Maude put a part of her front hair in her mouth, while she twisted her back locks into a massive coil. "He said you had lost your father and mother, and that made me feel for you at once, for I am an orphan, too; he said, also, that since their death, you had had a hard time generally, and was obliged to teach school, every item of which will apply to me. I am a poor school-ma'am,—which, in New York society, don't pass for much; and if Uncle Burton should close his doors upon me, I should have nowhere to lay my head, and so you see we ought to be friends. I wish you would hold that lock of hair, please; it bothers me to get the last new kink. Can you do it?"

She looked up suddenly at Edna, who was curiously studying this girl, who mixed things so indiscriminately, poverty, orphanage, friendlessness, and the last style of dressing the hair.

"I don't try. I curl my hair, and that is all. I don't know a thing about fashion," she said, while Maude, who had succeeded in winding her satin braids, coil after coil, about her head, until the last one came almost to her forehead, replied, "Your curls are lovely. I would not meddle with them. Fashion is an exacting dame, but Aunt Burton and Georgie make such a fuss if I do not try to be decent."

"Who is Georgie?" Edna asked, feeling guilty for the deception she was practising.

"Georgie is Aunt Burton's adopted daughter and niece,

while I am Uncle Burton's relation, which makes a vast difference," Maude replied. "She is a belle and a beauty, and an heiress, while I, as I told you, am poor, and a schoolma'am, and nobody but 'that young girl who lives with Mrs. Burton.'"

Edna had made no attempt at arranging her own toilet, but completely fascinated with her visitor, stood leaning on the bureau, watching the young girl who rattled on so fast, and who, while pleading poverty, arrayed herself in a soft, flowing dress of shining blue silk, which harmonized so admirably with her fair, creamy complexion.

"One of Georgie's cast-offs," she explained to Edna. "Most of my wardrobe comes to me that way. I am fortunate in one respect; fortunate in everything, perhaps, for everybody is kind to me. Look, please, at my beautiful Christmas present, the very thing of all others which I coveted, but never expected to have."

She took from the little box on the bureau a gold watch and chain, and passed it to Edna, who held it in her hand, and with a face as pale as ashes, turned to the window as if to see it better, while only the most superhuman effort at control on her part kept her from crying outright, for there lying in her hand, with the old familiar ticking sounding in her ear, was *her watch*, the one Charlie had given to her, and which she had left in Albany. There could be no mistake. She knew it was the very same, and through it she seemed again to grasp the dead hand of her husband, just as she had grasped it that awful night when he lay beneath the wreck, with the rain falling on his lifeless face. Edna felt as if she should faint, and was glad of Maude's absorption in a box of collars and bows, as that gave her a little time in which to recover herself. When she felt that she could speak, she laid the watch back upon the bureau, carefully, tenderly, as if it had been the dead body of a friend, and said:

"It is a charming Christmas gift. Your aunt's, I suppose?"

She knew she ran the risk of seeming inquisitive by the last remark, but she wanted so much to know how that watch of all others came into Maude Somerton's possession.

"No, you don't catch her making me as costly a present as that. She selected it, but Roy Leighton paid for it."

"Roy Leighton!" Edna exclaimed, her voice so strongly indicative of surprise, that Maude stopped short and glanced quickly at her, saying, "what makes you say 'Roy Leighton' in that tragic kind of way? Do you know him?"

The wintry light had nearly faded from the room by this time, and under cover of the gathering darkness, Edna forced down the emotion which had made every nerve quiver, and managed to answer indifferently:

"I have heard Uncle Phil speak of him. He owns the hotel here in town, I believe. He must be a very dear friend to make you so costly a present."

Edna could not define the nature of the pang which had shot through her heart when she heard that to Roy Leighton Maude owed the watch she had once called hers, and surrendered with so many tears. It certainly was not jealousy, for why should she be jealous of one who had never evinced any interest in her save such as was expressed in the ornaments of jet, and the words "My dear little sister." Edna did not know how closely those four words had brought Roy Leighton to her until she saw his costly gift to another.

"That's just what I told Aunt Burton that people would say," Maude replied; "and I expect Georgie will be highly scandalized, for she it is who expects to be Mrs. Roy Leighton, some day, and not poor, humble I. Mr. Leighton's half-brother, Charlie, was killed the very day he was married. Perhaps you saw it in the paper. It was a dreadful thing. I'll tell you all about it sometime. I was with poor Mrs. Churchill a few days, and Roy, who had a broken leg, and could not sit up, greatly overrated my services, and resolved to make me a present. He had heard me say once or twice that I wanted a watch which was a watch, instead of the great big masculine thing of Uncle Burton's, and so he concluded to give me one, and asked Aunt Burton, who was going up to Albany, to pick it out. I suppose I should be deceiving you if I did not tell you that the watch was second-hand, and the jeweller sold it a little less because he bought it of a lady who had seen better days. Auntie had admired it very much before he told her that, and she took it just the same. I was perfectly delighted, of course, though I have built all sorts of castles with regard to its first owner, *who* she was and how she looked, and I've even found myself pitying her for the misfortune which compelled her to part with that watch."

Maude's toilet was finished by this time, and as Uncle Phil's voice was heard in the south room below, she asked if they should not go down.

"Yes, you go, please. Don't wait for me, I have my hair to brush yet," Edna said, feeling that she must be alone for a few moments, and give vent to the emotion she had so long been trying to repress.

She opened the door for Maude to pass out, and stood listening till she heard her talking to Uncle Phil; then with a sob she crouched upon the hearth and wept bitterly. Maude's presence had brought back all the dreadful past, and even seemed for a time to have resuscitated her girlish love for Charlie, while in her heart there was a fierce hungering for Charlie's friends, for recognition by them, or at least recognition by Roy, who had called her his "dear little sister." It was the memory of these words which quieted Edna at last. He had had her in his mind when he sent the jet, and perhaps he would think of her again, and sometime she might see him and know just how good he was; and as Becky called to say supper was waiting, she hastily bathed her face, and giving a few brushes to her hair, went down to the room where Maude, full of life and spirits, was chatting gayly with Uncle Phil, and showing him the watch which Roy Leighton had given her.

As Edna came in, Uncle Phil glanced anxiously at her, detecting at once the traces of agitation upon her face, and as Maude suddenly remembered leaving her pocket-handkerchief upstairs, and darted away after it before sitting down to the table, he improved her absence by saying, softly:

"What is it, little *Lu?* Has Maude brought the past all back again? Yes, yes, I was afraid she would."

"Not that exactly," Edna said, with a quivering lip and smothered sob; "but, Uncle Phil, *that* was *my* watch once, —Charlie gave it to me, and—and—I sold it, you remember, in Albany. I knew it in a moment."

"Yes, yes. Lord bless my soul! things does work curis. Your watch, and Roy Leighton bought it for Maude! there couldn't a likelier person have it, but that don't help its hurting. Poor little Lu! don't fret; I'll buy you one, handsomer than that, when I sell my wool. You bet I will. Yes, yes."

He took a large pinch of snuff, and adroitly threw some of it in Edna's eyes, so that their redness, and the tears streaming from them, were accounted for to Maude, who came tripping in, all anxiety to know what was the matter with "*Little Dot,*—that's what I call her, she is so very small," she said to Uncle Phil, as she took her seat at the table, talking all the time,—now of her school, now of Aunt Burton, and Georgie who was in Chicago, and at last of Charlie Churchill's tragical death, and the effect it had on his mother.

When she reached this point Uncle Phil tried to stop her, but Maude was not to be repressed. Uncle Phil knew Charlie, and of course he must be interested to hear the particulars of his death. And she told them, as she had heard them from Georgie, and said she pitied the poor girl for whom nobody seemed to care,—unless it was Roy, who was lame at the time and could do nothing for any one. And Edna heard it all, with an agony in her heart which threatened to betray itself every moment, until Maude spoke of "the poor young wife, for whom nobody seemed to care but Roy." Then there came a revulsion; the terrible throbbing ceased; her pulse became more even, and though she was paler than usual, she seemed perfectly natural, and her voice was firm and steady as she said, "Then the wife did not come to Leighton?"

"Lord bless me! That is curis," Uncle Phil muttered to himself, as, having finished his dinner, he walked hastily to the window, while Maude, without heeding him, replied:

"No, and I was so sorry. I had her room ready for her, too,—Charlie's old room, because I thought she would like it best. You see, Mrs. Churchill was sick, and I had it all my own way, except as I consulted Roy, who evinced a good deal of interest, and I think was really disappointed that Edna did not come. That was her name,—Edna,—and I think it pretty, too, because it is not common."

Supper was over by this time; and the conversation concerning Charlie Churchill was not resumed until the two girls had said good-night to Uncle Phil, and were alone in their room. Their acquaintance had progressed rapidly, and, girl-like, they sat down before the fire for a good long talk before going to bed. Passing her fingers through Edna's flowing curls, Maude made some remark about Georgie's hair, and then added, "Georgie said Edna had handsome curls. Poor thing! I wonder where she is."

"Don't they know?" Edna asked, feeling that she must say something.

"No; they only know that she is somewhere working to pay the debt she fancies she owes to Roy."

"I almost wonder Roy told anybody about that; seems to me he should have kept it to himself," Edna said, feeling a little hurt that her affairs should be so generally known to strangers.

"Roy didn't tell of it," Maude replied. "Mrs. Churchill told it first to auntie, and then to Georgie. She tells them everything, and against Roy's wishes, too, I am sure; for he is not a gossip. Roy Leighton is splendid everyway,— the best man I ever knew."

Edna looked up at her with a peculiar smile, which Maude readily understood; and, shaking her head, she said:

"No; I am not in love with him. I would as soon think of aspiring to the moon; but I admire him greatly, and so does every one. He is very different from Charlie, with whom I used to flirt a little."

Edna would rather hear about Roy than Charlie; and so she asked:

"Do you think he cares anything about his sister-in-law?"

"Of course he does. He wrote her a letter to Chicago; but she had left before it reached there; and once, in speaking of her to Georgie, he called her 'a brave little woman;' and, if you believe me, I think Georgie didn't quite like it."

There were little throbs of joy quivering all along through Edna's veins, and softly to herself she repeated: "Brave little woman," trying to imagine how Roy looked when he said that of her, and how his voice sounded. She did not care for Georgie Burton's liking or disliking what Roy said. She did not care even if Georgie became his wife, as Maude said she probably would. If he only gave her a place in his heart as his sister, and esteemed her "a brave little woman," she was more than content; and in Edna's eyes there was a brightness not borrowed from the fire-light, as, long after Maude was in bed, she sat upon the hearth, combing her curls, and thinking of Roy Leighton, who had called her "a brave little woman," and acknowledged her as his sister.

Maude's visit did Edna a world of good, for it brought her glimpses of a life widely different from any she had known, and stirred her up to higher aims, by inspiring her with a desire to make herself something of which Roy should not be ashamed, if ever she chanced to meet him. And she should meet him sometime, she was sure of that; and Maude would be the medium, perhaps; for, if necessary, she would tell her everything, knowing she could trust her as her own sister. They grew to liking each other very much during the few days Maude stayed at the farm-house; and Edna roused herself from a certain morbid listlessness into which she had fallen, with regard to herself and her personal appearance, thinking it did not matter how she looked or what she wore, as black was black anyway. But Maude did not think so.

"Needn't look like a Guy, if you do wear black," she said.

And so she coaxed Edna into white collars and cuffs, and, spying the jet, made her put it on, and screamed with delight when she saw how it brightened her up, and relieved the sombreness of her attire.

"If you were a widow, you could not go into deeper mourning than you have," she said, as she was trying the effect of arranging Edna's curls a little more fashionably, and twisting in a bit of lavender ribbon taken from her own box.

"Oh, no, not that," Edna cried, as she looked at herself in the glass, and thought of the driving rain, the terrible wreck, and the white, drenched face beneath.

But Maude, who knew nothing of this as connected with

Edna, insisted upon the ribbon just for that evening, and managed to have Uncle Phil praise the effect, and say he liked bright, pretty things, and wished Edna would wear ribbons and jet all the time.

The next day was Sunday; and Maude suggested that Uncle Phil should drive herself and Edna over to St. Jude's, at Millville.

"Dot tells me she has never been there, and I think it's a shame," she said.

"Yes, yes; maybe 'tis; but she never came right out as you do, rough shod, on a feller. She reads her prayer-book at home, and adorns her profession that way. Yes, yes; you want to go to the *true* church," Uncle Phil said, adding that he "didn't think no great things of that persuasion, or leastwise never had till he knew Louise and Maude. They were the right stripe, if they were 'Piscopals; and maybe for once he'd go to the doin's; but they mustn't expect him to jine in the performance, nor bob his head down when he went in, nor keep jumping up like a dancing-jack. He should jest snuggle down in the pew, and sleep it out," he said.

Maude gave him full permission to do as he liked, and, just as the bell of St. Jude's was pealing forth its last summons, old Bobtail drew up in front of the church, and deposited his load upon the steps. Whether it was from a wish to surprise his young ladies, or because of the softening influence around him, Uncle Phil did not lounge or sleep in one corner of the pew, but, greatly to Edna's astonishment, took a prayer-book from the rack in front, and followed the service tolerably well for a stranger. Only in the Creed he was silent, and in the fourth response to the Litany; "The *Trinity* part," he "couldn't go;" and he took a pinch of snuff on the sly, and glanced furtively at the two young maidens kneeling so devoutly at his side.

"They act kinder as if they did mean it, and were not puttin' on, and thinkin' of their neighbors' bunnets," he thought, as he listened to the services, which he decided were "confoundedly long, and a very trifle tedious."

It was many a year since Uncle Phil had heard our church service; and something in its singular beauty and fitness impressed him as he never was impressed before. All those kneeling people around him were *not* "putting on." Some of them surely were earnest and sincere, and were actually talking to somebody who heard, and whose presence even he could almost feel, as he sat listening to the sermon, which was from the text, "For he loveth our nation, and hath builded us a synagogue." The sermon was a plain, straightforward one; and, as the clergyman took the ground, as an inducement for good works, that the building of a synagogue was the direct means of commending the centurion to the Saviour's notice, Uncle Phil, who believed more in works than in faith, began to prick up his ears, and to wonder if he hadn't better do something which would be put to his credit in Heaven's great book of record.

"I can't snivel, and say I'm sorry when I ain't, but I should like to have a balance sheet in my favor, when I get on t'other side," he thought; and then he began to wonder if "it wouldn't please the *gals*, and the Lord, too," if he was to build a chapel at Rocky Point.

If that synagogue had really been a help to the centurion, and led the Saviour to deal mercifully with him, what might not the building of a chapel do for Uncle Phil? He did not believe in the divinity of Christ; but he had a warm feeling in his heart for the *man* who had lived on earth thirty-three years, and known all the sorrows which could be crowded into a human life. He believed, too, in heaven, and, in a kind of mystical half-way, he believed in hell, or in purgatory, at least, and deemed it well enough, if there was a route which led away from that place, to take it. That chapel might be the very gate to the road of safety; and when, during the last prayer, he put his head down with the rest, his thoughts were on a little knoll, half way between his house and the village proper, and he was wondering how much lumber it would take, and if Carson would cheat his eye-teeth out if he gave him the job.

As from little streams mighty torrents sometimes flow, so from that Sunday at St. Jude's sprang the beautiful little Gothic structure, whose spire you may see just behind a clump of trees, as you whirl along in the cars through the mountain passes between Albany and Pittsfield. "St. Philip's," they call it, though the old man who planned it, and paid for it, and *run* it, as the people said, would have liked it better if "they had called it *St. Maude* or *St. Louise*, he didn't care which." Both girls were perfect in his estimation, though for a time he gave the preference to Maude, as having been the first who had torn the thick coating away from his heart, and made it vibrate with a human interest. He liked Maude wonderfully well, and when, on the Monday following the ride to St. Jude's, she said good-by to them all, and went back to her school on the Hudson, he stole out behind the smoke-house, and, after several powerful sneezes, wiped his eyes suspiciously upon his butternut coat-sleeve, and wondered to himself "why the plague he wanted to be a snivelin' when he didn't care shucks for the neatest woman in the land."

Uncle Phil was terribly out of sorts that day, and called poor Beck a *nigger*, and yelled furiously at some boys who were riding down hill on his premises, and swore at Bobtail because he didn't trot faster on his way from the depot, and forgot all about the chapel, and was generally uncomfortable and disagreeable, till Edna came from school, and he found her waiting for him in the south room, with the ribbon in her hair, just as he had said he liked to see it, and the jet brightening her up, and making her a very pretty picture to contemplate, as she came forward to meet him. Hearing from Becky how forlorn he was, she put aside her own longing for the girl, who had brought so much sunshine with her, and made herself so agreeable to her uncle, that the frown between his eyes gave way at last, or rather she kissed it away, telling him she knew why it was there, and did not like to see it, and was going to be just as much like Maude as it was possible to be.

"Bless my soul, a gal's lips feel mighty curis on such a tough old rhinoceros hide as mine," he said; but he caught the little hands which were smoothing his hair, and held them in his own, and talked of his dead sister, whom Edna was like, and of the old days at home when he was young; and then the conversation drifted to Aunt Jerusha and Roy Leighton, and the payments Edna hoped to make them both in the spring when her first quarter was ended.

She would have one hundred and fifty dollars, she said, and fifty should go to Roy, and one hundred to her aunt; and she drew a comical picture of that dame when the money was received, proving that her niece's promise had been no idle thing.

"And you don't mean to keep a cent for yourself, Dot?" Uncle Phil asked, adopting the name Maude had given to his niece, and which suited her so well.

"No, not a cent till my debts are paid. I've clothes enough to last until that time, I guess, if I am careful. At all events I shall buy nothing unnecessary, I assure you," Edna said; and then Uncle Phil fell into a fit of musing, and thought how for every dollar Edna paid to Jerusha Pepper and Roy, he would put a corresponding dollar in the Millville Savings Bank to the credit of Louise Overton, who might one day find herself quite a rich little woman.

CHAPTER XXIII.

PAYING DEBTS.

EARLY in April, Aunt Jerry received a letter from Edna containing a draft for one hundred dollars. "All honestly earned," Edna wrote; "and affording me more pleasure to pay it than you can well imagine. I have fifty dollars beside, which I enclose in an envelope, and wish you to send to Mr. Leighton; but don't tell him where I am, for the world."

Aunt Jerry was not in the best of spirits when she received the letter. She had been having a cistern dug under her back stoop, and what with hurrying Robbins, who dug it, and watching her clock to see that he worked his hours, she had worried herself almost sick; while to crown all, the poor old man, who at her instigation had spent nearly one entire day in wheeling the dirt to a safe distance from the house, where it wouldn't "stand round in a great ugly pile," found on sinking his hogshead that he had dug his excavation too large, and would need all, or nearly all, the dirt to fill it up again; and greatly to the horror of the highly incensed Miss Pepper, he spent another day in wheeling his dirt back again. It was of no use for Miss Jerusha to scold, and call the man a fool. She had ordered the dirt away herself, and now she listened in a half-frantic condition to the slow tramp, tramp of Robbins' feet, and the rattling sound of the wheelbarrow which brought it back again, and undid the work of yesterday.

"Shiftless as the rot," was Aunt Jerry's parting comment, spoken to herself, as, the cistern finally finished, Robbins departed, just as a boy brought her Edna's letter.

The sight of the money mollified her a little, and for a long time she sat thinking, with her pasteboard sun-bonnet on her head, and Tabby in her lap. At last, her thoughts found vent in words, and she anathematized Roy Leighton, and called him "a stingy hunks if he touched a dollar of that child's hard earnings. Don't catch me to do it, though I dare say *he* thinks I will!" and Aunt Jerry gave a contemptuous sniff at the mysterious *he*, whoever he might be.

The next day she went to Canandaigua, and got a new bank-book, with "Edna Browning's" name in it, and put to her credit two hundred dollars, and then at night wrote to her niece, telling her "she had done better than she ever s'posed she would, and that if she kept on she might in time make a woman, perhaps."

Not a word, however, did she say with regard to her disposition of the funds: that was a surprise for the future; but after finishing her letter, she caught up a half sheet of paper, in a fierce kind of way, and wrote hurriedly:

"PHILIP OVERTON :—I dare say you think me as mean as *pussley*, and that I kept that money Edna sent for my own, but I assure you, sir, I didn't. I put every dollar in the bank for *her*, and added another hundred besides.

"Yours to command,   JERUSHA PEPPER."

"P.S.—I hope, from some things Edna tells me, you are thinking about your depraved state, while out of the ark of safety.   J. P."

Edna never saw this letter, for Uncle Phil did not think it best to show it to her; but he read it many times with infinite satisfaction, and took a pinch of snuff each time he read it, and chuckled over it amazingly, and said to himself:

"There's now and then a good streak about the old gal. Maybe she gets it from the Church,—the ark she calls it.

Anyhow, I'll speak to Carson to-day about the plan. I couldn't please three wimmen folks better."

He answered the letter at once, and said:

"MISS JERUSHA PEPPER:—Well done, good and faithful servant. Many daughters have done well, but you excel them all. Three cheers and a tiger for you.

"P.S.—I ain't thinkin' particularly about my depraved condition, but I *am* thinkin' of building a chapel for you to enjoy religion in, when you come to visit Edna.

"PHILIP OVERTON."

Uncle Phil *did* see Carson, as he proposed doing; and as a result of the conference, a delegation of the leading men in the Unitarian Church called upon him the next morning, to know if it was true that he had abjured their faith, and was going to be confirmed at St. Jude's, and build a church in Rocky Point, and pay the minister himself. They had heard all this, and a great deal more; and unwilling to lose so profitable and prominent a member from their own numbers, they came to expostulate and reason with him, and if necessary use harsher and severer language, —which they did before they were through with him. For Uncle Phil owned to the chapel arrangement, and said he thought it well enough for a man of his years to be thinking about leaving behind him some monument by which he should be remembered; otherwise, who would think of the old codger, Phil Overton, three months after he was dead.

Then Squire Gardiner suggested that their own church needed repairing, and that a new and handsome organ would be quite as fitting a monument, and do quite as much toward wafting one to heaven as the building of an Episcopal chapel, and introducing into their midst an entirely new element, which would make fools of all the young people, and set the girls to making crosses and working altar-cloths. For his part, he would advise Mr. Overton to think twice, before committing himself to such folly.

Uncle Phil replied that "he didn't want any advice,—he knew his own business; and as to repairing the church, he wouldn't say but what he would give as much toward that as anybody else; but he'd 'be *darned*' if he'd buy an organ for them to fight over, as to who should or shouldn't play it, and how much they should have a Sunday. A choir was a confounded nuisance, anyway,—always in hot water, and he didn't mean to have any in his chapel. No, sir! he'd have *boys*, as they did over to St. Jude's."

"Ha, a Ritualist, hey?" and one of the number drew back from him, as if he had had the small-pox, asking how long since he had become a convert to that faith, and when he met with a change?

Uncle Phil told him it was "none of his business;" and after a few more earnest words, said, "the whole posse might go to thunder, and he would build as many churches as he pleased, and run 'em *ritual*, if he wanted to, for all of anybody."

This was all the satisfaction the Unitarians got; while the Orthodox, who, like their neighbors, rebelled against the introduction of the Episcopal element into their midst, fared still worse, for the old man *swore* at *them;* and when one of them asked "how soon he intended to be confirmed?" vowed "he would be the very first chance he got, so as to spite 'em."

Uncle Phil was hardly a fit candidate for confirmation, but the lion was roused in him, and the chapel was now so sure a thing, that before the first of June, the site was all marked out, and men engaged to do the mason-work.

Edna's school was still a success, and Edna herself was very happy in her work and her home. She heard from Maude frequently, and the letters were prized according to the amount of gossip they contained concerning Leighton Place and its inmates. Roy had written a few lines acknowledging the receipt of the fifty dollars, and asking her, as a favor, not to think of paying him any more.

"I'd so much rather you would not," he wrote; "I do not need the money, and it pains me to think of my little sister working so hard, and wearing out her young life, which should be happy, and free from care. Don't do it, Edna, please; and I so much wish you would let me know where you are, so that I might come and see you, and sometime, perhaps, bring you to Leighton, where your home ought to be. Write to me, won't you, and tell me more of yourself, and believe me always,

"Your brother, "ROY."

It was a very blithe, merry little girl which went singing about the farm-house after the receipt of this letter, which came through the medium of Aunt Jerusha; and Uncle Phil stopped more than once to look after her, wondering to see her so different from what she had been when she first came to Rocky Point. Then she was a sad, pale-faced woman, with a dreary, pitiful expression in the brown eyes, which now sparkled and danced, and changed their color with every passing emotion, while her face glowed again with health and girlish beauty. All the circumstances of her life at Rocky Point had been tending to this result, but it was Roy's letter which produced the culminating effect, and took Edna back to her old self, the gay, light-hearted girl, who had known no greater care than Aunt Jerry's rasping manner. From this she was free now, and life began to look as bright and beautiful to her as did the hill-sides and the mountain-tops when decked in their fresh spring robes.

She answered Roy's letter at once, and told him how glad she was to know that he had an interest in her, but that she must pay him every dollar before she could feel perfectly free again, and that for the present she preferred to remain where she was. In reply to this, Roy sent her a few hurried lines saying that early in June he should sail for Europe with his mother, whose health required a change. They might be gone a year or more, and they might return at any time. It all depended on his mother, and how the change agreed with her. Edna cried over this letter, and when she knew that Roy had sailed, her face wore a sober, anxious look, and she said often to herself the prayer for those upon the sea, and watched eagerly for tidings of the arrival of the "Adriatic" across the water. And when they came, and she knew Roy was safe, there was a kind of jubilee within her heart, and she offered a prayer of thanksgiving to Him who rules the winds and waves, and had suffered no harm to befall her brother, Roy Leighton.

CHAPTER XXIV.

GEORGIE AND JACK.

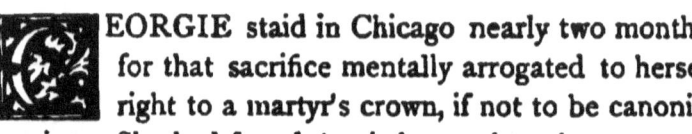

GEORGIE staid in Chicago nearly two months, and for that sacrifice mentally arrogated to herself the right to a martyr's crown, if not to be canonized as a saint. She had found Annie better than she expected, and that of itself was in some sort a grievance, as it implied undue anxiety, if not actual deception, on Jack's part. In order to get her there, he had represented Annie as worse than she was, Georgie thought; and at first she was inclined to resent it, and made herself generally disagreeable, to Jack and Aunt Luna, but not to Annie, whose arms closed convulsively around her neck, and whose whole body quivered with emotion when she first saw her sister, and knew she had really come. For two days Georgie sat by her, continually gazing at her, and listening to her prattle, until there came a softer look into her face, and her eyes lost somewhat of their cold, haughty expression. Annie told her everything she could think of about Mrs. Churchill, who had gone, no one knew where, and about herself and her little joys, and griefs, and faults. Everything bad which she had done was confessed, her impatience and fretfulness, and the falsehoods she had told, and then with a faltering voice Annie said:

"I have asked Jesus to forgive, and I most know He has, for I don't feel afraid of the dark any more, and I love to think He is here with me when my back aches, and I lies awake nights and can't sleep a bit. And will you forgive me too, sister Georgie; and did you ever tells a lie, though in course you never. You's always so good. I wonder what makes me bad? Do you know, sister Georgie?"

Oh, how abased and sinful Georgie felt while listening to this innocent little child, whose garment she was not worthy to touch, but who had exalted her so highly, and held her as something perfect. Perhaps she might have solved the mystery which troubled Annie so much as to what made her so given to the bad, when she wanted to be good. She might have told of blood, so tainted with deceit that a single drop of it in one's veins would make the fountain impure. But she did not; she kissed and comforted the child, and folding her arms about her said, with a gush of real, womanly feeling:

"Oh, Annie, my darling, what would I give to be as innocent as you; continue what you are; shun a lie or deceit of any kind as you would shun the plague, and pray for me that I may be half as good as you."

She lifted herself up, panting with emotion, while Annie looked wonderingly at her.

"Why, sister Georgie," she said. "You can't be bad. You are the goodest woman I know. I does pray for you that Jesus will take care of you, but never that He'd make you good, because I thought you were."

"No, child, I am not,—" and the proud Georgie sobbed aloud. "I'm not good, but I love you. I want you to remember that, Annie, whatever may happen; remember that I *do* love you, oh my darling, my darling."

There was some terrible pain tugging at Georgie's heart, —some fierce struggle going on, and for a few moments she cried aloud while Annie looked wonderingly on and tried to comfort her. After that she never gave way again, but was her old, assured self. Of the influences warring within her the wrong one had prevailed, and she had chosen to return to her formal life of ease rather than remain where her duty clearly lay, and where the touch of a little child's hand might have availed to lead her away from the ruinous path she was treading.

Between herself and Jack there was a stormy interview one night after Annie was asleep, and the brother and sister sat together before the grate, talking first of the past and then of the future. Jack had received, as he thought, an advantageous offer to go to Jersey City and enter an insurance office. There was a house there for sale on very reasonable terms, and Jack's friend urged him to buy it, and have a home of his own. How Jack's heart beat at the thought of a home of his own, with no constantly recurring rent-bill to pay, and no troublesome landlord spying about for damages! A home of his own, which he could improve and beautify as he pleased, with a sense of security and ownership, and where, perhaps, Georgie might be induced to stay a portion of the time. In Annie's present helpless condition it was desirable that she should not often be left alone, and as old Luna must at times be out, it seemed necessary that a third person should form a part of Jack's household, and who more fitting and proper than Georgie, provided she could be made to think so. Jack did not expect her to give up Aunt Burton's home, with its luxuries, altogether; only for a time he wanted her, and he was revolving in his mind how to tell her so, when she surprised him with the announcement that "she was going back to New York in a few days; that she had already stayed longer than she intended doing, especially after she found how well Annie was, and how little she needed her except for company."

Jack was astonished. He had fully expected Georgie to remain with him until spring, and he told her so, and told her further of his plans for the future, and his hope that she would be interested in his new home, if he had one, and stay there a portion of the time. Georgie heard him through, but there was an expression in her black eyes which boded ill to the success of Jack's plan, and her voice, when she spoke, had in it a cold, metallic ring, which made Jack shiver, and involuntarily draw nearer to the fire.

"*I* bury myself in Jersey City! you must be crazy to propose such a thing. Why, I'd rather emigrate to Lapland, out and out. I can't endure the place, and I don't see why you wan't to go there. You are doing well here, and these rooms are very comfortable."

The fact was Georgie did not care to have Jack and Annie quite so near to herself as they would be in Jersey City, and she quietly opposed the plan, without however changing Jack's opinion in the least.

"Are you not afraid that your return to New York will bring up old times? There are those there still who have not forgotten," she said, and in her eyes there was a kind of scared look, as if they were gazing on some horrid picture of the past.

"And suppose they do remember," Jack said, a little

hotly. "There's nothing in the past for which I need t[o] blush; and surely no one could possibly recognize in th[e] heiress Georgie Burton, the——"

"Hush, Jack, I won't hear what I was, even from you[r] lips," Georgie said, fiercely. "Perhaps there *is* no dange[r] for myself; but I never walk the streets even now, as th[e] daughter of Ralph Burton, without a fear of meeting som[e] one who remembers. Still I know that as Miss Burton, o[f] Madison Square, I am safe, but as your sister, in Jerse[y] City, I should not be; and I will run no risks."

"Not for Annie's sake?" Jack asked; and Georgie an[-]swered:

"No, not for Annie's sake," though her chin quivered [a] little as she glanced at the sleeping child.

Then they talked on and on, Jack trying to persuade hi[s] sister to stay with him a little longer, and she as persistentl[y] refusing, saying she must be home, that she had already los[t] too much time there in Chicago.

"Georgie," and Jack began to get in earnest, "by losin[g] time, I suppose you mean losing your chance with Ro[y] Leighton. I've never said much to you upon that subject[,] but now I may as well free my mind. If Roy Leighto[n] really cares for you he has had chances enough to make [it] known; and that he has not done so is pretty good proo[f] that he does *not* care. But supposing he does, and asks yo[u] to be his wife, will you marry him without telling him all?"

"Most certainly I will;" and Georgie's eyes flashed de[-]fiantly. "I need have no concealments from you, wh[o] know me so well, and I tell you plainly there's scarcely any[-]thing I would not do to secure Roy Leighton; and do yo[u] imagine I would tell him a story which would so surely thrus[t] him from me? A story, too, which only you know; an[d] you remember your oath, do you not?"

" She said the last words slowly, and her eyes fastened themselves upon Jack, as a snake's might rest upon a bird.

"Yes, I remember my oath;" and Jack returned her gaze unflinchingly.

Something in his manner made Georgie wince a little, and resolve to change her tactics. Sweetness and gentleness had always prevailed with Jack, when nothing else could move him, and so she tried them now, and her voice grew very soft, and reverent, and beseeching, as, laying her hand on his shoulder, she said:

"Don't let us quarrel, brother. I do want to do right, even if I cannot tell that dreadful thing to Roy. I am not going home either so much to see him as for another reason, of which I ought perhaps to have told you before. Jack, I am trying to be a better woman, and have made up my mind to be confirmed when our bishop comes to the little church near Oakwood, which will possibly be week after next. Aunt Burton is anxious for it, and is going to arrange to be there; and so you see I must go. You do not blame me now, I am sure. You respect religion, even if you do not profess it."

Her hand pressed more lovingly on Jack's arm, but he shook it off, and, starting to his feet, confronted her with a look which made her shiver, and turn pale.

"Blame you?" he began. "Respect religion? Yes, I do; and respect it so much that sooner than see you take those solemn vows upon you, knowing what I do, I would break my oath a hundred times, and feel I was doing right."

Georgie's breath came pantingly, and the great drops of sweat stood around her lips, as she asked:

"What do you propose to do?"

He did not answer her question directly, but went on to say:

"I do not profess to be good myself, or to have the first

principles of goodness, but my mother, who died there in that bed"—and he pointed to where Annie lay—"knew what religion was, and lived it every day; and when she died, there was a peace and a glory around her death-bed, which would not be around yours or mine, were we to die to-night. I am not judging harshly. By their fruits ye shall know them. He said so,—the man Jesus, whom mother loved and leaned upon, just as really as she ever leaned on me, and whom she taught Annie to love and pray to, until He is as much her companion when she is alone, as you are when you are with her. Georgie, there is something needed before one kneels at that altar, as you propose doing,—something which *you* do not possess. You do *not* care for the thing in and of itself. You have some selfish object in view, and I will not be a party to the deception."

"Will you drag me from the altar, or tear the bishop's hands from my head?" Georgie asked, beginning to grow both alarmed and angry at her brother, who replied:

"No; but this I will do: If you go to confirmation, and if before or after it Roy Leighton asks you to be his wife, and you do not tell him the whole truth, I will do it for you. He shall not be deceived."

"And your oath?" Georgie asked, in a choking voice.

"I break my oath, and do God service in breaking it," Jack answered.

And then there was silence between them for ten minutes or more, and no sound was heard except the occasional dropping of a dead coal into the pan, and the low, regular breathing of the little child, so terribly in the way of the woman who had so unexpectedly been brought to bay.

She gave up the confirmation then and there, and after a few moments arose and went to Jack, and putting her arms around his neck, cried aloud upon his shoulder, and called him the best brother in the world, and wished she was half as good as he, and a great deal more, which Jack took at its fair valuation. He was used to her moods, and knew about how to prize them. Still, in this instance, he had been a little hard on her, he thought, and he kissed her back at last, and said he was not angry with her, and bade her go to bed lest she should be sick on the morrow.

She staid a week after that, and when at last she went away, her diamond pin, ear-rings, bracelets, and two finger-rings, lay in the show window of a jeweller's shop where they bought such articles; and Annie held in her hand a paper, which contained the sum of one thousand five hundred dollars, and on which was written, "To help make the first payment on the new house."

Annie thought her an angel of goodness and generosity, while Jack, who understood now why he had seen his sister coming from Jachery's shop, said to himself: "There are noble traits in Georgie, after all;" and felt that the house in Jersey was a sure thing.

The bishop came to the little church near Oakwood at the appointed time, but Georgie Burton's proud head was not one on which his hands were laid. Aunt Burton, who had gone for a week or so up to her country house and taken Georgie with her, had urged her to it, and so too had the rector; and when Georgie gave as a reason for holding back, that she was "not good enough," the rector said she had set her standard far too high, while Aunt Burton wondered where the good were to be found if Georgie was not of the number, and cried softly during the ceremony, because of her darling's humility. What Georgie felt no one knew. She sat very quietly through the service, with her veil dropped over her face, and only turned her head a little when Maude, who was among the candidates, went up to the altar. But when Roy Leighton too arose, and with a calm, peaceful expression upon his manly face, joined the group gathering in the aisle, she gave a start, and the long lashes which dropped upon her burning cheeks were moist with tears. She had not expected this of Roy. He was not one to talk much of his deeper feelings, and so only his God, and his mother, and the rector, knew of the determination to lead a new and better life, which had been growing within him ever since Charlie's sudden death. "Be ye also prepared, for in such an hour as ye think not the Son of Man cometh," had sounded in his ears until he could no longer resist the Spirit's gentle wooings, but gave himself to God without reserve of any kind. There was a slight stir perceptible all through the congregation as Roy went up and stood by Maude. "He was a member worth getting; he, at least, was sincere," even the cavillers at the holy rite thought within themselves; and when it was over, and he came down the aisle, all noted the expression of his face as of one who was in earnest, and honest in what he had done. Georgie saw it, too, and for a moment the justice of what Jack had said asserted itself in her mind, and in her heart she cried out: "Roy ought not to be deceived, and yet how could I tell him, even supposing—"

She did not finish the sentence, but she meant, "Supposing he does ask me to be his wife."

And Georgie had again strong hopes that he would. He had seemed very glad to see her when she came to Oakwood; had called on her every day, and shown in various ways how much he was interested in her. There was about her now a certain air of softness and humility very attractive to Roy, and he had half hoped that when he knelt at the altar, Georgie might be with him, and he felt a little disappointed that she was not, and he told her so that night after the confirmation, when, as usual, he called at Oakwood, and they were alone in the parlor. Georgie had borne a great deal that day, and lived a great deal in the dreadful past which she would so much like to have blotted out. Her nerves were unstrung, and when Roy said to her so gently, and still in a sorry kind of way, "Why were you not confirmed, Georgie?" she broke down entirely, and laying her head upon the table, cried for a moment like a child.

"Oh, Roy," she said, at last, looking up at him with her eyes full of tears, "I did want to; but I am not good enough, and I dared not. But I'm so glad you did, so glad",—and she clasped her pretty hands in a kind of tragic way,—"for now you will teach me, won't you?"

Roy was a man, and knew nothing of that scene in Chicago, and Georgie was very beautiful to look upon, and seemed so softened and subdued, that he felt a strange feeling throbbing in his heart, and would without doubt have proposed taking the fair penitent as his pupil for life, if Maude had not just then come suddenly upon them and spoiled their *tête-à-tête*. Georgie's eyes were a little stormy now, but Maude pretended not to notice it, and seated herself very unconcernedly before the fire, with her crocheting, thus putting to an end any plan Roy might have had in his mind with reference to Miss Georgie Burton.

Maude had scarcely seen Roy since her visit to Rocky Point, and she told him all about Uncle Phil, who was his agent there, and of his niece, Miss Overton, the prettiest little creature, to whom she had given the pet name of "Dot," she was such a wee bit of a thing. And then the conversation turned upon Charlie and Charlie's wife; and Maude asked if anything had yet been heard from her, or if Roy knew where she was. Roy did not, except that she was teaching, and would not let him know of her whereabouts.

"How do you know she is teaching then?" Georgie asked; and Roy replied:

"I know through an aunt of hers, to whom I wrote last Christmas, asking her to forward a box of jet to Edna."

"Oh-h!" and Maude jumped as if she had been shot; then quickly recovering herself, she exclaimed: "That dreadful pin," and put her hand to her collar as if the cause of her agitation were there.

Maude had received an impression, which made her quiver all over with excitement, and sent her at last to her own room, where she bounded about like a rubber ball.

"I knew there was something queer about her all the time, but I never suspected that. Poor little Dot; how I must have hurt her feelings with my foolish talk of Charlie, if she really is his widow, and I know she is, for I remember now how interested she was in the Leightons, and how many questions she asked me about Roy and his mother; and then that box of jet. I'm sure of it,—perfectly sure; but, Dotty, if I can ferret out a secret, I can keep one too: and if you don't want Roy to know where you are, he never shall from me."

Maude wrote to Edna that night, and told her everything about the Leightons which she thought would interest her, and then with feverish impatience waited for her summer's vacation, when she meant to go again to Rocky Point, and satisfy herself.

Roy did not renew the conversation Maude had interrupted, but when in the spring he decided upon his trip to Europe, he half made up his mind to take Georgie Burton with him. He knew it would please his mother, and from all that had passed between himself and the lady he felt that he was in some sort bound to make her his wife; and why wait any longer? She was at Oakwood now. City air did not agree with her as formerly; she felt tired all the time, she told her aunt, who was ever ready to gratify her darling's slightest whim, consented to leave New York at least a month earlier than usual, but never dreamed that the real cause of Georgie's pretended weariness was to be found in the pleasant little house in Jersey City, where Jack Heyford was settling himself. Although constantly assuring herself that her fears were groundless, Georgie could not shake off the nervous dread that, by Jack's presence in New York, the black page of her life might somehow come to light. She went over to Jersey several times, for she could not keep away; but she took the Hoboken Ferry, and then came in the street car to the corner near which Jack lived, thinking thus to avoid meeting any one who knew her, and would wonder what she was doing in Jersey City. Still it was not so much through herself as through Jack that she dreaded recognition; and until he was fairly settled and at work, and swallowed up in the great Babel, it was better for her to be away; and so she went to Oakwood, and saw Roy every day, and was so soft, and sweet, and pious, and interesting in her new rôle of half-invalid, that Roy made up his mind, and started one morning to settle the important question.

His route lay past the post-office, and there he found the letter Edna had written in answer to his own, acknowledging the receipt of the money. He read it in the shadow of an old elm-tree, which grew by the roadside, and under which he dismounted for a moment. There was nothing remarkable in it, but it turned Roy's thoughts from Georgie for a time, and sent them after the frolicsome little girl whom he had once seen in the car, and who was now his sister. She wrote a very pretty hand, and seemed so grateful for the few crumbs of interest he had given her, that he wished so much he knew where she was. If he did, he believed he would take *her* to Europe, instead of Georgie; but not as his wife,—he never thought of such a thing in connection with Edna,—but as his sister, for such she was. And so, with her letter in his hand, he sat thinking of her, while his pony fed upon the fresh grass by the fence, and feeling no check from bit or bridle, kept going farther and farther away, until, when Roy's reverie was ended, and he looked about for his horse, he saw him far down the road, in the direction of Leighton Place, instead of Oakwood. Roy started after him at once; but the pony did not care to be caught, and seeing his master coming, he pricked up his ears and started for home, where Roy found him at last, standing quietly by the stable door, as if nothing had happened. That circumstance kept Roy from Georgie's side that day, and when on the morrow he saw her at his own house, he was guilty of a feeling of relief that he had not committed himself, and would have no one's luggage but his mother's and his own to look after in Europe.

He sailed early in June, and Georgie stood upon the wharf, and watched the vessel as it went down the bay, and felt such bitter pain in her heart as paled the roses on her cheek, and quenched some of the brightness of her eyes.

"Roy is lost to me forever," she said to herself, as she re-entered her aunt's carriage, and was driven back to Madison Square.

Still, as long as he remained unmarried, there was hope; and though her youth was rapidly slipping away, she would rather wait on the slightest chance of winning Roy Leighton, than give herself to another. And so, that summer,—at Saratoga, where she reigned a belle,—she refused two very eligible offers; one from the young heir of a proud Boston family; the other from a widower of sixty, with a million and a half of gold, and seven grown-up daughters.

CHAPTER XXV.

IN THE SUMMER.

MAUDE spent her summer vacation at Uncle Phil's, where she was received with every demonstration of joy by each one of the family, Uncle Phil dragging her off at once to see the "*suller hole*" of his chapel, or "synagogue," as he called it, which was not progressing very fast; "such hard work to get the men, and when they do come, they won't work more than half the time, and want such all-fired big wages, it is enough to break a feller; but then I'm in for it, and it's got to go," he said to Maude, who expressed so much delight, and called him a darling man so many times, and showed her trim, pretty ancles and dainty white tucks and ruffles with such *abandon*, as she stepped over the stones and sticks of timber, that Uncle Phil felt "curis again at the pit of his stomach," and did not care how much his synagogue cost, if Maude was only pleased.

Maude did not talk to Edna quite so much as usual at first; she was studying her closely, and trying to recall what she had heard Georgie say of Mrs. Charlie Churchill's looks. Then she began to lay little traps for her, and Edna fell into some of them, and then fell out again so adroitly, that Maude was kept in a constant fever of excitement, until one day, early in August, when, in walking by herself up the road which led to the hotel on the mountain, she met Jack Heyford, who had arrived the night before, and was on his way, he said, to call on her.

"I was up here a few years ago," he explained, as they walked back together, "and I retained so pleasant a remembrance of the mountain scenery that I wanted to see it again; so, as I could have a vacation of two weeks, I came first to

Oakwood, but it was lonely there with Georgie gone; she's off to Saratoga, you know, and hearing you were here, I concluded to come too. You are stopping at a farm-house. I have an indistinct recollection of Mr. Overton; a queer old fellow, isn't he?"

He talked very fast, and Maude did not hear more than half he said, for her tumultuous thoughts. If Louise Overton were really Edna Churchill, then Jack Heyford would recognize her, for he had been with her at the time of the accident, and had seen her frequently in Chicago.

"Yes, I have her now," Maude thought, as she said to Jack. " Mr. Overton has a niece living with him, Miss Louise Overton, a pretty little creature, whom you are sure to fall in love with. I hardly think she could have been here when you were at Rocky Point before."

"No, I think not. I have no recollection of seeing a person of that name. Pretty, is she?" Jack answered as indifferently as if he really had no idea of meeting any young lady at the farm-house, except Maude herself, and that his sole object that morning, was to call upon the girl chatting so gayly at his side, and telling him how pretty and charming and sweet Miss Overton was, and how he was certain to lose his heart at once.

"Suppose I have lost it already," Jack said, glancing at Maude, whose cheeks flushed a little, and who tossed her head airily and made him some saucy reply.

Of all the young men she had known, Maude liked Jack Heyford the best. She had thought him a little awkward and rusty when she first saw him at Oakwood, but had recognized through all the genuine worth and goodness of the man, and felt that he was true as steel. He was greatly improved since that time, and Maude was not unconscious of the attention she was attracting as she sauntered slowly on with the handsome stranger at her side. Edna saw them coming.

Indeed, she had watched all the morning for Jack, for she knew he was to have reached the Mountain House the night before, and that he would call on *Miss Somerton* that morning, and be introduced to her; and her conscience smote her for the part she was acting.

"If Uncle Phil was not so foolish about it, I should tell Maude at once," she thought, as after Maude's departure for a walk she made her toilet, in expectation of Jack Heyford's call.

She had schooled herself so well that when at last Jack came and was presented to her, she received him without the least sign that this was not their first meeting; and Maude, who watched them curiously, felt chagrined and disappointed that neither manifested the slightest token of recognition, but met as entire strangers.

"It's funny, when I am so sure," she thought; and for several days she lived in a constant fever of excitement and perplexity.

Regularly each day Jack came to the cottage, and stayed so long that Becky suspected him to be "Miss Maude's beau;" while Ruth Gardner, who was there frequently to help make up the game of croquet, interpreted his manner differently, and guessed that while he jested with and teased Miss Somerton, his preference was for Edna, who was evidently bent upon not encouraging him in the least, or giving him a chance to speak.

But Jack had his chance at last, on a morning when Maude and Ruth, with Maria Belknap and the Unitarian minister, were playing croquet upon the lawn behind the farm-house, and Edna was sitting alone on the stoop of the front door. Uncle Phil was gone, and as Aunt Becky was busy with her dinner in the kitchen, there was nothing in the way, and Jack told his story in that frank, outspoken way which characterized all he did. It was not like Charlie's wooing; it lacked the impetuous, boyish fire which refused to be denied, and yet Edna knew that the love offered to her now was worth far more than Charlie's love had been; that with Jack Heyford she should rest secure, knowing that no shadow of wrong had ever soiled his garments. And for a moment she hesitated, and thought of Annie, whom she loved, and looked up into the honest eyes regarding her so eagerly, and coming gradually to have a sorry, anxious expression as she did not answer.

"Won't you speak to me, Edna?" he said. "Won't you answer me?"

"Oh, Mr. Heyford," she cried at last. "I am so sorry you have told me this, for I don't believe I can say yes, at least not now. Give me till to-morrow, and then if I find that I can be to you what your wife ought to be, I will."

Jack did not press her further, and when the croquet party came round from the lawn, they found Edna sitting there alone, and Mr. Heyford gone back to the Mountain House.

That night, when Uncle Phil came from the post-office, he brought a letter from Aunt Jerry, enclosing one from Roy, who had written from a little inn among the Scottish hills. It was only a pleasant, friendly letter, telling of his journeyings and his mother's health, which did not seem to improve; but it sealed Jack Heyford's fate.

Edna had no thought of ever marrying Roy, but she could not marry Jack, and she sat down to tell him so on paper, feeling that she could do it in this way with less of pain and embarrassment to them both. And as she wrote, Roy's letter lay open beside her, and Maude came bounding up the stairs and stood at her side, almost before she knew that she was coming. With a quick motion she put Roy's letter away, but not until Maude's eyes had glanced at and recognized the handwriting.

"Eureka," she whispered softly; and then, to Edna's utter astonishment, Maude knelt down beside her, and putting her arms around her neck, said to her: "Dotty, don't be angry, will you? I always find out things, and you are Edna Churchill."

Edna felt as if she was suffocating. Her throat closed spasmodically, so that she could not speak, and for an instant she sat motionless, staring at Maude, who, frightened at the expression of her face, kissed her lips, and forehead, and cheek, and said:

"Don't take it so hard. Nobody shall know your secret from me; nobody, I assure you. I have guessed it ever so long. It was the *jet* which brought it to me. Roy spoke of his sister once last winter, and said he had sent her some ornaments of jet, and then it flashed over me that my little Dotty was the girl in whom I had been so interested ever since I first heard of her. Speak to me, Dot. You are not offended?"

"No," Edna gasped at last. "Only it came so sudden. I am glad you know. I wanted you to know it, it seemed so like a miserable lie I was living all the time."

And then the two girls talked a long, long time, of Edna's early life, of Charlie, and of Roy, whose letter Edna showed to Maude, and of whom she never tired of hearing. Thus it came about that Edna's note to Jack was not finished, and Edna gave him his answer verbally the next morning, when, punctual to the appointed time, he came and walked with her alone down to the clump of chestnut trees, which grew near the roadside. Something in Edna's face, when he first saw it that morning, prepared him in part, but the blow cut deep and hurt him cruelly. Still without love, Jack did not want any woman for his wife, and when Edna said, "I respect and like you more than any man I know, but cannot find in my heart the love you ought to have in return for what you give," he did not urge her, but took both her hands in his, and kissing them reverently, said:

"You have dealt fairly with me, Edna, and I thank you for it, and will be your friend just as I always have been. Let there be no difference between us, and in proof thereof, kiss me once. I will never ask it again."

He stooped down to her, and she gave the boon he asked, and said to him, in a choking voice:

"God bless you, Mr. Heyford, and you may one day find a wife tenfold more worthy of you than I can ever be."

They walked slowly back to the house, and found Maude waiting for them, with her mallet in hand, and Uncle Phil in close custody, with a most lugubrious expression on his face. Maude, who was nearly croquet mad, had waylaid the old man, and captured him, and coaxed a mallet into his hand, and was leading him in triumph to the playground, when Jack and Edna came up, and she insisted upon their joining her.

"A four-handed game was so much nicer," she said; "and Mr. Heyford and Uncle Phil were so fairly matched," and she looked so jaunty in her short, coquettish dress, and pleaded so skilfully, that Jack took the offered mallet, and, sad as was his heart just then, he found a space in which to think how pretty Miss Somerton was, and how gracefully she managed her mallet, and how small and well-shaped was the little foot she poised so skilfully upon the balls when bent upon croqueting.

Maude Somerton was very beautiful, and there was a power in her sunny blue eyes, and a fascination in her coaxing, winning ways, which few men could resist. Even sturdy Uncle Phil felt their influence, and under the witching spell of her beauty did things for which, when he was alone, he called himself "a silly old fool, to be so carried away with a girl's pranks."

Maude sported the first short dress which had appeared in Rocky Point, and she looked so odd, and pretty withal, in her girlish costume of white, trimmed with a pale buff, and she wore such stylish gaiters, and showed them so much with their silken tassels, that Uncle Phil confessed again to a "curis feeling in his stomach," and was not sure whether it was quite the thing for an old chap like him to let his eyes rest often on those little feet, and that trim, lithe form, which flitted so airily around the wickets, and made such havoc with the enemy's balls. It surely was not well for a young man like *Jack* to look at her often, he decided, especially when arrayed in that short gown, which made her look so like a little girl, and showed her feet so plainly.

They had a merry game, and Jack was interested in spite of himself, and accepted Uncle Phil's invitation to stay to dinner, and felt a queer little throb in his veins when Maude, acknowledging Edna and himself victors, insisted upon crowning them as such, and wove a wreath of myrtle for Edna's hair, while for him she gathered a bouquet, and fastened it in his button-hole.

She had said to Edna, "I shall tell Mr. Heyford that I know your secret. I must talk to somebody about it." And seizing the opportunity when Edna was in the house consulting with Becky about the dessert, she told him what she had discovered, and waxed so enthusiastic over "little Dot," and arranged the bouquet in his button-hole a little more to her liking, and stood, with her glowing face and fragrant breath, so near to him, and did it all so innocently, that Jack began to wonder he had never before observed "how very beautiful Miss Somerton was, and what pleasant ways she had," and when he went back to the Mountain House at night, his heart, though very sore and sad, was not utterly crushed and desolate.

He played croquet the next day and the next, sometimes

with Edna for his partner, but oftener with Maude, who, being the champion player, undertook to teach him and correct some of his faults. He must not *poke*, nor stand behind, nor strike too hard, nor go after other balls when he could as well make his wicket first. And Jack tried to learn, and do his teacher justice, and became at last almost as interested in the game as Maude herself, whom he sometimes beat. And when at the end of his two weeks' vacation he went back to his business in New York, he seemed much like himself, and Edna felt that he was bearing his disappointment bravely, and that in time life would be to him just what it had been before he thought of her.

Maude's departure followed close upon Jack's, and as she bade Edna good-by, she said, "I shall never rest, Dotty, till I see you at Leighton, where you belong. But I want you to go there first as Louise Overton. Take my word for it, you will succeed better so, with *la mère*, and possibly with *le frère* too. When they come home I am going to manage for you. See now if I don't. Adieu."

CHAPTER XXVI.

AFTER ANOTHER YEAR.

ROY LEIGHTON remained abroad little more than a year, and about the middle of July came back to his home on the river, which had never seemed so pleasant and attractive as on the summer afternoon when he drove through the well-kept grounds, and up to the side door where his servants were assembled to welcome him. Travelling had not greatly benefited his mother, who returned almost as much an invalid as when she went away, and to her ailments now added that of rapidly failing eyesight. There were films growing over both her eyes, so that she could only see her beautiful home indistinctly, and after greeting the domestics, she went at once to her room, while Roy repaired to the library, where he found several letters, which had come for him within the last few days. One was in Miss Jerusha Pepper's handwriting, and Roy opened that first, and found, as he expected, that it inclosed one from Edna.

She did not write in her usual cheerful tone, and seemed sorry that she had not been able to make him a single payment during the year.

"My school is not so large as at first," she wrote; "and I was anxious to pay another debt, of which I once told you, I believe. I *have* paid that now, except twenty-five dollars of interest money, and you don't know how happy it makes me that I can almost see my way clear, and shall soon owe no one but yourself.

"I am glad that you are coming home again, for though I do not know you, it has seemed lonely with you so far away, and I gladly welcome you back again. If I thought your mother would not be angry, I would send my love to her, but if you think she will, don't give it to her, please."

"I shall take the risk, any way," Roy thought; and carrying the letter to his mother, he read it aloud, and as she seemed interested, and inclined to talk, proposed going to see Miss Pepper, and ascertain, if possible, where Edna was.

Mrs. Churchill did not quite favor this plan, and still she did not directly oppose it, but sat talking of "the girl," as she designated her, until the summer twilight was creeping down the hills and across the river, and Georgie Burton came in with Maude Somerton. It was more than a year since Georgie had met Roy, and she assumed towards him a shy, coy manner, which rather pleased him than otherwise, and made him think her greatly improved.

Maude was her same old self, chatty, full of life and spirits, and a little inquisitive withal.

"Had Mrs. Churchill or Roy ever heard from Mrs. Charlie during their absence, and where did they suppose she was?"

Roy answered that "he had heard from her a few times by way of her aunt, but that he did not know where she was, as she still chose to keep her place of abode a secret from them."

Having said so much, he would gladly have changed the conversation, but his mother was not inclined to do so, and she talked about "the girl," and Roy's proposition to find her if possible, and bring her home with him.

"He thinks I need some young person with me all the time," she said; "and perhaps I do, for my sight is failing every day, and soon I shall be blind."

Her lip quivered a little, and then she added: "But whether *Edna* would be the one, I do not know. What do you think, Georgie? I must have somebody, I suppose."

There was a slight flush in Georgie's face as she replied, that "if Edna were the right kind of person, she should think it an excellent plan."

"And we will never know what she is until we try her," Roy rejoined, while Maude, who had been very quiet during this conversation, now spoke up and said: "In case you cannot find Edna, allow me to make a suggestion, and propose a dear little friend of mine; a charming person every way, pretty, and lady-like, and refined; in short, just the one to be with Mrs. Churchill. I refer to that Miss Overton, whom I met at Rocky Point last year, niece to Mr. Philip Overton, Roy's agent, you know. I wish you would take her, Mrs. Churchill; I am so sure you would like her."

Mrs. Churchill was not yet quite prepared for Edna, and as she really did feel the need of some one in the house besides the servants, she took the side of Miss Overton at once, and asked numberless questions about her, and finally expressed her willingness that Maude should write and see if the young lady would come. Georgie, too, favored the Overton cause, while Roy stood firm for Edna, and when the ladies arose to go he accompanied them to the door, and said to Maude in a low tone : " I would rather you should *not* write to that Miss —— what did you call her?—until I have seen Miss Pepper, as I fully intend doing in a short time. I am resolved to find Edna, if possible ; and having found her, to bring her and mother together, trusting all the rest to chance."

"Very well," was Maude's reply; but before she slept that night she wrote a long letter to "Dot" telling her what the probabilities were of her becoming, ere long, a member of Roy's household, and telling her also of Roy's intended visit to her aunt, who might as well be forewarned.

Four days after the date of this letter, which threw Edna into a great state of excitement, Aunt Jerry read with total unconcern that Roy Leighton was coming to see her and ascertain, if possible, where her niece was living.

"But don't tell him, Aunt Jerry, please," Edna wrote. "As Miss Overton I may possibly go to Leighton Place, and Mrs. Churchill is sure to like me better as a stranger than if she knew I was 'that dreadful girl' who ran away with Charlie ; so keep your own counsel, do."

"As if I needed that advice," Aunt Jerry muttered to herself, as she folded up the letter and put it in the clock, wondering "when the chap was coming, and how long he would stay."

"Not that I'm afraid of him or any other man, only I'd like to be looking decent on the girl's account," she said, as she glanced about her always tidy, well-kept house, to see what there was lacking. "The winders were awful nasty," she concluded, and she went at them at once with soap and sand, and rubbed them till they shone, and scoured her cellar stairs, and put fresh linen on the bed in the front chamber, in case he should stay all night, and carried water up there and a bit of Castile soap, and put a prayer book on the stand at the head of his bed, and wondered if he was high or low, and whether he would expect to ask a blessing at the table.

"I shall ask him to, any way," she said, and then she made a fresh cask of root beer, which she always kept in summer, and baked a huge pound cake, and made some balls of Dutch cheese, and wore her second-best calico every morning, and her best gingham every afternoon, in expectance of her guest, who did not appear for more than two weeks, and who took her at the last wholly unawares, as is so frequently the case.

She had given up his coming, and was making a barrel of soap in the lane, but so close to her front yard as to be plainly visible to any one who should stop at her gate. She did not wear her second-best calico that morning, but was arrayed in her cleaning-house costume, a quilted petticoat, patched with divers colors and kinds of calico, delaine, and silk, blue, green, and black, with here and there a bit of scarlet, the whole forming a most wonderful garment, which would at first sight remind one of Joseph's coat.

She never wore hoops in the morning, and her short, patchwork quilt, hung loose and limp about her feet, which were encased in what she called her "slips," a pair of low, cloth shoes, she had herself manufactured. A loose calico sacque, or short gown, surmounted her petticoat, and with the exception of the shaker on her head, with its faded brown cape, made from an old barege veil, completed her costume. She was equipped for her work, with no thought of Roy Leighton in her mind, and the fire was blazing brightly under her big iron kettle, and the soap was boiling merrily, and with her sleeves above her elbows, she stood, saucer in hand, stirring and cooling some of the glutinous mass, and had about concluded that it needed a little more lye, when the sound of wheels was heard, and a covered buggy and a gay, high-mettled horse came dashing round the corner of the church, and stopped before her gate, where a fine, stylish-looking man alighted, and seemed to be looking curiously about him, and possibly speculating as to whether he really had seen the whisk of a gay-colored skirt disappearing round the house or not.

Aunt Jerry had always expected Roy in the stage, and had never thought of his hiring a carriage at Canandaigua, and driving himself out; but the moment she saw him she guessed who it was, and in her surprise dropped her saucer of soap, and came near slipping down from setting her foot in it as she hurried out of sight.

"The very old boy! if that ain't Roy Leighton, and I lookin' more like an evil spirit than a decent woman!" was her first exclamation.

Then her natural disposition asserted itself, and instead of stealing into the house and effecting a change of toilet before receiving her guest, she resolved to brave it out, and make the best of it.

"I'm dressed for my work," she said, "and if he don't like my appearance, he can look t'other way." And holding her head very high, Aunt Jerry came round the corner of the house just as Roy was knocking, for the second time, at the open door.

He saw her, and could scarcely keep his face straight, as he asked "if Miss Pepper lived there?"

"Yes; I'm Miss Pepper." And Aunt Jerry began to unroll one of her sleeves, and button it around her wrist.

"Ah, yes; I am glad to see you. I am Roy Leighton,—Edna's brother-in-law."

"Oh, you be!" Aunt Jerry answered, rather dryly; and as he had come close to her now, and her soap was near boiling over, she darted toward the lye leech, and seizing a wooden dipper poured some of the dark fluid into the boiling mass, while Roy stood looking on, wondering what she was doing, for it was his first experience with soap-making, and thinking of Macbeth's witches:

> "'Double, double, toil and trouble;
> Fire burn, and caldron bubble,'"

he said, very softly, to himself, adding, in a little louder tone, as she threw in the lye:

> "'Cool it with a babboon's blood,
> Then the charm is firm and good.'"

Aunt Jerry caught the last line, and turning upon him, ladle in hand, she said, a little proudly:

"I suppose I look so like an old hag that you don't think I know anything about what you are muttering to yourself, but I do. I held that book before the Bible when I was young, and now,

> "'By the pricking of my thumbs,

I know that

> "'Something wicked this way comes.'"

Roy laughed merrily, and offering her his hand, said to her:

"Shakespeare with a vengeance; but I trust the pricking in your thumbs does not insinuate that I am the 'wicked something' which comes your way, for I assure you I come 'on peaceful thoughts intent,' but tell me, please, what you *are* doing in that seething caldron; and if the toad, and the bat, and the Jew's liver, are all in the poisoned broth?"

Aunt Jerry looked at him a moment, to see if his ignorance were real or feigned, and then replied:

"Where was you born, not to know *soft-soap* when you see it?"

"I was born in Bleecker street, New York, when that was the place where to be born," Roy replied; and with the ice thus broken, the two grew very sociable, and Roy made himself master of the mysteries of soap-making, and began to feel a deep interest in this strange woman, who made no movement toward the house until her soap was done, and the brands carefully taken from under the kettle.

Then she invited him into her kitchen, and disappearing in the direction of her bedroom, emerged therefrom in a few moments arrayed in her purple calico and white apron, which for several days she had worn in expectation of his coming. Aunt Jerry was something of a puzzle to Roy. Regarding her simply as an ordinary stranger, she amused and interested him, but when he thought of her as Edna's aunt, and remembered the first letter received from her, he winced a little, and wondered if her niece was like her. They spoke of Edna at once, and Roy told why he had come, and asked if Miss Pepper would give him her niece's address.

But Aunt Jerry was firm as a rock. "She never had told a lie since she joined the church," she said, "and she did not believe she should commence at this late day, with one foot in the grave. She promised Edna not to tell, and she shouldn't. The girl was doing well, and was more of a woman than she had ever 'sposed she could be. She has paid a good share of her debts," she continued, "leastwise she's paid nearly all she owes me; but if you think me mean enough to keep it,—and from what you wrote me once about a receipt I take it you do,—you are greatly mistaken. I've put every dollar of the four hundred in the Savings Bank, and as much more with it, in Edna's name; and when she's twenty-one, or if she marries before that time, I intend to give it to her. Let them that's richer do better if they will."

She jerked out the last words with a side motion at Roy, who took her meaning but said nothing of his own intentions with regard to Edna, further than his wish to find her and take her to Leighton Place. But he might as well have talked to a stone, for any effect his words produced on Aunt Jerusha.

"When Edna says I may tell, I will, and not before. I was harsh and unreasonable with her when she was young, perhaps, but I'll do my duty now," she said; then turning rather fiercely toward Roy, she continued: "My advice is that you let Edna alone, if you don't want to make more trouble for that mother of yours, who thinks her boy *stooped*. If I do say it that shouldn't, there's something mighty takin' about Edna, and every boy in these parts was bewitched after her before she was knee-high to a grasshopper. She ain't much more than that now, and she's a wonderful pretty girl, such as a chap like you would be sure to fancy. How old be you?"

Roy confessed to thirty, and Aunt Jerry complimented him by saying "she'd 'sposed him older than that," and then glancing at the clock, which pointed at half-past eleven, she asked him to stay to dinner, "and see how poor folks lived."

Roy's first impulse was to decline, but in spite of himself he was attracted by this queer woman, who boiled soap in so unsightly a garb, and quoted Shakespeare while she did it, and showed, in all she said and did, a striking originality of character, which pleased while it surprised him. He accepted her invitation to dine with her, and while she was making the needful preparations, looked curiously around the home which had once been Edna's. It was scrupulously neat and clean, and very comfortable, still he could imagine just how a bright young girl would pine and languish there, and long to break away from the grim stillness and loneliness of the house.

"Poor Edna," he said to himself, more than once, while

there awoke in his heart a longing to take the little girl in his arms and comfort her, after all she had borne of loneliness and sorrow.

Aunt Jerry's dinner, though not like the dinners at Leighton Place, was tempting and appetizing, and Roy did full justice to it, and drank two cups of coffee, for the cream, he said, and ate two pieces of berry pie, and a fried cake for dessert, and suffered from dyspepsia for the remainder of the day. Aunt Jerry asked him to spend the night, but Roy declined, and said good-by to her soon after dinner was over. His attempt to find Edna was a failure, and he went back to his mother, who, secretly, was glad, for she was not at all enthusiastic with regard to having her daughter-in-law for a companion. She greatly preferred Miss Overton from Rocky Point. Indeed, she had conceived quite a liking for that unknown young lady, and as soon as Roy came home and reported his ill success, she made him write at once to Miss Overton, asking if she would come, and what her terms were.

"Perhaps you'd better name three hundred and fifty dollars a year; that surely is enough," Mrs. Churchill said; and so Roy, to whom a few dollars more or less was nothing, and who felt that to be constantly with a half-blind, nervous invalid was no desirable position, made it four hundred dollars, and asked for an early reply.

CHAPTER XXVII.

EDNA ACCEPTS.

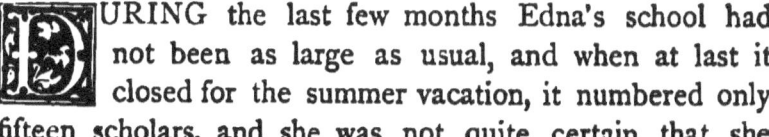URING the last few months Edna's school had not been as large as usual, and when at last it closed for the summer vacation, it numbered only fifteen scholars, and she was not quite certain that she

should open it again. She was as popular as ever. No one had aught to say against her, but Uncle Phil's "Synagogue" had gotten him into a world of trouble, and made him many enemies. So long as the work made little or no progress, the people were quiet and regarded the thing as a crazy kind of project which, let alone, would die a natural death. And for a time it did bid fair to do so, for what with the trouble to get men, and the fearfully high prices when he did get them, and the bother it was to see to them, Uncle Phil was inclined to take the matter easy, and after the cellar-wall was laid, there were weeks and months during which nothing was done, and Squire Gardner said, with a knowing wink, "We hain't lost the old man yet," and began to talk seriously of repairing his own church and having the ladies get up a Fair, of which his wife and Ruth were to be head and front. Accordingly Ruth came down one day to talk with Edna about it, and get her interested, as with her taste and skill she was sure to be a powerful ally if once enlisted in the cause. But Edna would not commit herself, and Ruth returned home disheartened and disappointed.

That night Uncle Phil was attacked with dizziness and a rush of blood to his head, which frightened him nearly out of his wits.

"I can't die yet," he said, when recovered somewhat, "but it came pretty nigh takin' me off. Yes, yes; had a narrer escape; but I can't go yet; it's no use talkin'. I ain't ready, and that synagogue business ain't moved a peg this two months; but if the Lord will set me on my legs agin, I promise to go at it at once. Try me and see if I don't."

He was taken at his word, and once well again he attacked the chapel with a right good-will, and brought out men from Millville, and boarded them himself, and kept them at work early and late, and proved so conclusively that he was in earnest, that his opponents took the alarm, and waiting upon him a second time grew so warm and even provoking that Uncle Phil blazed up fiercely, and said he wouldn't give a red toward any other church, nor ask anybody to give to his, and swore so hard that the Unitarians asked "how soon he intended to be confirmed;" while the Orthodox added that "it was of such materials the Episcopal church was composed," and then Uncle Phil wondered if he was not being "persecuted for righteousness' sake," and if it would not be put to his account as a kind of offset for the *hay* he had raked up and gotten into the barn away from the rain on two or three different Sundays which he could remember.

People did not mean to mix Edna up in her uncle's quarrel, but it affected her nevertheless, and on one pretext and another the Gardners left the school, while others gradually dropped off too, until Edna began seriously to think she might be obliged to seek employment elsewhere, and had some thoughts of going to New York and devoting herself wholly to her favorite occupation,—drawing and painting. She and Jack were the best of friends, and through him she hoped to get a situation in the city, and she was about writing to him with reference to it, when she heard from Maude of Roy's plan concerning herself, and then received his letter containing the offer, which she decided at once to accept. Among her other accomplishments, she numbered that of imitating, or adapting herself with great facility to different styles of handwriting, and this was a help to her now. Roy knew her natural handwriting, and it was necessary that she should take another. Next to her own, the style she used with the most ease was a pretty, running back-hand, and she adopted this in the letter she wrote to Mr. Leighton accepting his offer, and naming the first of

September as the most convenient time for her to come to Leighton, provided it suited Mrs. Churchill. It did suit Mrs. Churchill, who seemed much better now that she had something to look forward to, and who began to take a great interest in having everything comfortable and pleasant for the stranger.

"I shall want her near me, of course," she said to Georgie, who was often at the house; "and yet I do not wish her to feel as if she were a prisoner, tied close to my side. Here's this little room opening out of mine; but I think it is too small, don't you?"

Without waiting for an answer, Mrs. Churchill stepped into the hall, and opening a door directly opposite her own, continued:

"I have about decided to give her this one. It is near my own, and very pleasant too. Do you think she will like it?"

Georgie did not say that this room, with the bay-window and fine river view, was the one of all others which she would choose for her own, in case she was ever fortunate enough to reign as mistress of the house, but she did suggest that Miss Overton ran some risk of being spoiled if the best were given her at first. "I dare say the little room opening from yours is quite as good as she has been accustomed to, and will suit her very well," she said, but Mrs. Churchill did not think so. She felt a deep interest in the young stranger, and wished everything to be as pleasant for her as possible.

"If I could only see better, I should know if things were right," she said; "but I can't, and I wish you would superintend a little, and if anything is out of place, see that it is righted."

And so it came about that Georgie, instead of Maude, saw to the arranging of Edna's room, which, though not quite so handsomely furnished as some of the others, was the largest and pleasantest chamber in the house. Georgie had always coveted it, and now as she stood giving some directions to the housemaid, she felt a pang of envy toward the young girl who was to occupy it, and live under the same roof with Roy. She was too proud to acknowledge even to herself that she was jealous of a school-mistress, but she could not help envying her in some respects, and as she was very curious to see her, she waited with almost as much impatience as did Mrs. Churchill herself for the arrival of the stranger.

CHAPTER XXVIII.

EDNA GOES TO LEIGHTON.

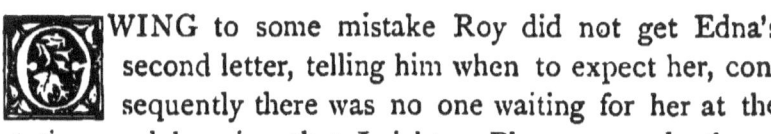OWING to some mistake Roy did not get Edna's second letter, telling him when to expect her, consequently there was no one waiting for her at the station, and learning that Leighton Place was only three-quarters of a mile distant, she determined to make the journey on foot. It was one of those bright, balmy days in early September, when nature, like a matron in the full maturity of her charms, reigns in all her loveliness a very queen. On the hills there was that soft, purplish haze, which only autumn brings ; and the sky above was without a cloud, save here and there a floating, feathery mist, which intensified the deep blue of the heavens, while the Hudson slept so calmly and quietly in the golden sunshine, that Edna involuntarily found herself recalling the lines :

"River, in this still hour thou hast
Too much of heaven on earth to last."

Indeed, everything around her seemed almost too much like heaven for her to keep it long; and when at last she reached the gate which opened into the Leighton grounds, she was obliged to stop and rest upon a rustic bench, beneath one of the maples which shaded the park.

She was there at last at Charlie's old home, and her eyes were feasting themselves upon the beauties, which had not been overdrawn either by Charlie's partiality, or Maude's enthusiasm. Everything was beautiful,—from the green, velvety turf, the noble elms, the profusion of bright flowers and shrubs, to the handsome house, with its broad piazza and friendly open doors, all basking in the warmth and sunlight of that autumnal morning. "It is like a second Eden," she said; and then, with a sad kind of a smile, born of a sudden heart-pang, she glanced toward the river, and saw what she knew must be the roof of the Gothic cottage, whither she once intended moving Roy and his mother, so they would not be in the way of the gayeties with which she meant to fill the house. That time lay far back in the past. And she had learned a great deal since then. Charlie was dead; and his grave was on a little knoll to the right of the house. Maude had told her all about it, and she could see the marble gleaming through the evergreens; and she shuddered as she always did, when she recalled the awful night of nearly two years ago. Still, time, which will heal almost any heart-wound, had been very kind to Edna, and though she always remembered Charlie with sadness and pity, thoughts of him had long since ceased to make her unhappy; and when at last she left her seat by the gate and pursued her way to the house, Roy was more in her mind than the boy Charlie, who slept under the evergreens, all unconscious that his wife was standing now at the very portal of his old home, and ringing for admission. Her ring was answered by the servant girl, who, inviting Edna into the library, bade her be seated while she carried her card to her mistress. Holding it close to her poor, dim eyes, Mrs. Churchill made out the word "Overton," and knew the expected stranger had come.

"How awkward that Roy should be gone," she said, as, declining the servant's offered aid, she made her way alone to the library.

It was a peculiarity of hers not to be helped by any one if she could avoid it, and there was something touching and pitiful about her as she walked slowly through the hall, trying to *seem* to see, with one hand partly extended in front, and making sundry graceful, cautious motions.

Edna heard her, and arose to meet her, her cheeks glowing and her breath coming pantingly at first, but when she saw the pale, languid woman, who stopped just inside the door, all her nervousness left her suddenly, and quick as thought she darted forward, and grasping the uncertain hand, exclaimed:

"Mrs. Churchill, here I am; Miss Overton. Let me lead you to a seat."

It was a blithe, silvery-toned young voice, expressive of genuine interest and sympathy for the poor blind woman, who did not refuse Edna's offered assistance, but held her hand, even after seated in her chair.

"I am glad to welcome you, Miss Overton," she said; "but am sorry you had to walk. We did not know you were coming to-day. You must be very tired."

Edna assured her she was not; and then Mrs. Churchill continued:

"I cannot see you as distinctly as I wish I could, for I like to know the faces of those I have about me. It is terrible to be blind!"

Her lip quivered as she said it, and instantly there awoke in Edna's bosom a feeling akin to love for this woman, who was her mother, in one sense of the word, and before whom she knelt, saying cheerily :

"Let me come nearer to you, then. Perhaps you will get an idea of me. I don't mind your looking at me as long as you like."

And Mrs. Churchill did look at the fresh young face held so close to her own, and passed her hand over the mass of golden brown hair, and lifted one of the heavy curls and held it to the light; then, with a gesture of satisfaction, she said:

"There, that will do. I think I know tolerably well how you look. I certainly know the feeling of your hands and hair. You are a little bit of a girl, and Maude rightly named you *Dot.* She is at Oakwood now with some young ladies from New York and a Mr. Heyford. They are having a croquet party, and Roy is there too. Maude is croquet-mad, I think."

Suddenly it occurred to Mrs. Churchill that her guest might like to see her room, and she arose, saying:

"I do not like being led; it implies too much helplessness; but I think I shall not mind using you for my guide. I can lean on your shoulder nicely. I am glad you are so short."

The soft, white hand rested itself softly on Edna's shoulder in a caressing kind of way, and the two went slowly from the library and out into the wide hall, through which blew the warm September wind, sweet with the perfume of flowers it had kissed in its passage across the garden. To Edna it seemed as if she had gained an entrance into Paradise, as through either open door she caught glimpses of the beautiful grounds, stretching away to the winding river in one direction and back toward the Catskill hills in the other. Slowly up the long flight of stairs they went, till they reached the hall above, and Mrs. Churchill, pointing to a door, said:

"That is Roy's room, and the one farther down, where

the door is shut, was Charlie's, my other son, who died two years ago. Yours is this way, opposite mine. I hope you will like it. Georgie Burton said it was all right."

They were in the room by this time, and with a cry of pleasure Edna broke away from the hand on her shoulder, and running to the window, from which the grounds, the river, and so many miles of country could be seen, exclaimed:

"Oh, I like it so much! It is all like fairy-land; and seems a dream that I should ever be in a place like this! I hope I shall not wake and find it so; that would be very dreadful!"

She was talking more to herself than to Mrs. Churchill, who nevertheless said to her:

"Have you seen so hard times that this place should seem so desirable?"

"Not hard in one sense," Edna said. "Almost everybody has been kind to me; but—" she hesitated a moment, and Mrs. Churchill added:

"Yes, Maude told me you had lost all your nearest relatives; was in black for your father, I think; but you have laid off mourning, I imagine, from the color of your travelling suit; and I am glad, for I would rather have you in bright colors. I am sure they suit you better," she said, laying her hand again on Edna's shoulder, and asking if she cared to dress for lunch; "because if you do not, there is no necessity, as Roy lunches at Oakwood. He will be home to dinner, and some of the young people may come with him."

This brought to light the fact that Edna's trunk was still at the station, whither Mrs. Churchill immediately dispatched a servant for it; then leaving Edna alone for a time, she bade her rest, and amuse herself in any way she liked until lunch was ready.

It was a very delicate lunch, and served in the prettiest of rooms, where the French windows opened upon a raised bed of bright flowers, whose perfume filled the room, as did the delicious air of that soft September day; and Mrs. Churchill was very kind and attentive to the young girl sitting opposite her, and wondering if it could be herself, there at last at Leighton Place, with only Charlie's monument shining through the distant evergreens to remind her that she was not the Miss Overton she professed to be.

They went out to the grave that afternoon. It was a habit of Mrs. Churchill's to visit it every day, and she asked Edna to accompany her, and leaned upon her as she went, and began talking to her of her poor boy, who was killed.

It would be difficult to tell just what Edna's emotions were as she stood by Charlie's grave, and read his name and age, cut deep into the marble. Mrs. Churchill had taken a seat on an iron chair which stood near by, and freed from her, Edna leaned heavily against the monument, and felt for a moment as if she was suffocating. But she never lost a word of what Mrs. Churchill was saying of her boy, or failed to observe how sedulously any mention of Charlie's wife was at first avoided. After a little, however, Mrs. Churchill said:

"As you are to be one of the family, you cannot avoid hearing Roy or some one speak of it, and I may as well tell you that Charlie left a wife,—a young girl, to whom he had been married that very day. Edna was her name; and they tell me she was pretty. I never saw her but once, and then scarcely noticed her. We don't know where she is. Roy cannot find her. She is teaching school, and keeps her place of residence a secret from us."

"You must be sorry for that," Edna replied. "It would be so pleasant to have her with you,—a daughter is better than a stranger."

"Yes, perhaps so," Mrs. Churchill answered slowly;

then, brightening a little, she said: "I felt hard toward her at first, but I do not now; and I think I should like once to see the girl Charlie loved and died for before I am wholly blind."

There was something so sad and touching in the tone with which Mrs. Churchill said this, that Edna involuntarily walked swiftly to her side, with the half-formed resolution to fall upon her knees, and cry out: "Oh, mother! Charlie's mother! I am she! I am Edna! Look at me! love me! let me be your daughter!" But she restrained herself, and Mrs. Churchill thought that the hand laid so softly upon her hair was put there from sympathy only, and felt an increase of interest in this Miss Overton, who was so kind, and gentle, and delicate in her attentions.

Mrs. Churchill liked to sit under the shadow of the evergreens, and they staid an hour or more by Charlie's grave, and then went slowly back to the house.

It was near dinner-time, and Edna went at once to her room and commenced her toilet for the evening. Mrs. Churchill had said that Roy would be home to dinner, and probably bring some of the young people with him; and Edna experienced a cold, faint feeling at her heart as she thought of the ordeal before her, and tried to decide upon a dress appropriate to the occasion. Her choice fell at last upon a soft gray tissue, which had been made by Ruth Gardner's mantua-maker, and praised by Ruth herself as faultless. It was very becoming to Edna, for the brilliancy of her complexion relieved the rather sober hue, while a bit of scarlet geranium, which she fastened in her hair, heightened the effect.

"Will Roy recognize me, or that Miss Georgie Burton?" Edna asked herself many times, and as often assured herself that they would not. "Roy probably did not notice me specially in the car," she thought; "while that bruise on my forehead and my terrible agitation and distress must have changed me so much, that Miss Burton will never dream I am the girl she looked at with such virtuous wrath."

There was scarcely a chance of detection except through the hair, and as that, instead of falling negligently around her face and neck, was brushed back from the forehead, and fell in masses of curls over a comb at the back of the head, Edna felt but little fear, and awaited, with some impatience, the return of Roy, hoping devoutly that Maude Somerton would be one of those who might accompany him from Oakwood.

The table was laid in the dining-room, and the dinner was waiting to be served, when down the avenue Edna caught the gleam of white dresses, and heard the sound of merry voices as Roy and his party drew near.

In her dress of rich black silk, with a soft shawl wrapped around her, Mrs. Churchill sat upon the piazza and kept Edna at her side, where she commanded a good view of the approaching guests, her heart giving a bound of joy as she recognized Maude Somerton, with Jack Heyford in close attendance. A little in advance of them walked a tall, straight, broad-shouldered man, whose manner proclaimed him the master, and who Edna knew at once was Roy; scanning him so curiously as almost to forget the brilliant woman at his side, who, if Roy bore himself like the master, bore herself equally like the mistress of Leighton, and pointed out to one of the party some fine views of the river and of the mountains in the rear. They were all in high spirits, talking and laughing and so absorbed in each other as not to see the two ladies awaiting their approach, until Maude suddenly exclaimed:

"Jack! Jack! there is some one with Mrs. Churchill. It is, it surely is little Dot!" and with her usual impetuosity Maude broke away from her companions, and bounding up the gravel walk and the wide steps of the piazza, caught Edna in her arms and nearly smothered her with kisses.

For an instant Jack's heart throbbed quickly at sight of the girl he had loved and lost, but Maude's pretty, saucy speeches were ringing in his ears, and his hand still burned with the touch of the soft, warm fingers, which had so deftly and so gently extracted an ugly sliver from his thumb, just before leaving Oakwood, and so the wave of memory passed harmlessly over him; and when Roy, who with Georgie was looking at and discussing the little figure in gray, said to him:

"Can that be Miss Overton?" he answered, "Yes, that is Miss Overton."

Roy hastened his movements then, and ere Edna knew what she was about he was shaking her hand, and looking down upon her in a curious, well-bred way, which did not make her one-half as uneasy as did the bold, prolonged stare which Miss Burton fixed upon her.

Maude introduced her as "Miss Overton, from Rocky Point," and all bowed politely to her, while Georgie, following Roy's example, took her hand and stood a moment looking at her, as if trying to solve some doubt or mystery. Maude, who was watching her, and saw the look of perplexity on her face, whispered, under her breath, "Old marplot, what if she should recognize her!"

But if to Georgie there had come any faint remembrance of that awful night on the prairie, and the little stunned, bewildered creature, whose eyes had in them such a look of hopelessness and terror, she put it away for the time, and gave no sign of what was passing in her mind.

It was Roy who took Edna in to dinner, and gave her a seat beside him, and treated her with as much deference and attention as if she had been an invited guest instead of the hired companion of his mother, who sat at the opposite end of the table, with Georgie at her side, acting a daughter's part to the poor, half-blind lady.

They were very gay during dinner; and Edna, whose spirits brightened and expanded in the atmosphere of kindness and good-breeding, joined in the gayety; and her sweet-toned voice and silvery laugh at some of Maude's queer sayings, reached Mrs. Churchill's ear more than once, and made her at last speak of the stranger to Georgie.

"Miss Overton has a very musical voice," she said; and Georgie, whose ear had been constantly turned in the direction of Edna, and who, without seeming to notice, knew exactly when Roy spoke to her, and how much attention he was paying to her, answered indifferently:

"Yes, very much like a child's voice. She seems a child too, in size, at least."

"Isn't she very pretty?" was Mrs. Churchill's next remark; and Georgie replied:

"Yes, though rather too small and *petite* to impress one very strongly. There is something familiar in her face; and I should say she looked a good deal like Mrs. Charlie Churchill."

"Oh, I'm glad," and Mrs. Churchill's hands made a little rattling among the china and silver, while her heart went out still more kindly toward the young girl who resembled Charlie's wife.

Georgie had not intended such a result, and she said no more of Miss Overton, or her resemblance to Edna Churchill; and, as if inspired with some new idea, she was very gracious to Edna, and after dinner was over, and they had returned to the drawing-room, she took a seat beside her, and questioned her minutely with regard to her journey and her home at Rocky Point. Had she always lived there, and was it not a charming place, with such delightful scenery?

"No, I have not always lived there. I was born in Ohio,

and lived there till my father died," Edna replied, fully alive to the danger of letting her interrogator too much into the history of her past life, and with a suspicion that Georgie was really making her out.

But the home in Ohio threw Georgie off the track, and ere she could resume it again Maude came to the rescue, bringing Roy with her, and urging Edna to favor them with some music.

"I have told Mr. Leighton how divinely you sing," Maude said, "and he is anxious to judge for himself; so please, Dotty, don't refuse."

Edna, who knew herself that she could sing, thought it impolite to refuse; and when Roy seconded Maude's request, and offered to lead her to the piano, she arose, and taking his arm walked the whole length of the long drawing-room to the alcove or bay-window, where the piano was standing. There was a mist before her eyes, and a visible trembling of her hands as she took her seat upon the stool; and then, by way of gaining time, pretended to turn over the sheets of music, as if in quest of something familiar. But when Roy, who saw her agitation, bent over her, and said so kindly and reassuringly, "Don't be afraid, Miss Overton. You have not a critical audience,—half of us don't know one tune from another," she felt her courage coming back, and her voice which, as she began to sing, trembled a little, soon gained strength and confidence, until it filled the room with such rich melody as held every listener silent, and made Mrs. Churchill brush away a tear or two, as she thought of Charlie and his grave beneath the evergreens. Edna was not permitted to stop with one song, but sang piece after piece, until thoughtful Roy interfered in her behalf, and said it was wrong to urge her further when he knew how tired she must be.

"Not that I could not listen to you all night, but it would

be the fable of the boys and the frogs over again," he said, as he led her from the piano and deposited her at his mother's side.

"You have given me a great deal of pleasure, Miss Overton," Mrs. Churchill said; "and I thank you for it. I am very fond of singing; and you have so sweet a voice. I shall often make demands upon it. I am glad you are here."

Mrs. Churchill, who seldom did anything by halves, had conceived a strong liking for her little companion, and her, "I am glad you are here," was so hearty and sincere, that Edna felt her eyes filling with tears, and wondered how she could ever have thought otherwise than kindly of this woman at her side.

Meantime, at the farther end of the room, Roy and Georgie were discussing the stranger and her style of singing.

"The sweetest voice I ever heard," Roy said; "and I am glad, for it will afford mother so much pleasure. I remember how delightedly she used to listen to poor Charlie's performance on his guitar when it almost drove me crazy."

"And that reminds me," said Georgie, "that Miss Overton looks a little like Charlie's wife. Indeed, the resemblance struck me at first as very strong. Wouldn't it be a funny joke if it were Charlie's wife in disguise?"

"A joke I should hardly relish," Roy replied; "for why should Edna come here in disguise when she knows the door stands open to her at any time?"

There was a lurking demon of evil in Georgie's black eyes as they rested upon Edna, sitting so quietly at Mrs. Churchill's side, and looking so young, and fresh, and innocent, and as she saw that her remark had awakened no suspicion in Roy's mind, she beckoned Jack to her side, and asked him if Miss Overton did not resemble Mrs. Charlie Churchill enough to be her sister.

"Why, no," Jack replied, running his fingers through his hair, and looking across at Edna. "I should not say she was her sister at all; and still, there is something in the expression of Miss Overton's mouth and eyes like Mrs. Churchill's, only not quite so sad and pitiful."

Jack spoke naturally enough, and met his sister's eyes without flinching, but inwardly he chafed like a young tiger, and when next he found himself alone with Maude, he said to her:

"Maude, Georgie has something in her mind which may mean mischief to Edna; and if she questions you, as she probably will, and presses you too close, tell her—" Jack hesitated a moment, and then continued: "Tell her that if she wants her secret kept she must respect the secret of others; in short, keep her tongue between her teeth."

Maude, who was very shrewd and far-seeing, had more than once suspected that there was something in Georgie's early life which the world generally did not know, and at Jack's remark she looked quickly at him, then nodded understandingly, while her mental comment was, "I knew there was something about Georgie, and sometime I'll find it out."

While this little by-play was going on, Roy had walked to a point in the room from which he could study Edna's face without being himself observed by her. Georgie's remark had awakened no suspicion whatever, but he felt more interested in one said to resemble his sister-in-law, and he stood for several minutes looking at the young girl, and mentally comparing her face with the one seen in the cars two and one-half years ago. Whether there were a resemblance or not he could not tell, for the face of the girl who had so sadly caricatured him and styled him a Betty, was not very distinct in his mind. Edna was very small, and so was Miss Overton, but he did not think his sister could be as beautiful as this girl, whose movements he watched so closely. He had not expected anything quite so fair and lovely in Miss Overton, and when at last, at a whispered word from his mother, she rose and led that lady from the room, he felt as if the brightness of the evening was suddenly clouded, and something lost from his enjoyment.

Mrs. Churchill's exit was soon followed by the departure of the young people from Oakwood, and Roy was left alone with his thoughts more upon his mother's hired companion than upon poor Georgie, whose star seemed to be waning, and whose heart, in spite of the lightness of her words and manner, as she walked back to Oakwood, was throbbing with a feeling nearly akin to hatred for the so-called Miss Overton, whom *she* knew to be Charlie Churchill's widow.

CHAPTER XXIX.

GEORGIE'S SECRET.

MAUDE SOMERTON had thrown her hat down in one place, her gloves and shawl in another, and donning her dressing-gown, stood by the open window of her room at Oakwood, looking out upon the beauty of the night, but thinking more of Jack and the words he said to her during their walk from Leighton, than of the silvery moonlight which lay so calmly upon the lawn below. They had lingered behind the others, and taken more time by half an hour to reach Oakwood, than the rest of the party had done. And Maude had been very quiet and gentle, and walked demurely at Jack's side, with her hand resting confidingly upon his arm, while he told her first the story of his love for Edna Churchill; then of his comparative poverty, and of the little crippled Annie, who must he his care as long as she lived. The Heyford name was a good and honorable one, he said, and never had been tarnished to his knowledge, and still there was in the family a shadow of disgrace, the nature of which he could not explain to her; he could only say that *he* had had no part in it, and it could by no means affect him or his future. Maude was morally certain that Georgie was in some way connected with this "shadow of disgrace," but she made no comment, and listened while Jack asked her, if, knowing what she did, she could consent to be his wife, and a sister to little Annie, who suffered so much for want of other companionship than that of old Luna, the colored woman, who kept his house for him.

There was a spice of coquetry about Maude Somerton; it was as natural for her to flirt as it was to breathe, but there was something in honest Jack Heyford's manner which warned her that he was not the man to be trifled with. She could play with silly Ned Bannister and drive him nearly wild, and make even poor Uncle Phil Overton's heart beat so fast, that the old man, who was mortally afraid of heart disease, had applied a sticking plaster to the region of inquietude, but she must be candid with Jack. She must tell him yes or no, without qualification of any kind, and so at last she answered "Yes," and Jack, as he stooped to kiss her upturned face, on which the moonlight was shining, felt as if Heaven had suddenly opened to his sight, and let the glory through.

And thus they were betrothed, and they lingered for a few moments under the shadow of the piazza at Oakwood, and whispered anew their vows of love, and when Jack asked it of her, Maude put up her lips and kissed his handsome face, and let her arm linger about his neck, and then started back like a guilty thing, as the door came together with a bang, and she heard the click of the key turning in the lock. It was Georgie fastening up, but she opened the door again at Jack's call, and looked sharply into their faces as they passed her, but said nothing except, "I supposed everybody was in."

"Tell her, Maude," Jack said, as he ran up the stairs to his room; while Maude walked leisurely to her own chamber, in which there was a door communicating with Georgie's apartment.

The two girls never slept together, but frequently, when Maude was in a very irrepressible mood, or Georgie unusually amiable and patronizing, they visited each other and talked together while disrobing for the night. Now, however, Maude felt more like communing with the moonlight and whispering her happiness to the soft September wind, which just lifted her bright hair as she leaned from the window, than talking with her future sister-in-law, and she feigned not to hear the knock upon the door and Georgie's voice asking if she might come in. But when the knock was repeated, and the voice had in it a note of impatience, she opened the door, and Georgie came in, brush and comb in hand, with her long black hair rippling over her crimson dressing-gown with its facings of rich satin. Everything Georgie wore was of the most becoming as well as expensive kind, and she made a very beautiful picture as she sat combing and arranging her glossy curls under a silken net. But there was a strange disquiet about her to-night, a feeling of unrest and vain longing for the years gone forever, the time when she was as young, and fresh, and pure as Maude Somerton or the girl at Leighton Place, who had so disturbed her equanimity, and of whom she had come to speak to Maude.

She found it hard, however, to begin, but at last made the attempt by saying:

"I say, Maude, what about that young lady at Leighton? Who is she; that is, what is her real name?"

"Her real name?" and Maude opened her blue eyes wonderingly. "She is Miss Louise Overton. You have known that all the time. Why do you ask me so queer a question?"

"Maude, this will never do," and Georgie's eyes had a stony look in them. "You pride yourself on ferreting out things, and you have not been at Rocky Point with the *soi-disant* Miss Overton so much for nothing. *You* know who she is, and I know too."

"And pray who is she?" Maude asked, her cheeks flushing and her temper beginning to give way.

"She was Edna Browning, and Charlie Churchill's wife. My memory is not so short that I have forgotten the girl at Iona, bruised and scratched as she was then. I recognized her almost immediately, and I wonder at her temerity in venturing to a place where she knew she would see me more or less. Why did she come,—that is, why has she taken another name than her own?"

There was no use for Maude to pretend ignorance any longer, and she frankly replied:

"Her coming here was my own plan. The change of name was long ago, when she first went to Rocky Point. Her uncle preferred and insisted that she bear his name, and so she joined her second to it which made her 'Louise Overton.' I want Roy and his mother to like her, and both, or rather Mrs. Churchill is more likely to do this if she knows her first as a stranger. Roy will like her any way; he cannot help it."

Maude had made her explanation and waited for Georgie's reply, which was:

"I think less of the girl now than I did before, and so will Roy and his mother when I tell them, as I shall."

"Tell them," Maude repeated, her blue eyes beginning to blaze with anger; "tell them, Georgie! You certainly cannot intend anything as mean as that! If Edna wishes to remain *incog.*, can you not, as a woman, respect her wishes, and keep her secret to yourself?"

"No; neither is it my duty to lend myself to the deception. I do not pretend to be one of the good ones, as you do, but I am a lover of truth, and should feel that I was acting a lie every time I addressed that girl as Miss Overton, or heard her addressed as such. She has some deep-laid design in what she is doing,—some design, which I shall take immediate steps to frustrate. I shall go to Mrs. Churchill to-morrow, and tell her who the girl is she has taken into such favor."

Georgie paused here and went on brushing her glossy hair, while Maude, who had been gathering all her forces for a grand onslaught and total rout of the enemy, said calmly:

"That is your decision, is it?"

"Yes, that is my decision, from which nothing can turn me."

"Then, Georgie, hear me," and Maude came close to Georgie, and looking her fully in the face, began: "You will not respect Edna Churchill's secret, and you talk grandly of being a lover of truth and hating to act a lie. *Georgie, your whole life is a lie, and has been for years!*"

Maude spoke very slowly and kept her eyes fixed upon Georgie, over whose face there crept a look of terror, and whose hands shook as they shed back the mass of hair from her forehead, where drops of perspiration were visible. In her excitement Maude had used rather stronger language than Jack's hint could warrant, but Georgie's manner convinced her that she could venture still further, and she continued:

"You have a secret, which you are guarding sedulously from the world, but, Georgie, just so sure as you breathe a word to any one against Edna, or tell that she is not Miss

Overton, or try, in any way, to prejudice either Roy or his mother, or anybody against her, just so sure people shall know that little passage in your life which you have hitherto succeeded in keeping from them. On the other hand, if you respect Edna's secret, yours too shall be respected, as it has been heretofore. Do you acquiesce in this? Is it a bargain between us?"

There was no need for Georgie to answer; her white, terrified face, from which her old assurance and haughtiness had fled, was a sufficient reply; and she sat for a moment staring at her companion in utter bewilderment. Then, with a tremendous effort, she recovered in part her composure, and said:

"I do not know what right you have thus to threaten me, or what you may have heard to my disadvantage from my enemies. I am not afraid of *you*, Maude, or of what you can do to harm me. Don't think I am, I beg; but if it's any favor to *you* or Jack, for I know he has something to do with it, I will let the girl remain in peace at Leighton, only devoutly hoping that the childish face which lured poor Charlie Churchill to his death will not also be the ruin of my brother, whose *penchant* in that direction I very strongly suspect."

"Spare your suspicions there," Maude said, and her voice was gentler now.

She had conquered Georgie wholly, and she began to feel a kind of pity for the proud woman who had been so terribly humbled, and who hereafter would inevitably stand somewhat in fear of her.

"Georgie," she continued, "I have no wish to quarrel with you. I loved Edna Churchill before I knew who she was. You will like her, too, when you know her better, but she will never be your sister. Don't fear for that, though Jack *did* love her once, and asked her to be his wife, up at Rocky Point last summer, and she refused him; and now the great, kind-hearted fellow has come to me to be consoled, and, Georgie, well,—I may as well tell you, for he said I might,—I am to be your sister some day, and I do not want to begin by quarrelling with you; I mean to make Jack a good wife and be a mother to little Annie; he told me about her, and I almost cried with thinking of the poor creature, sitting all day in her chair or lying in her crib so lonely, talking sometimes to herself, he said, and sometimes to you, for company, and again praying that Jesus will make her patient to bear the pain in her back and hip, which is dreadful at times. Yes, I mean to be kind to her, even if I worry Jack's life out of him. Speak to me, Georgie, and say if you are glad I am to be your sister?"

Maude had offered her hand to Georgie, over whom a curious change had passed. The expression of fear was gone, and as Maude talked of Annie, there came a softer look into her face, and grasping Maude's offered hand, she burst into such a passionate fit of weeping and bitter sobbing, that Maude, forgetting all her anger, knelt down beside her, trying to soothe and quiet her, and asking what was the matter, and if she had offended her.

"I did not want you to tell of Edna," she said, "and I was harsh with you about that; but, Georgie, I want to like you, and you must like me, for Jack's sake, if nothing else."

"I do, I will," Georgie gasped; "but Maude, oh, Maude, why did you open a grave I had thought closed forever? I am glad you are to be Jack's wife,—glad for him, and glad for Annie. She will have a mother in you, I know, and may God deal with you and yours as you deal with her; oh, my darling, my darling!"

In her excitement Georgie said more than she would otherwise have done, and with that passionate cry, "my darling, oh, my darling," she seemed suddenly to recollect herself, and, wresting her hand from Maude, she rose up swiftly and went back to her own room, leaving Maude more perplexed and confounded, and more kindly disposed toward Georgie withal than she had ever been in her life.

"I have sealed her lips with regard to Edna," she thought, "but I have wounded her cruelly somewhere. How she did cry about that little Annie, and what can the secret be that just the mention of it affects her so much?"

But wonder as she would, Maude was very far from the truth, and never dreamed of the cloud resting upon the woman, who in the next room sat with her head bowed down under a load of so bitter shame and humiliation, that it seemed as if she never again could lift it up as proudly and assuredly as she had done before. The world was very dark to Georgie then, and more evils than one seemed to be threatening her. Maude knew her secret, in part, if not in whole,—knew enough, at least, to blast her good name with Roy, should she dare to breathe a hint against Miss Overton. Her hands were tied in that direction, and when she remembered the admiring glances she had seen Roy give to Edna, and thought of all the opportunities he would have of seeing and knowing, ay, and of *loving* her, too, she writhed with pain, feeling an almost certain presentiment that this young girl, whom from the first she had to a certain degree felt to be her evil genius, had at last come between her and that for which she had waited and hoped so long. Purer, better thoughts, too, were stirring in Georgie's heart, —thoughts of little Annie, to whom Maude was to be a mother.

"And I am glad," she whispered; "for I know she will be kind to Annie, and, for Jack's sake, will keep my miserable secret. Oh, that I should ever have come to this, when a word from a weak girl can turn me from my purpose! Yet so it is, and Edna Browning is safe; but, heavens! how I hate her!"

Georgie's demon was possessing her again, and her black eyes blazed with passion as she thought of Edna Browning; but she could not do her harm, and she must pretend to like her, through her great fear of Maude, whom she felt as if she hated, too, until she remembered Annie; and then there came a gush of tears, which cooled her feverish passion, and made her more humble and subdued, as in her velvet slippers she paced the floor noiselessly, until she heard a distant clock striking the hour of two.

There was to be a croquet party at Leighton on the morrow, and knowing how mental agitation and loss of sleep told upon her looks, Georgie ceased her rapid walking, and bathing her flushed face profusely with water, crept shivering to bed, and by a strong effort of the will, such as but few can practise, she succeeded in quieting her nerves, and slept peacefully at last.

CHAPTER XXX.

AT LEIGHTON.

IT was a very pretty picture which greeted Roy's vision next morning, when, at an earlier hour than usual, he arose and sauntered out into the garden, glancing involuntary toward Miss Overton's window, and noticing that it was open, but seeing no signs of its owner near it. Edna was in the garden before him, gathering a bouquet for the breakfast table, and looking so fresh, and bright, and beautiful, with the flush of early girlhood upon her face, and the deep peace shining in her brown eyes, that Roy felt his pulse beat faster as he approached her and passed the compliments of the morning.

"You are an early riser," he said, "and your cheeks show the good effects of it; they are almost as bright as the rose in your hand."

"The fates forbid. So high a color as that would be vulgar, you know," Edna replied, laughing back at him, and then continuing: "Perhaps you think me a trespasser, or even worse, a thief; but I assure you I am neither. Mrs. Churchill told me yesterday to gather flowers whenever I liked, and I thought the breakfast table might be improved with a bouquet. I always used to get one for Uncle Phil, when I could."

Roy hastened to reassure her; and then, as he saw her trying to reach a spray which grew too high for her, he pulled it down himself, and in so doing scattered a few drops of dew upon her uncovered head; very carefully he brushed them off, noting, as he did so, the luxuriance of the golden brown hair, and the clear coloring of the neck and brow, and thinking to himself what a dainty little creature she was, and that Leighton was a great deal pleasanter for having her there. She was an enthusiastic admirer of everything beautiful, both in nature and art, and the grounds at Leighton filled her with delight, and she said out what she felt, while her eyes sparkled and shone, and almost dazzled Roy with their brilliancy, when, as was often the case, they were turned upward to his for assent to what she was saying. The gravel walks were still wet, and glancing down at Edna's feet, Roy saw that the little boots showed signs of damp, and stopped her suddenly.

"You are wetting your feet, Miss Overton," he said. "Let me go for your overshoes, and then I will take you around the grounds. It is a full hour before breakfast-time, and mother will not need you till then."

Edna was not at all averse to the walk, but she preferred getting her own overshoes, and ran back to the house for them, while Roy stood watching her and thinking how lithe and graceful she was, and that she must by birth and blood belong to the higher class; and then he thought of Edna, whom Georgie had said Miss Overton resembled, and wondered if she were half as pretty, and graceful, and bright as this young girl who seemed to have taken his fancy by storm. We say *fancy*, because if any one had then hinted to Roy Leighton that he was more interested in Miss Overton than men like him are usually interested in young ladies whom they have only known for twenty-four hours, he would have laughed at the idea, and if questioned closely, would have acknowledged to himself at least, that far down in his heart was an intention of ultimately marrying Georgie Burton. He rather owed it to her that he should make her his wife sometime, he thought; her name had been so long associated with his, and his mother was so fond of her; and knowing this of himself, he felt almost as if he were already a married man, and as such, could admire Miss Overton as much as he pleased. She was coming towards him now, her hat in her hand, and as she walked swiftly, her curls were blown about her face by the morning wind, recalling involuntarily to Roy's mind that scene in the cars more than two years ago, and the picture of himself in the poke-bonnet, which he carefully preserved. But Roy had no suspicion that the face confronting him was the same which had looked so saucily and curiously at him in the railway car, and had, with its witching beauty, been the means, through Providence, of that early grave toward which they were walking, and where poor Charlie slept. There was a shadow on Edna's face as they approached it, and when the gate to the entrance was reached, she stopped involuntarily, and laid her hand upon the iron railing.

"My brother's grave," Roy said, standing close to her side.

"Yes; your mother told me. I was here with her yesterday," Edna replied, hoping thus to prevent Roy from talking to her of Charlie.

She had felt guilty and mean when listening to Mrs. Churchill; and she should feel tenfold more guilty and mean, she thought, and find it harder work keeping quiet, if Roy, too, should tell her of his brother and his brother's wife. But Roy did tell her of them, and talked a good deal of Edna, *his sister*, whom he had never seen but once.

"Miss Burton tells me you resemble her," he said; "and that may be the reason why you seem so little like a stranger to me. I should be so glad to know Edna,—to have her here at home. Poor girl! I am afraid she is finding the world a harsh one, struggling alone as she is!"

He spoke so kindly that Edna had hard work to refrain from crying out: "Mr. Leighton, I am a liar, a cheat, an impostor! I am not what I seem. I am Edna, and not Miss Overton."

But she did not do it; and when at last she spoke, it was to ask if Mrs. Charlie Churchill had no friends or relatives, that she should be thus thrown upon her own resources.

"Yes; she has an aunt,—a Miss Jerusha Pepper, whose name is something of an index to her character," Roy said; and then, as there came up before his mind the picture of Aunt Jerry, as he first saw her, bending over her boiling caldron, and looking more like Macbeth's witches than a civilized woman, he broke into a low, merry laugh, which brought a flush to Edna's face, for she guessed of what he was thinking.

She had heard from Aunt Jerry herself of Roy's visit to Allen's Hill, and how he had found her employed.

"Dressed in my regimentals, and looking like the very evil one himself!" Aunt Jerry had written. And Edna, who knew *what* the "regimentals" were, and how her aunt looked in them, wondered what Roy thought of her, and if she herself had not fallen somewhat in his estimation. She knew he was laughing at some reminiscence connected with that soap-making in the lane; and she could not forbear asking him if just the thoughts of Miss Jerusha were sufficient to provoke his risibles.

"Well, yes," Roy answered; "I always laugh when I think of her arrayed in the most wonderful costume you ever saw, I reckon, and deep in the mysteries of soap-making. And still, no queen ever bore herself more proudly than she did, as she tried to feign indifference to her own attire and my presence.

"It was a pleasant enough place, or might be, with young people in it, though I fancy Edna must have led a dreary life there, and was thus more easily led to escape from it. Still, I am not certain, that in doing so, she has not proved, in her own experience, the truth of Scylla and Charybdis."

"Oh, no; I am sure she has not!" Edna exclaimed, so vehemently that for a moment Roy looked curiously at her, noticing how flushed, and eager, and excited she looked, and wondering at it.

Then suddenly there came to him the remembrance of Georgie's words: "Wouldn't it be funny if this Miss Overton should prove to be Edna in disguise?" and without at all believing that it was so, he resolved upon a test which should at once decide the matter, and put to rest any doubts which might hereafter arise.

Just across a little plat of grass Russell was busily employed with a clump of dahlias, and thither Roy turned his steps, with Miss Overton at his side.

Russell had seen Edna in Iona, and Roy had heard him say that he never forgot a face; so he stood talking to him several minutes, professing a great interest in the dahlias, but really watching him closely as he bowed very gravely to the young lady, and then resumed his work.

Edna had thought of Russell, and dreaded him as the possible means of her being detected; but in his case, as in Georgie's, she trusted that the change in her dress and the style of wearing her hair, and the expression of her face from one of terror and distress to peace and happiness, would effectually prevent recognition. Georgie evidently had not recognized her, and Russell certainly would not; so she stood quietly before him, seeming in no haste whatever to get away, and even asked him some questions about a new variety of dahlia which she had never before seen.

For once Russell's memory was at fault, for he did not know her; though he pronounced her a trim, neat sort of craft, as he stood for a moment watching her, as she walked away with Roy, who led her down a grassy lane toward the little cottage, where she had once thought to move him and his mother.

There was a half-sad, half-amused smile on Edna's face, as she recalled the days of her delusion, and looked at the cottage overgrown with ivy, where one of Roy's men was living, and with whom he stopped a moment to speak about a piece of work. It was nearly breakfast time now; and the two walked slowly back to the house, where Mrs. Churchill sat waiting for them in the cosey breakfast-room. The flowers Edna had gathered were upon the table; and Roy thought how bright they made everything look, and enjoyed his breakfast as he had not done for many a day. It was pleasant to have a young face opposite to him; pleasant to have a young life break up the monotony of his own; and Leighton Place seemed to him just now as it never had before; and, during the morning, while Miss Overton was engaged with his mother, he found himself thinking far more of her than of the croquet party which Georgie had planned, and which was to come off that afternoon.

CHAPTER XXXI.

OVER AT OAKWOOD.

MR. BURTON, of whom little has been said, was not a very frequent visitor at his own house in the country. He liked the dust, and heat, and noise of Wall street better than the green fields, and the tall mountains, and cool river, which encircled his country home in Oakwood. So the house on Madison Square was always kept open for him, and two or three servants retained to keep it, and there he slept, and ate his solitary meals, and lived his solitary life, while Mrs. Burton and Georgie were away enjoying the good which money and position can buy.

Occasionally, however, there came over him a desire for a change, and then he packed his valise, and took the cars or boat for Oakwood, usually surprising its inmates, who, never knowing when to look for him, were seldom expecting him. He had come up from New York thus suddenly the very morning after Georgie's interview with Maude, and announced his intention of spending the entire day, and possibly remaining over until the morrow, provided there was anything worth staying for. .

"Oh, there is! There's the croquet party at Leighton Place this afternoon, and you'll go, and I'll have you on my side, because you are capital at a long shot," Maude Somerton said, hanging about her uncle's chair, and evincing far more delight at seeing him than his wife had done.

Mrs. Burton was a very good woman, and a very proper woman. She always kissed her husband when he came to Oakwood, and when he went away, and inquired how he was, and how the servants were getting on, and asked for three or five hundred dollars, as the case might be, and deferred to him in a highly respectful manner, pleasant to behold. But she never hurried out to meet him as Maude was wont to do, nor threw her arms around his neck, nor smoothed the thin hair from his tired brow, nor said how glad she was to have him there.

Maude loved him as the uncle of her mother and the only father she had ever known, and almost the only heart-beats of affection the business man had felt in many a year, were called up by the touch of Maude's lips to his and the clinging of her soft fingers about his own. So, though he hated croquet and could see no sense in knocking about a few wooden balls, he consented to join the party; and then remembering that he had not seen Georgie yet, he asked where she was.

Georgie had a violent headache, and toast and tea had been carried to her room, and Mrs. Burton had been sitting with her when her husband came in, and reading her a letter received that morning from a man of high standing in Boston, who asked Mrs. Burton's consent to address her daughter.

It was an eligible offer enough, and but for one obstacle Georgie would have thought twice before rejecting it, for she knew better than any one else how fast her youth was fleeting. That obstacle was the genuine liking she had for Roy, and the hope that she might yet be fortunate enough to win him.

Never until this morning had she felt so much like talking freely with her aunt of her future, and her growing fear lest, after all her years of waiting, Roy Leighton should eventually be lost to her.

Nervous and weak from the effects of last night's interview with Maude, and the headache from which she was suffering, she could only bury her face in her pillow and cry when her aunt read the would-be-lover's letter, and asked what answer she should return.

"I had hoped to see you settled at Leighton ere this, but Roy does not seem as much inclined that way as he did some time ago," Mrs. Burton remarked.

And then the whole story came out, and Mrs. Burton understood just how passionately her niece loved Roy Leighton; and how galling to her pride it was to have had her name coupled with his so long, without any apparent result.

Mrs. Burton was roused, and resolved at once to strike a decisive blow. Roy had no right to play "fast and loose" with Georgie, as he certainly had done. Everybody supposed they were engaged, and he had given them reason to think so, and done enough to warrant Georgie in suing him for breach of promise if she would stoop so low as that, as of course she would not.

Mrs. Burton was not one to expose herself or family to public ridicule. What she did would be done quietly and with no chance of detection from the world, and she at once set herself to it, thinking it surely was a Providence which sent her lord home on that particular day. Kissing Georgie affectionately, and bidding her to think no more of the Boston match or of Roy either, as it was sure to come right, she sought her husband, and found him in the library with Maude, who had been telling him of her engagement with Jack Heyford, and whose face was suffused with blushes when her aunt came in.

Of course Mrs. Burton had to be told also, and she behaved very properly, and kissed Maude twice, and said she had done well; that Mr. Heyford, though poor, was a very estimable young man, and a brother of Georgie. This last was evidently his chief recommendation to the lady whose infatuation with regard to Georgie was something wonderful.

It was not Mrs. Burton's way to skirt round a thing or

to hesitate when a duty was to be performed; but on this occasion she did feel a little awkward, and after Maude was gone stood a moment uncertain how to begin. At last, as if it had just occurred to her, she said:

"Maude's engagement reminds me to tell you that Georgie has just received through me an offer from that young Bigelow of Boston, whom you may remember having seen at Saratoga last summer."

Mr. Burton was very anxious to resume the paper he had been reading, when Maude came asking an interview; but he was too thoroughly polite to do that with his wife standing there talking to him, and so he answered her:

"Maude first and Georgie next, hey? We are likely to be left alone, I see. Does he belong to the genuine Bigelow race?"

"Yes,—the genuine. You must remember him,—he drove those handsome bays, and his mother sat at our table, and said Georgie was the most beautiful girl at Saratoga."

"Georgie better take him, then, by all means,—she is growing older every day," was Mr. Burton's reply, as he rattled his paper ominously, and glanced at the "stock" column.

"But Georgie don't want him," Mrs. Burton rejoined, "and she does want some one else,—some one, too, who has given her every reason to believe he intended making her his wife, and who ought to do so."

Mr. Burton looked up inquiringly, and his wife continued:

"I mean Roy Leighton. His name has been associated with Georgie's for years, and at times he has been very devoted to her, and almost at the point of a proposal, then some interruption would occur to prevent it. His mother's heart is set upon it, and so, I must confess, is mine; while Georgie's,—well, the poor girl is actually sick with suspense and mortification, and I think it is time something was done."

Mrs. Burton was considerably heated by this time, and took a seat near her husband, who asked what she proposed doing.

"Nothing myself, of course,—a woman's lips are sealed; but you can and ought to move in the matter. As Georgie's father, it is your right to ask what Roy's intentions are, making Mr. Bigelow's offer, of course, the reason for your questionings. You are going to the croquet party this afternoon,—you can, if you try, find an opportunity for speaking to Roy alone, and I want you to do so."

At first Mr. Burton swore he wouldn't. Roy Leighton knew what he was about, and if he wanted Georgie he would say so without being nudged on the subject. It was no way to do, and he shouldn't do it.

This was his first reply; but after awhile, during which his spouse grew very earnest and eloquent, and red in the face, and called him "Freeman Burton," he ceased to say he wouldn't, and said instead, that "he'd think about it."

And he did think about it all the morning, and the more he thought the more averse he grew to it, and the more, too, he knew he would have to do it, or never again know a moment's peace when under the same roof with his wife.

"I wish to goodness I had staid in New York,—and I've half a mind to take the next train back,—upon my word I have; but then wife would follow me if I did, and hang on till I consented. She never gives up a thing she's set her heart upon; and if she's made up her mind that Roy must marry Georgie, he's bound to do it, and I must be the 'go-between.' I believe I'll drown myself!"

The poor man fairly groaned as he finished his soliloquy, and glanced from the window toward the river winding its way down the valley. His peace of mind for that day was destroyed, and not even Maude's blandishments had power to brighten him up as he sat in a brown study, wondering "what the deuce he should say to Roy, and how he should begin."

The party was not to assemble at Leighton until half-past three, and so he had a long time in which to arrange his thoughts,—longer indeed than he desired, and he was glad when at last the time came for him to start.

Maude, who seemed to be mistress of ceremonies, had been unusually quiet and reserved during the morning, but when at lunch her uncle formally announced to the guests at Oakwood her recent engagement with Jack, she became at once her old self, and entered heart and soul into the preparations for the party.

She had visited Georgie in her room, and kindly offered to bathe her head, or do anything which could in any way alleviate the pain.

Of the events of the last night not a word was said, and both felt that one page at least of that interview was turned forever. Maude, who had nothing to fear, was the more natural of the two, and talked freely of the croquet party at Leighton, and wished so much that Georgie could go.

"Perhaps you can," she said, "if you keep very quiet. Your headaches do not usually last the entire day."

But this was no ordinary case, and when the time came for the party to start, Georgie, though better, and able to sit up, declared herself too weak and nervous to dress for the occasion, and so they went without her, poor Mr. Burton lagging a little behind with his wife, who was very kindly instructing him as to the better way of opening the conversation with poor, unsuspicious Roy.

CHAPTER XXXII.

THE CROQUET PARTY.

THERE was not a finer croquet lawn in the neighborhood than that at Leighton Place, nor one with which so much pains had been taken. It was in shape, a long oval, bordered with low box, which prevented the balls from rolling off the limits, and surrounded entirely with a broad gravel walk, shaded by tall maples and evergreens, with rustic chairs and seats beneath, and here and there statuettes, and urns filled with luxuriant vines, and the shrubs which thrive best in the shade. At a little distance, the musical waters of a fountain were heard, as they fell into the basin, where golden fish were playing, while patches of bright flowers dotting the turf heightened the general effect, and made it one of the most delightful of resorts. Edna had almost screamed aloud, when, after breakfast was over, Roy took her there with his mother, who, though she never played, enjoyed nothing better than sitting in her favorite chair, and listening to the click of the balls, and the merry shouts which followed a lucky hit.

"Suppose, Miss Overton, that you and Roy try a game while I rest," she said to Edna, while Roy rejoined:

"Yes, do; then I can judge of your skill, and know whether to chose you first this afternoon. Miss Somerton and I are to be captains, I believe."

Edna had frequently played at Rocky Point; sometimes with Maude, sometimes with Ruth Gardner, and sometimes with Uncle Phil for an opponent, and except when playing against the latter, was generally beaten, so she took the mallet Roy brought to her with some hesitation, declaring her inability to interest a skilful player, much less to beat.

"Let me teach you then," Roy said. "You can learn a great deal in an hour."

To this Edna readily assented, and the game began with Roy as teacher. But Edna soon found that the uneven ground at Uncle Phil's, where the balls hid themselves in all sorts of holes and depressions, was a very different thing from the closely-shaven lawn which had been rolled and pounded until it was nearly as smooth as a carpeted floor. She could play here, and was astonished at her own success, and struck so boldly and surely, that Roy soon gave up the task of teaching her, and began to look after his own interests. She was such a little creature, and he so tall and big, that he almost felt as if playing with his daughter, though never did a father watch the motions of his child with just the same feelings with which Roy watched Edna as she moved from point to point, now showing her dimpled hands, and now poising her little boot upon her ball preparatory to croqueting it away. She was very lithe, very graceful, and very modest withal, and she beat Roy twice out of five games, and when at last they were through, and Roy led her to his mother, he said to her, laughingly:

"Remember you are engaged to me for the first game."

He was extremely kind and gentle, and though Edna had known him personally for only twenty-four hours, she had seen enough to understand just how thoroughly good and noble he was; how different from Charlie, who, had he lived, could hardly have satisfied her now. But Charlie was dead, and she went from the croquet ground to his grave, with his mother, and laid a cluster of flowers upon the sod which covered him, and felt like a guilty hypocrite when Mrs. Churchill pressed her hand and thanked her "for remembering my poor boy."

"I would like flowers put here every day," she said; "but my eyesight is so bad that I cannot see, while Roy's hands are not skilful in fashioning bouquets, and we have had no young lady staying here permanently until now."

"Charlie shall have flowers so long as they last," Edna replied with a trembling voice, while into her face there came a look of pain something like what it had worn on that dreadful night in Iona.

She had called him "Charlie," and the old familiar name carried her back to the Seminary days, when, aside from Aunt Jerry, she had not known what sorrow was,—and she was uncertain how Mrs. Churchill would take it. There was something very sad in the tone of her voice as she uttered the name, Charlie,—*pitiful*, Mrs. Churchill thought; and she deepened her grasp on Edna's hand and said, "Call him Charlie always when speaking of him to me. It makes it seem as if you had known him, and I can talk more freely to you than to a stranger. He was my baby, my poor boy; full of faults, but always loving and kind to his mother. Oh! Charlie, my darling. I wish I had him back. I wish he had not done so."

The tears were pouring over the poor woman's face, and Edna's kept company with them. She knew what the mother wished he had not done, and knew that but for her he would not have done it, and she felt for a few moments as if she were really guilty of Charlie's death; and could she then have restored him to his mother by going herself back to the house by the graveyard, and taking up her lonely life as it had been before she knew Charlie Churchill, she would have done so. But there was no going back when once death had entered in; and all she now could do was to comfort and love the helpless woman who clung to her so confidingly, and who seemed so much afraid of overtaxing or wearying her out.

"You have always been in school, I hear," she said, "after they had returned to the house, and Edna had read aloud to her awhile. "Teaching must be accompanied with more excitement than sitting here and amusing me, so I shall not tax you much at first, lest you get tired of me. Go, now, and enjoy yourself where you like. Perhaps Roy will take you to drive. I'll ask him; I hear his step now. Roy, come here, please."

And before Edna, who did not fancy being thrust upon Roy whether he would have her or not, could interfere, Mrs. Churchill had asked her son why he did not take Miss Overton for a drive, and he had expressed himself as delighted to do so. They were not gone long, for Roy had some matters to attend to before dinner, which was that day to be served at two, but during a *tête-à-tête* of an hour a young man and woman can learn a great deal of each other, and Roy's verdict with regard to Miss Overton, as he handed her out of his phaeton, was "A very bright, fascinating girl, with something about her which interests me strangely;" while Edna would not allow herself to put into words *what* she thought of him. He was something, as she had judged him to be from his letters, though better, she thought, and, as many a person had done before her, she wondered that he had lived to the age of thirty without being married. She did not now believe implicitly in his eventually making Miss Burton his wife. He could not be happy with her, she thought,—they were so dissimilar; and she unconsciously found herself extracting comfort from that fact, though she ascribed her motive wholly to the friendly interest she felt in Roy, and as she dressed herself for dinner, she warbled a part of an old love tune she had not sung since the days when Charlie Churchill used to stop by the Seminary gate to listen to her singing.

"I am nothing but a hired companion, a 'school-marm,' as that prig of a Jim Gardner said of me when he first came home from Germany, and of course these grand people from Oakwood have a similar opinion of me. I saw it in that

Miss Shawe's eyes, and so it is not much matter how I dress. Still I want to look as well as I can," she said, as she stood before the glass arranging her hair and wondering what she should wear. "Maude says there is everything in one's looks when playing croquet," she continued, "and perhaps she is right. I'll wear my white pique, with the little blue jacket."

She could not have chosen a more becoming costume, for the jacket was of that peculiar shade of blue which set off her fair complexion to the best advantage, and made her so pretty that Mrs. Churchill, blind as she was, remarked upon her dress when she came in to dinner, while Roy said she was like a bit of blue sky in June.

"You remember your engagement to play with me, of course," he continued; and when Edna suggested that she might be a detriment rather than a help to his side, he replied, "I want the best-looking ones at any rate, so that I can boast of beauty if not of skill. You and Miss Burton will go nicely together."

Edna did not relish her dinner quite as well after that speech, which showed that Roy claimed Miss Burton as something which by right belonged to him, and much as she despised herself for it, she knew that, inwardly, she had a feeling of relief when the party from Oakwood arrived, and reported Georgie as too sick to come with them. Roy said he was very sorry, and looked as if he meant it, and asked some questions about her as he led the way to the lawn where everything was ready. Maude, who was resplendent in white muslin, scarlet sash, and tall gaiters, seized at once upon Edna, and, drawing her aside, whispered to her of her happiness.

"He told me of his love for you, too, and I did not like him one bit the less. He couldn't help loving you, of course, when he saw you so helpless and alone. He is a splendid fellow, isn't he? Most as good-looking as Roy, and he is going to quit tobacco, and fit my room all up with blue, and we are to be married sometime next year if he is prosperous, and I won't have to teach the hot, sweating children any more. Oh, I am so happy. There he comes now. Hasn't he such a good face?"

And Maude beamed all over with delight as Jack came up and joined them, his eyes kindling, and growing very soft and tender, as Edna offered him her congratulations, and told him how glad she was.

"I knew you would be," he said. "Knew Maude would suit you better than any one else; and Edna, please remember that our home is yours also whenever you choose to make it so. Maude and I agreed upon that this morning."

They had reached the lawn by this time, and the ladies from New York were handling the mallets daintily, and decrying their own skill, and saying the side which claimed them was sure to lose.

"Then I run no risk," Roy said, laughingly; "and choose Miss Overton."

He had been drawing cuts with Maude to see which would have the first choice, and the lot came to him.

"Miss Overton," he called again, and Edna came forward, noticing, as she did so, the glances of surprise and dissatisfaction exchanged between the city girls, who, though very civil to her, did not attempt to conceal that they knew her only as a hired companion, whose rightful place was at Mrs. Churchill's side, rather than in the ranks with themselves as Roy Leighton's first choice.

Maude wanted to choose Jack first, but modesty forbade, and then, too, he sometimes made awful hits, and had a way of pursuing a ball, no matter where it was or into what enemy's quarter it took him. Jack was out of the question, and so she chose Uncle Burton, and Roy took Jack himself. Two of the New York girls came next, and the New York beau, and then the number was complete, and Miss Agatha Shawe and Beatrice Bradley retired in dignified silence, and taking seats by Mrs. Churchill, prepared to criticise the game. It was Roy's first play, and he drove his ball through the third wicket and in the vicinity of the fourth, while Maude, who usually struck so surely, started badly, and only made her second arch.

Miss Agatha, who was reporting to Mrs. Churchill, and whose sympathies were on Maude's side, said a little sarcastically:

"She is in no danger from her opponent, I fancy; Miss Overton plays next."

Edna heard the remark, and while it sent the blood to her face, it seemed to lend steadiness to her hand and coolness to her judgment, and her first stroke was through both of the wickets, while a shout went up from Roy and Jack, and was echoed by Maude, who, knowing that the city ladies looked upon Edna and herself as people belonging to the working class, rejoiced at her friend's success even though it should tell against her side. And it did tell sadly, for remembering Roy's teaching in the morning, Edna used her opponent's ball so skilfully as to reach the stake before stopping at all. But there she missed her stroke, and came back to her place by Roy, who commended her highly, while Miss Agatha began to change her tactics, and "guessed Miss Overton had played before."

Poor Mr. Burton was awkwardness itself. With the dread of talking to Roy before him, he hardly saw his ball, and made a "booby" of himself at once, and said to Maude, as he knocked his unlucky ball back to its place: "I told you so. I can't play any more than an elephant."

But he was good at long shots, as Maude had said, and he did some long shooting before he was through, for the game was a hotly-contested one. Maude recovered her skill with her second round, while Edna lost a little by being so constantly pursued by the city girl, who played the best, and who shared Miss Agatha's contempt for the plebeian. But Roy beat; and then they chose again, and Maude took Edna first, and Edna's side was always the winning one, until Miss Agatha suggested that "Miss Overton should play on both sides, and see what the result would be."

But Roy said Miss Overton was too tired to do that; besides, it was nearly time for refreshments; the servants were arranging the tables now; and he suggested that, for a time, they should rest, and go wherever they pleased. That broke up the group, which divided up in twos and threes, Maude walking away with Jack, Edna returning to Mrs. Churchill's side, and the city people making a little knot by themselves, under one of the tall shade-trees.

Mr. Burton was thus left alone; seeing which, Roy asked him to go and look at a fast horse which he had recently purchased, and which was accounted by connoisseurs of horse-flesh a very fine animal. And so it came about that, after the horse had been duly examined and admired, Roy found himself alone with Mr. Burton in a little rustic arbor, apart from all the rest of his guests, and where he could not well be seen, as the arbor was hidden from the greater part of the grounds by the evergreens which grew so thickly around it.

Now was Mr. Burton's opportunity. He had planned admirably to get Roy into this retired situation, and he gave himself considerable credit for his management. But how to begin was the trouble, and he grew very red in the face, and felt so warm and uncomfortable that the perspiration began to show itself in little drops about his forehead and mouth. And still he could not think of a word to say, until he saw by Roy's manner that he was meditating a return to the house. Then, screwing up his courage to the highest pitch, and holding on to the seat with both his hands, as if what he was about to do required physical as well as mental effort, he made a beginning.

"I say, Roy," he began, "I wonder you don't get married. You've everything with which to make a wife happy, and surely there are scores of girls who would jump at the chance of coming here to live."

Roy gave a little tired yawn, and answered indifferently:

"Perhaps so, but you see I don't exactly know where they are, and I should not care to be refused," and as he said it, visions of blue jackets, and white skirts, and little boots, mixed themselves together in his brain in a confused kind of way, and as was quite natural, a thought of Georgie, too, crossed his mind. He always thought of her when matrimony was suggested to him, but he had no suspicion that his companion was drifting that way. Poor Mr. Burton, who felt as if every particle of blood in his veins was rushing to his face and gathering around the roots of his hair, fidgeted from side to side, got up and looked behind him, spit several times, then sat down again, and said:

"You are too modest, boy,—too modest. I know of forty, I'll bet, that would not say no."

"Name one, please," Roy said, shutting his eyes indolently, and leaning against the trunk of a tree.

Mr. Burton hesitated a moment, and then replied:

"Well, there's Agatha Shawe for one, and Bell Bradley for another, and—and—(by Jove, I may as well blurt it out and done with it,) and Georgie, my wife's niece. (I'm in for it now, confound it.) She's a splendid girl; don't lack for offers; had one this morning from that young Bigelow from Boston."

"Ah, did she? and will she accept?" Roy asked, beginning for the first time to feel some interest in the conversation.

"Don't know. You can't calculate on a woman, but it's my opinion she won't. Roy, old boy, I'll be cussed if I mayn't as well say it; I do believe the girl likes you, and I'd rather have you for a son-in-law than any chap I know, and I'll be hanged if I don't think you've given her cause to suppose you meant something by hangin' off and on as you have this last year or two. Anyhow, people think so, and talk about it, and suppose you to be engaged, and that hurts a girl if it never comes to anything, and, well,—well,—blast it all,—as Georgie's father, so called, and as,—to be sure,—as Mrs. Burton's husband,—I feel called upon,—yes,—very much as the head of a family,—to inquire if you are in earnest, or not,—and if not,—why,—say it out, and let her alone, and not stand in the way of others. There,—I've out with it, and I sweat like rain."

The poor man wiped his wet face with his handkerchief, and looked anywhere but at Roy, who had managed to make out from rather confused jumble that he had done wrong to Georgie by allowing people to think there was anything serious between them, and that as Georgie's father, Mr. Burton had at last spoken to prevent more mischief in the future. While acknowledging to himself that Mr. Burton was right, and that Georgie had some cause for complaint, Roy still found himself in a quandary, and uncertain how to act. If he owed Georgie any redress, he ought as an honorable man to pay it, and perhaps he could not do better. She *was* a nice girl, he really believed, and would perhaps make him as happy as any one he could select. He meant to marry some time, and might as well do it now as to put it off to a later period. And then the Bigelow offer *did* trouble him a little, and he began to see that he had fallen into the habit of looking upon Georgie as something essentially his own when he chose to make up his mind that she suited him.

On the whole, she *did* suit him, and he would at once arrange with her, and have the matter settled. All this passed through his mind in much less time than it has taken us to write it, and he was about to put his thoughts into words, when across the lawn came the sound of a merry, girlish voice, which he knew to be Miss Overton's; and again blue jackets, and brown eyes, and little feet brought a throb of something he could not define to his heart, and Georgie did not seem quite so desirable as she had a moment before. But he must say something, and so he began to explain that he meant no harm to Georgie by his attentions; that he esteemed her highly, and could not deny having had thoughts of making her his wife; but that he found himself so comfortable just as he was, with her always available when he wanted her society, that he had put the matter off as a something in the future; and so, perhaps, had wronged her, but he would endeavor—

He did not finish the sentence, for a servant just then appeared around a clump of evergreens, telling him they were waiting for him upon the lawn, where the refreshments were ready to be served.

"Yes, I'll come at once;" and with a sense of relief, Roy jumped up, and turning to Mr. Burton, said: "You may be sure I shall do right in the future, whatever I may have done in the past. But tell me, please,"—and Roy's voice dropped to a whisper,—"did she know you were to speak to me? Did she desire it?"

"Certainly not," Mr. Burton replied, with some little asperity of manner, which Roy acknowledged was just, while at the same time he was glad to be assured that Georgie did not know.

She would have fallen in his estimation, if she had, and he wanted to think as well of her as he could; for, in his mind, as he walked back to the lawn, there was a rapidly forming resolution to propose to her immediately, and thus make amends for any harm done her heretofore.

The tables looked very pretty under the trees, with fruit, and flowers, and ices, and silver; and the guests were in their gayest moods; but something was the matter, and Roy felt as if oppressed with a nightmare as he did the duties of host, seeing nothing distinctly except Miss Overton's face, which, flushed with excitement, seemed prettier than ever. He did not care for Miss Overton that he knew of; certainly he had never had a thought of loving her, and yet he knew every time she moved, and what she did, and what she said, and something connected with her made it harder for him to concentrate his mind on Georgie, as he felt in duty bound to do.

The lawn tea was over at last, and the little party were talking of a game of croquet by moonlight, when down one of the gravel-walks came Mrs. Burton, her rich silk rustling about her, and her lace streamers floating back from her head. She had concluded to drive over in the carriage, she said, as some of the young people might be glad to ride home.

She was very affable and gracious, and when questioned with regard to Georgie, said she was better,—so much better, indeed, that she was up and dressed, and then, by various little subterfuges, she tried to decoy Roy into going to the house, and finally succeeded by insisting that his mother must have a shawl if she persisted in staying out there in the evening air. Wholly unsuspicious, Roy started for the house, and, looking into the parlor as he passed through the hall, gave vent to an exclamation of surprise at seeing Georgie Burton reclining upon a little divan standing in the bay-window. As Mrs. Burton had said, Georgie was better; her headache had disappeared, and she had thought often and regretfully of the party at Leighton, and wished herself with them. As she felt stronger, and her nerves became more quiet, the terror of the previous night, when her secret seemed in danger of being discovered, grew less and less. Maude was to be her sister, and, of course, it was for her interest to keep to herself whatever might be derogatory to any member of Jack's family; and, beside that, in thinking over all that had been said, Georgie was not quite sure as to how much Maude knew, and in that doubt was some comfort. Moreover, she meant to keep her part of the contract religiously, and Edna had nothing to fear from her for the present. If Roy should show a decided liking for her, while she, in turn, tried to practise on him the wiles which had lured poor Charlie to his destruction, she might, in some quiet way, warn him or Mrs. Churchill as to whom they were harboring. Anonymous letters were always available, and she should not hesitate a moment when it became necessary to act. But for the present she should be very gracious and kind to Miss Overton; and having thus decided upon her *rôle*, she felt extremely anxious to begin; and when her aunt suggested driving over to Leighton, she consented readily, and dressed herself with unusual care, thinking as she did so, that a little less color than she usually had, and a little heaviness of her eyes, was not unbecoming. And she was right; for the traces of her headache softened rather than detracted from her brilliant beauty, and she had seldom looked better than when Roy found her in the recess of the window, her face a little pale, and indicative of recent suffering, her eyes very gentle, and even sad in their expression, and her hands folded together upon her lap in a tired kind of way, as if she was glad to rest, and did not care to be disturbed even by Roy himself.

To do Georgie justice, she had no suspicion whatever that her uncle had been interfering in her behalf, and her face lighted up with a glow which made her wonderfully beautiful, as she sat with her shawl of bright cherry thrown around her shoulders, and showing well against her simple dress of soft black tissue.

Roy liked her in black; he had told her so once at Newport, when her dress was silken tissue, and her only ornament a spray of golden-rod twined among her glossy curls. She could not get golden-rod, but she had placed a white rose in her hair, and another upon the front of her dress, and Roy thought what a fine picture she made, with the setting sunbeams falling around her. And this picture might be his for the asking, he was very sure, and his heart gave a throb of something like pleasure at finding her alone.

"Why, Georgie!" he exclaimed, coming forward, and offering her his hand; "this is a surprise; I did not expect to find you here."

"Which does not mean, I hope, that I am not welcome?" Georgie said, with one of her rare smiles.

"Certainly not; you are always welcome. How is that poor head? better, I hope," Roy replied, still holding her hand and looking down upon her, while she blushed coyly, and affected to draw her hand away from his. "What makes you have such dreadful headaches, I wonder?" Roy said next, as he took a seat beside her, forgetful entirely of his mother's shawl, for which he had been sent.

Georgie did not know why she was so afflicted, unless it was from having too much time to think; she believed she would be better if she had some aim in life, some interest beside just living for her own gratification. She wanted something to do; something which would be of real benefit to mankind, and she had had serious thoughts of offering herself to the Freedman's Bureau as a teacher of negroes. That would rouse her up, and she should feel as if she were of use to somebody; now she was not, and she was getting tired of eternally thinking of fashion and one's self.

Georgie talked right along, clothing her sentiments in very appropriate language, and appearing as much in earnest as if she really had been meditating a trial of life among the negroes, whereas she knew in her heart that she would die sooner than sacrifice herself in that way, and that the idea had birth in her brain that very instant when she gave it expression. Accustomed to Roy as she was, she saw at a glance the change in his manner toward her, and always on the lookout for opportunities where he was concerned, she seized the present one and made the most of it.

Roy had highly eulogized some young ladies from Albany who had left luxurious homes, and given themselves to the wearisome task of teaching the freedmen; and knowing this, Georgie proposed to martyr herself just for effect, and her ruse worked well, for the true honest man at her side, who had never deceived a person in his life, had no conception of the depths of art and hypocrisy which she was capable of practising. He believed she did want something to occupy her mind, that she was tired of the idle, aimless life fashionable ladies led, and he felt himself drawn towards her as he never had before. She certainly could make him happy, and perhaps he might as well speak now, and have it settled. But before he had a chance to do so, Georgie suddenly assumed a troubled, perplexed look, and, after a little hesitancy said:

"Roy, you seem about as much like a brother to me as Jack does himself, and I want to ask you something in strict confidence. Do you know anything against Charlie Bigelow, of Boston, the one we met at Saratoga? He has proposed to a friend of mine, and my opinion is wanted in the matter. I rather liked him, but men sometimes know each other better than women know them, and as I am interested in my friend's happiness, I wish you to tell me honestly if you would advise her to accept him."

Georgie looked innocently at him, but her eyes drooped

beneath something which she saw in his, and her cheeks burned painfully, while the better side of her nature asserted itself for an instant, and cried out against suffering Roy Leighton to take the step she felt sure he was meditating. It was true that every word she had uttered since he had joined her had been spoken with a direct reference to this end; but she trembled now that she saw the end approaching, and half raised her hand as if to ward it off. The thought of losing Georgie made her more valuable to Roy, and he could not let her go without an effort to keep her. The blue jacket and the brown eyes and tiny boots were forgotten, and bending over the beautiful woman, he said :

"Georgie, something tells me that the young friend of whom you have spoken is yourself. Do you love Charlie Bigelow, Georgie?"

He spoke so kindly that the hot tears came with a swift rush to Georgie's eyes, which were very lustrous and beseeching, when for an instant they looked up at Roy, who continued :

"I don't believe you do; and if not, don't marry him for the sake of an aim in life. Better carry out your other Quixotic idea, and teach the Southern negroes. But why do either? Why not come here and live with me? I have always had an idea that you would come some time. Will you, Georgie?"

For a moment Georgie sat perfectly silent, looking at him with an expression of perfect happiness beaming in her eyes, and showing itself in every feature of her face; then gradually the expression changed, and was succeeded by one of terror and remorse, and the dark eyes turned away from Roy, and seemed to be looking far away at something which made them terrible while that fixed, stony gaze lasted. Wondering greatly at her manner, Roy said, "Georgie, won't you answer me?"

And this time he passed his arm around her, but she writhed herself from his embrace, and putting out both hands, said impetuously

"Don't, Roy; don't touch me; don't say the words again to me; take them back, please, lest it prove a greater temptation than I can bear, for, Roy, oh, Roy, I do—I do love you, and if I could I would so gladly live with you always; but—but—I can't,—I can't. I am—I was—oh, Roy, take the words back before I go quite mad."

He almost thought her mad now, and came a little nearer to her, asking what she meant, and why, if she loved him as she had said, his asking her to marry him should affect her so. And while he said this to her she began to recover her composure, and to be more like herself. The good impulse which had counselled her not to deceive Roy Leighton, and impose herself upon him without a confession of the past, was subsiding; and though there still were bitter pangs of remorse and terrible regrets for the past, she began to feel that she could not lose what she had desired so long, and to Roy's questionings, she answered: "I am not so good as you think me. I am not worthy of you. I am—you don't know how bad I am. You would hate me if you did."

She was growing excited again. All the good there was in the woman was asserting itself in Roy's behalf, and she continued :

"Everybody would hate me as I hate myself always."

He took a step backward as if she really were the creature she professed to be; but *now* it was her hand which was reached out to *him*. She could not let him go, and she gasped,—

"But Roy, with you, who are so noble and good, I could learn to be better, and I will. I swear it here, that if you make me your wife, I will be true and faithful, and do my best to make you happy. Try me and see if I don't."

Perplexed and bewildered with what he had seen and heard, and half inclined already to be sorry, Roy was still too honorable to draw back, and when she said so piteously, "Try me, Roy, and see if I don't," he took her offered hand and pressed it between his own, and answered her: "I know you will, Georgie. We all have faults, and you must make allowances for mine, as I will for yours, which, I am sure you overrate, or else I have strangely misjudged you. Why, Georgie, you would almost make one believe you had been guilty of some dreadful thing, you accuse yourself so unmercifully."

Roy laughed lightly as he said this, while Georgie felt for a moment as if her heart were in her throat, and it was only by the most powerful efforts of the will that she forced it back, and recovered her powers of speech sufficiently to say: "Don't imagine, pray, that I've murdered or stolen, or done anything that makes me amenable to the law. It is general badness;" and her old smile broke for the first time over her face, to which the color was coming back.

"You are so good, that nothing less than perfection should ever hope to win you, and I am so far from that; but I am going to be better, and the world shall yet say that Roy Leighton chose wisely and well."

She had settled it, and Roy was an engaged man; and as he looked down upon the beautiful face of his *fiancée*, he felt that the world would even now say he had done well without waiting for any improvement in his betrothed, who looked up at him in such a loving, confiding way, that he naturally enough stooped and kissed her lips, and called her his darling, and felt sure that he loved her, and was happy in doing so.

Georgie possessed the rare gift of going rapidly from one extreme mood to another. She had been very low down in the depths of humiliation, and in her excitement had almost told Roy secrets she guarded as she did her life; and from that depth she had risen to the heights of bliss, trembling a little as she remembered how near she had come to being stranded by her own act, and mentally chiding herself for her weakness in allowing herself to be so excited about something Roy never *could* know unless Jack or Maude betrayed her, as she was sure they would not. She had detected the wavering for a moment on Roy's part, and lest it should occur again, and work detriment to her cause, she said to him:

"I do not believe in secret engagements, and shall tell Aunt Burton at once, as you, of course, will tell your mother."

Then Roy *did* wince a little, and thought of Miss Overton, and wished Georgie was not in such a hurry to have it known that they were engaged, and told her she was right, and he would tell his mother that night, and asked if they should not join his guests upon the lawn. Georgie's languor was all gone, and, taking Roy's arm, she went with him through the house and out into the beautiful grounds, feeling as she went a sense of ownership in them all, which made her walk like a queen as she approached the group upon the lawn, and received their words of greeting.

CHAPTER XXXIII.

HOW THE ENGAGEMENT WAS RECEIVED.

ROY'S guests had missed him, and commented upon his absence, and Mrs. Churchill had wondered if he could not find her shawl, and Edna had offered to go herself for it. Then Mrs. Burton said that she had left

Georgie in the house, and probably she and Roy were deep in some learned discussion, as they usually got up an argument when they were together. She would go herself for Mrs. Churchill's shawl, as she knew just where it was.

But Mrs. Churchill would not suffer this. She preferred that Miss Overton should go; and accordingly Edna went, and in passing through the hall glanced into the drawing-room, and saw the couple at the farther end too much absorbed in themselves to know there was a witness to their love-making. Roy was kissing Georgie as the seal to their betrothal, and by that token Edna knew they were engaged, and felt for a moment as if the brightness of her life had suddenly been stricken out, though why she should care, she could not tell. She only knew that she did care, and that her heart was throbbing painfully as she fled noiselessly up the stairs in the direction of Mrs. Churchill's room. Once there, she stopped a moment to breathe and think over what she had seen, and ask herself what it was to her, that the heart-beats should come so fast, and the world should look so dark.

"Nothing, nothing," she said, "only he might have done so much better, and have been so much happier. I don't like her, and when she comes here I must go; and I could enjoy so much alone with Roy and his mother;" and having thus settled the cause of her disquiet, she found Mrs. Churchill's shawl, and left the house by another way than the one leading past the parlor door.

She had been very gay just before, so gay indeed that Miss Agatha, who did not believe in a plebeian's daring to be merry and free in the presence of superiors, had made some sarcastic remarks about "the wild spirits of that Miss Overton." But she was not wild when she returned to the lawn with the shawl, and her face was so pale, that Maude asked if she had seen a ghost that she looked so white and scared.

"No," Edna replied; "but I ran quite fast up and down the stairs."

"And did you see anything of my daughter," Mrs. Burton asked next, and Edna answered her evasively:

"I heard voices in the parlor, hers and Mr. Leighton's, I think."

"Oh, yes, there they come," Mrs. Burton rejoined, her face all aglow with the great delight it afforded her to sit and watch Georgie coming toward her so graceful and self-possessed, and looking so radiant and beautiful.

One could see her black eyes sparkle and shine even in the distance, as she leaned on Roy's arm, and smiled at something he was saying to her. Georgie was very happy for a few moments, and not a ripple of disquiet came to the surface until her glance fell on Edna, sitting upon a camp stool a little apart from the others, her hat on the grass at her side, her brown curls somewhat disordered, but falling about her face and neck in a most bewitching way, her hands folded listlessly together upon her lap, and her whole attitude and appearance that of some tired, pretty child. She *was* pretty, and Georgie knew it; and she looked so young, and fair, and innocent, that Georgie felt a sudden impulse of fear lest, after all, this girl, who would see Roy every day, should become her rival, and with that impulse came a thought that the sooner her engagement was known the better and safer for her. So clasping her white hand on Roy's arm, she whispered to him softly: "Perhaps we may as well have it off our minds and announce it at once; we shall both feel freer and easier."

Roy could not answer for her, but for himself he did not care to be in haste, especially with Miss Overton sitting there looking so eagerly at him. She was a restraint upon him, and he unconsciously wished her away while he made the announcement, for he was going to do it. Georgie was probably right. She usually was, he reflected, and without a second look at Edna, walked straight to his mother, and placing Georgie's hand in hers, said to her, "Mother I bring to you a daughter: Georgie has promised to be my wife."

"Heaven bless my soul!" Mr. Burton exclaimed, springing up from his chair and bobbing about like a rubber ball.

He had not expected Roy to act upon his hint so soon; in fact he was more than half afraid that nothing might come of it after all, and then Mrs. Freeman Burton would never cease to upbraid him with his awkwardness; but here it was fixed, settled, and announced, and he could not repress his feelings until a sharp pull at his coat-skirts from his spouse, and the whispered words, "Are you crazy?" brought him to his senses, and he sat down just as Georgie finished kissing Mrs. Churchill, and whispered to her what a good daughter and wife she meant to be.

Mrs. Churchill was glad, as it was something she had long desired, but now that Miss Overton had come she did not so much need a daughter. Still she was sufficiently demonstrative, and laid her hand in blessing on Georgie's head, while Mrs. Burton shed a few tears over the touching scene, and called Roy a naughty boy for stealing away her treasure, and said a deal more about the engagement generally, and Georgie in particular.

Maude came next with the New York girls, but there was a blank look of disappointment in her face as she kissed Georgie and offered her congratulations. She had not looked for this so suddenly. Once she had been constantly expecting it, but they had waited so long, and latterly Roy had seemed so indifferent, that she had hopes for him in another direction, and felt disturbed and sorry, and wondered how Jack would take it.

Jack was at some distance from the group of which Georgie was the centre, but he heard what Roy had said, and saw the demonstrations which followed, but did not join in them. Knowing what he knew, he could not congratulate Roy, who was being so deceived; and his breath came hard, and something like an oath escaped his lips, as he purposely drove a ball to the farthest extremity of the croquet lawn, and then kept on idly knocking it about. He meant to keep away as long as possible, and Georgie knew he did, and her cheek paled a little when at last he came near enough for her to see the troubled look upon his face, as he sat down by Edna and fanned himself with his hat.

The evening air was cool, but he seemed to be very warm, and constantly wiped the drops of sweat from his brow, as he sat talking with Edna. The announcement of the engagement had not been made to *her;* there was no need for her to do or say anything, and so she feigned indifference, and kept on talking to Jack until Georgie came that way. Jack saw her first, and, suddenly remembering that he had not put his mallet in the box, darted away just as his sister came up.

She was thus left alone with Edna, to whom she was excessively gracious and affable. Taking the seat Jack had vacated, she began to talk as kindly and familiarly as if all her life she had known Miss Overton as her equal. There was something wonderfully winning in Georgie when she chose to be agreeable, and it had its effect upon Edna, who began to like her better and to wonder at the change. It was a part of Georgie's *rôle* to treat Edna well,—part of her bargain with Maude; and she was resolved to fulfil her contract, and she sat chatting with her until Roy came up and said that Mrs. Burton thought it was time for her to go in from the night air. He did not say that *he* thought so, or evince any undue anxiety about her health, but he did say to Edna:

"Miss Overton, I am sure the damp air must be bad for you also; take my arm, please, and come with us to the house."

And so, with Georgie upon one side and Edna on the other, he led the way to the house, followed by Mr. Burton, who had his mother in charge, and by Mrs. Burton, who was lauding Georgie to Miss Shawe, and telling what an angel of perfection she was, how hard it would be to part with her, and how glad she was that she was to go no farther away than Leighton.

There was some music in the drawing-room, and afterward ice-cream and cake; and then, at about half-past ten, the little party broke up. Georgie was still in a gushing mood, and kissed Mrs. Churchill three times at parting, and even kissed Edna in the exuberance of her joy, and said she hoped to know her better in the future, and bade her take good care of dear Mrs. Churchill; and then she looked around for Roy, who led her to the carriage, and pressed her hand a little at parting, and said he should see her to-morrow.

Mr. and Mrs. Burton, Georgie, and Miss Shawe, occupied the carriage, while the other people walked; Maude and Jack lingering behind the others, so that it was nearer one than twelve when they at last reached Oakwood. But late as it was, Georgie was waiting for them. She *must* see Jack before she slept. He was to return to Jersey City on the morrow, and she might not have another chance.

So she sat by her window until she heard him coming up the walk, and then waited until the whispered interview on the piazza was at an end, and Maude was in her room. Then she passed noiselessly out into the hall, and on through a narrow corridor, until Jack's chamber was reached.

"Come in!" was answered rather sternly to her timid knock, and by the tone of his voice, she knew that Jack guessed who his visitor was, and she trembled as she advanced toward him, and laid her hand on his arm.

He did not smile, nor allow his face to relax a muscle,

even when she looked up at him in her most beseeching way, and began by calling him "dear Jack." But he *would* soften after a time, she was sure. He never had withstood her long at a time, and so she mustered all her courage, and began:

"Dear Jack, I've had no chance to congratulate you on your engagement, and I came to do so now, and to tell you how glad I am. I would rather have Maude for my sister than any one I know. You have chosen well, my boy."

"I am glad you think so," Jack answered stiffly; and then there was a painful silence, which Georgie broke by saying:

"Jack, have you no word of congratulation for me in my new happiness?"

The tears were swimming in her great, bright eyes, and she seemed the very embodiment of innocence and goodness; but Jack looked away from her, straight down at some slippers which Annie had embroidered for him, and asked:

"*Are* you happy, Georgie?"

"Yes, oh, yes; so happy that I feel as if I never could be thankful enough to the good Father who has been so kind to me."

"Pshaw!" and Jack spoke impatiently. "Don't, for gracious sake, try to come your *pious* strains on me, for I tell you they won't go down till you have done one thing. Have you told Roy?"

He looked at her now, and her eyes fell before his searching gaze, while her heart beat so fast that he could hear and count the throbs as her bosom rose and fell.

"No, Jack; I have not. I tried at first,—I meant to,—I really did; but I could not say the words, they choked me so. I couldn't tell him, Jack!" and her voice was very mournful in its tone. "Think, if it were yourself, and you felt sure that to tell would be to lose Maude's love, would you do it?—could you?"

She had made her strongest argument, and Jack hesitated ere he replied:

"It would be hard; but better so, it seems to me, than to live with a lie on my conscience, and a constant, haunting fear lest she should find it out."

"But he can't, Jack,—he never can,—unless *you* tell him, or Maude. How much does *she* know? Oh, Jack, have you broken your oath, sworn so solemnly to me."

There was a flash in her black eyes as they fastened themselves upon Jack, who replied to her, truthfully:

"Maude knows nothing, except that there is something you would hide from Roy, and from the world. I hinted so much to her, as a weapon of defence for Edna. Whether she or any one else ever knows more from me, depends upon yourself, and your treatment of Edna."

"I knew you would not betray me, Jack," Georgie rejoined, a heavy weight lifted from her mind. "I shall not harm Mrs. Charlie Churchill,—I shall try to like her, for your sake and Maude's. And, now, why need I tell Roy, when he never can, by any possibility, find it out, and to tell him would only distress him, and ruin me?"

"Perhaps not. If he loves you truly, as I love Maude, he can forgive a great deal. I should try it and see,—I should go to him clean and open-hearted, or not at all," Jack said; but Georgie shook her head.

Confessing her fault would involve too much, for more people than Roy would have to know, if full confession was made; Aunt Burton, who thought her so perfect, and her Uncle Burton, too, and, possibly, little Annie; and from that last ordeal Georgie shrank more nervously, if possible, than from telling Roy himself. She could *not* do it. She would rather die than attempt it, and she said so to Jack, who was silent for a moment, and then regarding her intently, asked:

"Has it ever occurred to you, Georgie, that possibly the

dead might come to life and witness against you? Such accidents have happened."

"The dead, Jack; the dead?" and Georgie's face was like the face of a corpse, and her voice was husky and thick. "That cannot be. I saw him in the coffin. I know just where he lies in Greenwood."

"I was not thinking of him, but of Henry; you did not see him in his coffin. You don't know where his grave is."

"No; but Jack, there can be no doubt. You made so sure yourself. You told me he was dead. Was it all a farce? Oh, Jack, do you know anything—"

She was kneeling to him now, with her proud head bent to his very feet, just as once she had crouched years ago when he was but a boy, and she a wretched woman suing for pity and begging him to stand by her in her need. Then her long glossy curls had swept the floor just as they swept it now, and Jack had lifted her up, and comforted her, and sworn to be her friend, and he wanted to do it again, though his heart was harder toward her now than it had been then. He could more readily forgive the sin committed through great temptation when she was young and without a counsellor, than he could forgive the many years during which she had lived a lie. Still he pitied her so much, and loved her so much, for she was his sister, and her great beauty had always exercised a wonderful power over him. He felt it even now as she lifted her white, tear-stained face to his, and as he had done that other time in the darkest hour she had ever met, so he did now; he stooped and raised her up, and tried to comfort her, and said that he "knew nothing and had heard nothing, only such things sometimes did happen, and it would be very awkward for her, as Roy's wife, to be some day confronted by Henry Morton."

"Don't, don't speak his name," she almost shrieked, while a shudder like a convulsion shook her frame. "I have been greatly to blame, but my punishment has been terrible. I have suffered untold agony in thinking of the past. I surely have atoned, and now if there is a haven of rest for me, don't try to keep me from it by harrowing up my fears. I *know* he is dead. I am sure of it, and I mean to be a good wife to Roy. He never shall repent his choice,—I'll bring every thought and feeling into conformity with his; and Jack, you must stand by me as a brother. Will you, Jack? As Roy's wife, I can help you so much, and I will. Annie shall no longer be an expense to you. I will support her entirely."

"And not let Roy know you are doing it?" Jack answered; and Georgie replied:

"I will tell him that, at least. I will not cheat him there. I'll arrange it before we are married, that I am to do something for Annie, and perhaps when he sees how I care for her he will propose that she live with us. Oh, if he only would."

Jack felt that on this point, at least, Georgie was sincere. She *did* love the little Annie, and his heart softened still more toward her; and when, as she was about to leave him, she said, imploringly, "Kiss me, Jack, once, as you used to do!" he put his arm around her, and kissed her white lips, which quivered with emotion, while the tears fell like rain upon her cheeks.

"You are a good brother, and I will try to be good, too, for your sake and Roy's," she said, as she bade him goodnight, and left the room.

He had not congratulated her, but she knew he would keep silent; knew, too, that she had comparatively nothing to fear from Maude; and but for one harrowing fear, which yet was not exactly a fear, she would have felt tolerably composed and happy, as she sought her own chamber.

Jack's words, "What if the dead should come back to

witness against you?" rang in her ears, and when, as she stood by the window, looking out into the moonlight, a shadow flitted across the grass, she trembled from head to foot, and turned sick with nervous dread. But it was only the watch-dog, Bruno, and as he bounded out into the light, she grew quiet, and even smiled at her own weakness.

"That cannot be," she said; and then, as if to make assurance doubly sure, she opened a trunk which always stood in her closet, and taking from it a box, touched a secret spring, and soon held in her hand three documents,— one, a newspaper, soiled and yellow with time, and containing a paragraph which said that a certain Henry Morton, who had managed to escape from justice, had recently died in a little out-of-the-way village among the Alleghanies, and that his friends, if he had any, could learn the particulars of his death, by inquiring at the place where he died. The other two were letters, one from the dying man himself, who wrote that, from the very nature of his disease, he had but a day or two to live; and one from Jack, who had gone to that out-of-the-way place, among the Pennsylvania hills, and learned that Henry Morton had died there at such a time, and then had written the same to his anxious sister at home. She had kept these papers carefully, and guarded them from every eye but her own, and occasionally she read them over to assure herself of the truth. But now she would keep them no longer, lest in some way they should come to light; and so, holding them to the gas, and then throwing them upon the hearth, she watched them as they crisped and blackened, and turned to a pile of ashes.

There was nothing now in her way, and, as was her constant habit, the woman who had sinned so greatly, but who was going to do better, knelt down and said her prayers, and thanked God for Roy, and asked, first, that he might never know what she had been; and, second, that she might be to him all that a good, true wife should be, and that he might be willing for Annie to live with her. This done, she felt as if she really were a very good woman, and that but for Jack, who had such straight-laced notions, she would be confirmed, by way of helping her to keep her resolution!

CHAPTER XXXIV.

HOW THEY GOT ON AT LEIGHTON.

ROY'S first thought on waking the next morning, was to wonder what had happened that he should feel so oppressed, as if a load were bearing him down. Then it came to him that he was engaged, and he wondered why that should affect his spirits as it did.

All the excitement of the previous night was gone, and he could reason clearly now, and remember how queerly Georgie had talked and acted at first, just as if she had done some horrible deed, which, if she should confess it, would prove a barrier between them. But she had not confessed, and she had recovered her usual composure, and accepted him, and was going to be his wife sometime, he hardly knew when, though he had a vague idea that there need be no undue haste. He had done his duty in asking her, and surely Mr. Burton would not urge an immediate marriage, neither would Georgie desire it ; girls never did ; and having fixed the blissful day at some period far in the future, Roy gave a relieved yawn, and went on with his toilet, quickening his movements a little when he saw from his window the flutter of a white dress, and knew that Miss Overton was already in the grounds.

"She is an early riser, and it must be that which makes her look so fresh, and bright, and young, though of course she is very young. I wonder, by the way, how old Georgie is. I never heard any one hazard a conjecture. Sometimes she looks all of twenty-eight, though that can't be, as she has only been out of school four or five years; and even if she is, I am thirty myself, and two years difference is enough, provided the husband has the advantage. Georgie will never look old with those eyes and that hair."

Roy was dressed by this time, and went out to join Miss Overton in her morning walk.

He found her in a little arbor, looking pale and tired, as if she had not slept; but she smiled brightly as he came up, and made some remark about the pleasant morning. He wanted her to talk of Georgie,—wanted to be reassured that he had done well for himself; but as nothing had been said to her on the subject, she did not feel at liberty to introduce it, and so the conversation drifted as far as possible from Miss Burton, and turned at last upon *Edna*, whom Roy hoped eventually to have at Leighton.

"She will come, of course, when I am married," he said. "She can then have no excuse for not coming."

"Perhaps your wife would not like her," Edna suggested, and Roy replied:

"I am sure she will. Georgie is not hard to please, and from Edna's letters I judge her to be a very bright, sprightly little body. There's a good deal of mischief about her, I guess. I saw her once in the cars with some of her schoolmates. I had been very sick and was still an invalid, nervous and irritable, and afraid of the least breath of air. Girl-like, they opened all the windows near them, and mother got a cinder in her eye, and I began to sneeze, and at last asked the sauciest looking one to shut the window, not pleasantly, you know, but savagely, as if I were the only person to be considered in the car. She did shut it with a bang, and then avenged herself by making a caricature of me, shivering in a poke-bonnet, and called me a Miss Betty."

"How did you know that?" Edna asked, looking up with so much surprise as almost to betray herself.

She had not thought of that sketch since the day when it was made, and she was curious to hear how Roy came to know about it.

"She dropped it as she left the car, either purposely or accidentally, and mother picked it up," Roy said. "I have it still, and if I ever see her and know her well, I mean to show it to her and have some fun with it," he continued, while Edna asked, a little uneasily:

"Then you were not angry with her for her impertinence?"

"Yes, I was at the time, very angry, and wanted to box her ears; but that only lasted a little time, and I was glad to see myself as others saw me. I do believe it did me good. She must be something of an artist, for even as a caricature the picture was a good one. I wish I knew where she was. I must write to-day, and tell her of my engagement."

He was trying to introduce that subject again, but Edna made no reply. His mention of the picture had sent her off on an entirely different train of thought, and she was glad that just then the breakfast bell rang, and brought their walk to an end.

Roy spent the most of the day at Oakwood, but he was home at dinner, and passed the evening there, and Edna heard him talking with his mother about his engagement, and asking if she were glad.

"Yes, very glad," was the reply; "though it does not matter quite so much now as it did before Miss Overton came. I am getting really attached to her, she seems so pleasant and refined, and knows what I want before I tell her. She is a very superior person, I think, and must have been well brought up."

Mrs. Churchill did nothing by the halves; she liked or disliked thoroughly; and, as she had conceived a great liking for her little companion, she was more inclined to talk of her than of Georgie; though she *did* ask when the marriage was to take place.

"Whenever it suits Georgie," Roy replied. "For myself, I am in no haste, and should prefer waiting until next spring. We are very comfortable now, and Miss Overton's presence precludes the necessity of having some one for company."

He did not seem a very ardent lover, impatient for the happy day; and, indeed, he was not, and much of his indifference was owing to Miss Overton, who experienced a feeling of relief in knowing that Roy would probably not bring his wife home until spring. She could not live with Georgie; and that lady's arrival as mistress would be the signal for her departure. So she hailed with delight anything which would put off the evil day; for, short as had been her stay at Leighton, she was very happy there, and shrank from leaving it, with all its refinement, and luxury, and ease. She did not mean to be a listener to any private conversation between Roy and his mother, but, situated just as she was, on the piazza, and directly under the window where they were sitting, she could not well help herself, and so she sat still, while their talk turned next upon Edna, whom Roy meant to have at Leighton as soon as Georgie came.

"I've never felt right about it at all," he said. "Poor little thing, knocking about the world alone, trying to pay a debt she foolishly thinks she owes me; and I am determined to find her at some rate, if I put the police on her track. Wouldn't you like to have her here when Georgie comes?"

Mrs. Churchill hesitated a little, and then replied:

"Wouldn't *three* ladies be in each other's way? for, Roy, I should not like to have Miss Overton leave even when Georgie comes."

"Nor I, nor I," Roy said, quickly, with a feeling that he should greatly miss the little girl, who could hear no more, lest her feelings should betray themselves, and who, crawling upon her hands and feet, crept away from the window and sought her own room, where she was free to indulge in a hearty fit of tears.

Why she cried she hardly knew, though she made herself believe it was for the pleasant home she must ere long give up, for after Roy's marriage she felt that she must go away, as she never could be happy with Georgie at Leighton as its mistress. The thought of leaving was a dreadful one, and she kept on crying in a desolate, homesick kind of way, until she heard Mrs. Churchill coming up the stairs, and knew her services would be needed. Remembering what had been said of her as Miss Overton, there was an added tenderness and gentleness in her voice and manner as she read the evening chapter to the half-blind woman, and then helped to disrobe her. To brush and smooth Mrs. Churchill's hair was one of her nightly duties, and her fingers moved caressingly over the thin locks and about the forehead, until the lady declared herself mesmerized, and drawing Edna's face down to her lips, kissed her affectionately, saying as she did so:

"Excuse the liberty, but you seem more like a daughter than a stranger; and, Miss Overton, you know of course I am to have a daughter by and by; Georgie is to be Mrs. Roy Leighton, and I am glad, and think my son could not have chosen better, or as well perhaps,—but—but—I want you to stay just the same, even if Edna, that is Mrs. Charlie

Churchill, comes too, as Roy means to have her. Will you, Miss Overton?"

"You may get tired of me by that time and glad to have me leave," Edna replied, evasively; and making some excuse to leave the room, she staid away so long that the conversation was not resumed when she returned with the medicine which Mrs. Churchill always kept standing by her bed at night.

Edna had not counted upon all the unpleasant things to which the peculiarity of her position would subject her. She had no idea that she should so often hear herself discussed, or be compelled to feel so continually that she was living and acting a lie, or she would never have been there as she was; and that night after leaving Mrs. Churchill she began seriously to revolve the propriety of leaving Leighton, and going back to Uncle Phil, who, she knew, would willingly welcome her.

After the departure of the city guests from Oakwood, Georgie spent several days at Leighton, and acted the sweet, amiable daughter and bride-elect to perfection, and petted Edna, and talked a great deal about "poor Charlie," and looked at Edna as she did so, and went with her when she carried flowers to his grave, and called her a dear kind creature to be so thoughtful for Mrs. Churchill.

"Of course it is not as if you had known him," she said; and her great black eyes looked straight at Edna, who colored scarlet, and turned her face away to hide her guilty blushes.

Georgie was bent upon torturing her, and, seating herself in one of the chairs, went over with all the harrowing particulars of the railroad disaster, the fearful storm, the body crushed beneath the wreck, and the young girl trying to extricate it. And Edna, listening to her, felt as if she should scream outright with pain, so vivid was the picture Georgie drew of that dreadful scene.

"Will she never stop," she thought, as Georgie went on to relate all that occurred at Leighton after the body was brought home, and told how Mrs. Churchill went into convulsions, and denounced the girl as Charlie's murderer. Georgie was drawing a little upon her imagination, but she was accustomed to that, and she had an object in what she was doing. It was not alone to wound and torture her auditor, though that was some satisfaction to her, but there was a fixed purpose in her mind that Edna should *not* remain at Leighton after her entrance there. She did not like the girl; she had a mean kind of jealousy toward her, and Mrs. Churchill's praises of her only made her more determined that the same roof should not shelter both. She dared not betray Edna's secret, but she could annoy and worry her, and she took a mean kind of delight in seeing poor Edna writhe as she went on to talk of that girl whom Charlie married, saying finally, that she hoped Roy would not insist upon bringing her home, as he now seemed resolved to do.

"Not that *I* should care at all. I probably should grow fond of her, for Jack insists that she is very nice, and little Annie nearly worships her; but for dear Mrs. Churchill's sake I should be sorry to see her here."

"Why so? She talks kindly of her always," Edna asked hotly, forgetting herself for a moment, in her indignation.

But Georgie was sweetly unconscious of her excitement, and replied:

"Yes, Mrs. Churchill is a noble woman, and tries to forgive the girl, and thinks she has done so; but I, who know her so well, can see the effort she makes to speak kindly of her, and just how she shudders when her name is accidentally mentioned. No, glad as I would be to help and befriend the girl, I am naughty enough to hope Roy cannot find her. But pray, Miss Overton, don't repeat what I have said. I hardly know why I have spoken so freely, unless it is that you have a way of taking our hearts by storm, and not appearing in the least like a stranger. By the way, you look a little like Mrs. Charlie Churchill; I thought of it the first time I saw you here, and spoke of it to Roy, and just for fun asked if it would not be a good joke if you were *Edna* in disguise."

"What did he say?" Edna asked, and, without looking at her victim, Georgie replied: "He seemed to take altogether a different view of the joke from what I did, and expressed himself decidedly against disguises of all kinds. It would displease him very much to have Edna do such a thing, he said. But I fear I have wearied you with talk which cannot interest you, of course. You look pale and fagged. It's the hot morning, I guess. Suppose we go back to the house. Ah, there's Roy now; I think I'll join him for a little walk upon the lawn."

If Edna had ever entertained a thought of staying at Leighton after Georgie was mistress there, it would have been swept away effectually by what Georgie had said to her, just as that nice young lady meant it should be. And what was worse than all, she could never let Roy know who she was, after having been so foolish as to come to him *incog.* Why had she done it? she asked herself many times. Why had Maude and Uncle Phil suffered it; aye, contrived and advised it, and why hadn't she listened to Aunt Jerry, who had opposed it from the first. But it was too late now. She was there as Miss Overton, and as such she must always remain to Roy and his mother. By her own act she had precluded the possibility of ever showing herself to them in her own proper person. Mrs. Churchill, who already disliked Edna Browning and looked upon her as Charlie's murderer, would hate her should she know the truth, and Roy would hate her too, and that was more than she could bear. She could not lose his respect, and so she must never claim him as her brother; never see him after she went away from Leighton. It was very hard, and Edna cried bitterly for a few moments, while away in the distance walked Georgie and Roy, up and down the wide lawn, but always where Georgie could command a view of the little figure sitting so disconsolately under the shadow of the grape-vine, and weeping, as she knew from the motion of the hands which went so often to the face. Georgie was glad. She had made Edna's exit from Leighton a sure thing, and her spirits rose proportionately with the mischief she had done. She was very gay for the remainder of the day; very attentive to Mrs. Churchill; very affectionate to Roy; very kind and patronizing to the servants, and very familiar with Miss Overton, whom she petted and caressed, and kissed gushingly, when, at night, she finally shook the dust of Leighton from her garments and departed for Oakwood.

CHAPTER XXXV.

LETTERS.

IN course of time there came a letter to Edna from Roy. It had been sent by him to Aunt Jerry, and by her to Uncle Phil, who forwarded it to his niece, together with a few lines of his own, telling how "all-fired lonesome he was, and how he missed her gab, and the click-clack of her high heels on the stairs, and the whisk of her petticoats through the doors."

"The synagogue is getting along slowly," he wrote, "for the *cusses*—" (he erased that word as hardly consistent for a man who was running a church, and substituted "cattle," so that it read) "the *cattle* are on another strike, what hain't gone over to work on the Unitarian meetin' house, which is havin' the greatest kind of overhaulin' inside and out. The persuasion meets now in the Academy, and go it kind of ritual, with the litany and some of the *sams*, which they read slower than time in the primmer. Ruth Gardner leads off, and is getting up another carouse to buy a *Fount* to dip the young ones in, and expects to catch the new minister. But let 'em run. Old Phil don't ask no odds of Unitarian nor Orthodox, nor nobody else. He'll build his own church and pay his own minister, if necessary, and burn *innocence* too, if he wants to.

"I send a letter from Roy, I guess, and it has done some travellin', too, having gone first to that remarkable woman, your Aunt Jerushy, who wrote to me as follows :

"'Philip Overton, forward the enclosed to Edna, and oblige, Jerusha Amanda Pepper.'

"Short and sweet, wasn't it? but like the old gal, as you described her. If Maude is there, tell her I am real hungry for a sight of her blue eyes and sassy face. Come up here, both of you, as soon as you can. Yours to command,
"PHILIP OVERTON."

This was Uncle Phil's letter, and Edna cried over it a little, and knew just how lonely the old man was without her, and half wished she had not left him, "though it would have been dreadful never to have known Roy at all," she said to herself, as she opened next Aunt Jerusha's letter, in which Roy's was enclosed, and read what that worthy woman had to say.

There was a good deal about her "neurology," and a sure

cure she had found for it, and about the new rector, who was as much too *low* as the other had been too *high*, inasmuch as he went to the Methodist prayer-meetings and took a part in them, and said he wasn't quite sure about the direct line down from the Apostles; it might be straight enough, but he guessed it had been broken a few times, and had some knots in it where it was mended, and he fully indorsed young Tyng, and believed in Henry Ward Beecher and Woman's Rights, all of which she considered worse than turning your back to the people, and bowing to the floor in the creed, and so latterly she had staid at home and read the Bible and Prayer Book by herself, and sung a hymn and psalm, and felt she was worshipping God quite as well as if she had gone to church and been mad as fury all the time. She hoped Edna felt better now she was at Leighton, though she was a big fool for going, and a bigger one if she staid there after that woman with a boy's name came as my lady.

"Roy was not satisfied with sending me a letter for *you*, but he must needs write to *me* too, and tell me he was going to be married; and that he should insist upon knowing where you were, so he could persuade you to live at Leighton, your proper place.

"So you see what's before you, and you know my advice, which, of course, you won't follow. You are more than half in love with Roy yourself; don't deny it; I know better; and that critter with the boy's name will find it out, if she has not already, and you'll hate one another like pisen, and it's no place for you. Better come back to Aunt Jerusha, and keep the district school this winter. They want a woman teacher, because they can get her cheap, and she'll do her work better, as if there was any justice in that. I believe in Woman's Rights so far as equal pay for the same work; but this scurriping through the country speech-making, and the clothes-basket full of dirty duds at home, and your husband's night-shirt so ragged that if took sick sudden in the night he'd be ashamed to send for the doctor, I don't believe in, and never will.

"According to orders, I send this to your Uncle Philip, and s'pose you'll answer through the same channel and tell if you'll come home about your business, and teach school for sixteen dollars a month, and I board you for the chores you'll do night and morning. Yours with regret,

"JERUSHA A. PEPPER."

"Go back to Allen's Hill, and teach school, and board with Aunt Jerusha, and do chores?" Edna repeated to herself, as she finished the letter; she might have added, "and leave Roy?" but she did not, though her face turned scarlet as she recalled the words, "You are more than half in love with Roy yourself."

Was that true? She could not quite answer that it was, and she tried to believe it was her attachment to Mrs. Churchill which made Leighton so dear to her, and that Roy had nothing to do with it, except as he helped to make her life very pleasant. She was *not* in love with him, she decided at last; if she were, she should think it her duty to leave at once, but as it was, she should remain until the wedding, which had not yet been appointed. Some time before Christmas, Georgie had told her, while Mrs. Churchill had said:

"Roy will not marry till spring."

And she believed the latter, because she wanted to, and saying to herself, "I shall stay till Georgie comes, for Mrs. Churchill's sake," she opened Roy's letter, and read the kind, brotherly message he had written to his "dear sister Edna, whom he wished so much to find." There were hot blushes on Edna's cheeks, and she felt a heart-throb of pain as she began to read, in Roy's own words, of his engagement to

Georgie Burton. She had known it all before, it is true, and had seen his betrothed almost every day, and received, each time she saw her, some little malicious stab through the medium of Edna Browning. She had also been witness, at divers times, to various little love-passages between the engaged pair, or rather of love-passages on Georgie's part, for that young lady was not at all backward in asserting her right to fondle and caress her promised husband, who was not demonstrative, and who never of his own accord so much as took Georgie's hand in his own, or laid a finger on her in the presence of others. He merely submitted to her fondlings in silence and did not shake her off, though Edna sometimes fancied he wanted to do so, when she hung so helplessly upon him, or put her arm around his neck, and smoothed and caressed his hair, and called him "Roy dear." How he demeaned himself toward her when they were alone Edna did not know, but seeing him always so quiet and reserved, she had never realized that he was engaged as fully as she did when she saw it in his own handwriting, and two burning tears rolled down her cheeks and were impatiently dashed away as she read:

"And now, my little sister, I have something to communicate which may surprise you, but which I hope will please you, inasmuch as I trust it may have a direct bearing upon your future. I am engaged to be married to the Miss Georgie Burton who was so kind to you and poor Charlie in Iona. She is very nice, of course, and the most beautiful woman I have ever met, unless it be a Miss Overton who is here as companion for mother."

Edna's face and neck were scarlet now, and there was a throb of ecstasy in her heart, as she read on:

"This Miss Overton is not at all like Georgie, but quite as beautiful, I think, and both mother and myself like her immensely. She is nineteen, I believe, but a *wee* little creature, with the roundest, sauciest eyes, the softest golden-brown hair rippling all over her head, and the sweetest, most innocent face, while her smile is something wonderful. Maude Somerton, whom I wish you knew, calls her *Dotty*, but to myself I call her 'Brownie,' her eyes and hair are such a pretty brown, just tinged with golden, and her complexion, though smooth and soft, and very bright, is still a little brownish."

"A pretty way to talk about *me*, and he engaged to Georgie," Edna said, but not impatiently.

Indeed, she would have been well satisfied to have read Roy's praises of herself for the entire day, and felt a little annoyed when he turned from Miss Overton's beauty, to his plan of having his sister at Leighton as soon as Georgie came, and begged her to tell him where she was, that he might come for her himself.

"Mother wants you," he wrote, "and surely for Charlie's sake you will heed her wishes."

Edna wished she could believe that Mrs. Churchill would love her when she knew who she was, but after Georgie's insinuations she could not hope to be esteemed by either Roy or his mother.

"They would hate and despise me," she said, "so I shall not let them know that *Edna* was ever here, and my easier way will be not to answer Roy's letter, now or ever; I cannot tell him I am rejoiced at his engagement, for I am not. I don't like her; I never shall like her; I almost think I hate her, or should if it were not so very wicked," and Edna's boot-heels dug into the carpet as she gave vent to this amiable outburst.

There was nothing more of Georgie or Miss Overton in the letter, but Edna had read enough to make her very happy. Roy thought she was beautiful, and called her "Brownie" to himself. Surely this was sufficient cause for happiness, even though his marriage with another was fixed for the ensuing spring. It was a long time till then, and she would enjoy the present without thinking of the future, when Leighton could no longer be her home.

This was Edna's conclusion, and folding up Roy's letter, she went to Mrs. Churchill with so bright a look in her face, that it must have shown itself in her manner, for Mrs. Churchill said:

"You seem very happy this morning. You must have had good news in the letter Russell brought you."

"Yes; very good news. At least, a part of it was," Edna replied, her pulse throbbing a little regretfully, as she remembered having seen, in Roy's own handwriting, that he was pledged to another,—he who called her "Brownie," and who, as the days went by, was so very kind to her, and who, once, when she was standing beside him, laid his hand upon her hair, and said:

"What a little creature you are! One could toss you in his arms as easily as he could a child."

"Suppose you try," said a smooth, even-toned voice, just behind him, and the next moment Georgie appeared in view, her black eyes flashing, but her manner very composed and quiet.

After that, Roy did not touch Edna's hair, or talk of tossing her in his arms. Whatever it was which Georgie said to him with regard to Miss Overton,—and she did say something,—it availed to put a restraint upon his manner, and caused him to keep to himself any wishes he might have with regard to Edna. But he watched her when she went out, and when she came in, and listened to her voice when reading or singing to his mother, until there would, at times, come over him such a feeling of restlessness,—a yearning for something he could not define,—that he would rush out into the open air, or, mounting his swift-footed steed, ride for miles down the river road, until the fever in his veins was abated, when he would return to Leighton, and, if Georgie was there, sit dutifully by her, and try to behave as an engaged man ought to do, and get up a little enthusiasm for his bride elect. But whether he held Georgie's white jewelled hand in his, as he sometimes did, or felt her breath upon his cheek, as she leaned her beautiful head upon his breast in one of her gushing moods, he never experienced a glow of feeling like that which throbbed through every vein did "Brownie's" soft, dimpled hands by any chance come in contact with so much as his coat-sleeve, or "Brownie's" dress sweep against his feet when he was walking with her.

He did not ask himself whither all this was tending. He did not reason at all. He was engaged to Georgie; he fully intended to keep his engagement; he loved her, as he believed, but that did not prevent his being very happy in Miss Overton's society; and as the days went by he drifted farther and farther from his betrothed, who, with all her shrewdness, was far from suspecting the real nature of his feelings.

During all this time, no answer had come from Edna to Roy, who wrote again and again, until he grew desperate, and resolved upon a second visit to Aunt Jerry Pepper, hoping by bribe or threat to obtain some clue to Edna's whereabouts. This intention he communicated by letter to the worthy spinster, who replied:

"Don't for goodness' sake come here again on that business, and do let Edna alone. She nor no other woman is worth the powder you are wasting on her. If she don't answer your letter, and tell you she's in the seventh heaven because of your engagement, it's pretty likely she ain't thrown off her balance with joy by it. She didn't fancy that woman with a boy's name none too well when she saw her in Iona, and if I may speak the truth, as I shall, if I speak at all, it was what she overheard that person say to her brother about you and your mother's opinion of poor girls like her, that kept her from going to Leighton with the body, and it's no ways likely she'll ever go now, so long as the thing with the boy's name is there as mistress. So just let her alone and it will work itself out. Anyway, don't bother me with so many letters, when I've as much as I can do with my house-cleaning, and making over comforters, and running sausages.

"Yours to command,
"JERUSHA AMANDA PEPPER."

It was Roy's duty to feel indignant toward one who called his wife elect, "that thing with a boy's name," and he made himself believe he was, and styled her a very rude, impertinent woman, and then he thought of what she had said about Edna's disapproval of the match, and of Georgie's treatment of her in Iona, and that hurt him far worse than Miss Pepper's calling his betrothed "that thing with the boy's name."

What could Georgie have said or done to Edna? She had always seemed so kindly disposed toward the girl, and since their engagement had warmly seconded his plan of finding her, and bringing her home. Once he thought to speak to Georgie herself on the subject, but generously refrained from doing so, lest she should be pained by knowing there was any one who was not pleased with the prospect of her being his wife. But Georgie, who was not overscrupulous with regard to other people's property, found the letter on the library table, where he left it, and unhesitatingly read it through, and then that same afternoon took occasion, in Edna's presence, to ask Roy if he had heard from his sister yet, and to express herself as *so* sorry that they could not find where she was.

13*

"Poor little creature, so young and so childlike as she seemed when I saw her at Iona," she said, flashing her great eyes first upon Roy and then upon Miss Overton. "And so shy too of strangers. Why, I almost fancied that she was afraid of *me*, she was so timid and reserved, and possibly she was, for in my excitement I might have been a little brusque in my manner."

"I do not remember asking if you urged her to come here at that time," Roy said, thinking of Miss Pepper's letter, while Georgie, thinking of it too, replied without the least hesitation:

"Certainly, I did. I said all I could consistently say; but she was too sick to undertake the journey, and then she had a nervous dread of meeting Charlie's friends. I've since thought it possible that she was too much stunned and bewildered to know exactly what was said to her, or what we meant by saying it."

Georgie had made her explanation, and effectually removed from Roy's mind any unpleasant impression which Aunt Jerry's letter might have left upon it. And she was satisfied; for it did not matter *what* Edna thought of her; and still Georgie could not then meet the wondering gaze of the brown eyes fixed so curiously upon her; and she affected to be very much interested and occupied with a cap she was finishing for Mrs. Churchill, and did not look at Edna, who managed to escape from the room as soon as possible, and who, out in the yard, had recourse to her old trick of digging her heels into the gravel by way of relieving her feelings.

Roy made one effort more to win over Miss Pepper, but with so poor success that he gave the matter up for a time, and devoted himself to trying to get up a passion for his betrothed equal to that she felt for him, and to studying and enjoying Miss Overton, who became each day more bewildering and enjoyable for him, while to Mrs. Churchill she became more and more necessary, until both wondered how they had ever existed without her.

CHAPTER XXXVI.

ANNIE HEYFORD.

EARLY in November the Burtons went back to their city home on Madison Square; and Edna was looking forward to a long, delightful winter alone with Roy. But Georgie decreed it otherwise. It was of no use to be engaged, and not have her lover at her disposal when she wanted him; and so she kept up a continual siege, until Mrs. Churchill signified her willingness, and even her wish, to spend a portion of the winter in New York, where she could have the best of medical advice for her eyes, that being one of Georgie's strongest arguments. Roy had sold his house in Fifth avenue the year before; and, as the elegant residence far up-town, on which Georgie had fixed her mind, was not now available, he had a suite of rooms in that prince of hotels, the Worth House, where his mother could have all the luxuries and all the quiet of a private house, with none of its annoyances.

And thither, in December, he came with his mother, and Miss Overton, and his mother's waiting-maid. It was late in the afternoon when they arrived, and took possession of their handsome rooms looking out on Madison Square; and, as in duty bound, Roy called at once upon his bride elect, who lived not far away. She did not know of his arrival in town, and seemed surprised and a little flurried at seeing him.

She had not expected him for a week or more; and all through the interview she was confused and absent-minded; and her thoughts were less with her lover than with little Annie, who up in her room was waiting her return, and wishing so much that she could see the gentleman whom "sister" was to marry.

Georgie had never been in the habit of visiting Jersey City often; but she had gone there immediately after her return to town in November, and had felt shocked at the great change perceptible in Annie. It was not so much a wasting of the flesh as a spiritualization of the whole face, which shone, as the faces of angels are supposed to shine, and which looked as if its owner were already through with the things pertaining to earth, and was realizing the joys of heaven.

"Tired all the time,—that's all," Annie said, when Georgie bent over her and asked what ailed her darling.

"Tired,—so tired," was all the child complained of; but it was evident to those who knew her that she was rapidly passing away; and Georgie saw it too, and her tears fell like rain, as she sat by Annie's couch, and listened to her childish talk.

"And you are to be married, Georgie?" Annie said; "and Jack will be married, too; and he has brought Maude to see me; and I loved her so much right away; and I am glad for Jack. But, Georgie, mayn't I stay part of the time with you when you are married to Mr. Leighton? I should be so 'streemly happy there, seeing you every day."

There was something very pleading in the tone of the voice; and Georgie's lip quivered as she replied: "Yes, darling, you shall. I'll have a nice room fitted up next to mine, and I'll call it Annie's Room, and put so many pretty things in it."

And then, by way of amusing the child, Georgie told how

she would furnish that room which was to be Annie's, picturing such a fairyland that Annie's eyes shone like stars as she exclaimed, " It will be most as good as heaven, where I am going before long; but not till I've lived a little bit of a while in that splendid room. O Georgie, I don't want to die till I've been there. And you won't forget, will you?"

Then she talked of Roy, and asked Georgie to bring him there some day; and Georgie promised that she would, without meaning at all what she said. She was very morbid upon the subject of an interview between Annie and her lover, so long as he was her lover. Once his wife, she should not care so much, she thought; and she was really in earnest in thinking that Annie should spend a portion of the time with her. Roy knew there was such a child; that in some way she was connected with the family, and that she called Georgie her sister; but he had never evinced any special interest in her, and Georgie did not mean that he should until she chose to have him. So when Annie asked if she might go over to New York at once, and spend a few days at Mrs. Burton's, Georgie hesitated, and calculated the chances of Roy's coming to see her, deciding finally that she was safe, and promising Annie that she should go if Jack was willing. He was willing, and was more friendly and cordial with Georgie than he had been before since her engagement. He always liked her best when she was interested in Annie, and he assented readily to the visit; and Georgie appointed the next day to come for the little girl. But one of the sinking turns to which the child was subject came on to prevent the visit, which was deferred until December, when it at last occurred; and Annie had been a week with Georgie, and was intending to stop a few days longer, when Roy suddenly made his appearance, and the visit was at an end.

Georgie could scarcely define to herself why she dreaded so much to have Roy see her sister; and when she received his card, and knew he was waiting for her in the parlor below, her first impulse was to bring him up at once to her room, and have the interview over; but with that impulse there came a feeling that she could not stand by Roy and see him talking so kindly to Annie as he would, without suffering such pangs of remorse and anguish as she was not willing voluntarily to incur. And so she merely said to him, when he remarked that she looked pale and tired, "I am a little worn, I guess. I have had Annie, my adopted sister, you know, here for a week or more, and, as she is a great invalid, it has kept me closer in my room than was altogether for my health. How is your mother? And are you comfortable at the Worth House? Though of course you are. I went through the rooms the other day, and almost envied you. Such elegance, with so much of home-comfort, is not to be found elsewhere in New York, or, one may almost say, in the world,—such a gentlemanly host as the man in charge, and then the proprietor himself. I went down into the bookstore, to get some note-paper I did not want, for the sake of seeing him. One of his authors has styled him the 'Royal George,' and he is fully entitled to the name. I wish I knew him intimately. I must manage it somehow, if I have to write a book."

She was talking very fast, for the sake of driving all remembrance of Annie from Roy's mind; but the ruse did not succeed, for, as soon as she ceased, Roy proposed taking herself and Annie for a drive to the park.

"It will do you good," he said, "and the little sick girl too. I've never seen her, you know; and I would like to make the acquaintance of all my relatives."

He spoke playfully; and Georgie's face flushed for a moment with pleasure at his allusion to their projected marriage, then grew pale again and troubled, as she declined the invitation both for herself and Annie. The latter was not well enough to bear the ride, she said, (forgetting that she had promised to take her there that very afternoon,) while *she* felt it her duty to stay and amuse the child, who was so fond of her. And so, Roy, thinking how self-sacrificing she was, and liking her the better for it, bade her a more affectionate adieu than usual, and drove his mother and Edna to the park that afternoon, never dreaming of the bitter disappointment which filled poor Annie's heart, when told in Georgie's most honeyed tones that it would be impossible for her to fulfil the promise of a ride, as her head was aching so hard, and she felt too sick to go out.

The largest, handsomest doll on Broadway was bought next morning as a peace offering to Annie; and then, as Georgie found that she owed a call in Jersey City, and would pass directly by Jack's house, she suggested that Annie should go with her and see Aunt Luna, while she was making her call.

"You can come back with me if you like," she said, smoothing the silken hair, and thinking how she would manage to prevent the coming back, in case Annie took a fancy to do so.

But Annie did not; her own home and easy chair looked so pleasant to her, and Luna was so glad to have her back again, that she at once expressed a wish to stay, and Georgie bade her a loving good-by, and drove directly to the ferry, leaving the call which had existed only in her imagination unmade!

That night Georgie went to the opera with Roy and Miss Overton, and occupied the most conspicuous seat in the box, and was more admired and commented upon than any lady in the audience, as she sat flushed, and brilliant, and beautiful, with diamonds on her neck and arms, and in her flowing hair. Roy was sufficiently attentive, and, proud of her position as his betrothed, she carried herself regally, and felt a very queen, as, leaning on Roy's arm, she made her way through the crowd after the play was over.

Close behind her, as she emerged into the open air, came another figure,—the figure of a man, who, all through the play, had watched the glowing beauty, with a look upon his bad face, which, had Georgie seen it, would have driven her to the verge of insanity. But Georgie did not see it, or dream of the shadow following her so fast, just when her sky was brightest, and her triumph seemingly sure. She *did* think of Annie, however, when she reached her room, and saw the little bed where the child had lain, and the thinking of her kept her from praying, as was her nightly custom.

She could not pray with Annie's face before her, as it looked when told that the Park must be given up, and she lay awake a long time trying to quiet her conscience by thinking how much she would do for Annie when once she was Mrs. Roy Leighton, with no fear of anything either in the past or future. She did not go to see Annie as she had promised to do. Her time was *so* occupied with Mrs. Churchill and Roy, and all her fashionable duties, besides which Mrs. Burton was about to give a party, which, for costliness and elegance, was to surpass anything which had been or would be seen in New York that winter.

Maude, on whose taste and skill in many matters both Mrs. Burton and Georgie relied, had obtained a vacation of a few days, and was busy with Georgie's dress, which was made in the house, where the ladies could give it their hourly inspection if they chose. Edna, who was to be included in the invitations sent to the Worth House, was also eager, and expectant, and supremely happy in the beautiful gauzy fabric which Mrs. Churchill had presented to her, and which was made by a fashionable *modiste*. It would be her first introduction to New York society, as seen at a brilliant party, and though she dreaded it somewhat, she was looking forward to it with eager anticipations, and was frequently in earnest consultation with Maude, who, like herself, was flushed, and excited, and happy.

The cards were already issued, and but two days intervened before the appointed night, when Georgie suddenly appeared at the Worth House, and asked to see Miss Overton. She was very pale, and there were traces of great mental agitation and distress in her manner, as she proceeded at once to her errand. A note had just come from Jack, who wrote that Annie was dangerously ill, and desired to see Georgie as soon as possible, while he too joined in the sick child's request, and wished his sister to bring several little delicacies which he named, and which he could not well find in Jersey City.

"It is impossible for me to go, with my dress and everything in its present condition, and the party to-morrow night," Georgie said, "neither can I spare Maude, and as it does seem necessary that Jack should have some woman there besides Aunt Luna, I came to see if you would be kind enough to go over just for to-day. You can, of course, return to-morrow, when Annie will, I am sure, be better. Jack is easily frightened, and has, no doubt, exaggerated the case. Will you go, Miss Overton, if Mrs. Churchill can spare you?"

She was holding Edna's hand, and squeezing it affectionately; in fact, she had held and squeezed it ever since she commenced talking, and she was so urgent and anxious, that Edna consented, feeling a genuine pleasure in the prospect of seeing the little girl who had been her pupil for a short time, and in whom she had been so much interested.

"Thank you so much. You don't know how you have relieved me, for I know you will do everything that is necessary, and Mrs. Churchill says you are a capital nurse,"

Georgie said, kissing Edna twice, and promising to send the carriage round at once with the articles Jack had ordered.

Edna had never seen Annie since she left Chicago, and she got herself in readiness immediately, and in less than an hour was standing in Jack Heyford's house, and explaining to him why she had come instead of Georgie.

"Not coming! Sent you in her place?" he repeated, appearing more angry and excited than Edna had ever before seen him. "She is a hard, unnatural woman, and if Heaven lets her prosper, I shall lose my faith in everything I have been taught to respect," he said, grinding his teeth together as he uttered the words, which seemed almost like a curse upon the proud girl, who at that very moment was trying on her party dress, and calculating the effect upon her guests when she appeared before them in her costly and becoming robes.

Still she did not forget Annie, and all the day long there was a dull, heavy pain in her heart, and a foreboding of evil, which at last prompted her to tell Maude of the note from Jack, and to ask her as a favor to go herself to Jersey City, and bring news of the sick girl. It was the first Maude had heard of Annie's danger, and she opened her eyes wide with wonder and surprise, as she asked:

"Why not go yourself, Georgie? Not that I am unwilling, but Annie wants *you*. Neither Miss Overton nor myself will answer the purpose."

"I can't," Georgie replied. "I might ride over this evening, if I was sure of coming back, but once there, Annie and Jack both would insist upon my staying through the night, and you know just how loss of sleep affects my nerves and spirits."

"And looks," Maude added, sarcastically, knowing that this was the real key to the whole matter.

Georgie must be fresh and bright for the next evening's

party; Georgie could not afford to peril her beauty by nursing a sick child who wanted her, and so she made herself believe that there was no immediate danger threatening the little girl, and she staid at home, and sent Maude in her stead, with injunctions to pass the night, if necessary, but to send back a correct account of Annie's condition, and excuse her to Jack as far as practicable.

"More comfortable, but very sorry not to see you. I shall stay all night, as will Miss Overton, also. Please get word to Mrs. Churchill."

This was Maude's message, which Georgie read aloud to Roy, whose interest in Annie's illness arose more from the fact that it had taken and was keeping Miss Overton away; and, handsome and elegant as were his rooms at the Worth House, they were not quite the same without the hired companion.

"I hope Miss Overton will not think of sitting up to-night. She does not seem very strong, and I want her to be as fresh as possible for the party," he said, and his manner betrayed even more annoyance than his words.

There was a threatening look in Georgie's eyes, and a very little impatience in her voice, as she said:

"I suppose I ought to have gone myself, and so spared Miss Overton."

"Certainly not," Roy said, earnestly. "It is more to me that you should look your best, and watching is not conducive to that. I trust, however, that nothing will keep Miss Overton to-morrow."

He would persist in bringing in Miss Overton, and Georgie fumed with inward rage and hate of the girl at that very moment bending over Annie's couch, and wiping the moisture from the pale, damp forehead.

Annie was very sick; so sick indeed, that although she expressed pleasure at seeing Edna, she manifested no surprise and did not ask where she came from. Neither did she say much when told that Georgie had not come, but with a low, moaning cry she turned her face to the wall, while her body trembled with the sobs she tried to suppress. When Maude came she seemed better, and nestling close to her, laid her head upon her arm and appeared to sleep quietly.

And while she slept, or seemed to, Jack freed his mind with regard to Georgie's selfishness. It had always been so, he said. She had left to others what she ought to have done herself.

"Why, my mother, who was in no ways connected to Annie, did far more for her than Georgie, even when she lived at home," he said, and then the great blue eyes opened wonderingly, and fixed themselves upon Jack's face, while Annie said faintly:

"Your mother—not mine too,—Jack? Did you say that?"

Jack was in a hard, desperate mood, and reckless of consequences, he replied:

"I did say it. Your mother was a far different woman from mine."

"Oh, Jack," and Annie put both her hands beseechingly toward him. "Oh Jack, who was mother, then, and where is she now, tell me?" she cried, while Maude and Edna both looked up reprovingly, and the former said:

"How could you be so imprudent, Jack, and she so sick and weak?"

"Because I'm a brute, I suppose, and feel sometimes like blurting out things I must not say," Jack replied, as he tried to quiet Annie, who insisted upon knowing "who and where her mother was."

"Ask Georgie, she may tell you, but I cannot," Jack answered her at last, and with that reply Annie had to be satisfied.

Both Maude and Edna staid by her during the night, forgetful of their own fatigue, and scarcely giving a thought to the brilliant party of the next evening, or the worn, tired faces they would carry to it, provided they went at all, which seemed very doubtful, as the daylight came creeping into the room, and showed them the change in their patient. She was not dying; she might linger for two or three days longer, the physician said, when at sunrise he came, but there was the sign of death upon her face, and she lay perfectly motionless, only speaking occasionally to ask what time it was; if it was to-night the party was to take place, and if Georgie would surely come after it was over. Her absorbing thought was to see Georgie once more, or "sister," as she still called her, for the idea did not seem to have entered her mind that Georgie was not her sister, even though the kind woman whom she remembered well had not been her mother.

Once, as Maude started to leave the bedside for a moment, Annie grasped her hand and said to her:

"You won't go too and leave me; nor you?" turning an appealing glance at Edna, then quickly adding: "Yes, you must, you may; you want to see the party, and you'll tell how Georgie looked, and bring her back with you."

But neither Maude nor Edna had any heart for gay festivities then; that white face with the stamp of death upon it would be ever present in their minds, and each came simultaneously to the same conclusion. They could not leave Annie, and so a hasty note was written by Maude and despatched to Madison Square, saying that though Annie was not in immediate danger, neither Miss Overton nor herself could think of leaving her unless their services were absolutely required in New York. Would Georgie see Mrs. Churchill for Miss Overton, and if possible send word to Jersey if she was comfortable, and was willing to be left alone another day.

Georgie read this note in her own room, and when she saw that Annie was no worse, an involuntary, "Thank God!" dropped from her lips, while her next remark was, "I knew Jack was more alarmed than he need be,—he always is;" and then she was conscious of a mean feeling of relief that Edna was to be absent that evening. The girl was too beautiful and attractive not to be noticed and admired, while Roy was altogether too much interested in her; and Georgie ground her teeth together as she recalled certain looks she had seen him give to "that hypocrite."

Mrs. Burton was greatly disappointed that Maude was not coming back; she depended so much upon her, she said, to fill up the gaps and amuse all the dull, prosy people. But Georgie quieted her down, and promised to do her own part and Maude's too, then went herself to see Mrs. Churchill, who, in a different way, was quite as sorry about Edna as Mrs. Burton had been about Maude.

"She is anticipating so much, and her dress is so pretty, and she is so sure to be appreciated and admired, that I cannot bear to have her lose it all," she said, smoothing fondly the gauzy folds of the party dress, which had been sent home, and was spread out upon her bed.

Georgie was *so* sorry, too, and felt almost as if she must go herself to Jersey, and take Dotty's place, only Aunt Burton would not hear of it; and it *was* a great relief to know that Annie was being cared for by nurses as efficient and kind as Maude and dear Miss Overton; neither of whom should lose anything by their unselfish kindness.

This was what Georgie said, and her voice was sweet, and low, and sad, and she kissed Mrs. Churchill tenderly, and bade her come over early, and then tripped back to the house on Madison Square, where the preparations for the coming night were going rapidly forward.

CHAPTER XXXVII.

THE NIGHT OF THE PARTY.

ROY was not at home when Georgie came with the news of Edna's intended absence, and, when he heard it from his mother, he evinced more dissatisfaction even than she had done, and finally after lunch drove over to Jersey City, determined to bring Edna back.

She was surprised and glad to see him, and there was a flush on her cheek, and a soft light in her brown eyes, which in spite of her worn, tired look, made her very beautiful as she stood, with her hand in his, in the reception-room, listening to his anxious inquiries as to how she had passed the night, and his intention of taking her home with him."

"Oh, I cannot do that," she said. "I cannot leave Annie now. You don't know how sick she is, or you would not ask it."

"But surely there are others whose duty it is more than yours to forego their pleasure," Roy rejoined, and Edna answered:

"She has no relatives except Mr. Heyford and Miss Burton, and she, you know, cannot be here; and, as I will not leave Maude alone, I must stay. I am sorry, for I did anticipate the party a little, but I think I am doing right."

Roy thought so too, and involuntarily pressed the hand which Edna had all the time been quietly trying to withdraw from his grasp. He did not urge her further, nor ask to see Annie. He was not specially interested in the latter, save as he would be in any sick person: and just at that particular time he felt her to be rather a *bother*, and wondered why she need have been sick when he wanted Miss Overton at home.

"Don't say anything to alarm Miss Burton, please," Edna said to him as he was about to leave. "We know she cannot come now, but to-morrow morning we shall expect her sure."

. . . .

Rapidly the day passed to the inmates of No. — Madison Square, where all was bustle and excitement, and eager anticipation; and rapidly, too, passed the day at No. — in Jersey City, where Jack, and Maude, and Edna watched the death-sign creeping slowly upon the face of the dying child.

All the afternoon she lay in a kind of stupor, never moving or speaking, except occasionally to utter Georgie's name; but about dark there came a change,—a great restlessness, with a continual asking for sister and mother.

"Oh! where and who was she? How shall I know her in heaven if I never saw her here? How did she look? Tell me, Jack, was my mother beautiful?" she asked, and Jack replied:

"Yes, damnably beautiful."

The last was under his breath, and Annie only heard the first word, and asked again:

"Beautiful as Georgie, Jack?"

A suppressed groan was Jack's only reply as he paced up and down the room, whispering to himself:

"Oh! why am I thus punished for *her* sin? It has been so always. I have suffered, and she has escaped. Is that just or right?"

He was questioning Heaven's dealings with himself, when suddenly there flashed into his mind the words, "Vengeance is mine; I will repay, saith the Lord," and he paused quickly in his walk, with a half shudder, as he thought how far from him was the wish for vengeance to overtake the woman who had sinned, and for whom he had borne so much,—ay, and for whom he was ready and willing to bear more, if need be.

He would not harm a hair of that beautiful head, and, with a softer look upon his face, he went to Annie's side, and soothed and quieted her until she fell asleep, resting this time for half an hour or more. Then the restlessness returned, accompanied with moments of delirium, in which she called piteously for Georgie to hold her aching head.

"Her hands are so soft and cool, and rest me so, and I love her so much. Go to her, Jack; tell her to come; tell her Annie is dying, and wants to see her again. She said I should have the nice room when she was married to Mr. Leighton, and I wanted to live so bad, and asked Jesus would He let me; but I'm willing now, only I must see Georgie first."

Thus she talked on until the clock was striking seven, and the attending physician came in. He saw at once that she was dying, and as he listened to her plaintive pleadings for Georgie, he said to Jack:

"If this Georgie can be reached, my advice is to reach her."

Jack hesitated a moment, glanced at the white, wasted form upon the bed, and then thought of the house on Madison Square, ablaze with light by that time, and of the brilliant woman who was undoubtedly decking herself in her fairest garb for the occasion, and whose black eyes would flash so angrily, perhaps, should he go for her then.

"I can't, I can't," he thought; but when the voice, fainter now than when it spoke before, said again, "Has Jack gone for Georgie?" he went to her and whispered: "Darling, I am going."

"And you won't come back without her? Promise, Jack."

"No, I won't come back without her; I swear it to you, Annie. I'll bring her, or not come myself."

One kiss he pressed upon the white face, feeling that it

might be the last, and then rushing swiftly down the stairs, and out into the street, he hailed the first car which passed, and was on his way to Madison Square.

. . . .

Georgie was dressed at last; every fold and flower, and curl, and jewel was in its place, and she stood before her mirror, flushed with pride and excitement, and thinking within herself that few that night could compete with her in beauty, even if the first freshness of youth was gone, and her face did show signs of maturity. Had Miss Overton been there, Georgie felt that she might have had a rival, for there was a wonderful power about the fair young girl to charm and fascinate. But she was away, across the river, doing what Georgie should have done; and when Georgie remembered that, she felt a pang of remorse, and wondered how Annie was, and said to herself, with a shudder,

"What if she should die to-night! I never could get over it."

There was a knock at the door, and the maid, who had left her a few moments before, handed her Jack's card. The bright color faded in an instant from Georgie's cheeks, as she felt what Jack's presence there at that time portended, and she leaned against her dressing-table heavily, as she said:

"Tell him I will see him here."

The girl departed with the message, and Georgie had time in which to recover herself a little before Jack entered the room. She could not go then, whatever might be the import of his errand, she had decided before he came in; but she moved rapidly toward him, and asked:

"What is it, Jack? is Annie dead? Tell me quick,—the suspense is horrible!"

"No, not dead, but dying, and keeps asking for you. So I came, though sorely against my will, and I have sworn not to return without you. Will you go!"

There was a sharp ring in his voice which exasperated Georgie, but she put the feeling aside, and answered him:

"How can I go? You know it is impossible." Then, as the realities of her position began to impress themselves more and more upon her, she wrung her hands in genuine distress, and cried: "Oh, why am I tortured so; I wish I had died years ago. What made you come here now, when you know I cannot go?"

She turned almost fiercely upon him, as if he had been in fault, but he met her eyes unflinchingly, and replied:

"I told you Annie was dying; that is why I came. I shall not go back without you."

"Then you must wait," she rejoined. "It is almost time for the guests to come; I must be here to receive them. Maybe she will revive. Doctors do not always judge aright. She may yet recover, or, at least, live for days."

"I tell you she was dying when I left her, else I had not come, knowing you as I do," Jack replied vehemently, and Georgie answered with a gush of tears:

"I *cannot* go until the party is over. Come for me then; come at two o'clock, and I will be ready."

He bowed in acquiescence and left the house, meeting, as he went out, a group of ladies, whose gay dresses brushed against him on the steps, and whose light laughter sounded like mockery in his ears. It was a glorious night, and the *élite* of New York turned out *en masse* to honor Mrs. Burton's invitation, until the rooms were full, and the light jest and merry repartee were heard on every side, and the gay dance began to the sound of sweet music. And amid it all moved Georgie, a deep flush on her cheek, and a glittering light in her eye, which attracted general attention, and was the subject of much comment among the guests. It was an insane, delirious kind of look, and Georgie *was* nearly mad, as with a heart full of bitter pain she tried to be natural, and smile upon those around her as sweetly and pleasantly as if there was no skeleton of death walking at her side, and pointing, with its bony fingers, across the distant river to where Annie lay dying and begging for her. She could hear the little voice even above the din of the gay throng, and when Roy asked what was the matter that she seemed so absent-minded, she felt for a moment as if she must shriek out her miserable secret before them all, and tell them of that little child in Jersey. She had spoken of her to many of the guests, and explained the cause of Maude's absence, but none of those who heard her guessed of the mental agony endured by the beautiful woman who was envied by so many, as the bride-elect of Roy Leighton, and the possessor of everything which can make one happy.

The party was over at last; every guest had said goodnight, and only one carriage stood before the door. That had waited there an hour, and while it waited the lights flashed out into the darkness, the soft music sounded on the night air, and the merry feet kept time in the dance; the driver nodded on his box, and the tall figure of a man walked up and down; up and down,—always to the same lamp-post and back,—a worn, anxious look upon his face, and an impatient, resentful expression in his eyes whenever he glanced up at the blazing windows, and then consulted his watch.

Jack had broken his vow not to return home without his sister. He had tried waiting at the hotel; had sat an hour and could have sworn it was ten; then with a feeling that he must know how it fared with Annie, had re-crossed the ferry and gone to his home.

"Still alive, but failing fast, and asking for Georgie," Maude had said to him, and then he waited another hour and a half until the clock struck twelve.

Georgie had said "come at two," and so he went, and

waited until the last carriage drove away, and then his hand was on the door before the tired servant could lock and bolt it.

"Did you leave anything, sir?" the man asked, thinking Jack one of the recent guests.

"No; I came for Miss Burton. Say her brother is here," Jack replied; but before the message could be delivered Georgie was standing by him and had heard the message: "Alive, but dying very fast. You have no time to lose."

And Georgie lost none. Speeding upstairs to her room she caught up a long water-proof, and wrapping it around her, said to her astonished maid:

"Tell mamma that Annie Heyford is dying; that my brother Jack came for me before the party, and I promised to go as soon as it was over. She must not be troubled about me. I shall come back or send some word in the morning."

"But your dress, Miss Burton! Surely, you will change that?" the girl said, thinking her young mistress demented.

It was the first thought Georgie had given to her dress, and with a shudder, as she drew up the folds of her elegant costume, she answered:

"I have not time to change it now. I told you she was dying."

And so with the diamonds glittering on her neck and arms and shining in her hair, Georgie went out to the carriage, where Jack put her in, his impatience and resentment beginning to subside when he saw the deep pallor of her face and the look of anguish in her eyes. Her head was uncovered, and the flowers she had worn were there still, but Jack drew the hood of her water-proof up over her hair, and adjusted it under her chin with a carefulness and gentleness which brought a gush of tears from Georgie, who had laid her head upon his shoulder, and said sobbingly:

"You are kind, Jack; I don't deserve that you should think of my comfort."

He did not reply, and the silence between them was not broken again until Jersey City was reached. There had been a delay at the ferry, and it was nearer four than three when Georgie stood at last by Annie's bedside.

She had thrown off her water-proof as she entered the house, or rather handed it to Maude, who met her in the hall, and who stared in surprise at the gay party dress, which seemed so out of place in that house of death. But for once Georgie never thought of her dress, nor minded in the least when her flowing lace caught on some projection and had a long rent torn in it. And so, in all the splendor of diamonds, and satins, and flowers, she floated into the sick room where Annie lay, breathing heavily, but with a look of peace upon her face, which told that for her all pain had ceased, except as it might return when the final struggle came. She had not asked for Georgie for more than an hour, but the instant the rustle of her sweeping garments, and the sound of her step was heard, she opened her eyes and exclaimed joyfully:

"Georgie, sister, come at last."

"Yes, darling; here at last, never to leave you again," Georgie said, as, stooping down, she gathered the little wasted form to her bosom and held it there, while she cried over and kissed it passionately, murmuring words of fond endearment such as made Edna, who was in the room, look up in surprise. She had not imagined Georgie to be capable of the deep feeling she was manifesting, and she felt a thrill of friendly liking for the woman who could so love a little child.

"I wanted you so much," Annie said, faintly, as she put her hand on Georgie's cheeks, "I am going to die,—Jack told you, maybe,—and I'll never be in that pretty room you said you'd fix for me; but I want you to fix it all the same, and call it Annie's room, and, if I can, I'll come sometimes to see you. You won't hear me, or know it, perhaps, but I guess it will be when the sun is the brightest, and the flowers are blooming, and you are thinking of Annie; then I'll be there with you."

A cold shudder ran from the crown of Georgie's head to her finger tips as she listened to Annie's plan of re-visiting her in the spirit, but she only replied with a closer embrace and a rain of tears, which Annie brushed away as she continued:

"I ain't a bit afraid to die now, Georgie. I was at first, but I asked Jesus so many times to take the fear away, and He has, and forgave me all the naughty things I ever did,— the lies I used to tell, and the exaggerations, which Jack said were bad as lies; and I'm going to Heaven, where you'll come some time, sister, won't you?"

"Oh, Annie, my darling, my darling, I don't know; I am afraid not. Heaven is not for such as I am," Georgie cried, piteously, while Annie continued:

"Why, sister? yes it is; and you are real good, and you'll come some day, and find me waiting for you right by the door; but, Georgie,"—and Annie's lip began to quiver as there suddenly recurred to her mind the perplexing question which had troubled her so a few hours before, and which Jack had said Georgie might answer,—"but, Georgie, lay me down, please; on the pillow, so,—that's nice; and now tell me where is my mother,—if Jack's and your mother was not mine."

The great blue eyes of the child were fixed intently upon Georgie, who started and staggered backward as if smitten with a heavy blow. Edna had stolen from the room, and only Jack was there, sitting in a distant corner. To him Georgie turned quickly, and asked, under her breath:

"What does this mean? Who has been disturbing her?"

"It was the merest accident," Jack said, coming forward at once. "A chance remark I made about her not being mother's own child. *Your secret* is safe, if that is what you fear."

He said the last in a low tone, and then walked back to his seat upon the sofa. For a few moments Annie lay quiet, and Georgie hoped she might have forgotten that her question was unanswered, but she soon roused up and returned to the subject so painful to Georgie.

"How will I know my mother if I never saw her here, and don't know how she looks nor who she was?" she said, and her eyes held as by a spell poor remorseful Georgie's, who faltered out:

"Your mother is not in Heaven, Annie."

"Not in Heaven?" and the paroxysm of terror was something fearful to witness as Annie writhed upon her pillow. "Where is she then? Not in the bad place? Not there? My mother! Oh Georgie, oh Georgie."

Every word was a moan as the frightened child clutched Georgie's hand and demanded of her whether her mother was lost forever. She did not seem to remember that she must have had a father, too; it was all "my mother, my mother," until Georgie could bear it no longer, and said to her in a whisper:

"Your mother is not dead. She is living somewhere."

"Then why don't she come to see me? Mothers always take care of their sick little girls, don't they?" Annie asked, and Jack, who could see the anguish written on his sister's face, pitied her as he had never done but once before in his life.

"Oh, Annie, you break my heart; don't ask me about your mother. I cannot, cannot tell. Oh, Father in Heaven, this is worse than death," Georgie moaned, as she knelt upon the floor by Annie's bed and covered her face with her hands.

But amid her pain she did not forget to be cautious, and said to Jack, "Please shut the door. I cannot have witnesses to my degradation."

He did as she bade him, and then said to her: "Had you been open, Georgie, from the first, this would have been spared to you."

Perhaps he was wrong to chide her then when her cup of wretchedness was full. She thought so at least, and replied to him:

"Don't taunt me now; don't try to make my agony greater than it is. I could not bear another jot. And, Jack, let me tell you, that truly as I live, there's nothing I would not do to save Annie's life."

"Nothing?" Jack said, questioningly.

His tone roused Georgie to such an unnatural state that she replied to him: "No, nothing; and here I swear that if Heaven will spare Annie's life and give her back to me, I'll tell Roy everything. Yes, everything. I mean it. Father in Heaven, hear me, hear the vow I make. Give me Annie's life and I'll tell everything. Try me and see."

She was praying now, while Annie, bewildered by what she had heard, looked first at her and then at Jack, saying imploringly:

"Tell what, Georgie? What does it mean? It makes me so dizzy and faint. Is it about my mother, and why she don't come when I am dying?"

There was no response to this, and Annie pleaded again:

"Where is she, Jack? Don't she love me any? Oh if I could see her once and hear her voice, and put my head in her lap, and call her mother, I'd pray to Jesus to make her good and let her come to Heaven if she was ever so bad. Was she bad, Georgie? Was my mother naughty?"

It was a strange spectacle, that white-faced, dying child, stretching her trembling hands toward that gayly-decked, but crushed, stricken woman, and demanding some knowledge of her mother, and Georgie shrunk back from the touch of the little hands, and wiped the sweat-drops from her own pallid face, and turned toward Jack as if for help in her distress. But Jack was powerless then; it was her hour of agony and she must meet it alone.

Suddenly there broke over her countenance a light as of some newly-formed resolution, and with a gasp she said to her brother:

"Go out, Jack, please, and leave us here alone. Keep them all away till I call to you to come. Annie is mine, now; mine; all mine."

She seemed more like a crazed creature, when, after Jack was gone, she bolted the door, and even looked out into the wintry night, as if fearing listeners there. But she grew calm again, and her voice, though low and sad, was tolerably steady in its tone as she sat down by Annie and said:

"Ask me anything you please, and I will answer you."

. . . .

Half an hour passed away, and the three waiting below heard the low murmur of voices,—one of surprise and eager inquiry, the other, mournful, heartbroken, and, as Jack knew, full of bitter shame. Then there was a sound of sobbing, with broken sentences of love, and then another silence, followed by a hasty call for Jack to come quickly.

They were in the room in a moment, and each one was struck with the expression of Annie's face, where wonder and surprise, sorrow and compassion, with love unutterable, were blended together. Tender and pitiful as is a mother towards her suffering child, she seemed toward Georgie, and though she could not speak, her eyes were fastened upon the head bowed down at her side, and her hands kept caressing the tangled curls which lay upon the bedclothes.

"Annie, you are almost home," Maude said, bending over her and kissing her white brow.

Annie nodded and raised her eyes once upon them all, as if in a farewell; then her head drooped lower and lower upon her breast; while her hand still smoothed and fondled Georgie's hair. A moment went by which seemed an hour, then over the dying child there passed a shudder of pain; the hand ceased its caressing motion, and buried itself in the mass of hair; the eyes glanced upward, and the quivering lips said, brokenly, "Thank you, Jesus, I have seen my mother," and then Annie was dead.

Old Luna, who was present, responded, "Yes, blessed lamb, no doubt her mother did come to meet her. It's apt to be the case."

This was Luna's solution of Annie's last words, while Maude had a different one; and when they were alone and Edna said to her, "Do you believe Annie's mother was with her when she died?" She answered, "*I know* she was!"

CHAPTER XXXVIII.

AFTER ANNIE'S DEATH.

MRS. BURTON had been greatly distressed at the account given her by the servant of Miss Georgie's going off in her party dress, without so much as telling her, and naturally enough felt a very little annoyed with the cause of her pet's anxiety.

"That child will be the death of Georgie," she said to her husband; and when he asked, "Who is she, any way, and what is she to Georgie?" she hardly knew what to reply, for she did not herself know just what Annie was to Georgie. "Not much, any way, second or third cousin," she guessed; and then she bemoaned Georgie's kind, tender, affectionate nature, which made her love everything young and helpless. She should go over in the morning herself, she said: and accordingly, as early as nine o'clock, she started for Jersey City, with a box of clothing for Georgie, who, with her water-proof wrapped around her uncovered shoulders, sat by the couch of the dead child, with a strange stony look upon her face, and in her red, swollen eyes.

She had not shed a tear since Annie died, and her own hands had made the little form ready for the grave.

"Don't touch her; she is mine; I will do all myself," she had said, almost fiercely, to Aunt Luna, when she first came in to care for the body.

She had also rejected Maude's and Edna's offers of assistance, and they had left her alone with her dead, and her own bitter thoughts, which nearly drove her mad, as she washed the little hands, and remembered when she had first felt their touch, and the thrill that touch had sent through every nerve. Then they were warm and soft, and she could have crushed them in her palm. Now they were cold and stiff, and she kissed them passionately, and drew the dainty white sleeves over the wasted arms, and combed, and brushed, and curled the silken hair, and felt glad that death had not robbed Annie of her beauty, as she finally laid her upon the couch, and then sat down beside her, unmindful that her rich dress was soiled and defaced, and her lace torn in more places than one. She took the tea and toast Jack brought her, because she knew he would insist until she ate, but she would not leave the room, and Mrs. Burton found her there, and called her a "poor dear," and wondered at her grief, and felt half glad that the child was gone at last out of Georgie's reach.

"I shall stay here till after the funeral," she persisted, in replying to her aunt's entreaties for her to go back to New York; and when Mrs. Burton asked where Annie was to be buried, she answered, "In Greenwood, of course."

"Has your brother a lot there?" was Mrs. Burton's next question; and Georgie replied:

"No, but he can have."

And after her aunt was gone she went to her brother, and giving him a costly diamond ring, said to him:

"It is my right and wish to bury Annie, and bear the whole expense. Convert the ring into money and see to it for me. I want her laid in Greenwood."

"In any particular spot?" Jack asked; and Georgie answered him:

"Yes, there's a vacant spot near *his* grave. It has been there for years."

Jack bowed, and turned away so as not to see the hot blushes on his sister's face as she gave her orders for Annie's burial.

That night Roy came himself to take Edna home. He was very sorry for Georgie, but, like Mrs. Burton, wondered at her love and grief for the little child.

"I would like to see the body. Can I?" he asked, and Georgie rose at once, and went with him into the darkened room where Annie lay.

Carefully, gently, she put back the thin covering, and then stood by Roy's side while he looked upon the child.

"She must have been very beautiful in life; and there is a look on her face like you," he said to Georgie, noticing for the first time how she shook as if in an ague chill. "You are sick; you have taken cold; this must not be," he said, and he put his arm around her to lead her from the room.

But she held back, and laying one hand on the pale, dead face, grasped Roy's shoulder with the other, and exclaimed:

"Not yet, Roy; wait a moment, please; hear me first; let me—"

He did not believe she knew at all what she was saying, and he cut her short and drew her forcibly away, just as she had, with a mighty effort, nerved herself to tell him *why* she had loved that little lifeless form so well.

"I meant to, I meant to, and he would not hear me. Surely it is not wrong to withhold it now," she said to herself, when Roy had taken her from the room; and then came a sense of relief that, after all, he did not know, and she never need to tell. "Had she lived I would have kept my vow, but now I am free from it," she thought, and there was a brighter look upon her face, and she moved about the house more like her olden self, but Maude, who watched her closely, saw that she shuddered every time Roy spoke pityingly to her, and that she seemed glad when at last he started for home, taking Edna with him.

The funeral was the next day, and Mrs. Burton came over in her carriage, and Roy came in his, bringing Edna and his mother with him. For once Georgie put fashion aside, and shocked her aunt by announcing her intention to go herself to Greenwood.

It was in vain that Mrs. Burton tried to dissuade her from it. She was determined, and the lady finally gave it up, and said she would go too, and take Mrs. Churchill and Edna in her carriage, suggesting that Roy go with Georgie, and Jack with Maude. And so it came about that Roy went as one of the chief mourners to Annie's grave, and while the coffin was lowered in the ground, and he stood near with uncovered head, he glanced, by accident, at the tall head-stone beside him, and read upon it:

"Richard Le Roy. Born in England, Jan. 5, 18—. Died in New York, Oct. 10, 18—. Blessed are the dead who die in the Lord."

Roy read it twice, and thought within himself, "I never knew before where Dick was buried. He was a pretty good fellow after all, but I *don't* believe he 'died in the Lord.'" And then Roy fell to wondering how many inscriptions upon tombstones were true, and in so doing failed to see how white and faint Georgie was, and how she trembled as she passed that grave on her way back to the carriage. It was a strange combination of things, Roy Leighton and Georgie Burton standing together with Annie's grave between them, and Richard Le Roy's just behind, but only two of the spectators knew *how* strange, and these gave no sign as they turned away and left the dead to their dreamless slumbers.

. . . .

The remainder of the winter was passed by Georgie very quietly and soberly. She was not well, and did not care to go out, she said, and she declined all invitations to large parties, and staid mostly at home or at the Worth House, with Mrs. Churchill, who liked her in this subdued mood better than ever before. She never spoke of Annie, but she seemed a good deal changed, and was really kind to Edna, except at times, when Roy's attentions in that quarter were a little too marked to suit her. Then her black eyes would blaze with a look which threatened harm to Miss Overton, who nevertheless enjoyed herself thoroughly, and passed a most delightful winter. Roy was very kind to her, and it had soon become known to his acquaintance that the pretty young lady seen with him so often in public was more of an equal to and friend of his mother, than a mere hired companion; and she was always included in the frequent invitations which came to the Leightons for dinners, and receptions, and parties, while it was a kind of mania with Mrs. Churchill to have her favorite dressed becomingly, and go with Roy, even when she was obliged to remain at home. And so in a certain way Miss Overton became a belle, and was sought after and courted and admired almost as much as Georgie herself.

Had she been an heiress, not fifty Georgies could have competed with her; but, being poor, she had this advantage, that the attentions of the male sex never became so serious as to require a check, and so she enjoyed it all, and to Roy seemed to grow more and more beautiful every day, while he even found himself at last growing jealous of the young men who surrounded her in such numbers the moment she entered a room; and he was glad when, toward the last of April, his mother signified her wish to go back to Leighton. Edna was glad, too, of the change; for she was pining for country air, and wanted so much to spend a few more delicious weeks at Leighton before she left it forever.

The wedding had finally been arranged by Mrs. Burton to take place in June, and as Mr. Burton had said that Maude should be married at the same time, and not have "two fusses," it was to be a double bridal, and take place at Oakwood, whither the Burtons removed about the time that Roy came back to Leighton.

CHAPTER XXXIX.

MAUDE AND EDNA VISIT UNCLE PHIL.

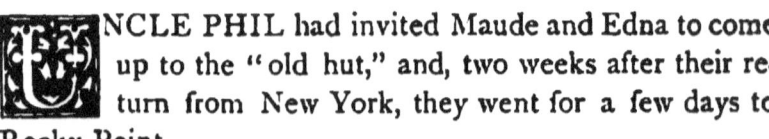UNCLE PHIL had invited Maude and Edna to come up to the "old hut," and, two weeks after their return from New York, they went for a few days to Rocky Point.

They found the old man not much changed from what he had been when they saw him last. A little stouter, perhaps, and a little grayer he looked, as, whip in hand, he stood waiting the arrival of the train, his face all aglow with delight, when the two young girls appeared upon the platform, looking so pretty and stylish in their new spring dresses, that he involuntarily gave a kind of low whistle, and said under his breath :

"Guy, ain't they stunners? They beat Ruth Gardner all hollow. And look at that gal's ankles, will you; it's enough to make a chap older than I am crawl, to see such things," he continued, as the tops of Maude's boots became visible in her descent from the car.

In a moment both the girls had caught him round the neck, making him very red in the face, and "awful ticklish at the pit of his stomach," as they kissed him more than once, and then kept hold of his hands while they asked him scores of questions.

"There,—there; yes, yes; let me be now, can't you; yes, yes," he said. "I'm about strangled with your hugs and kisses, and I not used to it, and the folks in the car lookin' on. It'll give a feller the dyspepsia to have his digester so riled up. These your traps, hey? Look like little housen; shall have to come back for 'em sure, for Bobtail can't carry all creation" he continued, as Maude pointed out her own and Edna's baggage.

Uncle Phil was very proud of his guests and very desirous to show them off, and making an excuse to see a man about re-setting a light of stained glass which some "tarnal boy had broken in one of the windows of his synagogue," he drove the entire length of the street on which 'Squire Gardner lived, and felt repaid for his trouble when he saw Miss Ruth looking at them from her chamber window. He did not find his man, but "Ruth saw the gals and the gals' *hats*, which he was so glad were not such all-fired lookin' things as she wore and tried to make folks think was the fashion. Maybe 'twas with a certain class, but needn't tell him that fust cut, who knew what was what, wore such 'bominable things. Why, Ruth's hat looks jest like a tunnel with a ribbon tied 'round it," he said to the young ladies, who accused him of having set up as a critic in dress; Maude promising to show him some fashions, "which would make him stare more than Ruth Gardner's tunnel had done."

They found the nicest, cosiest tea waiting for them, and Aunt Becky was quite as much pleased to see them as Uncle Phil had been. The front chamber was in perfect order, and Uncle Phil had tried his hand at a bouquet, made from daffodils and evergreens, and arranged in a broken pitcher.

They had come to spend a week, and the days flew rapidly, each one seeming to Uncle Phil shorter and happier than the preceding one. He had a great deal to tell them about his church, which was nearly completed, and would be ready for consecration in August, when the bishop had promised to be there.

"But I tell you what 'tis, gals," he said, as he sat with them inside the church, which he had been showing them, "if there's anything makes a chap feel like cussin', it's buildin' a meetin' house, and seein' to it yourself; not that I do swear right out loud," he added, as he saw Edna's look of surprise. "I hold on till I git the hiccups, and feel at my stomach some, as I do when you two are haulin' me over, only not quite so—so—tural-lural, you know; first, thar's the Orthodox pitchin' into me, and the Unitarians, who kind of claim me, you know; and then, if you'll b'leeve it, the Second Adventists held some meetin's in the school-house, and pitched right and left into my poor little chapel; called it one of the *ten horns*, and a *ritual*, and the Lord knows what; but the wust of all was the divinity chap from New York, who came out here, and preached a spell last winter; sort of a candidate, though he sniffed high at the idee, and said he'd never stoop to that. He preached in the Town Hall, and Ruth Gardner came up from New York, where she spent a month, with her head fuller of jimcracks than brains, and she jined the Episcopals, and helped run the machine, and rolled her eyes up till you could see nothin' but the whites, and got after the minister, and set to callin' him 'Father,' when, bless my soul, he wasn't a half-a-dozen years older than she ! And between 'em they raised the very old Harry with their processions, and boys dressed like girls, and flags, and crossin's, and curtcheys, which they called *Jenny*-something, and the land knows what they didn't do or would have done if I hadn't raised a row, and said they could do what they liked in the Town Hall, and go to the old driver with their flummeries, but in *my* synagogue I'd have no such carryin's on. I was a miserable enough sinner, and was willin' to own it, and had done a lot of things I didn't orto have done, and when I went to meetin, I wanted to hear now an' then a word about that Man who died over on Calvary a good many years ago, and not all about *the church, the church,* and the *fathers,* and the *medival* age. You orto have seen how the priest and Ruth Gardner looked at me when I got right up in meetin' and spoke my piece, for, I vum, I couldn't stan it when they give the bread and wine first to widder Jones's two little boys, the wust scamps in town, who rob gardens, and orchards, and birds'-nests in the summer, and who, only the day before, had broke my gate, and denied it up hill and down. I couldn't keep still no how, and freed my mind and quit, and the next day the priest and Ruth called on me,— he in his long frock coat, and she with a chain and cross as long as my arm, I'll bet. They as't me what I *did* believe, and I said I believed the Creed, word for word; and the Bible, and the Prayer-Book ; and more than all the rest, I believed in the Man that died; and I knew He never had any such goin's on in that upper chamber, nor on the deck of the ship, nor up on the mountain, nor in that house in Bethany where He loved to stay. Everything with Him was simple and plain as A B C. When the folks was tired, and sick, and sorry, He said, 'Come to me and rest,' and He didn't drive 'em crazy with forty-'leven ceremonies. 'Come to *me;* believe on me, that I can save you; that is all,' and He will. I'm just as certain as that my name is Philip. I'm a wicked old rat, but I do mean to be better; and I've took to readin' my Bible some, and I say the Lord's Prayer every night when I ain't too sleepy."

He was talking more to himself now than to the girls at his side, but they both felt that though there was still much of poor sinful nature clinging to the old man, he was making an effort to do better, and was drawing nearer to Him whom he so touchingly spoke of as the "Man who died."

The building of the church had evidently been a great trouble to him, but that was nearly over now.

The priest from New York had, soon after Uncle Phil's "piece spoken in meetin'," given up Rocky Point in disgust, and returned to the city, leaving the field clear for another man. That man Uncle Phil was anxiously looking out for, as he said he meant to have things in running order as soon as the house was consecrated.

It was a very pretty little edifice, and did credit to the good taste of Uncle Phil, or his architect, or both. As yet he had no name for it. Neither *St. Maude* nor *St. Edna* would do, and *St. Philip*, which both girls proposed, sounded too egotistical.

"He wasn't a saint," he said, "and never should be, perhaps, and they must try again."

Then he asked, in a kind of indifferent way, the name of the church at Allen's Hill, where Edna had formerly attended. *St. Paul's* suited him better, and he guessed "he'd have it christened after that curis chap who had that thorn in the flesh."

The next day when alone with Edna, he said to her:

"I kind o' hoped at one time that you or Maude might be married first in my new church, but she tells me there's to be great doin's at Oakwood for her and that girl, George, who, it seems, is to marry Roy, when I'd picked him for you."

"For me?" and Edna's cheeks were scarlet. "Roy would never think of me, and, Uncle Phil, I want to tell you I can't stay there after Miss Burton comes. I made up my mind to that a long time ago."

"Of course not," Uncle Phil replied. "One house can't hold three wimmen, so come back to the old hut as soon as you please.; there's always a place for you here. I shall be down to the weddin', I s'pose; I promised Maude I would, only you mustn't try to put gloves on me, nor stick me into a swallow-tail."

Edna laughingly promised to let him have his own way in dress, and two days after this conversation she said good-by to the old man, and, with Maude, went back to Summerville, where the preparations for the great event had commenced in earnest.

CHAPTER XL.

GETTING READY FOR THE BRIDAL.

ONLY once since Annie's death had Maude and Edna spoken together of the suspicion, amounting almost to a certainty, which had come to them both as they watched Georgie Burton at Annie's bedside. Then they had talked freely, and settling one point as a fact, had wondered *when*, and *where*, and *who*, and had both repelled the worst charge which can be brought against a woman. Annie had been born in wedlock, they fully believed; but if so, why so much reticence and mystery, they asked each other; and did Roy know, or would he ever know the truth?

"Somebody ought to tell him, and I've half a mind to do it myself," Maude said; but Edna advised her to keep her own counsel, as after all they knew nothing certainly.

Whatever Georgie might have been, she was greatly improved since Annie's death, and even the servants at Oakwood noticed how kind and gentle she was to every one around her. She did not visit Leighton as much as usual, and there was in her manner towards Roy a reserve, which became her better than her former gushing style. And still Roy was not satisfied, and often wondered at the feeling of *ennui* he experienced in her society, and the satisfaction he felt when he found her, as he frequently did, suffering from headache, and unable to see him, leaving him free to go back to Miss Overton, who never wearied him, but seemed always fresh and new. Before he left New York he had been a great deal with her, and he knew in his heart that the hours he enjoyed most were those spent alone with "Brownie" after his mother had retired. He had no intention of proving false to Georgie, and he did not stop to consider the wrong he was doing both to his bride-elect and Edna, until his mother gently hinted to him that possibly he might be doing harm by so much attention to Miss Overton. Though nearly blind, she could judge pretty well of what was passing around her, and could feel just how anxious and expectant Edna was when Roy was not present, and how flushed and excited and gay she became the moment he appeared, and she raised a warning voice, and said it was not fair to Georgie, that he ought to stay more with her, and less with Miss Overton.

"Had you chosen Dotty first," she said, using the pet name which she had caught from Maude, and adopted as her own. "Had you chosen Dotty, I do not think I should have objected, for the girl is very dear to me; but you took Georgie, and now I would have you deal honorably with her, and not give her any cause for complaint, and, above all, I cannot have Dotty harmed."

She spoke more for Edna than for Georgie, and Roy saw it, and wondered if it were true that Brownie cared for him, or could have cared, if there had been no Georgie in the way. There was perfect bliss for a moment in the thought that she might have been won, and then, good, honest, true-hearted man that he was, he said to himself:

"I have no right to lead her into temptation; no right to run into it myself; I am bound to Georgie. I will keep my vow, and keep it well, and Brownie shall not be the sufferer."

After that there were no more interviews alone, no more hours by the piano, or reading aloud to her from the books they both liked best. Georgie had him all to herself, and if ever man tried to get up enthusiasm for another, Roy tried to do so for Georgie, and tried to make himself believe that he loved her and could be happy with her. It was easier to believe this in her present softened mood, and by being constantly with her, and shutting from his heart that other, fairer picture of a brown-eyed, sweet-faced maiden, he succeeded pretty well, and was tolerably happy and content until Edna went for the week to Rocky Point.

Then he awoke to the fact of all she was to him, and how dreary Leighton would be without her. It had been a satisfaction when returning from Oakwood to know that *she* was at his home waiting for him. Very delightful, too, it had been to have her opposite him at his table, pouring his coffee, and making his tea for him, as she had done all winter, his mother being now far too blind to see to do it; she had such pretty little dimpled hands, and she managed so gracefully, and fixed his coffee so exactly to his taste, that it was not strange he missed her quite as much as his mother did, and hailed with joy the day which brought her back to him.

He met her at the station himself. He certainly could do so much, he thought, especially as Georgie was at home with a nervous headache, and he had been sitting by her an hour, bathing her head, and reading to her until she fell asleep. He certainly had earned the right to go for Brownie, and hold her hand a moment in his own, after he had lifted her to the ground.

He did not tell her how glad he was to get her back; but she saw it in his face, and felt it in his manner, as he drove her slowly home.

It *did* seem like coming home, when Mrs. Churchill met her with kisses and loving words, and told how lonely she had been, and how rejoiced she was to see her again.

As they sat alone that evening, after Roy had gone to inquire after Georgie's head, she recurred again to the forlorn week she had passed, and said, a little hesitatingly:

"I seem to be nothing without you, and what I want to say is this: I notice, sometimes, when Georgie is with me, that you go out, as if you thought I would rather be alone with her. I like her, of course, very much; but when she comes, please let it make no difference; I want you with me just the same. I am accustomed to you. I feel, somehow, *rested*, when you are with me."

Edna did not reply, but she felt a great throb of something like homesickness rising in her heart as she thought of going away forever from the gentle lady, who, she was sure, did love, and would miss her so much.

Roy returned from Oakwood earlier than usual, reporting Georgie better, and telling of a burglary which had been committed the previous night, at a house up the mountain-road. Nothing of value was taken, he said; but it showed that thieves were around, and he charged Russell to be very careful in securing the house.

"I would not like to suffer again, as we did in New York," he said; and then he told Edna how, years ago, his house in New York had been entered, and a quantity of plate and jewelry carried off, notwithstanding that Russell grappled with the thief in the lower hall, and gave him a black eye, by which he was afterward identified and brought to justice. "He must have been a very ingenious villain," he said, "as, after he was tried, and found guilty, and sentenced to the penitentiary, he managed to break out of prison, and is still at large, and for aught I know, is the very scamp who robbed the house last night."

Edna was not cowardly, and forgot all about Roy's burglar until the next day, when Georgie came over to Leighton, and the story was told again by Mrs. Churchill, who had been a little timid the previous night, and thought, once or twice, that she heard something around the house.

Georgie was interested, and excited, and frightened.

"We had a burglar in our house once," she said; "and since then I cannot even hear the word without its setting every nerve to quivering."

"Then let's talk of something pleasanter,—those trunks, for instance, which I saw in the express office this morning, and which must have contained the wedding finery, eh?" Roy said, playfully.

His allusion to the "wedding finery" was a fortunate one, and diverted Georgie's thoughts from burglars to the beautiful dresses which had that morning come up from New York for herself and Maude, whose trousseau was purchased by Mr. Burton himself, and was to be scarcely less elegant than that of Georgie. Edna was to be one of the brides-maids, and Mrs. Churchill was having her dress made in the house, and taking as much pride in it as if Edna had been her daughter.

And Edna tried hard to be happy, and sometimes made herself believe that she was, though a sense of loneliness and pain would steal over her whenever she saw Roy riding down the avenue, and knew where he was going, and that soon it would be a sin for her to watch him thus. Charlie's grave was visited oftener now, and the girlish widow tried to get up a sentimental kind of sorrow for the dead, and to think that her heart was buried with him, knowing all the while that a hundred living Charlies could not make up for that something she craved so terribly.

The bridal day was fixed for the 20th of June, and Edna felt that she should be glad when it was over. She had no thought, or even wish, that anything would occur to prevent the affair, which was talked of now from morning till night in Summerville, and was even agitating the higher circle in New York ; for many of Georgie's friends were coming out to see her married, and rooms were engaged for them at the hotel and every other available house.

And now but three days remained before the 20th. A few of the city guests, Georgie's more intimate friends, who were to be bridesmaids, had already come, and were stopping at Oakwood; and on the afternoon of the 17th, they went with Roy and Georgie to a pleasant point on the river, where they had a little pic-nic, and dined upon the grass, and made merry generally, until a roll of thunder overhead, and the sudden darkening of the sky warned them to hurry home if they would escape the storm, which came up so fast, and so furiously, that the horses of the carriage in which Georgie rode, frightened by the constant lightning and rapid thunder crashes, became unmanageable, and dashed along the highway at a rate which threatened destruction to the occupants of the carriage.

GETTING READY FOR THE BRIDAL. 339

"We are lost! we shall all be killed!" Georgie shrieked, just as from a thicket of trees a man darted out, and, seizing the foaming steeds by the bridle, managed, by being himself dragged along with them, to check their headlong speed, and finally quiet them.

"Thank you, sir. We owe our lives to you. Please give me your name and address," Roy said, but the man merely mumbled something inarticulate in reply, and slouching his hat over his face so as to shield it from the rain, walked rapidly away, just as the other carriage driven by Russell came up.

Roy's ladies were very much frightened and excited, especially Georgie, whose face was white as ashes, when Roy turned to speak to her, and who shook as if she had an ague chill.

"I am so very nervous," she said, by way of explanation, when, after she was safe at Oakwood, Maude commented upon her extreme pallor, and her general terrified appearance.

Through the blinding rain, which fell in torrents, she had caught a glimpse of the stranger's face, as he sprang toward the horses, and that glimpse had frozen her with horror for a moment, and made her very teeth chatter with fear, and her hair prickle at its roots. Then, as she remembered how impossible it was for the dead to rise and assume a living form, she tried to reassure herself that she had not seen aright. It was a resemblance, nothing more; a mere likeness which she in her weak, nervous state had magnified into a certainty. *He* was dead, the curse of her life; she had nothing to fear; she was Roy's wife, or would be in a few days, and there was no lawful reason why she should not be so. Thus she tried to reassure herself, until she became more quiet, and dressed for the evening, and met Roy, when he came, with a kiss and smile, and asked him in a rather indifferent manner if he knew who the stranger was who had come so bravely to their aid.

Roy did not know, but thought it very possible he was some workman on the farm near by, though his appearance was not quite that of a common laborer.

"Didn't he have queer eyes? Wasn't one of them turned, or put out, or something?" was Georgie's next query, and Roy answered laughingly:

"Really, you were more observing than I was. Why I don't know whether the man had two eyes or four. I only know that we owe our lives to him, whoever he may be."

He did not tell her all that had transpired at Leighton with regard to the stranger, or how, when he left home, Russell was busy nailing windows which had no fastenings, and barricading doors, and doing numerous things, which indicated that from some quarter he was apprehending a night attack upon his master's property. Russell, too, had seen the stranger's face more distinctly than Georgie had, and he could have sworn, ay, did swear, that he had seen it before, and had his fingers on that throat down in the basement of his master's house, years before, in New York.

"I know it is the same, and he'll be here to-night, maybe, to try his luck again," he said, to Roy and Edna, who made light of his fears, and told him he was always seeing burglars in the shade of every tree and around every corner of the house.

Remembering Georgie's nervousness, Roy kindly suggested that she should not be told of Russell's suspicion, and so he answered her lightly when she questioned him of the stranger, but felt a little startled when her description of the disfigured eye tallied so exactly with what Russell had said. He did not stay late at Oakwood that night, but returned earlier than usual to Leighton, which he found bolted, and barred, and locked, as if it had been some fortified castle ready to be besieged; but Russell's burglar did not make his appearance, a little to the disappointment of the good man, who narrated to Edna the particulars in full of his encounter with the midnight robber, who managed to break away, and escape from justice after all.

"What was his name?" Edna asked, more by way of saying something than because she was specially interested in the subject.

"John Sand he gave, though we didn't believe it was correct; we thought he took an assumed name to spare his wife. They said he had one, a very handsome young girl, and I think she was in the court-room when he was tried."

Just then Edna was called away by Mrs. Churchill, and Russell was left alone to think over the one adventure of his life, his conflict with the robber, of which he was never weary of talking.

What Georgie had endured the previous night no one guessed. Tortured with doubts which nearly drove her wild, she paced her room for hours, going over again and again in her own mind all the evidence she had ever received of *his* death, the *his* referring to the original of the spectre haunting her so cruelly now.

"It must be that he is dead," she said again and again, and then as she grew more quiet, she calmly asked herself what she would do if her fears proved true, and her answer was, "If already married to Roy, I will abide by his verdict: if not, if I know for sure before the twentieth, I'll kill myself."

There was a suicidal expression in her eyes as she said this, and she had the look of a woman capable of doing any thing if once driven to bay. It was nearly morning before Georgie slept, if indeed that state can be called sleep, in which so much of horror and fear is mingled as there was in her troubled dreams.

She was very pale and haggard when she came down to breakfast, and complained of her head, which she said was aching badly. She had suffered a great deal from nervous headache since Annie's death, and had sometimes expressed a fear that she should one day be crazy. She almost looked so now, with her unnaturally pallid face and glittering black eyes, and Mrs. Burton, always alarmed when anything ailed Georgie, made her lie down in a quiet, shaded little room in the rear of the house, and then sat by her all the morning, until Roy came and asked to see her. Then Georgie made a great effort to shake off the incubus which had fastened upon her, and dressing herself with the utmost care, went down to her lover and friends, and tried to be merry and gay, and felt a great load lifted from her spirits when Roy said:

"I think I have ascertained who our deliverer was. It is a poor man living near the spot where we were providentially saved from destruction, and I have charged Russell to see him, and remunerate him properly. He has a large family of children, I believe."

"How did you hear who it was?" Georgie asked, and Roy replied: "I saw a man this morning from that vicinity who told me."

After that Georgie did not longer doubt, and long before Roy left her, her headache passed away and the bright color came back to her cheeks, and one could almost see the filling up of her shrivelled flesh, and the fading of the dark circles beneath her eyes. Georgie was happy again, and that night her sleep was undisturbed by troubled dreams, or horrid dread of retributive justice overtaking her at the very moment when the cup of joy was in her grasp and almost at her lips.

CHAPTER XLI.

THE BURGLAR.

IT was the 19th; the very day before the bridal. All the city guests had arrived, and there was a grand dinner at Oakwood, where the three long tables were set upon the lawn beneath the maples, the bright silver, and the gay flowers showing well through the surrounding shrubbery, and seeming to curious passers-by, who stopped a moment to look on, more like a fairy scene than a reality. And Georgie, in her elegant white dress, was queen of the banquet, and quite overshadowed Maude in her simple muslin, with a few flowers in her hair. As some beautiful rose, which has drooped and pined beneath the fervid heat of a hot summer day, revives again after a refreshing rain, and seems fairer than ever; so Georgie, with her mind at ease, blossomed with new grace and beauty, looking so well and appearing so well that none ever forgot her as she was on that afternoon, the last she was to know in peace.

Anticipating the festivities of the next night, the guests did not tarry late, but dispersed soon after dinner was over, each making some pleasant remark to the brides-elect, and wishing them as bright a to-morrow as to-day had been. Roy was not feeling well, and he, too, went early, telling Georgie that he should not come again until he came to claim her.

There was a moon that night, but occasionally a rift of fleecy clouds obscured its brightness, and it was just as it had passed into one of these misty ridges that Roy met in the avenue with two men, one carrying a bundle, a little in advance of the other, who was walking slowly toward Oakwood. Without a thought as to who they were, Roy bade them a civil good-evening, as was his custom with every one, and then went on his way, while the two men did the same. One was a man sent with some work which had been done for Georgie in town, the other a stranger, who eyed the house curiously as he approached it, and who hesitated a moment when he saw his neighbor go round to a side door and ring the bell. Standing in the shadow, he waited until the ring was answered, and he heard the man say: "A bundle for Miss Burton, from Slosson's, and the bill."

Taking them both, the servant bade the young man wait a moment while he carried them to Miss Burton, who had gone to her room. The bill was paid, and the messenger from Slosson's departed, while the stranger stepped to the door, and asked for "Miss Georgie Burton."

"Gone to her room," was the reply, as had been anticipated, while the stranger added: "Please hand her this—other bill," and he held out a sealed envelope, addressed to Miss Georgie Burton, adding, when the servant asked if an answer was required: "Not to-night; to-morrow will do as well."

The next moment the stranger had disappeared under the dense shadow of the trees; and the servant was on her way to Georgie's room.

Georgie was very tired, and had signified to Maude her intention of retiring early. The arrival of the Slosson bill had retarded her movements somewhat, and she had just locked her door and let down her long flowing hair, when a second knock interrupted her, and she looked out a little impatiently to see what was wanted.

"Another bill, which the man said could wait till to-morrow," was the girl's laconic remark, as she handed her mistress the note, and then walked away.

"Another bill? I did not know there was another," Georgie thought, as she relocked her door, and went back beneath the gas to open the envelope.

But what was it which made her turn so white, and reel like a drunken creature, while her heart gave such violent bounds that she felt as if it were forcing itself into her throat. There could be but one handwriting like that, and she stood for a moment perfectly rigid, with her eyes glued to the name, "Miss Georgie Burton;" then with fingers from which all the blood had receded, leaving no feeling in them, she tore open her letter and read:

"DEAR LU:

"If you wish to avoid exposure, meet me to-night at twelve o'clock in the woodbine arbor at the foot of the garden. I have no desire to harm you, or spoil the fun to-morrow, *but money I must have*, so bring whatever you have about you, or if your purse chances to be empty, bring jewelry. I saw you with some superb diamonds on one night at the opera last winter. Don't go into hysterics. You've nothing to fear from me if you come down generous and do the fair thing. I reckon you are free from me, as I've been gone more than seven years.
"Yours, "H. M.".

There was a gurgling sound in Georgie's throat, as her first impulse was to scream, while a prickly sensation ran like lightning all through her right side, and she felt as if her mouth was twitching and turning toward her right ear; but she did not stop to question the meaning of these strange symptoms. She only thought of the fatal letter and its signature, and how *she* was ruined forever. The evil she had so much dreaded, and from which she had thought to escape, had come upon her at last. *He was not dead;* he still walked the earth; he lived and breathed not very far away, and had summoned her to meet him, and she must go. She had no thought of doing otherwise, and with the fearful agony gnawing at her heart, she consulted her watch to see how long before twelve. Nearly one hour and a half, and she clasped her hands together so tightly that the nails broke the skin in more than one place. But she did not feel it, or know that the blood was trickling from her nose until she saw the stains upon her white dressing-gown and on her long black hair. Mechanically she walked to the marble basin and washed and bathed her face until the flow had ceased; then she took up the letter again and read it a second time, while every fibre quivered and throbbed, and her eyes felt as if protruding from their sockets. And all this time she had uttered no sound; but when by chance she saw upon her table Roy's picture, which, since her engagement she had kept in her room, the magnitude of the calamity which had overtaken her, burst upon her at once, and with a low moan she fell prostrate upon her face, whispering to herself, "Roy is lost,—lost,—and so am I."

She knew that was so; knew there was no help, no escape for her now, and again that prickly sensation ran through her side, and a keen pain like a knife cut through her temples, where the veins were swelling and growing purple with the pressure of blood. Fortunately for her, unconsciousness came at last to her relief, unconsciousness which lasted until half-past eleven, and everything and everybody in the house was still. Then she roused herself, looked at her watch again, and prepared for action. He had written:

"Bring jewels if you have no money:" and knowing his rapacious disposition, she took her costly diamonds, necklace and all, her emeralds and pearls, and placing them in a little box, hunted up her purse, and laughed a kind of delirious laugh to find there were one hundred dollars in it.

She had no hope of Roy; it was impossible now that she

should be his wife; there was a bar between them,—a living bar,—raised, as it were, from the dead; and, though possibly, nay, probably, silence with regard to the past could easily be bought, and Roy need never know her secret even now, she was not bad enough at heart to let him take her to his arms while that man waiting for her outside lived and roamed through the world.

She had given Roy up when she lay upon her face, with the prickling sensation in her side, and the terrible pain in her heart; had buried forever that dream of happiness, and now the worst she would ever endure was past. No phase of suffering could come to her like what she had already felt, unless, indeed, Roy should hear the story of her shame, and that he must never do. She could guard against that; she knew the nature she had to deal with, and so she took her richest jewels,—thousands of dollars in value,—and throwing around her the same water-proof she had worn to Annie's bedside, went noiselessly out into the hall, and down the stairs, and on through another hall, the outer door of which communicated with the garden, and was far removed from the sleeping apartments of the family.

The night was a glorious one, and the moonlight lay like waves of silver upon the green-sward, and the shrubs, and the beds of bright June flowers, while the perfume of the roses filled the air with sweetness. But Georgie saw nothing of all this, and the night might have been one of thick darkness, so little she recked of it, or knew of the beauty around her. The woodbine arbor was all she thought about, and she sped swiftly down the broad, gravelled path, uttering a low scream as she saw the figure of a man rising to meet her.

One quick, searching glance she gave him to make sure it was he, then with a gasp she staggered forward, and would have fallen at his feet, had he not caught her by the arm and held her firmly up.

"Sit down, Lu," he said, not unkindly, and he drew a chair for her. "Don't take it so hard," he continued, as he saw how white she was, and how rapidly her heart was beating. "I do not mean to harm you; upon my word, I do not; though I've no special reason for doing you a favor except that you are a woman, and I once loved you too."

Georgie shuddered then, and pushed her chair a little farther from him, as if afraid he might touch her. But he had no such intention. However much he might have loved her once, he was well over the feeling now. He had summoned her to a purely business interview, and seating himself upon a stool not very far from her, he continued:

"I see I am to do all the talking. You do not even ask me how I chance to be *alive* instead of dead."

"It does not matter. I know you are alive, and that is sufficient," Georgie said, her words coming painfully, and her black eyes flashing upon him a look of bitter scorn.

"It was a mean thing to do, I know," he continued, without heeding her indifference; "but it made you happier thinking I was dead,—made you what you are, a grand lady,—the finest I have ever seen. Had you thought yourself tied to me, you could hardly have held your head so high as Miss Georgie Burton. Confess, now, that I have given you some years of happiness."

She would not answer him save by a moan of pain, and he went on:

When I wrote that letter to you, Will, my cousin, was sick, and going to die, and I was taking care of him among the mountains of Pennsylvania. By some chance, we had changed names; he was Henry Morton, I was Will Delong; and it occurred to me that here was a chance for my life. I'd throw the hounds off my track, and breathe again a free man; so I wrote that I was dying, and after Will was dead

I caused to be published in several papers the notice that Henry Morton, the man who was arrested for burglary, and tried as *John Sand*, and broke from his prison, had recently died. I saw the notice copied into other papers, and felt that I was safe so long as I staid away from those who knew me, and would recognize my blind eye. To remedy this defect, I took to wearing glasses, which answered very well. I travelled West and South, and crossed finally to England, then to Scotland, where I got me a little home among the heather hills, and tried to be a decent man."

"Why didn't you stay there?" Georgie asked; and he replied:

"I wanted to know if you were living or dead."

"Me!" she exclaimed, and for the first time since she had been there alone with him, a fear of him crossed her mind.

"Did you think me dead?" she asked; and he replied:

"I dreamed so; dreamed it three times in succession, and so I came to see, and found you surrounded with every luxury that money can procure. Young still and beautiful, a belle and an heiress, your old name of Louise Heyford changed for Georgie Burton, your old self all put out of sight, and you engaged to marry Mr. Leighton. Do you know it was his house I robbed in New York that night?"

"No, no; oh, heaven, no! I never dreamed of that; and I must have heard the name too, but forgot it again, everything was so horrible. *Roy's* house, and I was to be his wife to-morrow!"

She rocked to and fro in her anguish, while the man confronting her began at last to pity her; to wish vaguely that he had staid among the heather hills of Scotland, or at least had not shown himself to her. But anon, another woman's face arose before his mind, the woman for whom he had risked this interview, and he ceased to care so much for wounding Georgie, though his manner was conciliatory, and he spoke kindly and respectfully as he went on :

"I wondered at the engagement if you *did* know; and wondered too if he had ever heard of me as connected with you."

"Never, never! and Henry, oh Henry!" she stretched her hands toward him now, and the expression of her white face was pitiful in the extreme ; "whatever you do or make me suffer, don't subject me to that; don't let him know. I have lost him, but I cannot lose his esteem. Roy must not despise me. I wronged you once ; I know I wronged you in the tenderest point where a woman can wrong a man, but I meant to be a good wife, and would have been if you had forgiven and tried me. You would not do that; you thrust me from you, and though I have seen much of prosperity, there has been a skeleton in every joy. I have been fearfully punished every way. Annie is dead, did you know that?"

She said the last humbly, beseechingly, and a flush of red crept into her white face.

"I supposed she was. I saw the name of Annie Heyford on a stone in Greenwood, close by Le Roy's grave. And Mr. Leighton never knew of her either, I suppose?"

"Not what she was to me. Nobody knows but Jack and you," she answered mournfully, while a sudden flame of passion leaped into the one sound eye of the man beside her, as he said :

"Up to your old tricks again, I see; marrying with a lie on your soul, just as you came to me."

She did not resent the taunt at all. She was too thoroughly crushed for that, and she answered gently, "Yes, I was going to do the same thing again. I am everything that is bad, I confess ; but, oh, how could I tell, when all these years nobody has known, and I was so different, and the old life lay far behind, and I did love Roy. Oh, if I've sinned deeply, I am cruelly punished at the last. Think, Henry, to-morrow, ay, to-day, for it is to-morrow now, I was to have been his wife; everything is in readiness, the guests are here, and now it cannot be, and I,—oh, what reason can I give to Roy for holding back at the very altar?"

"What reason? No reason. Why should you hold back? Marry him just the same. I shall not interfere. I did not come for that. I came for money, and took this time in order to get what I want. I thought I hated you, but upon my soul, I don't. I am sorry for you, to see you feel so bad, but there's no cause for it. Swallow your conscience a little lower down. Act a bigger lie, and all will be right; for I tell you I am not here to claim any right I may have had in you. I dreamed you were dead. I'll be honest and say I hoped it was true, for over the sea among the heather hills is a little blue-eyed, brown-haired Scotch lassie whom I call Janet, and who thinks she is my wife. There are also two children in the home-nest; *mine*, too, as well as *hers*," he added, and again that red flush of shame crept into Georgie's face, while the stranger continued; "I tried to reform over there for her sake. She is pure and good, and she loves me, and the fraud I practise upon her cuts me sometimes to the quick, and when I dreamed you were dead so many times I got to hoping you were, for then I'd do *her* justice. So I came to see, and tracked you out, and found you on the topmost pinnacle, and felt angry when I saw your silks and satins and jewels and remembered Janet's two dresses, one for every day and one for Sunday, and thought of my little boy Johnnie, who might be cured if I had the money. We are poor, very poor, and Janet thinks I am making my fortune here in America, for I told her it was for her sake and the bairns' I came, and she is waiting for me so anxiously, and I am going to her soon; within a week at the farthest, but cannot go empty-handed. I did not enter that house on the mountain-road, as you probably think I did. I know nothing of the robbers. I quit' such things after my escape from prison, and since I have known Janet I have tried to be honest and decent. I have been hanging about in this neighborhood for two weeks or more, trying to make up my mind whether to seek an interview with you and risk detection or not. I saved your life and Mr. Leighton's too, but did not know when I seized the horses who was in the carriage. If I had, I should have done the same, though your death would make Janet an honest woman, for by finding some flaw in our first marriage ceremony I should coax her to go through with it again over the border in England."

"Oh, if you had let me die then," Georgie moaned faintly, and her companion rejoined, "Nonsense; you are making too much of the matter. There's no reason in the world why you should not marry just the same. I shall not trouble you, provided you do the fair thing by me. I want money. You want silence. It is a fair bargain. Did you bring anything with you?"

"Ye-es," Georgie said slowly, clasping her hands to her head. "I brought my diamonds and emeralds, worth thousands of dollars, but—don't—don't think they are to cover my marriage. I am not so bad as that. I have given Roy up, but I must keep his respect at any cost. Oh Henry, by the love you bear this Janet and the little ones, I beseech of you, leave the country at once, and never let my name be on your lips again. I've brought the jewels, enough to make you rich. Look at this—and this—and this!"

She opened the box, and held up one by one her diamond pin, and earrings, and necklace; and the man's eyes sparkled with eagerness as he saw them flash in the moonlight, and thought how valuable they must be. He had not expected so great a price, and he was generous enough to say so, and gave her back her pearls and emerald pin.

"The diamonds will do," he said, "and the hundred dollars will take me home. Thank you, Lu; there is something good about you after all; but how are you to get out of the scrape if you refuse *in toto* to take the man, and how will you account for the loss of your diamonds?"

"Leave that to me," she said. "Only I warn you, that *you* must not be found near here, or anywhere, when the alarm is given."

"Yes, I see; a *burglar* got into your room," and he nodded knowingly. "I shall cross the river in a little skiff which is anchored just below here. Once on the other side I fear no one. I know your room; its windows look out on the river; watch for the boat, and when it is fairly across, do what to you seems best! only screen me, as I will screen you, now and forever."

"You swear it," Georgie asked, and he replied, "Yes, I swear by the love I bear Janet, and the little ones, and the hope I have of seeing them again, never to breathe a word to any living being, that I ever heard of you save as the belle and heiress."

He offered her his hand, and loath as she was, she took it, and the compact between them was sealed.

"One o'clock, and I must be off," he said. "Good-by, Lu. Take my advice; marry Roy, and be as happy as you can."

She did not reply, and he walked rapidly down the garden across the road, and out into the field-path, which led to the river. Slowly, as if all the life had gone from her body, Georgie dragged herself back to her room, leaving the outer door unfastened and open, the better to answer the end she had in view. Her own door too was left ajar, and then drawing a chair by the window overlooking the river, she watched until a boat shot out into the stream, and by the moonlight she recognized the form of her late visitor as he bent to his oars and rowed the skiff swiftly across the water.

An hour went by; it was nearly half-past two, and before very long the early summer morning would be breaking in the east. What she did must be done quickly, and with a calmness born of utter despair she made her preparations. The box in which her diamonds were kept was laid empty in her drawer, which stood open, its contents tossed up promiscuously, and her empty purse lying upon the table. The emeralds and pearls were put carefully away unharmed, as were some smaller articles of jewelry. Then with trembling, ice-cold hands she made herself ready for bed, and laid her throbbing head upon her pillow just as the clock struck three. She had taken from a shelf, and looked at a bottle of laudanum, and thought how easy it would be to end it all, but she dared not do it when she thought seriously about it. She believed in a hereafter; in the Heaven where Annie had gone, and she could not deliberately throw away all chance of ever entering there.

"I may repent; the thief did at the last hour," she said, as she drew the bedclothes about her, and felt that she was ready for the first scene in the strange drama about to be acted.

CHAPTER XLII.

THE ALARM.

NEITHER Mrs. Burton nor Maude had slept very soundly that night. Both had been haunted with a conviction that they heard something about the house, stealthy footsteps Mrs. Burton thought, and she shook her snoring spouse vigorously, and tried to make him get up, receiving for reply, " Pish, only one of your fidgets ; go to sleep, do, and let me alone."

And so poor, timid Mrs. Burton listened until her ears ached, and, hearing nothing more, made up her mind that she had been mistaken, and there really was no cause for alarm. Maude, too, had taken fright, and knocked softly at Georgie's door, but Georgie was in the woodbine arbor, and did not hear her, and she went back to bed and fell asleep again, and was just dreaming that her wedding had proved to be her funeral, when a piercing shriek rang through the house, followed by another and another, each louder, more appalling than the other, until every sleeper was awake and huddling together in the halls, demanded what it was, and where the screams came from.

Jack was the first to decide that the noise was in Georgie's room, and entering through the unlocked door, he saw his sister sitting up in bed ; her eyes rolling wildly, her long black hair falling over her night-dress, and her whole face the very image of terror, as she shrieked, " The burglar— the man—been here—in this room—look—where he went and what he did. Oh ! Jack, Jack, I am dying, I shall die ! "

She continued her wild ravings until Jack succeeded in quieting her so far that she was able to tell her story, amid a series of moans and gasps and sobs. She had been suddenly awakened by some slight sound in her room, and saw a man wearing a mask, standing, revolver in hand, close at her bedside, and evidently watching her. Before she could scream, so paralyzed was she with fear, his hand was over her mouth, and his hot breath on her face, as he bent close to her and said, "Be perfectly quiet, if you wish to save your life. Scream once, or make any sound which shall attract attention, and you are a dead woman before I leave the room. I have no wish to harm *you*, but your diamonds I must have. Frozen with terror she had not dared to move, but lay perfectly still while the villain searched her dressing-bureau, and took, she did not know what.

"Look, Maude," she gasped; but Maude had already looked, and found the diamonds gone, and the purse empty; but the emeralds and pearls were there safe,—a state of things accounted for on the supposition that the robber had been startled by some noise, and left his depredations unfinished. He fled through the door, Georgie said; and having finished her tale, she fainted entirely away, while the male members of the house dispersed outside to hunt for the thief, and the ladies staid to minister to the fainting woman.

There was no shamming now. Georgie had borne so much, and suffered so much, that the faint was real; and she lay so long unconscious, and looked so white and corpse-like, that Mrs. Burton went off into hysterics, declaring her darling was dead. As soon as possible, a physician came, and after carefully examining his patient, and listening to the story of the robbery as related by each of the dozen women in the house, appeared to be greatly puzzled, and said he hardly knew what to think. It was scarcely possible that a sudden fright, however great it might have been, could have thrown the whole nervous system so completely out of balance as Miss Burton's seemed to be. Had she been perfectly well heretofore?

Then Mrs. Burton remembered how nervous and fitful she had been ever since Annie died. "She took a violent cold at that time," the lady said, "and has never been or looked well since."

"I thought there must be something behind. A person in perfect health could hardly be struck down like this by mere fright. She does not seem to have the free use of her limbs. Miss Burton"—and he turned to his patient—"lift your right hand if you can, or speak to me and tell me who I am."

The great black eyes were wide open, and fixed upon his face with an expression which showed that Georgie heard; but the right hand did not move, and the white lips only gave forth a queer kind of sound, as they tried in vain to repeat the doctor's name.

"What is it, doctor? Oh, tell me what ails my darling?" Mrs. Burton asked, terribly frightened at the look on Georgie's face, and the peculiar expression of her mouth.

"Auntie," Maude said, in a low whisper, "come with me; I'll tell you;" and leading her frightened aunt into the hall, she told her as gently as possible that Georgie was paralyzed.

It was true. The long-continued strain upon mind and nerve, which she had endured in guarding her secret, with the skeleton of detection always threatening her, added to the terrible shock of the previous night, had been more than nature could endure without a loud protest; and the prickly sensation she had felt creeping through every vein was the precursor to the fearful thing which had come upon her, striking her down as the lightning strikes the oak, and leaving just one-half of her helpless, motionless, dead. There was no feeling in any part of her right side; no power to move the soft, white hand, which lay just where they put it ; no power to speak audibly in the pale lips whose last act had been to frame a tissue of falsehoods whereby she could steer safely through the labyrinth of woe in which she was entangled. Poor Georgie! There were hot tears shed for her that bright June morning, when the sun, which should have shone upon her bridal day, came up over the eastern hills, and looked in at the windows of the room where she lay so helpless and so still, knowing perfectly well what was doing and saying around; but having no power to tell them that she knew, save by the feeble pressure of the fingers of her left hand, and the slow shutting of her eyelids.

Wistfully Georgie's eyes followed each movement of the people around her, as if imploring aid, and resting longest upon Jack, who wept like a little child over his stricken sister. All her faults and errors were forgotten in this great calamity which had come so suddenly upon her ; and he remembered only that she was his sister, the beautiful girl whom he had loved, and petted, and befriended, and chided, and scolded, and blamed, ever since he had been old enough to read her character aright. There were no scoldings, no chidings, no blaming now ; nothing but love and tenderness ; and the hot tears rained in torrents over his face, as, in obedience to a look in her eye, which he construed into a wish for him to come nearer to her, he bent his face to hers, and felt the cold lips trying to kiss his cheek, while the left hand crept feebly up to his head, and stroked and parted his hair. No one of all those present thought Jack one whit less manly for the great choking sobs which he smothered on Georgie's neck, or the tears which dropped so fast upon her hair and brow.

With a trembling grasp she held his face close to her own and tried to tell him something. But it was all in vain that he strained every nerve of his ear to understand what she meant. There was nothing to be made out of the mumbling noise, the only sound she could articulate. It would not always be thus, the doctor said. She would recover her powers of speech, partially, if not in whole, and possibly recover the use of her limbs. He had seen far worse forms of paralysis from which there was entire recovery. She was young, and naturally healthy, and had every reason to hope for entire restoration to health.

"Be of good courage," he said to her kindly, for he saw she understood him, and hung eagerly upon his words; "be of good courage, and you will yet be a happy bride, though perhaps not to-day."

There was a sound then from the pallid lips, a low, moaning sound, and a spasm of pain contracted every muscle of the white face, while in the dark eyes there was a look of horror, as if the doctor's words had not been welcome ones. Maude, who was standing by her, and chafing her lifeless hands, said to her next, "We have sent for Roy, Georgie. Do you want to see him?"

At the mention of Roy's name, the dumb lips spoke with an agonized effort which brought the great sweat-drops upon cheek and brow.

"No, no, no; Ja-ack," they said, and the sound was more like the moan of some wounded animal than like a human cry, while the eyes seemed as if trying to leap from their sockets, as they fastened themselves upon Jack.

"What, sister? What is it?" he asked, and with another mighty effort the lips moved slowly, and one by one made out the words, "Don't—let—Roy—"

They could not articulate any more, but Jack thought he comprehended her meaning, and said, "Not let Roy see you yet? Is that it, sister?"

She clutched his hand nervously in answer to the question and held it tightly in her own. She did not want to see Roy then or ever. She could not bear it, she thought; could not endure to look upon what she had loved and lost just as it was within her reach. Guilt, remorse, and shame were busy at work, and those who watched by her little dreamed of the bitter anguish which was rending her soul and sending out that rain of perspiration which wet her night-dress about the neck, and wet her long, black hair, and the pillow on which she lay, and which was the means eventually of doing her bodily good. The profuse perspiration seemed in some way to grapple with, and partially subdue the disease, so that after an hour or more she could speak more distinctly, and the little finger of her right hand moved once as Maude was rubbing it.

"You are already better, Georgie. We will soon have you well," Maude said encouragingly, while one of the ladies in attendance carried the good news that Georgie had spoken, to Mrs. Burton, who was in strong hysterics on the sofa in her own room, and over whom poor, ignorant Mr. Burton had emptied by turns the water-jug, the camphor-bottle, the cologne and arnica, in his awkward attempts to help her.

Limp and wet, with her false curls as straight as an Indian's hair, and her under teeth on the floor where the hapless husband planted his boot heel upon them, and crushed them out of shape, the poor woman received the news, and in her joy went into another hysteric fit worse than any which had preceded it. Frightened now out of his wits, and taking advantage of the presence of some one with whom he could leave his spouse, Mr. Burton retreated precipitately from the room, wondering why the deuce the women wanted to raise such a row as his wife and Georgie were doing.

"Hanged if I don't take the first train for New York, and stay there, too, when I get there," he said, as he rushed out into the back yard, where he met Roy, just dismounting from his horse, and looking very anxious and disturbed, though *not* as unhappy as one might expect of a man who had just heard that his bridal, for that day at least, was impossible, and his bride a paralytic.

CHAPTER XLIII.

ROY.

HE had not slept much the previous night. Indeed, but for the dream which came to him in the early morning, he would have sworn he had not slept at all since parting from Miss Overton, just as the clock struck twelve. He had left Georgie at an early hour, and tried, as he kissed her cheek, to believe himself happy in the possession of so much grace and beauty, and he wondered, as he rode slowly home, at the strange disquietude which possessed him, the feeling of something lost, or losing very fast from his life; something which could have made him happier far than he was now, for he was *not* happy, and as he went through his beautiful grounds up to his handsome house, he would have given all his fair heritage to have been free again, and as he was one year ago; ay, less than a year ago, on that September day when his mother's hired companion first greeted his sight as he came up the avenue, and saw her standing upon the vine-wreathed piazza. As she had been there then, so she was now, with this exception: his mother had retired, and Edna sat alone, enjoying, or thinking she was enjoying, the glorious summer night, and trying to make believe that she was happy; that there was no hidden pain in her heart; no lingering regret for what could never be; no *love*,—to put it in plain words,—for the man riding toward her, and whose wedding-day was on the morrow. He saw her, and his heart gave a bound such as it never gave at sight of Georgie, and then his quick eye noted next that she was alone, and he was conscious of a glad kind of feeling that he had left Oakwood so early. It was the very last interview he would ever have with Miss Overton, and he meant to improve it, never stopping to reflect that there was in his heart disloyalty to Georgie, who might with reason have complained, could she have seen how his face lighted up, and how eagerly, after disposing of his horse, he bounded up the steps of the piazza, and drew a chair near to Edna's.

It was a long, long talk they had together, and though there was not, perhaps, a word spoken which might not with safety have been repeated to Georgie, there were certain tones of voice, and glances, which would not have borne strict inspection; and Roy carried to his room that night a heavier heart than men usually carry on the very eve of their marriage. Had he made a mistake after all? The question kept insinuating itself into his mind in spite of his efforts to drive it out. Had he, at the last, been too precipitate, and pledged himself to one who could never be to him what another might have been? And then he went over all the particulars attending his engagement with Georgie, remembering how sudden it was; how but for Mr. Burton it would probably not have been at all, and how strangely Georgie had conducted at first, and how soon she had recovered herself and taken things for granted. Then he looked on the other side, and thought of Georgie's beauty, and goodness, and amiability, and her love for him, which he could not doubt, and in so doing, drew a little comfort to himself, and felt that it was his own fault if he were not happy with her. He could not think of Miss Overton; that is, he dared not dwell upon what she was, and think how fully she satisfied him in the very points where Georgie failed. It would be folly, yes, a sin to do that now; and he resolutely put all such tormenting reflections aside, and then, sorry for any doubts and misgivings which had tortured him, he prayed earnestly that the thing which looked so dark to him now, might be made clear as the day; that wherever he had wronged Georgie, even in his thoughts, he might be forgiven, and be to her all that a kind, true husband should be.

"I can make her happy, and I will," he said to himself at last, as he fell into a troubled sleep, and dreamed, not of Georgie, but of "Brownie," who seemed to be with him, and in some trouble, too.

With a start he awoke, trying to make out where he was, and who was calling him so anxiously, with so much terror in the tone. It was Brownie's voice, sure; that was no dream. Brownie was at his door speaking to him, and what she said was this:

"Mr. Leighton, Mr. Leighton, wake up, please, and come as quickly as you can. Something dreadful has happened."

Swift as lightning his thoughts turned to his mother; something had happened to her, and dear as she was to him, and much as he would do to ward evil from her, he was half-conscious of a pleasurable sensation, a feeling of hope that the something which had happened might give him a little longer respite. He was soon dressed, and out in the hall with Edna, whose face was very white, and whose voice trembled as she said to him:

"I have bad news for you, and I am so sorry that I should be the one to tell it, but your mother is sleeping quietly and I would not rouse her. A servant has just come from Oakwood, and says that Miss Burton,—oh, forgive me that I must tell you,—Miss Burton has had a stroke of paralysis, and can neither move nor speak."

He was not glad, and it was not a sense of freedom which made him clutch Edna's shoulder so firmly, as if he saw already a path which led toward her. He was shocked, frightened, and filled with remorse as he remembered all the past, and how he had wished to escape.

"Paralysis, and she seemed so well when I left her! When was it? How was it?" he asked, and Edna told him of the burglar, and what she had heard from the Oakwood servant.

"You will go at once," she said as he made no movement, and that roused him to action.

"Yes, certainly," he answered, and then hurried down stairs, and out into the yard, where his horse was already saddled and waiting for him.

Edna had given orders to that effect before she called him, and she stood watching him as he galloped down the avenue and turned toward Oakwood.

Georgie seemed better; had spoken once, and moved her fingers just a little, they told Roy, in answer to his inquiries; but when he asked if he could see her, he was put off with the excuse that a sight of him might excite her too much at present, and then he asked for Mrs. Burton, and was going to her room, when Mr. Burton exclaimed:

"Don't for thunder's sake go there. She's in the awfulest hysterics, I reckon, you ever run against, and the old boy generally is to pay."

But Mrs. Burton *would* see Roy, and so he went to her, and at sight of him she went off into another cramp, and clutched him round the neck, and cried and sobbed over him, and called him her poor, dear boy, and spoke so touchingly of Georgie, that Roy, always sympathetic, felt the tears rush to his own eyes as he tried to comfort her. The house was full of guests, some of whom were huddled together in groups, talking over the terrible calamity, while others were packing their trunks preparatory to leaving on the first train for New York. There would be no wedding that day, of course, so all the morning the baggage wagon came and went, as guest after guest departed, both from Oakwood and the hotel, until Summerville generally was emptied of its strangers, and an air of gloom settled down upon it, as the citizens thought of the sad change a few hours had wrought.

They had told Georgie of Roy's presence in the house, and how he cried in Mrs. Burton's room. Then every muscle of Georgie's face was convulsed, and Jack, who was with her constantly, never forgot the look of anguish which came into her eyes, or the quivering motion of her lips as she tried in vain to speak again. What she thought no one could guess, and she was powerless to tell, as she lay there all the day listening so eagerly to all they said about the hunt for the burglar, which was still going on.

"They will be pretty sure to find him; he cannot escape," Jack said, and then Georgie gave forth a cry which curdled his very blood, and made him turn quickly towards her, trying to read what she wanted in her eyes.

But he could not, though he thought he understood that talking of the burglar distressed her, and he forbade the mention of the subject in her presence again. Even that did not satisfy her. There was the same strange look in her eyes when they rested on his face, the same evident desire to say something to him, and after a time she succeeded. They were alone, he and she, for he would not leave her, and she would not suffer it if he would. She had seemed to be sleeping, and all had left the room but Jack, who sat rubbing her hand, and marvelling at the great change in her face within so short a time.

"Ja—ack," she said, and after a pause added, "Don't—"

Then she waited again, and Jack asked: "Don't what, sister! Don't leave you? Is that it?"

She shook her head and managed to say "Catch."

Still Jack had no idea of what she meant, but he put the two words together and asked: "Don't catch what?"

"Ma—an," she gasped with a tremendous effort, and there came a horrible suspicion across Jack's mind.

It could not be possible either, he thought, though if it were true it would account for the terrible shock to Georgie.

"Did you think you knew the man?" he asked; and Georgie nodded her head, while the tears gathered in her eyes and rolled down her cheeks.

Jack asked her no more questions then. He hoped and believed she was mistaken; but when later in the day the men who had gone in pursuit came back reporting their ill success, he managed adroitly to cool their ardor a little, and threw what obstacles he could in the way of their continuing the search. He was to write a notice for the papers, but he conveniently forgot it, and put it off until the following day, and Georgie's face looked brighter when he told her what he was doing. She had not seen Roy yet, though he had been in the house all the time, now sitting with Mrs. Burton, who had taken to her bed, and was more troublesome than Georgie, and now walking slowly up and down the piazza, with his head bent forward and his hands clasped together behind his back. Of what he was thinking, all guessed, but none knew how full of remorse he was when he remembered the previous night when he had shrunk so from his fate, and half wished that something might arise to save him from it. Something had arisen, a terrible something, and to himself he said, as he walked up and down, "I did not want this to happen; did not want Georgie harmed, and if I could, how gladly I would save her."

His heart was very full of pity and tenderness, and almost love, for the poor girl, who never forgot him for a moment, and who felt comforted in knowing that it was his step she heard so constantly passing beneath her window. She had intervals when speech was easier, and in one of these, which came toward the sun-setting, she beckoned to Jack, who was at her side in an instant, trying to comprehend her meaning.

"Roy," she said, then paused a moment, and added, "Free—free;—tell him—now."

Jack understood her, but did not go at once.

"Wait awhile before doing that," he said. "You may get entirely well; the doctor says so."

"Ne-e-ver," and Georgie shook her head and touched her helpless hand. "Ne-e-ver,"—de-ad," touching again her hand and arm; then pointing to her face and heart she continued, "Shall—die—soon;—tell—Roy—f-ree—n-ow."

She was growing excited, and Jack left her with Maude, and went out to Roy, who stopped in his walk and asked how Georgie was, and when he might see her.

"Not yet," Jack said. "She seems morbid on that subject; perhaps because her face is not quite natural, and she thinks it might distress you to see her beauty so marred. And, Roy, she sent me to tell you that you are free. She insisted that I should come," he added, as he met Roy's look of surprise. "She was growing excited, and to quiet her I came to tell you that you are free from your engagement."

For an instant Roy experienced a feeling of relief, a lifting of his spirits, but he quickly put it aside, and said to Jack:

"Tell your sister that only her death or mine can sever the tie between us. She was to have been my wife to-night, and as such I look upon her, no matter how maimed and stricken she may be. Tell her I am waiting to see her, to help you take care of her, that I think I have a right superior to yours. Ask if I may come."

This was his answer, which Jack carried to Georgie, who, with a frantic effort, tried to raise her helpless hand to clasp within the other, while her lips quivered and the tears rolled in torrents down her cheeks.

"Don't—de-serve—it," she managed to articulate, and Jack, who knew her so well, felt that she spoke truly, but pitied her just the same, and tried to quiet and comfort her, and asked her if she would see Roy then.

She shook her head; but when Jack said, "Is it a comfort to you to know that he is here?" she nodded twice; and so, though he could not see her, Roy staid all night at Oakwood, and for hours walked slowly up and down the piazza, always in the same attitude, with head bent forward and his hands locked behind him. They had told him that Georgie was quieter when she heard his step, and that when it ceased she seemed to listen for it; and so, unmindful of his own fatigue, he kept up the same weary round, until the moon, which should have lighted him to the altar, was past the zenith, and down toward the west. Then Jack came out and told him Georgie was asleep. So he paused in his walking, and sinking into a chair began to feel how worn and tired he was.

Edna had come over late in the afternoon, and with Maude and Jack was watching by Georgie's bedside. She had not seen Roy since the morning when she had broken the tidings to him; but when Jack came in and told how exhausted he was, she poured a glass of wine from a decanter on the sideboard, and placing it with some crackers on a little silver tray, carried it out to him.

"You are tired, Mr. Leighton," she said, "and I have brought you this; try and take some of it."

He had not heard her step, but at the sound of her voice he started, and the weary look upon his face disappeared at once. He drank the wine and took one of the crackers, and thanked her for her thoughtfulness, and asked if she too were not very tired.

"Sit down and rest," he said, offering her his chair, and bringing another for himself. "Jack told me she was sleeping. You are not needed there now. Stay with me awhile."

So she sat down beside him, but neither talked much to the other, and when they spoke it was of Georgie and the fearful thing which had come upon her. Roy was very tired, and after sitting awhile in silence, Edna knew by his breathing that he had fallen asleep. "If he only had a pillow, or something at the back of that chair for his head, he would rest so much better," she thought, and going into the hall, she brought out her own shawl and adjusted it so carefully, that he did not awake, though he stirred a little and said something which sounded like "my darling." Of course he meant Georgie, and Edna left him there to dream of the poor girl who was sleeping also, and who was better in the morning when she woke.

The twisted look about the mouth was nearly gone, and her right eye was much like the other in its expression. Still she could not use her hand at all, or speak except with difficulty, and she persisted in refusing to see Roy, who went home to breakfast with his mother, and then returned to Oakwood, where for several days he spent most of his time, until at last Georgie signified her willingness to see him. She was looking quite bright and natural, and Maude had made her neat and tidy in one of her prettiest white wrappers, while Edna, who was there also, had combed and curled her long black hair and put a white rosebud in it, and had said to her encouragingly, "You look very sweetly, Miss Burton, and I am sure Mr. Leighton will think so too. Shall I hold the glass for you to see yourself?"

Georgie shook her head; she was satisfied with the verdict of her young nurse, and nodded her readiness for Roy. Both Maude and Edna left the room as he came in, and so no one witnessed that first interview between them, when, far more lover-like than he had ever been before toward her,

Roy kissed her pallid lips, and called her dear Georgie, and told her she was better, and would soon be well.

Then she spoke slowly, painfully: "Ne-ver, Roy, ne-ver—well; nev-er—your—wife; be-lieve—it—can-not—be, even—if I—should—live. I shall—die. Am—afraid—to die; pray, Roy;—pray—for—me."

And Roy did pray beside her bed, and with her hand in his, he asked in a choking voice that God would spare her life. But Georgie stopped him short, and gasped:

"Not that, Roy; pray—I may be—ready; pray Him to —forgive; and there's—more to—forgive—than—you know; pray for *me*,—for that."

Roy's voice was very low, and sad, and earnest now, as he asked forgiveness for the stricken woman before him; that, whether living or dying she might be God's child, and find the peace she sought.

"Can you say 'Our Father,' with me?" he asked; and Georgie tried to follow him, her lips making a queer sound, and repeating twice, "forgive our trespasses,—my trespasses; my sin."

"My sin," was her burden; and Roy, who did not understand, prayed for her generally until she seemed quiet, though the great tears kept dropping from her eyelids and she tried to disengage her hand from his, and shrank so evidently from his caresses, that he ceased at last, and only sat by her as a stranger would have done.

After a while Jack, who had been resting, came up, and then Roy went away to Leighton with Georgie's farewell words ringing in his ears: "Pray, Roy; pray for *me*."

She did not again refuse to see him, and he visited her every day, and sent her fruit and flowers, and tried sometimes to think she was improving, but Jack knew better. There was no life in her right side now, nor ever would be again. Her speech had come back to her, so that she talked less painfully, but she was fast wasting away, consumed, the doctor said, by a slow fever which he could not understand. Indeed, he did not understand her case at all, and puzzled his brain over it, while she grew weaker, more helpless, and more restless, too, begging to be moved so often, that even Jack's strong arms grew tired at last, but never for that relaxed one whit in their efforts to do for her. Tender and faithful as a mother to her sick and only child, he gave up his whole time to her, feeling repaid for all he did when he saw how she clung to him, and how much better she seemed when he was with her. No one could fill his place, not even Roy, who spent a great deal of his time at Oakwood, where everything was overshadowed in gloom, and where the inmates just lived on from day to day, waiting for, and wondering what to-morrow would bring.

CHAPTER XLIV.

LAST DAYS.

THE wedding had been appointed for the 20th of June, and it was now the 20th of July; just one month from the day when so fearful a calamity had overtaken poor Georgie. Every one, even to Mrs. Burton, had ceased to hope for her now. They knew she could not live, and waited anxiously for the final shock which should terminate her life. All the old restlessness and desire to be moved continually was gone, and she would lie for hours just where she was put, with her well hand clasped over the feeble one, and her eyes closed, though they knew she was not asleep; for occasionally the pale lips would move, and those nearest to her caught whispered words of prayer, and knew that at the last the soul so near to death was seeking for that peace without which to die is terrible. Her speech was more natural, and could easily be understood, but it tired her to talk; and when Roy came to see her, she would only press his hand and nod her thanks for the flowers or fruit he always brought her. She was greatly changed in more ways than one. Her glorious beauty, of which she had been so proud, was gone; and her long black hair was streaked with gray.

But Georgie cared for none of these things; her interest was elsewhere, and the intensity of her anguish and remorse so great that often when she lay with her eyes shut, Jack saw the great drops of sweat standing upon her brow and about her mouth. To Jack as well as to Roy she had said, "Pray for me," and Jack did not repel her now with scorn, but, unworthy as he felt himself to be, tried to pray for his poor sister, promising to be himself a better man if peace were given to her. And peace came at last, and brought a brighter, happier expression to the worn face, and drove the look of terror from the eyes, and then Georgie talked freely with her brother.

It was the night of the 20th, and he alone was watching with her. Again there was a moon, and its silvery light came in through the open window and shone on Georgie's face, and made it seem to Jack like the face of an angel, as she drew his head down to her and kissed him so lovingly, saying to him, "Dear Jack, let me tell you while I can just how it was that night a month ago. I told you all a *lie ;* there was no one in my room. I made it up to screen myself, for I must have some excuse for Roy, some reason why I could not marry him. You told me once the dead might come to life to witness against me. Jack, he did; Henry is not dead; he was here in the garden; I saw him and talked with him, and gave him my diamonds to keep him quiet. But Jack, oh, Jack, don't think *that* of me," she cried, as she saw the look of horror on his face and guessed of what he was suspecting her.

"I never for an instant thought to marry Roy after I knew Henry was living. I only did not want him to know about it. I don't want him to know now. Oh, Jack, can't I go to Heaven unless I tell Roy everything?"

She was getting greatly excited, and Jack tried to quiet her, and brought her a glass of wine, and then, when she was better, listened, while in her slow way she told him what the reader already knows, of her interview with Henry Morton; of all he said to her; of her utter despair and agony, and her planning the story of the robbery to account for her fearful excitement and the sudden illness she meant to feign so as to put off her marriage.

"But God planned for me better than I could plan for myself," she said; "and sent the paralysis as a sure means of separating me from Roy. Henry told me it was Roy's house he robbed in New York, years ago. I never knew that, or if I heard the name, I forgot it afterward. Did you know it, Jack?"

"I knew the name was Leighton, but thought it another family," Jack said; and Georgie continued:

"Had I known it, I could not have done as I did, it seems to me, though I was bad enough for anything. But I hope God has forgiven me. I feel so differently, so sorry for the past; the fear of death is gone, only I don't know about telling Roy, and Aunt Burton, too. Must I, Jack? Do you think I ought?"

Jack did *not* think so. Telling them now could do no good, and would only add to their wretchedness, he said, and much as he liked the truth, he could not see that she was bound to a confession of what could in no wise benefit any one, especially as there was no possibility of her secret ever being known except to himself.

"For, Georgie," he continued, "I have something to tell you, which I have withheld, because I was not sure how much you knew, or how certain you were who it was that took your diamonds. Henry Morton is dead,—really, truly dead; for I saw him myself about a week ago, when I went with Roy to New York for a day. He could not have sailed as early as he told you he intended doing. Perhaps he was afraid of detection, and kept quiet awhile in the city. At all events, he was booked in the Scotia as Tom Anderson, and in going on board the night before she sailed, either lost his footing, or made some misstep, and was drowned before he could be reached. On examining his person, a handsome set of diamonds was found secreted about him, and as they answered to the description given of yours, a telegram was at once forwarded here, and Roy and myself went immediately to New York, Roy swearing to the jewels, while I mentally swore to the man, though outwardly I made no sign. Your diamonds are here with Mrs. Burton, and Henry is in his grave. You have nothing to dread from him. You are free to marry Roy, if ever—"

He did not finish the sentence, for Georgie put up her hand, and said quickly: "Never, Jack; don't, please, speak of that; never now, even if I should live, which I shall not; I could not marry Roy without telling him everything, and death is preferable to that. If I die, he need not know who or what she was whom he thought to make his wife. Nobody need know but you and Maude, for I want you to tell her. Don't let there be a secret between you. But do not tell her till I am gone; then do it as kindly as you can, and excuse me all you can. I was young and foolish when I knew Richard Le Roy, and he flattered and turned my head, and promised to make me a lady, and I hated to be so poor, to stay all day in that little school-room, with that set of tiresome children, and I envied his sisters when I saw them going out to parties so elegantly dressed, and knew they had whatever they liked best. There was nobody to warn me ; nobody who knew what he said to me, or how he lured me on to ruin, and made me believe in him more than in Heaven, and so I fell, and he died before he could make me a reparation; for, had he lived, I do believe he would have saved me from disgrace. He said he loved me ; I believe he did; tell Maude so; tell her not to hate me, for Annie's sake. Annie was not to blame,—darling Annie. Shall I meet her, Jack?"

She was very much exhausted, and Jack bade her rest and not talk any more then; but she was not through with all she had to say.

"Let me tell you while I can," she whispered; "tell you what I want you to do. He told me of a *Janet* over in Scotland waiting for him, and a little blind boy whose sight he hoped to have restored, now he had the means. Find them, Jack, they live in ——, not far over the border. When you and Maude are married, go there on your bridal trip. I have money of my own,—ten thousand dollars, which Aunt Burton gave me. It is all in bonds. I shall give it to you, and a part of it you must give to her, to Janet and her little ones. That is something I can do, and it will make me die easier, knowing somebody will be benefited by me. Promise, Jack, to find her, or get the money to her in some way, but never let her know she was *not* his wife. Tell her his friends sent you."

She could talk no longer then, for her speech was failing her, and her utterance so thick that it was with difficulty Jack could understand her. He made it out, however, and promising compliance with all she asked, soothed and quieted her until she fell into a sleep, which lasted several hours, and from which she awoke with a fresher, better look upon her face and in her eyes. But this did not deceive her, nor delude her with vain hopes. She knew that life was not for her, neither did she desire it now. Hoping and believing, though tremblingly, that all would be well with her hereafter; that the God against whom she had sinned so deeply had, in His infinite mercy, pardoned even her; she looked forward calmly, and even longingly, to the death which was to free her from all the bitter pangs of remorse which, should she live, would be hers to endure continually. The sight of Roy and her aunt was a constant pain and reproach, for she knew how unworthy she was of the fond love manifested for her by the one, and the extreme kindness and delicate attentions of the other.

"If I could tell them,—but I cannot, and Jack says I need not," she thought often to herself, praying earnestly to be guided aright, and not to be allowed to leave undone anything necessary to her own salvation.

Once when Roy was sitting by her, she said to him hesitatingly:

"Roy, you are a good man, one in whom I have confidence; tell me, please, if a person has done something very wrong, ought he to confess it to everybody or anybody, unless by so doing he could do some good, or repair an injury?"

Roy did not think it necessary, he said, though he was not quite sure that he fully understood the case. There were great sweat drops on Georgie's face, and her lips twitched convulsively as she said:

"There was something in my early life which I meant to keep from you and which I want to keep from you now. It would distress me greatly to tell it, and pain and shock you to hear it. Do you think I must? that is, will God love me more if I tell?"

Instantly there came back to Roy a remembrance of Georgie's strange conduct at the time of their engagement, and he felt certain that whatever was now preying on her mind was then trembling on her lips. What it was he did not care to know; it could not affect him now. Georgie was passing away from him to another, and, as he believed, a better world. He had never loved her as he ought to love one whom he meant to make his wife; but during the days he watched beside her and saw how changed she was, and how earnestly she was striving to find the narrow way, even at the eleventh hour, he felt that he liked her as he had never done before, and he did not care to hear anything which could lower her in his opinion, and so he said to her, "Georgie, if the something in your past life does not now affect any one, keep it to yourself. I do not wish to know it. Neither, I am sure, would Mrs. Burton, if the telling it would trouble you. Be satisfied with my decision, and let us remember you as you seemed to us."

He bent down and kissed her while her pale lips whispered, "Bless you, Roy; bless you for the comfort you have given me. Think of me always as kindly as you can, but as one who has erred and sinned, and hoped she was forgiven, and who loved you, Roy, so much, for I do, I do, better than you love me. I have known all along that I was not to you what you are to me, and in time you will find another to take my place; find her soon, perhaps, and if you do, don't wait till I have been dead the prescribed length of time, but marry her at once, and bring her to your mother, if she is not already there."

Georgie said the last slowly, and looking into Roy's eyes, saw that he understood her, and went on:

"She is a sweet girl, Roy; pure and womanly. Your mother loves her as a daughter, and I give her my right in you. If you succeed, don't forget, please, what I say; if you succeed, remember that I told you *I knew all about her.* Don't forget."

A violent fit of coughing came on, and in his anxiety and fear, Roy paid little heed to what Georgie had said with regard to Miss Overton, who soon came into the room, and signified her readiness to do whatever she could for the suffering Georgie.

CHAPTER XLV.

DEATH AT OAKWOOD.

THE August morning was a glorious one, and every shrub, and flower, and plat of grass at Oakwood seemed fairly to laugh, as, glistening with the raindrops which had fallen through the night, they lifted their heads to the beautiful summer sunlight which came up the eastern hills, and bathed the earth in a sea of mellow light. The air, purified by the thunder-shower, was cool and sweet, and laden with the perfume of the many flowers which dotted the handsome lawn, while the birds almost burst their little throats with gladness as they sang amid the trees, and flew about the house, from whose door knobs knots of crape were streaming, and whose shutters were closed to shut out the glorious day which only mocked the sorrow of those who wept that morning for their loved and lost one. Georgie was dead. Just as the lightning-flash and the thunder-roll passed away, and the young moon broke through the rift of dark storm-clouds, she looked her last good-by to those around her, and her spirit fled to Him who would deal justly with her, and of whom she had no fears as she went down the river-bank and launched out into the stream whose waters never return to lave the shores of time.

It was a very easy death she died; so easy, that Jack, who held her in his arms, only knew the moment of her departure by the sudden pressure of her hand on his, and the falling of her head upon his bosom. She had said good-by to every one, and left for all a friendly word, and tried, as far as possible, to repair any wrong she might have done. To Edna, who was often with her, she had said once when they were alone:

"I have something to tell you. I knew you from the first, and but for Maude and Jack, should have told Roy who you were. I disliked your being there, and meant to do you harm. I purposely worried and annoyed you by talking so much of Charlie's wife, and I exaggerated matters when I told of Mrs. Churchill's feelings toward her daughter-in-law, and what Roy said about her coming in disguise. You remember it, I think. I wanted to make sure that you would neither remain at Leighton, nor divulge your real name to them. Forgive me, Edna, won't you? I have much need of your forgiveness."

And Edna had stooped and given her the kiss of pardon, feeling, as she did so, that a load was lifted from her heart, and that she could now make herself known to Charlie's friends.

"Do it at once," Georgie said. "Don't put it off, but let Roy know who you are."

And Edna promised that she would; and then, with another kiss for the repentant woman, she went back to Leighton, and when next she looked on Georgie, she was cold and pale in death, but lay like one asleep upon her pillow, with white lilies in her hand, and a look of perfect peace upon her face. The pinched, disturbed look was gone, and in its stead death gave back to her much of her beauty. The bright color had faded from her cheeks; there were threads of snow in her black hair, and her glorious eyes were closed forever; but otherwise she looked the same, and poor Mrs. Burton wrung her hands distractedly, as she bent over her beautiful darling, and called upon her to waken and speak to the mother who loved her so much. They dressed her in her wedding robes, and Roy kissed his pale, dead bride with a great sob of pain, and forgot for once when Brownie's step was near, and did not hear when she spoke to him. It was a grand funeral,—the largest ever known in Summerville, for the circumstances attending Georgie's death had been so strange and sad that hundreds had gathered from a distance, and came to show their respect for the mourning family. They carried her to Greenwood, and laid her by the side of Annie. This was Jack's thought and wish.

"She was my sister," he said; "nearer to me by blood than any one else. I surely may have my wish."

So Mrs. Burton, who had in her mind a fashionable lot, with a monument, setting forth her daughter's virtues, and costing from ten thousand to twenty thousand dollars, gave way, thinking within herself that the monument was still available, even for that rather obscure spot, and wishing that neglected-looking grave, so near to poor, dear Georgie's, might be removed to another part of Greenwood.

"Whose grave is it, and who was Richard Le Roy?" she asked, after they had returned to her house in New York, where she had proposed spending a few days until Oakwood could be cleansed from the recent atmosphere of death.

Jack, who knew more of Richard Le Roy than any one present, made no reply, and so it devolved on Roy to ask if she did not remember an English family which years ago lived on Fourteenth street, and had so many handsome daughters.

Mrs. Burton did remember something about them, especially a piece of *old lace* which Mrs. Le Roy used to wear, and whose value was immense.

Richard was the only son, Roy explained, a fast young man, though very genial and companionable. He died quite suddenly, and at the time of his death was engaged to an elder sister of Miss Agatha Shawe; at least, so it was said. The Le Roys had returned to England long ago, he said, and that was all the information he could give concerning the occupant of the lone grave, which Mrs. Burton felt was in her way. She was satisfied, however, with what Roy told her, and never suspected the cause of Jack's sudden rising, and walking to the window, where he stood for a time looking out into the summer night, and thinking strange thoughts of the three graves in Greenwood, where slept, side by side, Richard Le Roy, Georgie Burton, and the little Annie.

CHAPTER XLVI.

JACK'S MARRIAGE AND JACK'S STORY.

TWO days before Georgie's death she had asked to see her Uncle and Aunt Burton alone for a few moments, and during that interview she talked with them of Maude and Jack, telling them that to the latter she had given all her possessions, and asking them to receive Maude as a daughter in her place, and give her a part at least of what had been intended for herself.

"And mother," she said to Mrs. Burton, "it is my wish that they be married at once. Do not let them wait because I am dead. It is better for Jack to have a wife. Let them marry immediately. Say it was my dying wish."

Too much broken with grief to oppose anything which Georgie asked, Mrs. Burton promised compliance with everything, and so it came about that three weeks after Georgie's death, there was a very quiet wedding at Oakwood, and Maude was made Jack Heyford's wife. Aside from the family, only Mrs. Churchill and Roy were present, together with Edna and Uncle Phil, who, at the earnest solicitation of Maude came down to the wedding, looking very smart and trim in the new coat bought for the occasion, and the white vest, and big white handkerchief tied about his neck, giving him the appearance of a Methodist minister. Mrs. Burton was a little shocked with his manners, and was glad there were no more guests present to see him. But Mr. Burton enjoyed him thoroughly, and took him all over his farm, and went with him to drive a fast horse which he had just bought, and which came near breaking the necks of both the old men. Roy, too, who had seen him at Rocky Point, was very polite to him and made himself so agreeable, that Uncle Phil prolonged his stay to a week, and when he left, he had Edna's promise to visit him in October, while Roy was to come for her when her visit was over.

Remembering the widowed Janet among the Scottish hills, and the promise made to Georgie, Jack planned a short trip to Europe, and when on the day following his bridal, the Scotia sailed out of the harbor of New York, he stood upon the deck with Maude at his side, her face radiant with happiness and joyful anticipations of the new world to which she was going. She had as yet heard nothing of Janet, or Jack's message to her, but one bright, balmy day, when the sea beneath them was like glass, and the sky overhead as blue as Maude's laughing eyes, Jack led her to a retired part of the steamer, and seating himself beside her, told her Georgie's story, and why he was going to Scotland.

Georgie had been very beautiful in her fresh girlhood, he said, and they had been so poor, living on one floor of a tenement-house down on Varick street. She was older than Jack by a few years; was his half-sister, whom he had loved devotedly ever since he could remember anything. His father had died when he was a mere boy, and soon after his death, Georgie, who then was known as Louise, her real name being Louise Georgiana, had sought for a situation in a milliner's establishment on Canal street. But her face, and her natural love of coquetry was against her, and after both sons of the proprietor had owned themselves in love with her, she had been dismissed as one who did not know her place. Through a kind friend who was interested in the beautiful girl, she went next to a dry-goods establishment, where she met with HENRY MORTON, a good-looking young man, whose virtues were rather of the negative kind, and whose infatuation for Louise Heyford was unbounded. She meant to marry rich, and while waiting upon customers, her thoughts were always intent upon the future, when she too could wear her satins and diamonds, and have her carriage waiting at the door, while she purchased what she liked, irrespective of the cost. Henry was poor, and as such did not gain favor very fast with the young girl, although while building her Spanish castles she managed to hold him fast in her meshes, making of him a perfect tool, to come and depart according to her pleasure.

Suddenly the firm failed, and again Georgie was without employment, with a greater love for dress and admiration than ever before, inasmuch as she had been so flattered and caressed. Her next situation was that of nursery governess in the family of Mr. Le Roy, who lived on Fourteenth street, and who had seven daughters, and one only son. Here, in this family where a governess was but little more than an ordinary servant, and where she was seldom or never admitted to a glimpse of the gay world, save as she saw it in the rich dresses the young ladies wore, or heard it in the snatches of talk in which they sometimes indulged in her presence, she lived a dreary, monotonous life, always sitting, and eating, and sleeping in the nursery, where she washed and dressed, and taught and hated the three little Le Roys, who were the fruit of a second marriage, and who did all they could to worry their young teacher's life away.

It was getting to be intolerable, and Georgie was beginning to think seriously of giving up the situation, and either returning to the home on Varick street, or accepting Henry Morton, when the only son of the house, Richard Le Roy, came home from Europe, and everything was changed as if by magic. They met first in the nursery, where Richard came for a romp with his little half-sisters. He was very fond of children, and as the little ones were nearly crazy over their tall, handsome brother, waylaying him at every corner, and dragging him with them, it came about naturally enough that he was often in the school-room, where a pair of the most beautiful eyes he had ever seen, soon began to brighten when he came, and a young face to blush and half turn away when it met his admiring gaze. Perhaps he meant no harm at first, for he was not vicious or bad at heart. Georgie was a poor little lonesome thing, who was shamefully neglected by his proud sisters, and who would be far more in place in the drawing-room than in that pent-up hole with all those young ones worrying her to death, and if he could do anything to ameliorate her condition, it was his duty to do it.

Thus he reasoned, and acted in accordance with his reasoning, and spent a great deal of time with the *children*, and sometimes took them to drive, always insisting that the governess should accompany them. She needed air and exercise as much as they did, he said, and to Miss Elinor Shawe, to whom he was said to be engaged, he talked very freely of Louise Heyford, and his charitable labors in her behalf. And because of his frank, honest manner, no one suspected evil, or dreamed of the fearful results of his deeds of charity. Henry Morton's face wore a sober, disappointed look those days when Louise snubbed him in the street,—and was always engaged, or had a headache when he tried to see her; while Louise herself expanded each day into new freshness and beauty, and her eyes shone like stars, and seemed fairly to dance in the exuberance of her happiness. Richard promised her marriage,—honorable, though *private* marriage, because of his family,—and their future life was to be spent in Europe, where none would know that he had not chosen his bride from his own social rank. All Louise's castles were about to come real, and in her own mind she had settled her bridal trousseau, and her style of dealing with her husband's family, when suddenly, as a thief in the night, the blow came, and Richard Le Roy was stricken down with a prevailing epidemic,—cholera, some called it. In twenty-four hours from the time when his kiss was warm on Georgie's lips, he lay a corpse in the room where he had died, with only Georgie and his father with him. His step-mother and sisters had in the first alarm fled to their chambers, and locked themselves in from the dreadful pestilence, though not until Sophie, the eldest sister, had begged of the despised governess to go to her brother and help him if she could.

"Cholera does not often attack healthy girls like you, but it would kill me sure," she said, wringing her hands in great distress, while Georgie stood motionless, with her face and lips as white as ashes.

It was *fear*, Sophie thought, and she tried to reassure the young girl who needed no reassurance, and who went swiftly to the room where her lover lay. He knew she was with him, and clasped her hands in his, and tried to tell his father something,—but the words were never spoken, and before the sun went down he was dead; and Georgie lay upon her face in her own solitary room trying to fight back the horrid fear which amounted almost to a certainty, and which within three days drove her to the store where Henry Morton was a clerk. He saw her as she meant he should, and the sweetness of her smile, and the great change in her manner toward him, drew him again to her side, and revived all his love for her. There was a chance meeting next day in the street, a long walk in the evening, followed by another and another, and ere Richard Le Roy had been in his grave a month, Henry Morton and Louise Heyford were man and wife. Contrary to the usual course of things, she had been the one to urge an immediate union. There was no necessity for delay; they could earn their living better together, and she did so want a home of her own, if only one room. He should see what a nice housekeeper she could be, she said, when he proposed waiting a few months until he had more laid up.

So they were married, and they rented two rooms, and fitted them up as prettily and cosily as his limited means would allow, and there he brought his handsome bride in November, and there, early in the following May the little Annie was born. She was a full-grown, healthy child, with no resemblance to the father, who, troubled and mystified, looked at her curiously, and then at his young wife, and then went away alone, and thought it all out, while as he thought there came over him a change which awoke all the evil passions of his nature, and transformed him into a demon of rage and jealousy. There was a stormy interview between him and his wife, a full confession from her, and then he cast her from him and drove her into the street, where, with her baby in her arms, she wandered half the night until it was no longer safe for a respectable woman to be abroad.

Faint, and tired, and sick, she stepped from the car, and turned toward the home in Varick street.

"I'll try it," she said. "I'll tell them the whole truth, and if they too turn me off, I'll go to-morrow to Greenwood and die on Richard's grave."

As yet, neither her step-mother nor Jack knew of her disgrace, for the former had been sick, and Jack had not been to see her since Annie's birth two weeks before. Jack slept soundly that night, and dreamed that some one called his name. Waking at last, he listened, and heard Georgie's voice, calling him to come, and telling him she was dying. That was no dream, and in a moment he was dressed and at the door, where he met his sister with her baby in her arms, and her face so white and ghastly that he uttered a cry of alarm, which brought his mother to his side.

"Louise, it *is* Louise," he said, taking her by the shoulder, and pulling her into the room. "It is Louise, mother; but what brings her here at this time of the night, and what, what is this she holds so tight?"

An infant's wail told him what it was, and ere he could step forward, Georgie held the baby to him and cried:

"Take her, Jack; take her before I die."

And so it was Jack who first received the little unwelcome child. Jack's arms, which held her close, and Jack's voice, which tried to hush her plaintive moans. As she entered the room Georgie had sunk down upon the floor, and when her step-mother tried to assist her she pushed her off, exclaiming:

"No, no, not yet; let me lie here in the dust until I tell you all and you know how vile I am."

Then, amid tears and sobs she told them the truth; how she had sinned, and deceived her husband, who had driven her from him with the fury of a madman.

"I have been in the street, out in the dark ever since," she said, and I thought once to go down to the river and end my miserable life, but the touch of baby's hands kept me from it, and at last I come to you. Oh Jack, don't turn from me now," she sobbed, as she saw the look of horror on his face. "I know what I am, but don't you turn against me. You are all I have in the world. Forgive me, Jack. Take me in. Try me, for the baby's sake. You may learn to love her sometime, and to pity me."

She was at the boy's feet now, and her hands held him fast, as she begged thus for his pardon. And Jack forgave her then and there, and laying the baby upon his mother's lap, he lifted Georgie up and strove to comfort her, and said so long as he could work she should have a home. He was earning good wages now; he supported his mother, and with a little more self-denial on his part, a little overwork out of business hours, he could support her. He did not kiss her; he could not do it then; but he kept his hand upon her neck while he talked to her, and Georgie did not feel one-half so desolate when she felt the touch of that boyish hand. Jack had saved her; Jack would stand by her; Jack would shield her as far as possible. And he did; and, with his mother's help, managed so well, that none of their few acquaintances guessed the real cause of the separation between Georgie and her husband, or why the former kept so carefully out of sight with her baby when any of them called. It was mortification, and a natural shrinking from meeting old friends, they thought, and so excused it in her, and gradually forgot to speak of her and her affairs at all.

At first there was in Henry Morton's face and manner a kind of sullen, brutish ferocity, which made him so unpopular that he was finally dismissed by his employer, and cast upon the world, a desperate man, with nothing to do, nothing to live for, his home desolated, his wife lost, and himself dishonored. Falling in with a set of the New York roughs who live mostly by theft and fraud, he went rapidly from bad to worse, becoming such an expert in robbery that he was always put to do the work inside, while his comrades watched without. Thus it happened that he was found in Roy Leighton's house, and afterward identified by Russell, who knew him by a defect in his right eye, which had been put out when he was a boy. Although he gave an assumed name, it came out at the trial who he was, and that he had a wife, whom he had abandoned. Then came the verdict of the jury, the sentence to the penitentiary, followed swiftly by escape, and the forgetfulness by the public, as is usual in New York; where robberies are so common, and escape from justice not unfrequent.

A year went by, and Georgie received a letter from her husband, telling her he was dying of an incurable disease, among the Alleghany Mountains. Then came a paper containing a notice of his death, and then Jack went himself to the little inland town to make sure that the wretched man was dead. There could be no mistake about it, he thought, and Georgie breathed freer, and urged her brother's removal to the West, where they were unknown to every one, and where she could begin life anew as GEORGIE HEYFORD, instead of Louise Morton.

And so westward they went, settling first upon a farm which Jack worked upon shares, taxing his strength too much, until his health began to fail, and the farm had to be abandoned. The next move was to Chicago, where Jack procured work as half porter, half errand boy, in the store, and rising gradually to a higher place of trust as clerk, and gaining the good opinion of all who came in contact with him. Georgie and his mother supported themselves by plain-sewing and fancy needle-work, while the little Annie was known as the orphan child of a friend of Mrs. Heyford, and Georgie passed for a young girl. Very few people knew her, as she seldom went out except to get or carry work, and her life bade fair to go on in the same quiet, monotonous way, when there came a letter, which changed at once her whole destiny.

It was from Mrs. Freeman Burton, whose only sister had been the first Mrs. Heyford, and Georgie's mother. As girls the two sisters had been strongly attached to each other. Early orphaned, they had clung together, and by needle-work and teaching supported themselves respectably, until a rich old man, who might have been Mrs. Burton's grandfather, had fallen in love with and married her, thus raising her to a position of wealth and importance, and furnishing a home of luxury both for her and her sister Annie. The latter, however, had given her affections to young Heyford, who, though poor, had this in his favor, that he was young and well connected, and that she loved him devotedly, which was more than could be said of the gray-haired husband of Mary, the elder sister, who had sold herself for gold, and who set herself against the Heyford match. But love won the day, and with her sister's farewell words, " never come to me if you are starving," ringing in her ears, the young wife went willingly with her husband, and for his sake bore cheerfully a life of comparative poverty, and tried to do her duty by her husband and the little child born to them within the first year of their marriage.

When she heard that her sister's husband was dead, she wrote her a letter expressing her sympathy, and offering to go to her in case she could in any way comfort or console her. To this letter no answer came, but a year after, Mrs. Heyford was surprised at receiving a call from her sister, who came in quietly, and unattended by carriage or servant. She had married a second time, and was now Mrs. Freeman Burton, of Madison Square. Knowing that her sister was in New York, she had found her out, not to renew acquaintance, but rather to *prevent* it. She was very frank and open, and said what she had to say in a manner which left no doubt as to her meaning. "Their paths in life were very different," she said. "As the wife of Mr. Freeman Burton she was entitled to, and should take, the very first place in society, and as her sister was situated so differently, it would be unpleasant for them to meet each other often, and they might as well make up their minds to it first as last. She should come occasionally to see Mrs. Heyford, but should not feel badly if her calls were not returned, and she greatly preferred that Mrs. Freeman Burton should not be known as the sister of Mrs. William Heyford, who lived on the upper floor of a tenement house far down town, and made dresses for a living." That was decisive. The sisters never met again, and when at Christmas time Mrs. Freeman Burton sent a check for one hundred dollars to Mrs. William Heyford, it was promptly returned, and the intercourse ended entirely when Mrs. Heyford died, as she did, not long after. The husband sent a paper containing a marked notice of the death to Mrs. Freeman Burton, and a second time that lady mounted the three flights of stairs, and knocked at No. ———. But the rooms were shut up; the child Georgie was with her father's friends, and Mrs. Freeman Burton stole back to her fashionable house, and cried all the morning over the memory of other days, when she and her dead sister had been the world to each other.

Six months later, and she received another paper containing a marked paragraph. Mr. Heyford had married again, and lived now on Varick street, whither Mrs. Burton ventured to go, crying over the little Louise, who had a look like the dead sister, and appearing far more friendly toward the second Mrs. Heyford than she had toward the first. Still, there was no wish expressed for further intercourse, and the families for years knew nothing of each other except through the little presents of books and clothes which were occasionally sent from Madison Square to the little Louise, and which Mrs. Heyford kept.

When Georgie was thirteen, she heard that her aunt had gone abroad, and in the exciting scenes of the ensuing years which followed, she almost forgot the existence of such a relative until a letter came from her, saying she had returned to New York and reopened her house, and was coming in a few weeks to Chicago to find her *dear niece.*

"I have been a very proud, wicked woman," she wrote, "but I hope I am trying to do better, and wish to make some amends for my treatment of my poor sister by being kind to her child."

This was the secret of the whole. Mrs. Burton did believe herself a better woman, and perhaps she was. An ardent admirer of Dr. Pusey, she had in her the elements which made her afterwards a devoted Ritualist, and she wanted to do something which should prove her reform to herself. Upon inquiry in the neighborhood where she had left her sister's family she could learn nothing of them, so completely had they dropped out of memory. Remembering at last the name of Mr. Heyford's former employer, she went to him and heard that her brother-in-law was dead, and the family in Chicago; that was all the man could tell her. Of Georgie's marriage he knew nothing. Mr. Heyford died years ago, he said, and he had taken the boy Jack into his employ until he went West, since which time he had heard nothing from him.

In this dilemma, Mrs. Burton wrote to Georgie, directing to Jack's care, and then waited the result. For days the letter lay unclaimed, and then appeared among the list of advertised in one of the daily papers. It caught Jack's eye, and he immediately went for it and carried it to Georgie, who counted it the brightest day of her life when her aunt came to their humble home, and offered to adopt her as her daughter and give her every advantage which the heiress of Mrs. Freeman Burton ought to have. There was no hesitancy on Georgie's part. Dearly as she loved little Annie, she loved ambition more, and said at once, "I will go."

To Jack's suggestion that she tell her aunt of her marriage, at least, she turned a deaf ear. No one must know that. To go to New York as a widow with a child would seriously mar her plans, and then in the winning, fascinating way she knew so well how to use, she persuaded Jack into taking an oath that he never would reveal her secret to any living person unless she first gave him permission to do so. From her step-mother a promise of silence was all she could obtain, but she knew Mrs. Heyford well enough to feel sure that she was safe; and casting the past behind her, she said good-by to Jack, her mother, and Annie, and went with her aunt, who had no suspicion that the beautiful young creature, who seemed so soft, and gentle, and innocent, had a hidden history, from which she would have shrunk in dismay.

What Mrs. Burton hated she hated cordially, and what she loved she loved as cordially, and she lavished upon her niece all the affection which she had withheld from her sister and both her husbands.

At first she had her taught at home under her own eye, and then when she felt that she had acquired a little of the polish and knowledge of the world, which would be expected from Mrs. Freeman Burton's daughter, she sent her to a fashionable boarding-school, from which she emerged a finished young lady, and became a belle at once. Her after career is so well known to the reader that it is useless to repeat it here, though Jack told Maude of the deep love there had always existed between his sister and the little Annie, who worshipped her as some superior being; "and I loved her, too," he said, as he finished the sad story, to which Maude had listened wonderingly, "loved her as few brothers have ever loved their sisters. I knew she had many and glaring faults, and sometimes in my anger I was almost desperate in my feelings toward her, but a touch of her hand, a tone of her voice, or a beseeching glance of her eye, had power to quiet me at once, and I would almost have walked over burning coals for her sake, when in her softest mood. I knew, too, that she loved me,—honestly, truly loved me,—and now that she is gone it is a comfort to remember it, for there were times when I was very harsh with her. Poor Georgie; in many things she was a splendid woman, and though she greatly erred, I feel that at the last she was sorry for it and repented most sincerely, and I believe she is in heaven now, with Annie and my mother."

There were tears in Jack's eyes, and his voice shook so for a few minutes that he could not go on with his story; but after a little he continued, and told Maude about the burglar at Oakwood, and why he was going to Scotland. It was on a mission for Georgie; and Maude entered heart and soul into it, and would scarcely let him rest a day in England, so anxious was she to find the Janet among the heather hills, and the fatherless little bairns. They found them at last,—a rosy-cheeked, brown-haired little woman, and two fair young children with her, one clinging to her dress behind, and peeping shyly out as the strangers came in, and the other turning his sightless eyes toward them. Their errand was soon told; and when Jack saw how bitterly poor Janet wept, he felt that Henry Morton had been a kind, loving husband to her, even if in secret he had done her wrong. After arranging about the money which Georgie had sent to the widow, who supposed it came from her husband, Jack and Maude repeated their offers of assistance whenever it was necessary; and then promising to see Janet again before returning to America, he bade her good-by, and started on their tour through Europe.

CHAPTER XLVII.

ROY FINDS EDNA.

EDNA had promised Georgie that not a long time should elapse before she would make herself known to Roy and his mother. She had also promised Uncle Phil an early visit to Rocky Point; and within a week or so after Jack's departure for Europe, she asked and obtained permission from Mrs. Churchill to go to her old home. It was very lonely at Leighton without her; and Roy found the time hanging heavily on his hands, and was trying hard to make himself believe that his property at Rocky Point required personal looking after, when he received through Miss Pepper a letter from Edna, expressing her sympathy with him in his recent loss, and saying that if he would come to Allen's Hill, at such a time, she would be there to meet him.

Roy had not heard from Edna before in a long, long time. Indeed, she had written to him but once since his engagement with Georgie. Then she had sent him a hundred dollars toward the payment of her debt, and had said a few words about his intended marriage, hoping he might be happy with his bride, but declining to tell him where she was living. And that was all he knew of her; and he was not quite as enthusiastic on the subject as he had once been. Miss Overton was his absorbing thought. Still he felt glad that at last he was to see and know his mysterious sister-in-law, and felt especially glad of any excuse which would take him away from home and into the vicinity of Rocky Point; for he meant to go there first. It would be only a short run from Albany, and detain him but a day at the most, and Brownie was sure to be glad to see him. It is true she had never said much to him of Edna, or evinced any great interest in her; but she would be glad because he was glad; and he hoped the two young girls would like each other; for of course Edna would now live at Leighton, which was also to be Brownie's home forever. He had settled that last point satisfactorily with himself, and he meant to settle it with Brownie before long. Georgie herself had hinted it to him. Georgie had been willing, and had bidden him not to wait because she was dead. And he would not; he would speak to her and tell her of his love; and if she could love him in return, they would wait a reasonable time, and then he would make her his wife, and install her mistress of Leighton, where Edna should always have a place as the sister of the house.

This was his plan; and he found his pulse quickening as he drew near to Rocky Point, where he expected to find his Brownie. But the bird had flown,—had gone, Uncle Phil said, to visit some of her kin. And when Roy asked where her kin lived, the old man answered, "Oh, in forty places. She is goin' to Albany first, and then to Schenectady, and Utica, and Canestoty, and Syracuse, and Auburn, for what I know. You'd better let her run a spell whilst you hunt up t'other one; two gals at a lick is too much."

There was a knowing twinkle in Uncle Phil's eyes; but it was lost on Roy, who, in his disappointment, did not once think that Uncle Phil had mentioned the different points along the railroad line through which it was necessary to pass in order to reach Allen's Hill. He only felt that he must bear his suspense a little longer, and that it was hard to do so.

The next day he took the train for Canandaigua, where he spent the night, and the following morning drove himself out to Allen's Hill, just as he had done once before, when

Edna as now was the object he sought. There was no soap boiling in the caldron kettle this time, and no Macbethian witch bending over it in wonderful costume, as Roy came round the corner of the church, and tied his horse to the post. Aunt Jerry was expecting him, and welcomed him cordially, and invited him in, and then tortured him by talking for ten or fifteen minutes upon every topic but the one uppermost in his mind. At last, when he could wait no longer, he said to her, abruptly:

"Your niece wrote me that she would meet me here any day this week, and I have lost no time in coming. She will not disappoint me now, I trust. I am very anxious to find her."

"Yes, I s'pose so. She's here, though not in the house this minute. She went to the woods an hour or so ago."

"Can I find her there, do you think? Show me the way, please, and I'll try it," Roy said with sudden animation, rising to his feet, and seeming full of eagerness and impatience.

It could not have been anything in Aunt Jerry's manner which communicated itself to him, nor anything in the atmosphere of the house. It was rather a presentiment of the coming happiness, a remembrance of Uncle Phil's demeanor and mysterious hints, which, put together, came over Roy with a sudden suspicion of the truth, or rather a suspicion that it might be just possible, nothing more. It was too delightful a possibility to be true; and he must not harbor the hope for a moment, he said to himself, as, waiting only for Aunt Jerry's somewhat indefinite directions, he started for the west woods, where Edna was to be found.

"There's a brook down there, and a bank under a tree: maybe you'll find her there," Aunt Jerry had said, and Roy kept on his way down the hill, past the site of the old school-house where Edna had learned her alphabet; through the bars, which he did not wait to let down, but over which he vaulted at one bound; and on across the grassy patch until the border of the woods was reached, and there he paused a moment to look about and reconnoitre a little.

It was one of those balmy, autumnal days when earth and sky seem more beautiful even than in early summer. A recent frost had just tinged the leaves of the maple with scarlet, and here and there a leaf was falling from the trees, and a ripe, brown nut was dropping through the hazy air down to the ground, while the murmur of the brook was plainly heard as it ran singing on its way, now through the bed of ferns whose broad leaves dipped themselves in its cool waters, and now widening out into a broader channel, with little fishes playing in it, and tall trees reaching their arms across it, making a delicious shade, on that warm, sunny morning. Roy followed the brook until he reached the point where it began to widen, then a little farther on, and then he stopped again, and felt every nerve quivering with an ecstasy of delight, so great and overpowering, that for an instant he leaned for support against a tree, while his lips framed the words, "I thank Thee, my Heavenly Father, for this great joy of which I never dreamed."

Twenty rods or so in advance, and sitting under a tall maple, with her hat on the ground beside her, and her back to Roy, was a little girlish figure, which Roy was certain he knew. The attitude, the poise of the head, and more than all, the curls of golden brown, and the dress of blue cambric, which he had always admired so much in Brownie, proclaimed that it was Brownie herself, the woman whom he felt at this moment he loved more than his life. Everything he had said to Georgie concerning his disapproval of disguises, was forgotten in that moment of supreme delight, when, with a few rapid strides he reached the figure on the bank, and met the soft, laughing eyes he knew so well, and saw the blushes deepen on the beautiful face upturned to his when Edna first became aware of his close proximity to her.

"My darling," was all he said, all he could say, as he took her in his arms, and laid his mouth to the sweet lips which kissed him back without a moment's hesitation.

There was little need for more open declaration and acceptance of love than was expressed in that first embrace. Roy had confessed himself in the kisses he rained upon her lips, her forehead and her hands, while she, in suffering it, had accepted him; and both felt that they were pledged to each other, when at last Roy released her and drew her to a seat beside him on the grass.

"Now, tell me," he said, as he put his arm around her, and held her hand in his, "tell me the whole story, why you deceived us so, and how you did it so successfully?"

"You are not angry with me then, for being such an impostor? Oh, Mr. Leighton, I have hated myself so much for the imposition," she said; and Roy replied:

"Angry? I should think not; but please drop that formal Mr. Leighton. Let me be Roy to you."

She always called him Roy to herself, when thinking of him, and the name came readily enough.

"Well, Roy, then," she began, "I wanted you and your mother to like me, and I fancied I should succeed better as a stranger, than as Charlie's wife;" and then she told him of her life at Uncle Phil's; of Maude's recognition of her; of the watch she sold, and which by some strange chance had come round to Maude, who did not know until just before she sailed whose watch it was she was carrying; of Uncle Phil's wish that she should take another name than her own; of Maude's arranging for her to go *incog* to Leighton; and of the various devices she had resorted to in order to keep up the delusion, and mystify him with regard to her whereabouts.

She uttered no unkind word against poor Georgie. She merely said, "Had you married Miss Burton, I should have gone away at once, and never have let you know who I really was. *She* knew me from the first, but kindly kept my secret."

"Ye-es," Roy rejoined, between a sigh and a groan, for he remembered many things Georgie had said in Edna's presence, and which were far from being kind in her if she knew, as it seemed she did, who Miss Overton was.

But Georgie was dead; he had buried her from his sight, and he would put from him even the memory of her faults, and remember only that at the last she had sanctioned his love for the young girl beside him, whose bright head he drew to his bosom, while he kissed the white brow, and said, "Never to have found you, darling, would have been a calamity, indeed, both to my mother and myself. She could not love an own daughter better than she loves you, and I long so to see her joy when she learns the truth, and that you are ours for ever."

Then they talked of that adventure in the cars, and laughed over the Miss Bettie Edna had so hurriedly dashed off, and spoke sadly and softly of poor Charlie in his far-off grave; and then, bending his head so low that his face touched hers, Roy said, "Georgie foretold this thing, and bade me not to wait because she was dead. Shall it not be as she said, my darling? Shall we be married at once?"

Then Edna's love of mischief broke out, and withdrawing herself from him, she answered saucily, "Married! who has said anything to me about marriage? Surely not you, and here you ask for an early day. I am astonished at you, Mr. Leighton."

"Edna," Roy said, bringing her again to his side, and holding her so closely that she could not get away. "This is no time to trifle. You know well what my kisses meant when I first saw you here, and found that Edna was the same with the girl whom I named Brownie to myself, and whom I now think I have loved almost since I first saw her standing at my mother's side, and answering to the name of Miss Overton. But lest you misunderstand me, and deem yourself not wooed *au fait*, I formally ask you to be my wife, feeling confident that after what has passed between us you will not refuse me."

She wanted to tease him dreadfully, but something in his manner forbade it; she must deal openly with him, and so she replied frankly and honestly, " I do love you, Roy, and am willing to be your wife, only I had promised myself never to marry until the whole of my indebtedness to you was paid. I have been extravagant since I have been at Leighton, where I saw so much of dress. I have not paid you as fast as I might have done. I still owe you——"

" Seventy-five dollars, I believe," Roy said, interrupting her, and adding, laughingly: " It was a foolish thing, your trying to be so independent, but since you have been, and there is still something my due, suppose we make it an even thing, and you give yourself in lieu of the money——"

" Which will make me worth just seventy-five dollars to you. I hoped you valued me higher than that," Edna said, pretending to look aggrieved, while Roy bent down and kissed her pouting lips, and said that to her which told that money could not liquidate the price at which he held her, and that to lose her now would be to lose the very brightness of his life, and leave it all a blank.

While they sat there too much absorbed in each other to heed the lapse of time, or hear first the bell, and then the tin horn, which Aunt Jerry in her impatience had used alternately as a reminder of dinner, that worthy spinster herself suddenly appeared before them, her brow clouded, and her mouth puckered up in the peculiar fashion which Edna knew was indicative of displeasure.

Aunt Jerry's first act after Roy had left the house in quest of Edna, was to unhitch the check-rein of the horse standing at the gate, and her second to give it water and handfuls of the tall grass growing near. Kindness to brutes was a part of her nature, and nothing which had life was ever in danger of being ill-used where she was, unless it were a child. For children she had not a great deal of love; but where animals were concerned she was a second Bergh, and she cared for Roy's horse and patted its neck, and when she saw how high it threw its head at first, and how it shrank from her, she said:

"Poor critter! I know by the way you act that your keeper abuses you. No horse kindly used is ever as nervous as that. The wretch! I wish I had him by the nape of the neck!"

When the horse was cared for, the dame, with thoughts intent on dinner, pounced upon a group of fowls feeding at her back-door, and catching the youngest, fattest one, had its neck off in a trice, and picked, and dressed, and had it in the pot within an hour after. Aunt Jerry's forte in cookery was *pot-pie*, and she now did her best, and made such a crust, as, to use a common culinary phrase, would almost "melt in one's mouth." White and light, and flaky, it looked like bats of cotton wool, and her spirits rose proportionably as she arranged her table and prepared her vegetables.

Everything was done at last. The baked tomatoes were browned just right; the corn pudding was white, and creamy, and sweet; the custard was delicious, and the coffee sent a fragrant odor through the house; but the guests did not come. She had rung the bell, and blown the horn, and at last, as the clock struck one, she started herself for the delinquents, exclaiming when she saw them, "Well, you are smart!" but ere she got farther, Roy arose, and taking Edna's hand in his, said to her:

"I have found her, you see, and she has promised to live with me always. She is to be my wife, if you do not object."

"Umph! a pretty time of day to ask if I object, after it's all cut and dried, and dinner spoiling in the oven. Didn't you hear the bell, nor the horn I blew an hour ago?"

Both culprits pleaded guilty, and both made haste to follow Miss Jerusha, who never spoke again until the house was reached, and contrary to her prediction, she found that the pot-pie was not spoiled, though she insisted that it would have been better half-an-hour before.

By the time dinner was over, Aunt Jerry was completely mollified, and after her dishes were washed and put away, and her floor swept, and the cat fed, and the horse watered again, she was ready to hear Roy on the subject uppermost in his mind. He loved Edna; he wanted her for his wife; and wanted to know if Miss Pepper had any objections to the match.

"It's most too late to give them, if I have," Aunt Jerry said. "But that's the way nowadays. Young folks have got the whip row of us, and will keep it, I suppose. No, I have no objections. If she must marry, and I suppose she must, I'd as soon she'd have you as anybody, and she won't go to you poverty-stricken either. Every dollar she paid me, I put in Beals's bank, in her name, and added another to it, so that she has now as good as a thousand laid up. I shall give her another thousand, too, and a feather bed, and I want it secured to her and her heirs forever."

"Oh, auntie, how kind you have been to me, when I thought, sometimes, you did not care," Edna said.

The money in the bank was new to her, and she felt the tears rush into her eyes as she thought how she had misjudged her aunt. As for Roy, he could scarcely repress a smile at the woman's eagerness to have the two thousand dollars settled on Edna beyond his reach, but he promised to see that it was done, and then said it was also his intention to give his bride, out-and-out, such a sum as would make her independent in case of his dying insolvent, a catastrophe by the way, which he did not anticipate. When he asked for an early day, and named Christmas as the time when he hoped Edna would come to him, Aunt Jerry demurred.

"It was not decent," she said, "and did not show proper respect for that dead woman with the boy's name."

Roy reassured her on that point by telling her what Georgie's wish had been, and she gave way at last, but her face wore a very forbidding look, and reminded Edna of the days when she used to cut carpet-rags up in the back chamber. Roy could not tear himself from Edna at once, so he remained all night, and made himself thoroughly at home in Aunt Jerry's house, and interested himself in whatever he saw interested her. First, however, he wrote to his mother that he had found Edna, and that he should stop at Allen's Hill a few days, and then bring her home with him. He wished to surprise her, and so did not tell her *who* Edna was. He only wrote, "You will like her. She is a pretty little creature, and will be a great acquisition to our family circle. I need not bespeak a welcome for her, I am sure, for you will receive her as a daughter, I know, and love her with a mother's love."

It was rather late when he retired, and he would not have gone when he did, if Aunt Jerry had not told him it was after her bedtime, and she shouldn't sit up any longer for anybody. Roy felt that he would gladly have dispensed with her company, and enjoyed himself quite as well, but he refrained from giving expression to his thoughts, and taking the lamp she brought him, went to his room at the end of the hall.

Meantime, Edna had been longing for some expression of sympathy from her aunt. Her heart was so full of happiness that she wanted to share it with some one, to talk with some one, who ought to know something how she felt; and after Roy had said good-night, she drew a little stool to her aunt's side, and laying her head in her lap, as she had never lain it before, said to her :

"Auntie, have you no word of congratulation, for me? Are you not glad because I am so happy, oh, so much happier than I ever thought I could be, when—"

Here she stopped abruptly, feeling that she was treading on dangerous ground, but her aunt took up the unfinished sentence and said, "When you lived with *me*, and I made a little nigger of you ; that's what you mean. Don't spoil a story for relations' sake. I was hard on you at times, and mean as pussly, too. But, Edna," and the voice began to tremble, "I never meant to be bad. I didn't understand children, or that they could grow up to be a comfort, as I know now you would be, and since you come back I've thought how nice it would be to have you live with me, and now he's come, and you'll go with him, and the old woman will be alone again, all alone."

There was a pitiful sound in Aunt Jerry's voice, and it brought the tears to Edna's eyes, but before she could speak, Aunt Jerry went on. "I am glad for you, child ; it's the ordained way to marry, and you've got a good man, I believe, and you'll be happy with him. You think, of course, old Aunt Jerusha don't know what it is to love, but I do. I was nearer once to being married than you are now ; so near, that the day was set, and my wedding dress was made, and my hot temper got the better of me, and we quarrelled about a trivial thing, and I wouldn't yield an inch, and got so mad at last that I vowed I'd never marry him, and I never have, and we have lived our lives alone, he in his way, I in mine."

"Oh, auntie, I never suspected such a thing; and he is living yet, you say, and maybe sometime—you'll—"

"No we shan't," and Aunt Jerry spoke quickly. "I ain't such a fool as that. We have not met in thirty years, and the sight of me now would make him sick at the stomach. I was young then, and not bad-looking either; now I'm old and wrinkled, and hard and gray, and he is old, and fat, and queer, and pussy, I have no doubt. No, child, don't build castles for me. Be happy yourself and I am satisfied."

She stroked Edna's hair softly for a moment, and then said abruptly but kindly, "There, now, you've got just what you wanted; be off to bed. Don't you see it is going on to twelve o'clock."

So Edna left her with a good-night kiss, and stole up to her room, there to muse over her own great happiness, and to think of the story Aunt Jerry had told her of her early love affair, which terminated so disastrously. Who, and where was the man, she asked herself without ever a thought of the truth, and while speculating upon it, and thinking how queer it seemed that Aunt Jerry was ever young and had a lover like herself, she fell asleep and dreamed that the lover was Mr. Freeman Burton!

CHAPTER XLVIII.

MRS. CHURCHILL AND EDNA.

IT was Saturday morning, and Mrs. Churchill was feeling very lonely and desolate, and missing her late companion more than she did Roy.

"It is strange how she has grown into my love, and how much she is to me," she said softly to herself, as she feared that her dress was not quite as it should be, and her hair somewhat awry.

She had depended altogether upon Miss Overton to care for her personal appearance, and felt her absence more sensibly for it.

"A letter, ma'am," her maid said, bringing it in and placing it in her hand.

Mrs. Churchill was sure that Roy had written nothing which a third person might not see, so she asked her maid to read it, and listened with a strange feeling to what Roy said of Edna.

"Thanks: you may go now," she said to her maid, who went out and left her alone.

Roy would be there Monday night, and with him Charlie's wife.

"Poor Charlie," she whispered to herself, and tried to believe that the tears which rolled down her cheeks were prompted by sorrow for him, instead of sorrow for the fact that Edna was found and was coming there to live. "I mean to be glad, and I am glad. I am going to like her, and I do like her," she said to herself; but she did not sleep much that night, and nearly all the next day she sat out by Charlie's grave, trying by thinking of him and his love for

Edna Browning, to awaken a feeling of genuine affection in her own breast.

But she could not do it. The most she could effect was a determination to be very kind to the girl, and to make it as pleasant for her as possible. To this end she gave orders that the largest and best sleeping-room in the house should be prepared for her on Monday, and as far as her sight would admit, gave it her personal inspection.

"If it was only Miss Overton coming to-night, how happy I should be," she said, when after all was done, and the day nearly gone, she sat down by the fire in the library to wait for the travellers.

It was very quiet and lonely there, and she fell asleep at last, and did not hear the carriage when it went to the station nor when it returned. But Roy soon found her, and putting both his arms around her, kissed her forehead lovingly.

"Wake up, mother," he said, and there was a ring of some great joy in the tone of his voice. "Wake up, mother; I have brought Edna to you. Here she is,—right here; let me put her hand in yours and see if you have ever felt one like it."

Roy was greatly excited, and something of his nervousness communicated itself to his mother, who trembled like a leaf, and whose sight seemed dimmer than ever as she turned her eyes toward the little figure, the rustle of whose dress she heard, and whose hands took hers in their own and held them fast, while a voice, which thrilled through every nerve, said, "Mother, dear mother, Charlie's mother and mine,— the only one I ever knew! You liked me some, I know, as Miss Overton; love me, won't you, as Edna, and forgive the deception."

Mrs. Churchill was pale as death, and for an instant could not speak; but she held close to the soft hands, and bent her face down over the young girl who had knelt before her, and whose head was in her lap.

"What is it? How is it? I do not understand at all. Roy, tell me what it means. You bring me one you say is Edna, Charlie's wife; and she calls me mother with Miss Overton's voice. Is it, can it be they are the same? That the girl I already love as my daughter is really mine?"

"Yes, mother, really yours in more senses than one," Roy said; and then as briefly as possible he told Edna's story, and why she had come to them in disguise, and how he had loved her even when pledged to another, and that she had promised to love him in return, and was to be his wife.

"Oh, I am so glad, so glad! Kiss me, Edna," Mrs. Churchill said, adopting the new name at once, and holding her daughter to her in an embrace which assured Roy that all was well between his mother and his future wife. "You would think me foolish if you knew how I did dread your coming here," Mrs. Churchill said to Edna when she was a little composed and could talk about the matter calmly. "I was afraid it would not be so pleasant for Miss Overton and myself with a third party, but I am so glad now, so glad."

"It is so nice to have you back, and to know you will never go again," she continued; and then Edna told her of her promise to Aunt Jerry to return to Allen's Hill and remain there for a time at least before her marriage.

"She has some claim on me; she is all alone, and I must do so much for her," Edna said, while Mrs. Churchill did feel a little chill when she thought of the woman with the dreadful name who had written so familiarly to her, and who was Edna's aunt and had a claim on her.

But she loved the niece well enough to tolerate the aunt, and suggested that the latter should come there if she wished for her niece's society. But Edna knew this would

18

never do, and persisted in her plan of returning to the Hill after a few days at Leighton and a flying visit to Uncle Phil. Mrs. Burton, who called next day, received the intelligence quite as well as could be expected. The fact that Georgie had known who Edna was, and had indorsed her too, and even spoken to Roy about her, and given her consent, went a long way toward reassuring her. What Georgie sanctioned was right, and she kissed Edna kindly, and cried over her a good deal, and said she should like her for Georgie's sake, and hoped she would try to *fill* poor Georgie's place in Roy's heart, and be a comfort to Mrs. Churchill.

In order to keep Edna with them as long as possible, Roy telegraphed for Uncle Phil to come to Leighton, and the next day's train brought the old man with his quaint sayings and original style of dress. He knew how it was going to end, and was not surprised, and he wished Edna much joy, and congratulated Roy upon his good fortune in securing so great a happiness.

"The neatest, prettiest girl in the world, with the trimmest ankles except one,—that's Maude; and Roy, Edna must be married from my house, and in my church. I claim that as my right. Never should have built the pesky thing that's been such a plague to me if it had not been for Maude and Edna, and that sermon about the synagogue. Not that I'm sorry, though the bother has worn me some thin. We've got a nice man, too, now; had him *two weeks*, and like him tip-top. Neither one nor the other; Ritual nor anti-ritual, but common sense. Don't mind Ruth Gardner more than if she was a gnat. Yes, yes; a good fellow, who speaks to everybody, slaps you on your back sometimes, and acts as if he liked the old man; and he must marry Dotty. She'll be the first bride in church, and I'll have it trimmed if it costs me my farm. Yes, Dot must go from my house."

Edna favored this, and as Roy did not object, it was arranged that after a few weeks stay with Aunt Jerry, Edna should go to Rocky Point and be married in Uncle Phil's church. Christmas was the very latest time of which Roy would hear. "Georgie said I was not to wait," was the argument which he used with all, and which finally prevailed; and so, after a week at Leighton, Edna returned to Allen's Hill, accompanied by Roy, who, during the six weeks that she staid there, spent nearly half his time there and on the road. "He was as tickled as a boy with a new top," Aunt Jerry said, but she liked him nevertheless, and paid him every possible attention, and made Parker House rolls and Graham muffins alternately, and used her best dishes every day, and hired a little girl to wait upon the table when he was there, because he "was used to such fol-de-rol," and it pleased Edna too. Aunt Jerry seemed greatly changed; and if uniform kindness and gentleness of manner could avail to blot out all remembrance of a past which had not been pleasant, it was surely blotted from Edna's mind, and she felt only love and gratitude for the peculiar woman who stood upon the doorstep and cried when at last the carriage which was to take Roy and Edna to the train, drove away from her door and left her all alone.

CHAPTER XLIX.

THE WEDDING.

"NOBODY now, Tabby, but you and I," said Aunt Jerry, as she re-entered her lonely house, and taking her cat in her arms, she cried like a child over the dumb creature, which tried in so many ways to evince it's appreciation of this unusual caress.

She had said it was doubtful whether she went to the wedding or not; in fact she didn't much believe she should; it would be cold and blustering, and she should get the neuralgia, and be in the way, and nobody would miss an old dud like her. She should of course visit Edna once any way, in her own house; but to the wedding she shouldn't go. This was her decision till the receipt of a certain letter which came to her within a few days after Edna's departure, and which changed her intentions at once.

"Don't be a fool, but come. I rather want to see if you look as bad as I do. P. O."

That was the letter, and it sent Aunt Jerry to the glass, where she inspected herself for some little time, and decided that she was not so very bad-looking, and she'd show him that she was not, too! So she wrote to Edna that she had changed her mind and was coming to the wedding; and she went over to Livonia, and from thence to Rochester, and having inquired for the most fashionable dressmaker in the city, went to her at once, and told her where she was going, and that she did not want to disgrace her relations, and asked what she should get, and if she would make it, and how much she would charge. The price staggered her a little, and made her stop for a moment before committing herself, but remembering a recent rise in stocks which had affected her, she concluded to stand the expense, and when next she wrote to Edna she announced that she had a new black silk, making at Mrs. Baker's, and a gray morning dress, velvet cloak, and black alpaca for travelling, and that they were to be made in style, too, and she shouldn't shame any one. She did not add that she had indulged in a handsome set of lace and furs, and even committed the extravagance of getting a waterfall! This last article of fashion and luxury came near being the death of the poor old lady, who could not make it stay on without a whole box of pins which stuck into her head, and pulled her hair, and drove her nearly wild as she persisted in wearing it when alone, so as to get used to the horrid thing before going among the fashionables. The chest upstairs, where the yellow satin and the faded wreath were lying, was visited more than once, and the good dame in her abstraction forgot to shut the lid, and when she went again to her Mecca, she found that Tabby had made the chest and its contents into a nice bed and playhouse for the two fat, pretty kittens which for three or four weeks had lived under the woodshed floor, and only came out at intervals. The chest was locked after this and not visited again before Aunt Jerry's departure for Rocky Point, with her new clothes, and trunk, and satchel. The dresses fitted admirably, especially the silk, which was elegant in its way, and trailed far behind the good dame, who felt more at home in her short alpaca suit, which made her look full ten years younger than her wont, and a few years younger than she really was. Some of the neighbors who enjoyed her outfit, and the remarks she made concerning it, suggested a round hat as a fitting accompaniment to her suit, but this Aunt Jerry repelled with disdain, hoping she was not such a fool as to put her old snuff-colored face under a round hat, not she. She had a nice velvet bonnet, for which she paid the 'bominable price of fifteen dollars; she should wear that, and her thread-lace veil; and she looked so nice and stylish that Edna, who was waiting for her at the station, did not recognize her at first, and looked twice at the fashionably dressed woman, holding so fast to her check, which the hackman was trying to get from her.

"Why, auntie," she cried, when the turn of the velvet bonnet showed her Miss Pepper's face, "how pretty, and young you look. I did not know you at first."

"Fine feathers make fine birds," was Aunt Jerry's reply; but she did not seem ill-pleased with her niece's compliment as she followed on to the little pony-carriage waiting for her, and which Edna had driven down herself.

"Is this his,—Mr. Overton's, I mean?" Aunt Jerry asked, in some surprise; for Edna's account of Bobtail and the square-backed buggy did not quite tally with this stylish turnout.

Edna explained, blushingly, that the establishment was her own,—a gift from Roy, who had driven it up to Rocky Point two weeks before, and left it for her use while she was there.

"Love in the tub, just now; but wait till by and by," Aunt Jerry said; but Edna had no fears of the by and by; and her face was radiant with happiness as she drove her aunt through the main street of Rocky Point, in the direction of Uncle Phil's.

"That is the place," she said, as they turned the corner which brought the old farm-house in view. "Uncle Phil talks of building a new house in the spring,—a Gothic cottage, —only, he says if he does, there is nobody to live in it but himself and Aunt Becky."

"The nigger, you mean," Aunt Jerry said, rather crisply; and, as one of the ponies shied a little just then, Edna said no more of the Gothic cottage, but gave her attention to her horses, until they drew up before the unpretentious building, which Aunt Jerry eyed sharply, keeping her veil closely drawn over her face, and feeling a decided trembling in her knees, as she walked through the gate and up to the front door, where she intended waiting till Edna could tie her ponies, and was ready to usher her in.

But,—greatly to her surprise,—the door swung open, seemingly by itself,—for she saw no living being; only a voice, which came from behind the door, and sounded a little smothered, said to her: "Walk in, Jerry, and make yourself at home."

Then she walked in; and, as the owner of the voice emerged into view, and offered her his hand, she said: "How do you do, Philip?" as naturally as if it had been yesterday they parted, instead of thirty years before.

Poor Uncle Phil had been quite as much exercised on the subject of his wardrobe as Aunt Jerry had been with hers. He wanted to go decent to the wedding, and not disgrace Dotty's grand relations, he said. "He'd been looking like a codger long enough, and he meant to fix up, and pay the fiddler." Nothing in Rocky Point, however, would answer his purpose; and when Edna suggested Millville, he sneered at that, and even spoke contemptuously of Albany and its tailors! Where did Roy get his clothes made? Wan't it in New York, and why couldn't *he* go there as well as anywhere? Accordingly the old man went to New York, from which place he returned so metamorphosed that the boys in the streets followed him as a natural curiosity, and the men hollowed after him to know what had happened, as he walked from the depot home, arrayed in his new suit of clothes, which made him look so trim and youthful, with his turn-over collar, and his necktie, and soft hat. Even his shoes and shirts were city made; and he looked very nice, and very much ashamed as he hurried home, glad to be out of sight of the curious, impertinent boys, and wondering what they would say "to his t'other suit,—his very best, with the little tail-coat, and the stove-pipe hat," for he had indulged in these extravagances, as they were safe in the trunk which the backman left at the door.

Edna was delighted to see him, and complimented him greatly on his personal appearance, and never dreamed why all this change had been made by her eccentric uncle, or guess how nervous and excited he was on the day when Aunt

Jerry was expected. She had asked him to accompany her to the depot, but he had declined, and after she was gone had donned his second-best suit, and put on one of his new neckties, and indulged in cuffs and cuff-buttons, and a white pocket-handkerchief, which he grasped in his hand as tightly as if it had been the spar which was to keep him from drowning. When he heard the whistle of the train, he was sitting in his arm-chair by the fire, but quick as if he had been shot, he sprang to his feet, exclaiming: "The Lord help me!" while, in the palms of his hands, and under his hair, were little drops of sweat, wrung out by sheer nervousness and excitement. He saw the carriage when it turned the corner, but the young girl with the jaunty hat and feather, holding the reins so skilfully, and managing the horses so well, was nothing to him then. He only saw the tall, erect woman at her side, with the veil over her face, and the rich furs about her shoulders.

"Straight yet as an Injun, and as gritty, too, I'll bet you," he said to himself, as, stationing himself by the window, he watched Aunt Jerry's descent from the vehicle, and then as he saw her come up the walk, he ran behind the door and opened it for her with the salutation we have recorded elsewhere.

Edna was close behind, so close indeed, that she saw the look in Uncle Phil's face, and heard Aunt Jerry's, "How do you do, Philip?" and in an instant the truth flashed upon her, taking her breath away and rendering her speechless for a moment. Then confronting them both, she exclaimed; "Oh, Uncle Phil,—Aunt Jerry,—I never knew,—I never guessed,—I never thought,—"

"Well, don't think now, or if you do, keep your thoughts to yourself," was Aunt Jerry's characteristic reply, as she walked into the sitting-room with Uncle Phil following after her, standing first on one foot, then upon the other, spitting a great deal, and flourishing his handkerchief almost in her face in his zeal to make her welcome.

"Come upstairs," Edna said; and glad to escape from the curious eyes of the fidgety little man, whom she had mentally pronounced "fat and pussy,—just as I knew he was," Aunt Jerry accompanied her niece to her room, while Uncle Phil said softly to himself: "Yes, yes; better go before I bust the biler; good-lookin' craft, though, you bet," and he nodded at the figure-head of the tall clock in the corner as if that knew and appreciated his feelings.

Alone with her aunt, Edna could not refrain from saying, "Aunt Jerry, it *was* Uncle Phil; I saw it in his face; I know it all; I wish, I believe—"

"You needn't wish nor believe anything, for as true as you do, I'll take my duds home in double-quick time. I ain't quite such an old fool as that. Philip Overton and I have had our day, and lost it; let us alone;" Aunt Jerry answered so fiercely that Edna came to a sudden halt with her intentions of doing something for this odd, lonely couple, whose lives had once been so near to flowing in the same channel, but had drifted so far apart.

They were wholly unlike each other, Edna thought, as she watched them closely during the evening, when with the first reserve worn off, they talked together of old friends whom in their youth they had known, and who were now many of them dead and gone. It was strange what a softening effect the talking of these old times had upon Aunt Jerry, who hardly seemed herself as she sat there with the firelight falling on her smooth hair, and giving a rosy tinge to her cheek.. Her eyes were always bright, and they shone now with much of their olden fire, and made Uncle Phil "squirm," as he expressed it, whenever they rested on him.

"If I only could bring them together. I mean to get Roy to help me," Edna thought; and when next day Roy came, the story was eagerly told to him, and his assistance asked in the matter.

Roy was interested, of course, but declared himself no match-maker. He had been more than thirty years making one for himself, he said, and he advised Edna to let the old couple do as they liked, adding that he was not at all sure it would be a good or happy thing for two people so peculiar to come together. This was a damper to Edna's zeal, and she affected to pout for a little, but soon forgot it all in her delight at the diamonds which Roy had brought to her. They had been his mother's, and had always attracted great attention from their size and brilliancy, but she never cared to wear them again, and at her request they had been reset for Edna, who tried their effect with Roy standing by and admiring her sparkling face more than the flash of the rich jewels, and proving his admiration by a kiss, notwithstanding that Aunt Jerry was looking on, and pursing up her mouth with so queer a look that Roy kissed her too, whereupon Uncle Phil, who had come in just in time to see the last performance, exclaimed in an aside: "By George, the chap has more pluck than I have," while Aunt Jerry deliberately wiped and rubbed her cheek, and said, "I should s'pose you'd as soon kiss a piece of sole leather."

They were very gay and merry at Uncle Phil's during the few days which preceded the wedding; and nothing was wanting to complete their happiness but the presence of Maude and Jack. From them, however, a kindly message came on the very morning of the bridal; and Edna read it with Roy's arm around her waist, and Roy's face looking over her shoulder. Only a few friends from Rocky Point were invited to the lunch given at the house after the ceremony; but all were welcome to go to the church, which was filled to its utmost capacity. Ruth Gardner presided at the organ, and did herself great credit with the music she made, as the party went up the aisle,—Uncle Phil and Edna, Roy and Aunt Jerry, whose rich black silk was stepped on two or three times by those who followed in her train. Mrs. Churchill was not there. She was far from well; and as there was to be a grand reception at Leighton that evening, she preferred to receive her children at home, and staid to see that everything was in readiness for them when they arrived. Uncle Phil was at first a little stiff in his New York clothes, and wondered what the chaps did who dressed up every day; but this soon wore off, and he was the merriest and youngest of the party which took the train for Albany, going thence down the river to Leighton, which they reached just as the twilight shadows were beginning to fall, and the stars looked out upon another Christmas Eve.

It was not a crowded party, but very pleasant and select; and Edna moved among her guests like some little fairy, clad in her bridal robes of sheeny satin and fleecy lace, with only pearls upon her neck and arms, and the wedding-ring upon her finger. It was a far different bridal from her first one; and she felt it to be so, and wondered if it was wicked for her to be so happy, when just a little way from the bright lights and sounds of festivity Charlie lay sleeping, with the young moon shining on his grave. Roy, too, thought of Georgie, in far-off Greenwood, and thought of her, too, with a softer, tenderer regret than Edna could give to Charlie; for he only knew of the good there had been in her; the bad was buried with her, and he remembered her as she had seemed at the last,—amiable, loving, and good. But he could not wish to exchange his bride for her; and once, when they were standing a little out of sight, and a thought of what had almost been, came over him, he involuntarily wound his arm tightly around Edna, and drew her to him in a quick, passionate embrace, as if he would thus assure himself that she was a reality, and not a myth which would vanish from his side.

The chimes from the church tower had pealed the hour of midnight, and Merry Christmas had passed from lip to lip, ere the party broke up, and the last guest was gone. An hour later, and every light had disappeared from Leighton; but the moon and the stars which heard the angels sing eighteen hundred years ago shone over the place, and seemed to breathe a benediction upon the newly-wedded husband and wife, whom all had pronounced so well-suited to each other.

CHAPTER L.

CONCLUSION.

TWO years later, and again the Christmas chimes were ringing from many a tower, and the words, "Peace on earth, good-will to men," were sung by many a voice, while many a welcome greeting was given to returning friends, and to none a warmer or more welcome one than was extended to Jack and Maude, who came from their home in Jersey to keep Christmas at Leighton, where Edna presided as mistress, with no shadow on her bright face, or sorrow in her heart. Hers had been a happy life since the day Roy called her his wife; and no ripple, however small, had broken the smooth surface of the matrimonial sea on which she sailed so pleasantly. All in all to each other, neither she nor Roy had cared to leave their pleasant home; but had remained there all the time, with the exception of an occasional trip to New York, and a visit of a few days to Rocky Point and Allen's Hill.

"Oh, I am so happy that I sometimes tremble lest I should wake some morning and find it all a dream," Edna said to Maude, as she led the way to the suite of rooms which had been prepared for Mrs. Jack, with her nurse and babies, for Maude had reached that honor, and the cares of maternity sat very gracefully upon her.

"Edna Browning" she had named the expected stranger, and had held all sorts of consultations with Mrs. Roy concerning the christening robes and the christening dinner, and had talked quite confidently of what her daughter would and would not do. How, then, was she amazed and confounded when the result proved to be *twins*, and boys at that! Two great, red-faced, sturdy boys, at whom she looked askance, and from whom she shrunk at first as from something appalling, and of which she was ashamed.

Edna Browning was a Betsy Trotwood affair now, and they named the babies John and Roy, but the father always called them Jack and Gill. And they were spending their first Christmas at Leighton; and Mr. and Mrs. Freeman Burton were there also, the latter still in black for her darling Georgie, whom she talked about a great deal, wishing so much that she could be with them as she used to be.

"Not that I want you away, my dear," she would add, laying her hand on Edna's shoulder, or wish that things with you and Roy were otherwise, only I miss poor Georgie so much, but Maude is a great comfort to me."

And this is true, for to some degree Maude has taken Georgie's place in her aunt's affections. She spends a good deal of time at Oakwood with her boys, to whom Mr. Burton calls himself grandpa, while his wife is the grandma; and it is said that in his private drawer there is a will giving all his worldly possessions to his beloved niece, Mrs. John Heyford, and her heirs forever; so Jack is doing well in a worldly point of view, and is talking of building a handsome country seat, where Maude can keep her ponies, and her children, and be what she desires to be, a farmer's wife in comfortable circumstances. Uncle Phil is also at Leighton keeping the Christmas holidays, and playing with the twins, and rallying Edna on Maude's surprising success. But Aunt Jerry is not there. "Got the rheumatism in her hip, and is crosser than four bears," Uncle Phil said, and then Edna knew that he had been to Allen's Hill, and looked at him so inquiringly, that he replied, "No use, no use,—and I may as well tell you that I've made a prodigious fool of myself, and been after that snap-dragon again. She looked so trim and neat when you were married, that my heart kept thumpin' under my jacket; and I was so lonesome with you and Maude both gone for good, that I—yes—well—I—yes, yes —asked her again, and said I was 'Piscopal now, and told her I'd build a Gothic cottage, and we might take comfort yet, for it was lonesome and awful cold winter nights, and she called me an old fool, and told me to let her alone, and I did, but kept thinkin', and hankerin', and rememberin' how slim and straight she looked, and I've begun the Gothic house, you know, and it will be finished in the spring, and— and—yes, yes—the upshot is, I went out there two weeks ago and found her on crutches, and tried her again with the 'Piscopal and the Gothic, but no go. She didn't dislike me, she said, and she was lonesome at times, but she wouldn't be a laughing-stock for nobody; and she gave me the mitten the third time, and I've give it up for good."

Edna tried to console him, and told him her aunt might change her mind yet, but he did not think she would, and said he could stand it if she didn't; and was the merriest of them all at the dinner, where Maude and Edna appeared in evening dress, looking as young and beautiful as in their girlish days, while Roy and Jack seemed and were perfectly happy and altogether satisfied in the choice they had made.

And now, saying good-by to Leighton, we glance for a moment at poor Aunt Jerry, who ate her dinner alone and let one single tear roll down her cheeks as she thought of the party at Leighton, and of herself, so lonely and forlorn. As the night deepened without, and the shadows crept into every corner of the room, she tried, by caressing her tabby-cat, and watching the fire-light flickering on the wall, to get up a little enthusiasm for her surroundings, and believe that she was happy and content. But it would not do; there was a craving in her heart for other companionship than that of cat and cow, and putting the former from her lap she hobbled to the window and looking out into the night, thought of the Gothic cottage, and the man who had offered it to her acceptance, and called her Jerry as he did so.

"It might be better than living here alone, and it might be worse," she soliloquized. "There's nothing bad about him, and I do believe, that as far as he knows, he is a good churchman now, but he *is* short, and fat, and stumpy, and if you'd let him, would be silly enough to keep your stomach riled the most of the time. No, Tabby and I'll try it a spell longer anyway, and then if he is fool enough to ask again, I—don't—know— ; it's about an even thing;" and the good woman went back to her chair by the fire, and Tabby crept again into her lap, and purred her content with things as they were, and the kettle from which Aunt Jerry was to have a cup of tea when the clock struck eight, sang upon the hearth, and made, with the snapping of the wood, a pleasant, cheery sound which lulled Aunt Jerry to sleep at last, and there we will leave her, not knowing any better than the reader, whether that Gothic cottage at Rocky Point will ever have a mistress or not, though we have a suspicion that it will!

THE END.

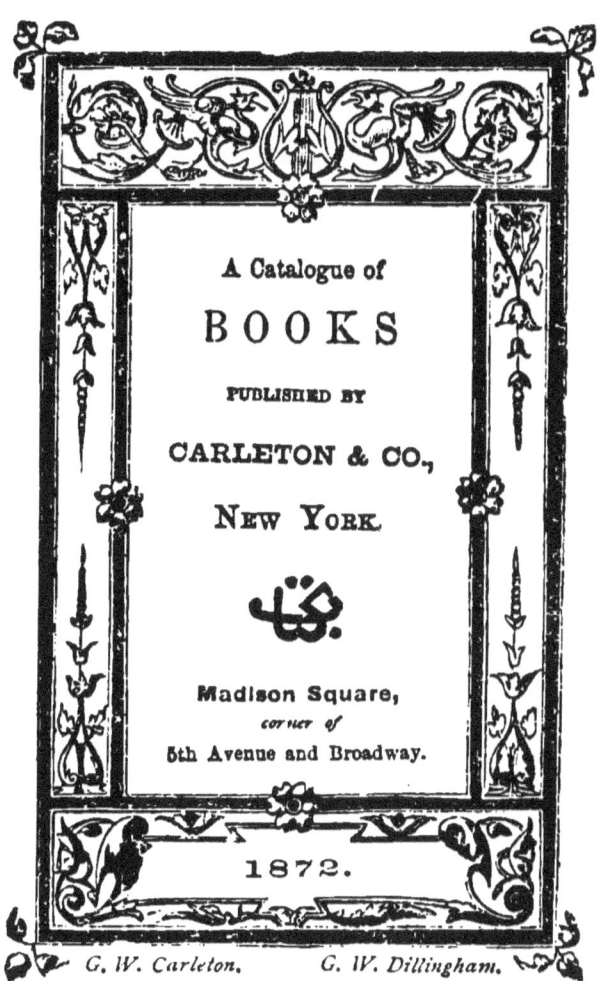

A Catalogue of
BOOKS
PUBLISHED BY
CARLETON & CO.,
NEW YORK.

Madison Square,
corner of
5th Avenue and Broadway.

1872.

G. W. Carleton.   G. W. Dillingham.

"*There is a kind of physiognomy in the titles of books no less than in the faces of men, by which a skilful observer will know as well what to expect from the one as the other.*"—BUTLER.

NEW BOOKS

Recently Published by

G W. CARLETON & CO., New York,

Madison Square, Fifth Avenue and Broadway.

N.B.—THE PUBLISHERS, upon receipt of the price in advance, will send any of the following Books by mail, POSTAGE FREE, to any part of the United States This convenient and very safe mode may be adopted when the neighboring Booksellers are not supplied with the desired work.

Marion Harland.

ALONE.—	A novel.	12mo. cloth.	$1.50
HIDDEN PATH.—	do.	do.	$1.50
MOSS SIDE.—	do.	do.	$1.50
NEMESIS.—	do.	do.	$1.50
MIRIAM.—	do.	do.	$1.50
AT LAST.—	do. *Just Published.*	do.	$1.50
HELEN GARDNER.—	do.	do.	$1.50
SUNNYBANK.—	do.	do.	$1.50
HUSBANDS AND HOMES.—	do.	do.	$1.50
RUBY'S HUSBAND.—	do.	do.	$1.50
PHEMIE'S TEMPTATION.—	do.	do.	$1.50
THE EMPTY HEART.—	do.	do.	$1.50
TRUE AS STEEL.—	do.	do.	$1.50

Miss Muloch.

JOHN HALIFAX.—A novel. With illustration. 12mo. cloth, $1.75
A LIFE FOR A LIFE.— . do. do. $1.75

Charlotte Bronte (Currer Bell).

JANE EYRE.—A novel. With illustration. 12mo. cloth, $1.75
THE PROFESSOR.—do. . do. . do. $1.75
SHIRLEY.— . do. . do. . do. $1.75
VILLETTE.— . do. . do. . do. $1.75

Hand-Books of Society.

THE HABITS OF GOOD SOCIETY; nice points of taste, good manners, and the art of making oneself agreeable. 12mo. $1.75
THE ART OF CONVERSATION.—A sensible work, for every one who wishes to be an agreeable talker or listener. 12mo. $1.50
ARTS OF WRITING, READING, AND SPEAKING.—An excellent book for self-instruction and improvement. 12mo. clo., $1.50
A NEW DIAMOND EDITION of the above three popular books.— Small size, elegantly bound, and put in a box. - $3.00

Mrs. A. P. Hill.

MRS. HILL'S NEW COOKERY BOOK, and receipts. 12mo. cloth. $2 00

Mary J. Holmes.

LENA RIVERS.—	A novel.	12mo. cloth,	$1.50
DARKNESS AND DAYLIGHT.—	do.	do.	$1.50
TEMPEST AND SUNSHINE.—	do.	do.	$1.50
MARIAN GREY.—	do.	do.	$1.50
MEADOW BROOK.—	do.	do.	$1.50
ENGLISH ORPHANS.—	do.	do.	$1.50
DORA DEANE.—	do.	do.	$1.50
COUSIN MAUDE.—	do.	do.	$1.50
HOMESTEAD ON THE HILLSIDE.—	do.	do.	$1.50
HUGH WORTHINGTON.—	do.	do.	$1.50
THE CAMERON PRIDE.—	do.	do.	$1.50
ROSE MATHER.—	do.	do.	$1.50
ETHELYN'S MISTAKE.—	do.	do.	$1.50
MILLBANK.—	*Just published.*	do.	$1.50

Augusta J. Evans.

BEULAH.—	A novel.	12mo. cloth,	$1.75
MACARIA.—	do.	do.	$1.75
ST. ELMO.—	do.	do.	$2.00
VASHTI.—	do.	do.	$2.00
INEZ.—	do.	do.	$1.75

Louisa M. Alcott.

MORNING GLORIES.—By the Author of "Little Women," etc. $1.50

The Crusoe Library.

ROBINSON CRUSOE.—A handsome illus. edition.		12mo.	$1.50
SWISS FAMILY ROBINSON.—	do.	do.	$1.50
THE ARABIAN NIGHTS.—	do.	do.	$1.50

Captain Mayne Reid.—Illustrated.

THE SCALP HUNTERS.—	} Far West Series	12mo. clo.,	$1.50
THE WAR TRAIL.—		do.	$1.50
THE HUNTER'S FEAST.—		do.	$1.50
THE TIGER HUNTER.—		do.	$1.50
OSCEOLA, THE SEMINOLE.—	} Prairie Series	do.	$1.50
THE QUADROON.—		do.	$1.50
RANGERS AND REGULATORS.—		do.	$1.50
THE WHITE GAUNTLET.—		do.	$1.50
WILD LIFE.—	} Pioneer Series	do.	$1.50
THE HEADLESS HORSEMAN.—		do.	$1.50
LOST LENORE.—		do.	$1.50
THE WOOD RANGERS.—		do.	$1.50
THE WHITE CHIEF.—	} Wild Forest Series	do.	$1.50
THE WILD HUNTRESS.—		do.	$1.50
THE MAROON.—		do.	$1.50
THE RIFLE RANGERS.—		do.	$1.50

Comic Books—Illustrated.

ARTEMUS WARD,	His Book.—Letters, etc.	12mo. cl.,	$1.50
DO.	His Travels—Mormons, etc.	do.	$1.50
DO.	In London.—Punch Letters	do.	$1.50
DO.	His Panorama and Lecture.	do.	$1.50
DO.	Sandwiches for Railroad.		.25
JOSH BILLINGS	ON ICE, and other things.—	do.	$1.50
DO.	His Book of Proverbs, etc.	do.	$1.50
DO.	Farmer's Allmanax.		.25
FANNY FERN.—Folly as it Flies.		do.	$1.50
DO.	Gingersnaps	do.	$1.50
VERDANT GREEN.—A racy English college story.		do.	$1.50
MILES O'REILLY.—His Book of Adventures.		do.	$1.50
ORPHEUS C. KERR.—Kerr Papers, 4 vols. in one.		do.	$2.00
DO.	Avery Glibun. A novel.		$2.00
DO.	The Cloven Foot. do.	do.	$1.50
BALLAD OF LORD BATEMAN.—Illustrated by Cruikshank.			.25

A. S. Roe's Works.

A LONG LOOK AHEAD.—	A novel	12mo. cloth,	$1.50
TO LOVE AND TO BE LOVED.—	do.	do.	$1.50
TIME AND TIDE.—	do.	do.	$1.50
I'VE BEEN THINKING.—	do.	do.	$1.50
THE STAR AND THE CLOUD.—	do.	do.	$1.50
TRUE TO THE LAST.—	do.	do.	$1.50
HOW COULD HE HELP IT?—	do.	do.	$1.50
LIKE AND UNLIKE.—	do.	do.	$1.50
LOOKING AROUND.—	do.	do.	$1.50
WOMAN OUR ANGEL.—	do.	do.	$1.50
THE CLOUD ON THE HEART.—	do.	do.	$1.50
RESOLUTION.—	do.	do.	$1.50

Joseph Rodman Drake.

THE CULPRIT FAY.—A faery poem, with 100 illustrations. $2.00
DO.   Superbly bound in turkey morocco. $5.00

"Brick" Pomeroy.

SENSE.—An illustrated vol. of fireside musings.	12mo. cl.,	$1.50
NONSENSE.— do. do. comic sketches.	do	$1.50
OUR SATURDAY NIGHTS. do. pathos and sentiment.		$1.50
BRICK DUST.—Comic sketches.		$1.50
GOLD DUST.—Fireside musings.		$1.50

John Esten Cooke.

FAIRFAX.— A brilliant new novel.	12mo. cloth,	$1.50
HILT TO HILT.— do.	do.	$1.50
HAMMER AND RAPIER.— do.	do.	$1.50
OUT OF THE FOAM.— do. *Just published.*	do.	$1.50

Victor Hugo.

LES MISERABLES.—-The celebrated novel, 8vo. cloth. $2.50
" Two vol. edition, fine paper, do. - 5.00
" In the Spanish language, do. - 5.00

Algernon Charles Swinburne.

LAUS VENERIS, AND OTHER POEMS.—Elegant new ed. - $1.50
FRENCH LOVE-SONGS.—By the best French Authors. - 1.50

Author "New Gospel of Peace."

THE CHRONICLES OF GOTHAM.—A rich modern satire. - $ .25
THE FALL OF MAN.—A satire on the Darwin Theory. - .50

Julie P. Smith.

WIDOW GOLDSMITH'S DAUGHTER.—A novel. 12mo. cloth. $1.75
CHRIS AND OTHO.— do. do. - 1.75
THE WIDOWER.— do. do. - 1.75
THE MARRIED BELLE.— do. (in press). - 1.75

Mansfield T. Walworth.

WARWICK.—A new novel. - - - 12mo. cloth. $1.75
LULU.— do. - - - do. - 1.75
HOTSPUR.— do. - - - do. - 1.75
STORMCLIFF.— do. - - - do. - 1.75
DELAPLAINE.— do. Just Published. do. - 1.75

Richard B. Kimball.

WAS HE SUCCESSFUL?— A novel. - 12mo. cloth. $1.75
UNDERCURRENTS.— do. - do. - 1.75
SAINT LEGER.— do. - do. - 1.75
ROMANCE OF STUDENT LIFE. do. - do. - 1.75
IN THE TROPICS.— do. - do. - 1.75
HENRY POWERS, Banker.— do. - do. - 1.75
TO-DAY.— do. - do. - 1.75

M. Michelet's Remarkable Works.

LOVE (L'AMOUR).—Translated from the French. 12mo. cl. $1.50
WOMAN (LA FEMME).— do. - do. - 1.50

Ernest Renan.

THE LIFE OF JESUS.—Trans'ted from the French. 12mo. cl. $1.75
LIVES OF THE APOSTLES.— do. do. - 1.75
THE LIFE OF SAINT PAUL— do. do. - 1.75
THE BIBLE IN INDIA— do. cf Joccoliot. 2.00

Popular Italian Novels.

DOCTOR ANTONIO.—A love story. By Ruffini. 12mo. cl $1.75
BEATRICE CENCI.—By Guerrazzi, with Portrait. do. - 1.75

Geo. W. Carleton.

OUR ARTIST IN CUBA.—With 50 comic illustrations. - $1.50
OUR ARTIST IN PERU.— do. do. - 1 50
OUR ARTIST IN AFRICA.—(In press). do. - 1 50

Miscellaneous Works.

THE DEBATABLE LAND.—By Robert Dale Owen. 12mo.	$2.00
RUTLEDGE.—A novel of remarkable interest and power.	1.50
THE SUTHERLANDS.— do. Author of Rutledge.	1.50
FRANK WARRINGTON.— do. do.	1.50
SAINT PHILIP'S.- do. do.	1.50
LOUIE.— do. do.	1.50
FERNANDO DE LEMOS.—A novel. By Charles Gayarre.	2.00
MAURICE.—A novel from the French of F. Bechard.	1.50
MOTHER GOOSE.—Set to music, and with illustrations.	2.00
BRAZEN GATES.—A new child's book, illustrated.	1.50
THE ART OF AMUSING.—Book of home amusements.	1.50
STOLEN WATERS.—A fascinating novel. Celia Gardner.	1.50
HEART HUNGRY.—A novel. By Maria J. Westmoreland.	1.75
THE SEVENTH VIAL.—A new work. Dr. John Cumming.	2.00
THE GREAT TRIBULATION.—new ed. do.	2.00
THE GREAT PREPARATION.— do. do.	2.00
THE GREAT CONSUMMATION.—do. do.	2.00
THE LAST WARNING CRY.— do. do.	1.50
ANTIDOTE TO "THE GATES AJAR."—	25
HOUSES NOT MADE WITH HANDS.—Hoppin's Illus.	1.00
BEAUTY IS POWER.—An admirable book for ladies.	1.50
ITALIAN LIFE AND LEGENDS.—By Anna Cora Ritchie.	1.50
LIFE AND DEATH.—A new American novel.	1.50
HOW TO MAKE MONEY; AND HOW TO KEEP IT.—Davies.	1.50
THE CLOISTER AND THE HEARTH.—By Charles Reade.	1.50
TALES FROM THE OPERAS.—The Plots of all the Operas.	1.50
ADVENTURES OF A HONEYMOON.—A love-story.	1.50
AMONG THE PINES.—Down South. By Edmund Kirke.	1.50
MY SOUTHERN FRIENDS.— do. do.	1.50
DOWN IN TENNESSEE.— do. do.	1.50
ADRIFT IN DIXIE.— do. do.	1.50
AMONG THE GUERILLAS.— do. do.	1.50
A BOOK ABOUT LAWYERS.—Bright and interesting.	2.00
A BOOK ABOUT DOCTORS.— do. do.	2.00
WOMAN, LOVE, AND MARRIAGE.—By Fred. Saunders.	1.50
PRISON LIFE OF JEFFERSON DAVIS.—By J. J. Craven.	1.50
POEMS, BY L. G. THOMAS.—	1.50
PASTIMES WITH MY LITTLE FRIENDS.—Mrs. Bennett.	1.50
THE SQUIBOB PAPERS.—A comic book. John Phœnix.	1.50
COUSIN PAUL.—A new American novel.	1.75
JARGAL.—A novel from the French of Victor Hugo.	1.75
CLAUDE GUEUX.— do. do. do.	1.50
LIFE OF VICTOR HUGO.— do. do.	2.00
CHRISTMAS HOLLY.—By Marion Harland, Illustrated.	1.50
THE RUSSIAN BALL.—An illustrated satirical Poem.	.25
THE SNOBLACE BALL.— do. do.	.25
THE PRINCE OF KASHNA.—Edited by R. B. Kimball.	1.75

Miscellaneous Works.

A LOST LIFE.—A novel by Emily H. Moore	$1.50
CROWN JEWELS.— do. Mrs. Emma L. Moffett.	$1.75
ADRIFT WITH A VENGEANCE.— Kinahan Cornwallis.	$1.50
THE FRANCO-PRUSSIAN WAR IN 1870.—By M. D. Landon.	$2.00
DREAM MUSIC.—Poems by Frederic Rowland Marvin.	$1.50
RAMBLES IN CUBA.—By an American Lady.	$1.50
BEHIND THE SCENES, in the White House.—Keckley.	$2.00
YACHTMAN'S PRIMER.—For Amateur Sailors.—Warren.	50
RURAL ARCHITECTURE.—By M. Field. With illustrations.	$2.00
TREATISE ON DEAFNESS.—By Dr. E. B. Lighthill.	$1.50
WOMEN AND THEATRES.—A new book, by Olive Logan.	$1.50
WARWICK.—A new novel by Mansfield Tracy Walworth.	$1.75
SIBYL HUNTINGTON.—A novel by Mrs. J. C. R. Dorr.	$1.75
LIVING WRITERS OF THE SOUTH.—By Prof. Davidson.	$2.00
STRANGE VISITORS.—A book from the Spirit World.	$1.50
UP BROADWAY, and its Sequel.—A story by Eleanor Kirk.	$1.50
MILITARY RECORD, of Appointments in the U.S. Army.	$5.00
HONOR BRIGHT.—A new American novel.	$1.50
MALBROOK.— do. do. do.	$1.50
GUILTY OR NOT GUILTY.— do. do.	$1.75
ROBERT GREATHOUSE.—A new novel by John F. Swift.	$2.00
THE GOLDEN CROSS, and poems by Irving Van Wart, jr.	$1.50
ATHALIAH.—A new novel by Joseph H. Greene, jr.	$1.75
REGINA, and other poems.—By Eliza Cruger.	$1.50
THE WICKEDEST WOMAN IN NEW YORK.—By C. H. Webb.	50
MONTALBAN.—A new American novel.	$1.75
MADEMOISELLE MERQUEM.—A novel by George Sand.	$1.75
THE IMPENDING CRISIS OF THE SOUTH.—By H. R. Helper.	$2.00
NOJOQUE—A Question for a Continent.— do.	$2.00
PARIS IN 1867.—By Henry Morford.	$1.75
THE BISHOP'S SON.—A novel by Alice Cary.	$1.75
CRUISE OF THE ALABAMA AND SUMTER.—By Capt. Semmes.	$1.50
HELEN COURTENAY.—A novel, author "Vernon Grove."	$1.75
SOUVENIRS OF TRAVEL.—By Madame Octavia W. LeVert.	$2.00
VANQUISHED.—A novel by Agnes Leonard.	$1.75
WILL-O'-THE-WISP.—A child's book, from the German.	$1.50
FOUR OAKS.—A novel by Kamba Thorpe.	$1.75
THE CHRISTMAS FONT.—A child's book, by M. J. Holmes.	$1.00
POEMS, BY SARAH T. BOLTON.	$1.50
MARY BRANDEGEE—A novel by Cuyler Pine.	$1.75
RENSHAWE.— do. do.	$1.75
MOUNT CALVARY.—By Matthew Hale Smith.	$2.00
PROMETHEUS IN ATLANTIS.—A prophecy.	$2.00
TITAN AGONISTES.—An American novel.	$2.00

www.ingramcontent.com/pod-product-compliance
Lightning Source LLC
Chambersburg PA
CBHW051735300426
44115CB00007B/568